Demokratie, Sicherheit, Frieden

Democracy, Security, Peace

edited by Prof. Dr. Ursula Schröder

DSP   Volume 224

A publication of the Institute for Peace Research
and Security Policy at the University of Hamburg

Ulrich Kühn

The Rise and Fall of Cooperative Arms Control in Europe

Nomos

The Deutsche Nationalbibliothek lists this publication in the
Deutsche Nationalbibliografie; detailed bibliographic data
are available on the Internet at http://dnb.d-nb.de

ISBN   978-3-8487-6207-1 (Print)
        978-3-7489-0323-9 (ePDF)

British Library Cataloguing-in-Publication Data
A catalogue record for this book is available from the British Library.

ISBN   978-3-8487-6207-1 (Print)
        978-3-7489-0323-9 (ePDF)

Library of Congress Cataloging-in-Publication Data
Kühn, Ulrich
The Rise and Fall of Cooperative Arms Control in Europe
Ulrich Kühn
414 pp.
Includes bibliographic references.

ISBN   978-3-8487-6207-1 (Print)
        978-3-7489-0323-9 (ePDF)

Onlineversion
Nomos eLibrary

1st Edition 2020
© Nomos Verlagsgesellschaft, Baden-Baden, Germany 2020. Printed and bound in
Germany.

For there is no durable treaty which is not founded on
reciprocal advantage, and indeed a treaty which does not
satisfy this condition is no treaty at all, and is apt
to contain the seeds of its own dissolution.

François de Callieres, On the Manner of Negotiating With Princes (1716), translated by A. F. Whyte (Boston: Houghton Mifflin, 1919), pp. 109-10

Political action must be based on a coordination
of morality and power.

Edward Hallett Carr, The Twenty Years' Crisis: 1919-1939. An Introduction to the Study of International Relations (London: MacMillan, 1939), p. 97

The only remedy for a strong structural effect
is a structural change.

Kenneth Neal Waltz, Theory of International Politics (Reading: Addison-Wesley, 1979), p. 111

Table of Contents

Acknowledgements

This book is the result of ten years of intense and often interrupted periods of hard labor, scientific nomadic existence, and the final homecoming to where it all began in 2009. There are many persons whom I owe my gratitude for their steadfast support during this important decade and in the process of forging this volume, which directly builds on my PhD thesis. I apologize for my incapacity to those that I forgot to mention here.

Above all, I want to thank my parents to whom I am deeply indebted for their endless love, their unalterable patience, and their continuous support. No less, I want to thank my wife Mona for her unshakable love, her belief in me, and for making me a better man – every day a little bit. This book is most of all a dedication to my parents' and Mona's personal qualities that have shaped my way of thinking and living.

Further on, I want to thank Wolfgang Zellner who persuaded me to follow the academic path; Michael Brzoska for his thoughtful guidance and knowledgeable advice on my PhD thesis, Götz Neuneck for giving me the opportunity to work on arms control; Michael Staack for his trust in my abilities; Catherine Kelleher who would always support my various endeavors no matter what; James Acton for reminding me that besides scientific rigor, scholars should speak truth to power; Tristan Volpe for one of the most fruitful partnerships I entered thus far; Laura Rockwood and Elena Sokova for bringing me back to Europe; and to Susanne Bund for her love of detail when checking the galleys.

Further on, I am deeply indebted to the Evangelisches Studienwerk e.V. Villigst and IFSH for paying my PhD bills; the Stanton Foundation for gratuitously allowing me to better understand the "Washington bubble;" and the John D. und Catherine T. MacArthur Foundation for helping me bridge a crucial period in my life by focusing on my home country.

This book is dedicated to my beloved aunt Christel and my uncle Werner whom I miss.

Hamburg, 2019

Abbreviations

ABM	Anti-Ballistic Missile Treaty
ACFE	Agreement on Adaptation of CFE
A/CFE	meaning the CFE Treaty and the Agreement on Adaptation of CFE
AIAM	Annual Implementation Assessment Meeting
APEC	Asia-Pacific Economic Cooperation
ATTU	Atlantic to the Urals
CAC	Conventional Arms Control in Europe
CBM	Confidence-Building Measures
CDE	Conference on CSBMs and Disarmament in Europe
CFE	Treaty on Conventional Armed Forces in Europe
CFE-1A	Concluding Act of the Negotiation on Personnel Strength of CFE
CIA	Central Intelligence Agency
CIS	Commonwealth of Independent States
C/OSCE	Meaning CSCE and OSCE
COW	Correlates of War Index
CPC	Conflict Prevention Centre
CSBM	Confidence- and Security-Building Measures
CSCE	Conference on Security and Co-operation in Europe
CST	Treaty on Collective Security
CSTO	Collective Security Treaty Organization
CTBT	Comprehensive Nuclear-Test-Ban Treaty
EAPC	Euro-Atlantic Partnership Council
EC	European Community
EPAA	European Phased Adaptive Approach
ES	English School
ESDP	European Security and Defense Policy
EST	European Security Treaty (Medvedev initiative of 2009)
EU	European Union
FSC	Forum for Security Co-operation
GDP	Gross Domestic Product
GNP	Gross National Product
GOP	Grand Old Party (Republican Party)
G8	Group of Eight (see also G6, G7, and G20)
IDP	Internally Displaced Person
IFSH	Institute for Peace Research and Security Policy Hamburg
IGO	Intergovernmental Organization
IISS	International Institute for Strategic Studies
IMF	International Monetary Fund
INF	Intermediate-Range Nuclear Forces

IO	International Organization
IR	International Relations
JCC	Joint Consultative Commission
MAD	Mutual Assured Destruction
MANPADS	Man-Portable Air-Defense Systems
MBFR	Mutual and Balanced Force Reductions Talks
NACC	North Atlantic Cooperation Council
NATO	North Atlantic Treaty Organization
New START	New Strategic Arms Reduction Treaty
NGO	Non-Governmental Organization
NRC	NATO-Russia Council
NSNW	Non-Strategic Nuclear Weapons
NTM	National-Technical Means
ODIHR	Office for Democratic Institutions and Human Rights
OSCE	Organization for Security and Co-operation in Europe
OSCC	Open Skies Consultative Commission
PC	Political Committee (of NATO)
PD	Prisoners' Dilemma
PfP	Partnership for Peace
PJC	NATO-Russia Permanent Joint Council
PMSC	Political-Military Steering Committee
POL-MIL	Political-Military
PPP	Purchasing Power Parity
R&D	Research and Development
REACT	Rapid Expert Assistance and Co-operation Teams
SALT	Strategic Arms Limitation Talks
SALW	Small Arms and Light Weapons
SC	Security Community
SG	Secretary General
SMM	OSCE Special Monitoring Mission to Ukraine
SORT	Strategic Offensive Reductions Treaty
TFT	Tit-For-Tat
TLE	Treaty-Limited Equipment
TUR	Turkey
UK	United Kingdom
U.S.	United States of America
USSR	Union of Socialist Soviet Republics
VD	Vienna Document
WEU	Western European Union
WMD	Weapons of Mass Destruction
WTO	Warsaw Treaty Organization

List of Charts and Tables

Charts

Tables

Prologue

A chilly eastward wind crept through the streets of Manhattan. It had drizzled since the early hours. New York's hectic aura was only about to unfold on this Wednesday morning. A still young-looking man climbed the stairs of the United Nations Headquarters. Even though he was not as young anymore as he appeared to be on television – he would soon turn 58 – his moves were still energetic. Surrounded by a bunch of people, security guards and various broadcast teams, his thoughts remained focused on the first sentences he was about to deliver to the General Assembly. Until the very morning hours he had been pondering the weight his words would carry. He was certain that the coming weeks would change the course of history. Though, an awkward feeling which kept him awake at night made him shiver when imagining the future. He was not sure what the future would hold for him and his people. Only two events of comparable magnitude had come to mind when he was writing his speech.

A few minutes later, routine had gained the upper hand. The golden quadrangle behind his back, some hundred eagerly looking eyes before the podium, he started to formulate the first words that would set the scene; the words which would make the audience aware that a historic moment was about to unfold. 'Two great revolutions, the French revolution of 1789 and the Russian revolution of 1917, have exerted a powerful influence on the actual nature of the historical process and radically changed the course of world events.' He paused. From now on, nothing would be the same anymore...

That day – December 7, 1988 – the man by the name of Mikhail Sergeyevich Gorbachev announced that the Soviet Union would reduce its military presence in Eastern Europe by half a million soldiers. Considerable numbers of tanks and other conventional arms would be withdrawn in the years to come. The world held its breath. What had been unthinkable for decades was about to happen in a blink: the Soviet retreat from Eastern Europe.

Probably more than any other event in the following years, that cold December morning marked the beginning of the end of the Cold War. It was the irreversible sign that the politics of *Glasnost* and *Perestroika* had become reality. It was the moment Moscow relinquished its trump card in the military standoff with NATO. It was the signal for the other Warsaw Pact members that the Kremlin would not constrain their foreign and security policy choices the way it did in the past.

The subsequent years would see the fall of the Berlin Wall, a reunited Germany, and the break-up of both the Warsaw Pact and the Soviet Union. Gorbachev's initiative would pave the way for a comprehensive treaty on the conventional military equipment of both blocs, resulting in the largest disarmament initiative of all times. Based on the mutual reduction of arms, a new system of cooperative security in Europe emerged. Diplomats from the East and the West, for years trapped in ideological trench warfare, now rushed to the various negotiation tables to elaborate a dense network of interlocking agreements, designed to cement the new understanding and to avert a relapse into old confrontational times. The 1990 Charter of Paris of the CSCE stated with overt enthusiasm, 'ours is a time for fulfilling the hopes and expectations our peoples have cherished for decades: steadfast commitment to democracy based on human rights and fundamental freedoms; prosperity through economic liberty and social justice; and equal security for all our countries.' Centuries of bloodshed in Europe seemed to end within a few years only. The future promised security through partnership and cooperation.

Almost 20 years later, in 2007, the same Mikhail Gorbachev – now an old and disenchanted pariah to his own people – applauded the Kremlin's leaders for their decision to give up on the CFE Treaty. 'It would be absolutely illogical for Russia to be the only state to abide by the treaty and for others not to even ratify it', he noted. The preceding years had seen the rise of American unipolarity, the sellout of Russian greatness followed by an economic recovery under the autocratic Vladimir Putin, and the slow erosion of the system of cooperative security in Europe.

Only a few months after the end of CFE, Russian troops crossed the border to the former Soviet Republic of Georgia. The five-day battle was the first international war between two recognized states on geographical Europe after the surrender of Nazi Germany. During the early hours of the Russian campaign, a hawkish U.S. Secretary of Defense seriously weighed the option of limited air strikes against the advancing Russian tanks. What seemed to be a long-gone specter of the past was in a sudden a conceivable scenario: a potential military standoff between Russia and an enlarged NATO.

While those five days seemed to be an unexpected "historical hick-up", a sudden relapse, owed to the complicated settings in the South Caucasus and not intended to significantly change Europe's security, the Russian incursion into Georgian territory turned out to be the writing on the wall that the West and Russia were again drifting apart. In March 2014, in a breathtaking coup of Machiavellian impudence, Vladimir Putin ordered the annexation of Crimea to halt Western influence in what the Kremlin sees as part of its *Near Abroad*. Shocked by the events, Western policy-makers slowly realized that there was no positive engagement strategy left in their dealings with Russia anymore. Belligerent language followed belligerent action and sanctions followed the unlawful presence of Russian soldiers on what was Ukrainian soil for the past 22 years. A quarter of a century after Gorbachev's bold speech, West-Russian relations had hit rock bottom.

What went wrong? What happened to the enthusiasm that had inspired leaders in the East and the West? And why was the neatly established system of cooperative arms control agreements in Europe incapable of impeding the return to confrontation? Traces to the answers are spread across three continents and three generations of political leaders. Some of them date even back to a past long before the cold and rainy Manhattan winter day.

1   Introduction

For more than a decade now, Europe's once unique security institutions are in decay. (Cf. for example Dunay 2008; Steinmeier 2008; Euro-Atlantic Security Initiative 2012; Mützenich and Karádi 2013) To different degrees, this development affects almost all institutions under the rubric of cooperative security. In particular, the realm of cooperative arms control is negatively affected.

Significant legally and politically binding arms control agreements under the auspices of the Organization for Security and Co-operation in Europe (OSCE) are either stagnating, deadlocked, or in retreat. The most prominent example is the Conventional Armed Forces in Europe Treaty (CFE). OSCE participating States remain unable or unwilling to successfully overcome the deadlock in arms control institutions. Mirroring this development, cooperative security institutions between the North Atlantic Treaty Organization (NATO) and the Russian Federation have largely ceased to function. With the war in Ukraine ongoing, prospects for reversing this trend are rather low for the moment.

The rise and fall of cooperative arms control in Europe raises the question, why its institutions are eroding. Unfortunately, scholarly research on the issue is incomplete. On the one hand, scholars have failed to pay long-term attention to the volatile evolution of cooperative security institutions. On the other hand, they missed to comprehensively link institutional decay to the general foreign and security policies of the main actors involved. As a result, previous research has either concentrated on issue-specific institutions, while leaving out the conundrum why the broader schemes behind institutionalized cooperation changed over time, or it has focused on the broader politics while ignoring the issue-specificity of relevant institutions.

The rise and fall of cooperative arms control in Europe is therefore a promising research subject to analyze the volatility of institutionalized cooperation between the West and Russia, both from a theoretical and a policy-oriented angle. By concentrating on the establishment, maintenance, and decay of institutionalized cooperation in this specific sphere of Euro-Atlantic security, common interests, divergent interpretations, and critical structural changes come to the fore. Understanding the volatile process of institutionalization of cooperative arms control in Europe will not provide a blueprint for taking on current and future challenges. However, it could help to avoid repeating those policies that led to its current state of decay.

This book analyzes the policies of cooperative arms control in Europe and their institutionalization from 1973 to 2014, the year of Russia's illegal annexation of Crimea. It tries to explain not only the rise but also the fall of cooperative arms control by examining what forms of institutions compose cooperative arms control in Europe, and why those institutions are in decay.

Its focus is on institutions established between 1973 and 2014 with the aim of reducing the potential for military conflict between a number of actors: (1) between the United States and NATO on the one hand and the Soviet Union/The Russian Federation and the Warsaw Treaty Organization (WTO)/the Collective Security Treaty (CST) on the other; (2) between NATO and the post-Soviet states; and (3) amongst OSCE participating States. Special emphasis is placed on the respective politics under the auspices of the Conference on Security and Cooperation in Europe (CSCE) and its successor the OSCE as well as under the NATO-Russia framework. Intra-alliance arrangements of NATO, the coordinating politics of the Common Foreign and Security Policy of the European Union (EU), the Western European Union (WEU), or bilateral U.S.-Russian arms control arrangements from the realm of weapons of mass destruction (WMD) are not part of the analysis.

Within this sphere of multilateral politics, special emphasis is put on two actors: the United States and the Soviet Union/the Russian Federation. This focus is due to the quasi-hegemonic roles both held during the Cold War (cf. Leffler and Westad 2010), the United States' quasi-hegemonic position in post-Cold War NATO (Rauchhaus 2000: 175), and Russia's national identity as the prime successor to the Soviet Union. (Cf. also Aggarwal 2000: 71)

Indeed, the politics of cooperative arms control in Europe are neither exclusively shaped by these two actors nor are their foreign and security policies identical with or limited to cooperative arms control in Europe. While further research is needed to fully understand the multilateral dimension of the evolution of cooperative arms control in Europe, concentrating on those two states that helped to substantially shape it is beneficial from a structural point of view. As McKenzie and Loedel (1998b: 8) have put it, 'the United States and Russia remain the key states in determining the outcome of the debate over European security: the United States as the only power with a global reach; Russia because of its ability to threaten its neighbors and to thwart attempts at institutional change.'

1.2   Why Focus on Cooperative Arms Control in Europe?

Five fundamental reasons speak for focusing on the rise and fall of cooperative arms control in Europe. The first reason is a *lack of comprehensiveness in current research*. Analysts and researchers have not provided a complete picture of the volatility of institutionalization, including establishment, maintenance, and decay of institutions. At the same time, exclusive foci on specific institutions, such as the CFE Treaty (cf. Zellner, Schmidt, and Neuneck 2009), the OSCE (cf. Ghébali and Warner 2006), or NATO (cf. Pouliot 2010), prevail. Analysis of institutional overlap is underrepresented. No multi-level holistic approach on cooperative arms control in Europe exists so far.

The second reason is a *lack of theoretical research*. Current and past research has often avoided grounding issue-specific analysis in sound theoretical analysis. While early scholars of arms control have applied clear-cut theories in support of their analysis (cf. Schelling and Halperin 1961), current arms control research often tends either to overemphasize purely policy-driven approaches (cf. exemplary Andreasen and Williams 2011) or uses approaches that lack a well-researched and reasonable combination of theory and research issue (cf. exemplary Durkalec, Kearns, and Kulesa 2013: 9-10; for a good exception from the rule see Mutschler 2013). In turn, theoretical research of IR scholars has largely evaded the topic of arms control since the end of the Cold War. No sound scholarly research on the rise and fall of cooperative arms control in Europe exists so far.

The third reason is a *lax use of terminology*. Researchers, political analysts, and decision-makers often employ terminology from the theoretical concept of *regime* (for an analysis of the concept see Chapter 4) when referring to cooperative arms control in Europe without any proof that it really suits their requirement, both from a conceptual point of view and with respect to the topicality of the theoretical concept as such. No genuine research has either verified or falsified the regime claim in relation to the issue. The reasons behind this shortcoming are a general shrinking interest in theoretical research on arms control (cf. opening remarks by Alexei Arbatov, EU Non-Proliferation and Disarmament Conference 2014) and a specific lack of originality in conjunction with the issue.

The fourth reason is a *lack of research on regime decay*. As earlier said, cooperative arms control is now in decay. Directly deriving from the lack of comprehensiveness in current research on the issue is the fact that researchers are struggling to explain institutional decay, both from a more narrow issue-specific and from a broader theoretical perspective. Issue-specific research either remains with descriptions of the current problems (cf. exemplary Zellner 2012) or approaches the wider spectra of U.S.-Russian relations without going into the cumbersome procedure of searching for the reasons behind its poor state (cf. exemplary Walt 2014). Theoretical research based on the regime episteme has a somewhat different problem. Decay is simply not an equally represented part of regime scholars' research agenda. The result is an incomplete picture. So far, studies about the reasons for regime decay are underrepresented.

The fifth reason is the *topicality of the issue*. Policy-makers, researchers, and analysts alike agree that the decay of cooperative arms control in Europe is a severe problem for the continent's security (cf. exemplary Sikorski, Westerwelle, and Sovndal 2013). The Ukraine conflict has only helped to make the pre-existing problems even more pressing (cf. Ischinger, Pifer, and Zagorski 2014). However, future-oriented policy analysts based on sound theoretical research on the issue and designed to address the unraveling of institutions is absent. Issue-specific and theoretical lack of research will not alter this shortcoming. A comprehensive and theory-based approach might help to shed light on long-term policies that led to the current state. It might also help to formulate alternative policy concepts.

1.3   Shortcomings of Previous Research

When analyzing previous research on the issue, three important shortcomings come to the fore. (1) Previous research lacks a commonly agreed terminology when referring to the institutions of cooperative arms control in Europe. Without a commonly agreed terminology, actors might not know whether they talk about the same issues. (2) With regards to institutions, scholars often employ the regime terminology without any proof that the very institutions are in fact regimes. Furthermore, their applications of definitions are often imprecise and contradictory. Without proof, definitions become irrelevant. (3) Theoretical works on the issue are either highly outdated or they pay considerably less attention to the fact of institutional decay. Without up to date research and a holistic approach to institutionalization, research remains incomplete.

1.3.1   Fuzzy Terminology

It is impossible to find a commonly agreed term in either scholarly research or everyday politics describing the very research subject at hand. Instead, diversity prevails. Often, architectural or artisan paraphrases are employed to describe institutionalization. Already in 1994, Walker (p. 13) issued a warning that 'the talk of security "architecture" is misleading; "patchwork" is a better metaphor for the plethora of shifting and overlapping experiments under way'. Particularly the term 'security architecture' features prominent in the literature (cf. Czempiel 1998: xi). The absence of clear terminology has opened up the doors for diverse interpretations. Whereas some speak of 'Euro-Atlantic security structures' (Zellner 2009: 18) or a 'full fabric of European security' (Gottemoeller 2008: 7), others refer to a 'multilayered security architecture that incorporates [...] NATO, EU, WEU, OSCE, and the CFE regime' (Auton 1998: 153).

With a view to the OSCE, Rupp and McKenzie (1998: 120) see 'a web of interlocking institutions in post-cold-war Europe'. During his first term in office, Federal Minister of Foreign Affairs Steinmeier (2009: 11) termed the result of 'the cooperative approach to arms control [...] a network of mutually supporting and complementary arms control agreements.' In addition, former German Ambassador Hartmann (2009: 54) describes a 'CFE system [...] complemented by a [...] network of confidence- and security-building measures'. Krause (2003: 1) dubs the post-Cold War European order simply a 'liberal peace'.

Fuzzy terminology is a problem for research because it opens the door to misunderstandings. How can participants in a scholarly debate know that they talk about the same issue without a common terminology?

1.3.2   Theoretical References without Evidence

When talking about the rise and fall of cooperative arms control in Europe, IR scholars have regularly referred to regime theory or at least its terminology without providing actual empirical evidence. Chung (2005: 187) classifies the OSCE as a 'security regime' based on the general assessment that 'regimes can have formal structures as well'. Zellner (2012: 15) refers to a 'European arms control regime' and the CFE Treaty as 'the regime's core' (Zellner 2009: 12) without elaborating a regime-analytical line of argument. Contradicting these assumption, in another article, he labels CFE itself a 'regime' (cf. Zellner 2010: 67). Auton (1998) views confidence- and security-building measures (CSBMs) and CFE as 'multilateral security regimes' without analyzing what their possible regime quality generates in terms of institutional interdependence. None of these authors nor any other author who uses the regime label with reference to cooperative arms control in Europe, has ever made the effort to embark on a sound regime-analytical line of analysis. Their observations are mere assumptions.

Theoretical references not backed up by evidence are a problem for academic credibility and for the potential cognitive effects such research generates. As Thomas Hobbes noted in *Leviathan*, the abuse of speech happens 'when men register their thoughts wrong, by the inconstancy of the signification of their words; by which they register for their conceptions that which they never conceived, and so deceive themselves.' They are also a problem for the possible consequences of issue-specific research. If the forms of the institutions of cooperative arms control in Europe deserve the regime label – as most IR scholars claim – than the decay of certain institutions, such as the CFE Treaty, might have different effects on other potential regimes or regime networks than perhaps anticipated by scholars so far.

1.3.3 Incomplete Theoretical Research

Terminological fuzziness and theoretical references not backed up by evidence have their roots in the lack of theoretical research on cooperative arms control in Europe. First, there are only a handful of studies on the research subject which rely on a sound theoretical basis at all. Second, of those few studies almost all employ regime theory. Other theoretical approaches are rare. Third, researchers have not analyzed the institutionalization of cooperative arms control in Europe over a longer period. Instead, the very few theoretical accounts are either incomplete or highly outdated.

Nye (1987: 392-3) sees the CSCE as a 'U.S.-Soviet security regime' and argues 'that at least a weak regime exists in Europe and that its broad principles and norms are the division of Germany, the legitimate role of the United States and the Soviet Union in European security, and mutually recognized spheres of concern. The implications and implementation of these principles are spelled out in various ways, including the Berlin agreements and the Final Act of the Conference on Security and Cooperation in Europe.'

Janice Stein (2003: 17, footnote 5) claims that the provisions of the 1986 Conference on Confidence- and Security-Building Measures and Disarmament in Europe (CDE) led to a 'limited security regime designed to build confidence in central Europe.' Efinger, Rittberger, and Zürn (1988: 174) conclude in late 1988 that the regime conduciveness in the realm of limitation of conventional armaments is 'presumably non-existent'. In a study on CSBMs, Rittberger, Efinger, and Mendler (1988: 28) admit that 'East-West relations have rarely been considered as a field for 'regime analyses.' They infer that an East-West CSBM regime exists as 'a stabilizing element in the still highly militarized security situation in Europe.' (Ibid: 30) In two other studies, Efinger (1989: 343-84; 1990: 117-50) traces the evolving CSBM regime back to the formative days of the Helsinki Final Act.

Without much further elaboration, Müller (1993a: 133-4) rates the Helsinki Final Act and the 1990 OSCE Charter of Paris as regimes that consolidate the territorial order in Europe and concludes that the policies of regulating military capabilities in Europe through means of CSBMs and CFE have reached a certain level of regime quality. In another account, he (Müller 1993b: 361) identifies a security regime in the realm of European military order, including 'INF Treaty, Stockholm/Paris agreements on confidence-building, CFE Treaty, 2+4 Treaty, practices such as doctrine seminars and mutual visits of military personnel, the Crisis Control Centre, and the recent mutual promises of unilateral reductions of short-range nuclear weapons'. Kelleher (1994: 318) sees an emerging 'cooperative security regime [...] in the Northern Hemisphere.' In the same account (ibid: 326) she refers to 'the intersecting regimes set in place under the CFE, the CSCE, and the Open Skies agreements in 1992.'

Ropers and Schlotter (1989) have contributed the most elaborate account of the 'negotiation system of the CSCE' so far. They conclude that the system has led to generate regimes of differing scope and quality, with the military realm of CSBMs being the most established (ibid: 333). Furthermore, they anchor the regime demand in the inability of the United States and the Soviet Union to establish all-European hegemony and in the subsequent bloc confrontation which underlined the need for regulating political, military, economic, and human issues. Through employing issue linkages within and outside the CSCE system, the two blocs were able to establish the CSCE as reinforcing processual institution. The CSCE in its entirety, they conclude, can be classified as a 'declaratory regime'. Schlotter (1999) views the evolution of CSBMs as the only full-fledged regime in the CSCE process.

Neuneck (1995) has contributed a novel approach towards one aspect of cooperative arms control in Europe by applying a Game Theory approach to conventional stability and arms control measures. His approach has a sound mathematical basis. The downturn is that it concentrates mostly on conventional forces stability and leaves out the wider political evolution which has shaped the process of conventional force limitations as well as the multitude of CSBMs in the C/OSCE framework beyond the Vienna Document (ibid: 228-59; see Annex II for a list of the relevant CSBMs).

Incomplete theoretical research is a problem for the arms control research agenda. The decay of cooperative arms control cannot be comprehensively explained without an encompassing and up-to-date approach based on a sound theoretical frame. Instead, approaches towards the research subject would have to rely on assumptions.

Summing up the three previous paragraphs, up-to-date and comprehensive theoretical accounts are missing. In addition, a common terminology based on sound theoretical research is absent. It is therefore important, first, to arrive at a clear definition of the research subject at hand.

1.4   Definitions of Key Terms

So far, this study has employed the term *cooperative arms control in Europe* without further elaboration. It is indeed important to explain its origin for two reasons: (1) in order to avoid repeating the mistake of the diverse and confusing use of terminology of previous research; and (2) because the term is a neologism[1] by the author – an attempt to unite the various terminological concepts under one definition.

---

1   The term is not a mere translation of an earlier definition of arms control ('kooperative Rüstungssteuerung') provided by German Cold War scholars based in Hamburg (cf. von Baudissin and Lutz 1979: 5-6). In contrast, there is no stringent causal reference to nuclear deterrence.

Defining a subject of research should start with scrutinizing a number of concepts and definitions. Cooperative arms control in Europe appears within the issue-area of Euro-Atlantic cooperative security. The 'issue-area'[2] itself should by no means be confused with the issue of cooperative arms control in Europe or the boundaries of a specific regime or a network of regimes (cf. Orsini, Morin, and Young 2013: 30).

1.4.1 Cooperative Security

The first term in need of definition is *cooperative security*. Cooperative security has been defined differently (cf. Mihalka 2005: 113-4). In this book, the concept of cooperative security is understood to include a number of central aspects: increasing *mutual* security and predictability by means of reciprocity, inclusiveness, dialogue, a defensive orientation, transparency, confidence-building, and arms limitations (cf. Carter, Perry, and Steinbruner 1992; Nolan 1994a,b; Mihalka 2005; Dewitt and Acharya 1996: 9-10; Jervis 1999). The aim of cooperative security is to generate interstate relations 'in which disputes are expected to occur, but they are expected to do so within the limits of agreed-upon norms and established procedures.' (Nolan 1994b: 5) Zartman provides an explanation of the just distribution of gains in security policy negotiations aimed at increasing mutual security. It captures well a basic definition of cooperative security:

> Both negotiation and security policy are too often presented as tools for maximizing single party gain, when they should be presented as ways of maximizing two (or multi) party gain, jointly if possible, separately if necessary. Negotiations that provide something for everyone, or that trade off differentially valued goods, and security measures that provide security for all, or that tie my security to your security, are likely to lead to more favorable, stable, productive, and just results. (Zartman 1995: 892)

The politics of cooperative security in Europe have often been identified with the institution of the OSCE (cf. Krause 2003). Therefore, a large part of the analysis of this study will concentrate on policies achieved under the auspices of the OSCE and its predecessor, the CSCE. However, the focus here is not limited to this organization but instead tackles cooperative policies of NATO as well. This is particularly due to the fact that the different layers of security institutions and policies have come to increasingly overlap in the aftermath of the Cold War (cf. Flynn and Farrell 1999: 505). Bauwens et al (1994: 21) have thus argued that 'it is difficult to distinguish NATO's enlarged mandate

---

2   Keohane (1984: 61) defines issue-areas as sets of issues that are 'dealt with in common negotiations and by the same, or closely coordinated, bureaucracies.' Ernst B. Haas (1980: 365) defines an issue-area as 'a recognized cluster of concerns involving interdependence not only among the parties but among the issues themselves.'

from the overall approach of the Conference on Security and Cooperation in Europe.'

The OSCE's approach to security is basically holistic (cf. Krause 2003). So is the concept of cooperative security. It encompasses "hard" security issues in the military realm, economic and environmental, as well as human security aspects. It does not stop with the legal concept of the sovereign nation state but views intrastate developments as well as transnational and transboundary threats as key factors affecting the security of others – that is states *and* the individual human being.

Even though the holistic approach of cooperative security together with the encompassing security approach of the OSCE is of particular importance for the argument of this book, only a certain spectrum – arms control – is under consideration. Hence, the concept of cooperative security rather serves as the normative background against which a particular set of arms control institutions and the policies directed to them are analyzed. The following table comprises the aims and means of the concept of cooperative security.

TABLE 1

AIMS AND MEANS OF THE CONCEPT OF COOPERATIVE SECURITY

Aims	increasing mutual security and predictability
Means	reciprocity inclusiveness dialogue-based defensive orientation transparency confidence-building arms limitations

1.4.2 Arms Control

The second term in need of definition is *arms control*. Bull (1961: 4-5) sees 'peace through the manipulation of force' as the grand scheme under which to place the concept theoretically. In its most practical sense and in relation to the early period of the bipolar arms race, arms control's foremost objective was the prevention of (nuclear) war (cf. Schelling and Halperin 1961: 3; Bull 1961: 3-4).

Historically speaking, arms control in the bipolar context existed before the emergence of the paradigm of cooperative security during the 1970s.

However, the two became almost equated (cf. Dunn 2009: 175). Nolan (1994b: 5) concludes: 'at the practical level cooperative security seeks to devise agreed-upon measures to prevent war and to do so primarily by preventing the means for successful aggression from being assembled'. This quote reads almost like a description of the concept of arms control. Carter, Perry, and Steinbruner (1992: 6) refer to 'a commitment to regulate the size, technical composition, investment patterns, and operational practices of all military forces by mutual consent for mutual benefit.' Again, they do not refer to arms control but to cooperative security. These examples show how closely intertwined the two concepts are. Arms control has thus become an integral part or means of the "toolbox" of cooperative security. In recent years, the paths of the two concepts have somewhat drifted apart with arms control being questioned particularly in the United States (cf. Larsen 2009: 11 et seq) and cooperative security seen mostly through the prism of Constructivist theory (cf. Müller and Wunderlich 2013). In this book, a rather broad definition of arms control is used. Arms control is understood to be

> *any agreement among states to regulate some aspect of their military capability or potential. The agreement may apply to the location, amount, readiness, or types of military forces, weapons, or facilities. Whatever their scope or terms, however, all plans for arms control have one common factor: they presuppose some form of cooperation or joint action among participants regarding their military programs.* (Larsen 2009: 1)

Military-to-military contacts, military exchange programs, and the democratic control of forces, usually subsumed under the headline of CSBMs[3], are all part of this definition. In this sense, arms control 'should be thought of as encompassing all aspects of the military dimension' in order 'to prevent conflicts within states as well as between them.' (Walker 1994: 6-7)

1.4.3   Europe

Europe is the third term in need of definition. The term as such resembles 'a concept as well as a continent, and the borders of both oscillate wildly.' (Jacobs 2012) In this book, Europe is neither used in purely geographical nor in cultural terms. It is a linguistic reference to a historical-political development.

As already stated, cooperative security in Europe has always been in close vicinity to the CSCE/OSCE. Zagorski (2010: 58) argues that the contemporary understanding of cooperative security should not be confused with the indivisibility of security from the early documents of the CSCE. Nevertheless, the post-Cold War approach towards cooperative security in Europe

---

3   For a discussion about the validity of distinguishing between arms control and CSBMs see Holst 1991 and Wright 2000: 4-5.

can only be understood against the specific historical European background (cf. Krause 2003: 4).

As will be explained later, the politics and institutionalization of cooperative arms control in Europe took off shortly before and in parallel to the early CSCE framework. Even though the end of the Cold War triggered a fundamental shift in the political goals pursued and in the composition of parties to a number of agreements and organizations, the historical provenance of the concept of cooperative arms control in Europe is European. This book argues, however, that the concept is not limited to the OSCE but stretches across a densely institutionalized area, including NATO, and involving 56 states from Vancouver to Vladivostok.

Hence, this book is not about regionalism. Snyder (2012b: 312) defines regions as 'groupings of states that share either geographic proximity or have sufficient cultural/historic ties that bind them together.' In the vast OSCE area, stretching across three continents, this is not the case, neither from a cultural nor from a geographical point of view.

1.4.4 Cooperative Arms Control in Europe

The result of these observations is the novel term of *cooperative arms control in Europe*. It shall serve the purpose of combining cooperative security and arms control in a specific European historical-political setting. Cooperative arms control is not simply a merger of two already closely connected concepts (i.e. cooperative security and arms control). It is also not a reference to the earlier German definitions of arms control. Instead, it is an attempt to link institutionalization in a specific sphere of arms control to a strongly normative concept of European origin.

1.4.5 Institutions and Regimes

So far, this study has made continued references to *institutions* and *institutionalization*. As Thomas Risse (2002: 605) correctly noted, 'there are at least as many definitions of (international) institutions as there are theoretical perspectives'. The term *international institution* is often applied in IR to cover diverse social concepts such as treaties, organizations, regimes, or conventions. Duffield (2007) has addressed this terminological diversity by differentiating between ontological and functional forms of international institutions. Accordingly, ontological forms refer to intersubjective elements such as "norms". Functional forms refer to formal elements such as "rules". (Ibid: 8) Following his typology, regimes, in a general understanding, fall under ontological forms while agreements and formal IGOs fall under functional forms. (Ibid: 15) Throughout this book, these three types of international cooperative interaction – regimes, agreements, and IGOs (or IOs) – will be covered by the term institutions, while the process of their establishment, maintenance, and, in a more general understanding, their evolution will be captured by the term institutionalization.

International institutions are in close vicinity to the theoretical concept of regime. Often, institutions are equated with regimes. Before this study will provide an analysis of the concept of regime, it will be important for the further research process to provide a first, though incomplete, definition of the concept.

> *Regimes can be defined as sets of implicit or explicit principles, norms, rules, and decision-making procedures around which actors' expectations converge in a given area of international relations. Principles are beliefs of fact, causation, and rectitude. Norms are standards of behavior defined in terms of rights and obligations. Rules are specific prescriptions or proscriptions for action. Decision-making procedures are prevailing practices for making and implementing collective choice.* (Krasner 1982: 2)

1.5 The Theoretical Basis

Previous research has failed to comprehensively analyze what forms of institutions compose cooperative arms control in Europe and what their relationship is. As a consequence, decay has not been comprehensively explained. Possible reasons for decay which might have to do with the institutional form (e.g. linkages between regimes) remained unconsidered. Since cooperative arms control in Europe – the name already implies it – is based on international cooperation, IR approaches which analyze and explain international cooperation will provide the theoretical basis of this book. Different theories have tried to explain international institutionalized cooperation (cf. Schieder and Spindler 2010).

This study employs a multi-theory approach for explaining the rise and fall of cooperative arms control in Europe and the related foreign and security policies of the United States and the Soviet Union/Russia. Such an approach seems more promising for analyzing long-term cooperation than a single-theory approach, for IR's three grand theories put different emphases on the various aspects of cooperation and competition – all of them containing valuable insights (cf. Schieder and Spindler 2010). Realism, for instance, has always been skeptical with regard the durability of cooperation due to the constant competition states seemingly face. Regime theory, an offspring of Liberalism, has described how states cooperate using international institutions – however, mostly by focusing on trade and the environment while neglecting the realm of classical security policy (cf. Hasenclever, Mayer, and Rittberger 1997). Constructivism is particularly apt to explain cooperation taking into account the impact of cognitive repercussions such as emotions, knowledge or socially constructed images of oneself and "the other" (cf. Ross 2006).

This study relies particularly on Realism and regime theory. It combines these two theoretical approaches with the essentials of the concept of Security Communities, the English School, and Constructivist analyses of norm dynamics. Together, this multi-theory approach will provide the necessary broad analytical perspective on the rise and fall of cooperative arms control. This approach seems also particularly valuable given the long period covered by this study.

One alternative possibility to approach international cooperation would be the heuristic device of a Game Theoretical 2 x 2 matrix (cf. Mutschler 2013). However, examples of repeated and long-term cooperation involving different layers of cooperation and different situations would have to include a variety of multi super games with different payoff structures (cf. McGinnis 1986). Such real-world examples would be extremely difficult to model. In addition, explanations along the lines of a rational choice approach would most likely suffer from its overly static and rigid framing (cf. Hopmann and Druckman 1991: 273).

The following paragraphs will shortly highlight the five theoretical approaches chosen for this study.

1.5.1 Realism

Realism's skepticism towards international cooperation and its occupation with the impediments to successful cooperation provides the necessary critical basis, for the institutions of cooperative arms control in Europe are in fact in decay. Russia's foreign and security policy has regularly been characterized as following Realist rationales (cf. Mearsheimer 2014). Realism would thus be a good basis for better understanding contemporary Russian foreign and security policy (cf. Jonsson 2012: 450). Further on, the Ukraine conflict has triggered a revival of the Neoliberal vs. Neorealist debate amongst some U.S. scholars (see Mearsheimer 2014; McFaul, Sestanovich, and Mearsheimer 2014; Charap and Shapiro 2014a,b) about which U.S. and/or Russian foreign policy orientation (Liberal vs. Realist) is to blame for the conflict. Realism is therefore a very timely approach. In addition, Realism's occupation with conflict seems appropriate given the fact that the U.S.-Soviet/ Russian security relationship has undergone recurring periods of competition and conflict. Last but not least, the role of power remains central to understanding international cooperation (cf. Müller 2013).

1.5.2 Regime Theory

Regime theory makes for a reasonable approach due to the widespread recognition of cooperative arms control as either a single regime or as a network of interlinked regimes in both, the existing research literature and in official documents; even more so, because no research has ever proven the regime assumption. In addition, Realism is biased when it comes to international institutions and limited in its approach to explaining the persistence of international institutions, particularly in times of change or crisis. Regime theory simply provides more answers to this phenomenon. Beyond that, regime theory was an effort by Neoliberal scholars to bring the Neorealists on board in their effort to explain and accept international institutions. Regime theory thus builds on a number of distinct Realist assumptions and can be viewed as the Neoliberal "extension" to Neorealism (cf. Crawford 1996). Last but not least, regime theory can be applied as a method for classifying international institutions.

However, before we can speak of regimes when referring to cooperative arms control in Europe, the term regime will be handled with great care. Instead, the term *cooperation clusters* (Young 1996) shall be applied until the very form of institutions of cooperative arms control in Europe has been fully analyzed and clarified.

1.5.3 Security Communities, the English School, and Constructivist Analyses

Since decay is a prominent part of this study, particularly such theoretical approaches that also take account of the wider cooperation spectra which drive institutionalized cooperation might provide an additional basis for understanding the reasons for and effects of decay. As will be discussed later on, regime theorists have not comprehensively explained institutional decay. The consequences of this shortcoming make it necessary to look into other theoretical approaches explaining the volatility and, hence, the decay of international institutionalized cooperative efforts. Amongst them is the concept of Security Community, the English School, and Constructivist analyses of norm dynamics.

1.6 Methodology

This study applies mostly an inductive approach as outlined in Aristotle's *Nicomachean Ethics* (2008). It does not aim at theory building. Instead, it tries to either verify or falsify whether cooperative arms control in Europe can be characterized along the lines of the regime concept. This leads to instances of abductive analysis where inductive and deductive methods go hand in hand (cf. Daase et al 2008: 152).

The reason for this approach is rooted in the inadequate state of previous research. As already stated, a plethora of institutions under the broad rubric of cooperative arms control in Europe has already been labeled *regime* by various IR scholars. The diverse use of terminology and the lack of sound theoretical research has led to a cacophony of definitions. Of course, one could simply describe the institutions and the phenomenon of decay empirically. However, that would mean that any theoretical insights going beyond the descriptive stage would be left out. As an example, certain institutions might share significant characteristics of the regime concept. If that would be the case, the decay of specific agreements such as CFE would have a stronger effect on other agreements which might be part of the same potential regime (see the effects of 'negative reverberation' described in Alter and Meunier 2009). Before any questions about institutional decay can be answered, it has to be either verified or falsified that the form of the institutions of cooperative arms control in Europe actually deserves the regime label.

The methodological approach chosen for this study proceeds in a number of sequential stages. First, a Realist model for understanding international cooperation is developed. Then, the empirics of 41 years of cooperative arms control in Europe are assessed and analyzed, using the Realist model. Next, the main findings and assumptions of regime scholars are introduced and applied in order to classify the empirics. That way it will be possible to test whether and which institutions of cooperative arms control in Europe deserve the regime label. Finally, the question shall be answered whether regime theory can produce meaningful results with regards decay or whether other theories of cooperation have more explanatory power.

1.6.1 A Realist Model of International Cooperation

First, a Realist model for understanding international cooperation will be developed in order to explain what international cooperation is and why it is so problematic from a Realist point of view. The model will consists of five variables determining a number of processual sequences of international cooperation. It has been developed by the author specifically for this study in order to assess repeated instances of U.S.-Soviet/Russian cooperation on cooperative arms control in Europe during the last 41 years. The model shall help to shed light on the origins and consequences of cooperation and institutionalization. Its application shall allow for assessing reasons for, strategies of, and states' evaluation of gains from cooperation. By highlighting these factors, a preliminary comparison with the essentials of regime theory shall become possible.

1.6.2 First Abductive Test

After comparing the empirical evidence with the main claims of regime scholars, Steven Krasner's (1982: 2) typology of regimes ('principles', 'norms', 'rules', and 'decision-making procedures') will be used as a model to qualitatively classify 36 agreements with direct relevance to cooperative arms control in Europe. Identifying possible shared principles and norms, this is to test whether the form of institutions deserves the regime label. Thus, a final assessment about a potential regime quality of the institutions of cooperative arms control in Europe will become possible. In addition, regime scholars' findings about indicators of decay will be compared with the empirical evidence in order to assess whether the institutions of cooperative arms control in Europe display any such signs of decay. This test will be abductive, for it will combine the inductive process of extrapolating from potentially shared principles and norms to a general regime quality with the deductive process of extrapolating from general findings of regime scholars about decay to the specific state of certain institutions.

1.6.3   Second Abductive Test

Principles and norms are a significant part of regime theory. Their condition as regards topicality and relevance will then be analyzed in a second abductive test. As part of that second test, 51 statements by U.S. and Soviet/Russian delegations to the C/OSCE between 1990 and 2014 will be analyzed using quantitative and qualitative content analysis (cf. Krippendorff 1980) before being compared to twelve key principles and norms that shape cooperative arms control in Europe. That way, it should be possible to determine what principles and norms are still reflected in the statements, which ones are not reflected anymore, and what other general policy topics are on the two states' agendas. Thereby, potential additional reasons for the decay of cooperative arms control in Europe shall be highlighted. That second test is abductive as well since it combines the inductive process of extrapolating from the use of key principles and norms to a general assessment of their political relevance with the deductive process of extrapolating from general policy topics of the two states to the specific state of key principles and norms.

1.6.4   Comparison with Other Theories

Regime theory has a number of shortcomings, both from a conceptual as well as historical point of view. Additional approaches deriving from the theoretical concept of Security Communities, the English School, and Constructivist analyses of norm dynamics might help to broaden the regime concept in order to better explain the general volatility of international cooperation. Analyzing the empirics using those other theoretical approaches, a more holistic perspective, less exclusively bound to Realism and regime theory, shall be gained. That way, a hopefully complete picture of the reasons behind the rise and fall of cooperation on arms control in Europe will emerge.

2 International Cooperation from a Realist Viewpoint

This chapter is about international cooperation from a Realist point of view. Its main research question is: How do states, according to Realism, arrive at international cooperation and which factors complicate their efforts?

The aim of this chapter is to understand the problems associated with international cooperation. Different theoretical approaches try to explain and understand cooperation and the institutionalization of cooperation among states in an environment which lacks any central authority such as a world government. Among them is the Realist approach – the most cooperation-skeptical of all major IR theories. Realism has provided powerful arguments speaking against the probability of repeated, stable, and long-term cooperation, particularly in the realm of security. At the same time, Realism assumes a number of prerequisites which should be in place in order to achieve international cooperation. This chapter develops a novel model for understanding international cooperation from a Realist viewpoint. It shall help to understand and assess the policies of cooperative arms control in Europe.

2.1   Introductory Remarks

Before turning to Realism, one should first define cooperation. The Oxford Dictionary (Oxford University Press eds. 2014) defines *cooperation* as 'the action or process of working together to the same end'. Studying the behavior of animals, Clements and Stephens (1995: 527) define cooperation as 'joint action for mutual benefit'. Both definitions tell only little about the process other than that it is based on a reason and that it involves more than one entity engaged in a certain activity with at least another entity. The reason behind it, the nature of the entities, their activity, the surrounding environment, and their relationship towards the reason, towards their activity, towards each other, and towards the environment, remain a matter of speculation or, better, of definition and explanation.

Explaining *international cooperation* is not possible without first reflecting upon the nature of the entities and the environment in which international cooperation takes place. Since the Westphalian Peace, a particular system of sovereign *nation states* has developed, first in Europe and since the end of Colonialism also globally (cf. Reinhard 2009). Major elements of this system are states' sovereignty, the mutual recognition of sovereign equality, the non-interference in internal affairs of the nation state, diplomatic conduct amongst states, and war (cf. Bull 1977).

Ideally, the modern nation state has an internal monopoly of power which works to establish and uphold order. The domestic monopoly of power can have different forms. The most common forms during the last centuries were democracy, autocracy, monarchy, and oligarchy (cf. Hobsbawn 1992). No central authority (e.g. a world government) exists in the environment in which states operate. If they want to cooperate with each other, they have to find ways to deal with the consequences of the absence of a central authority. All major schools of IR thought recognize this fact to varying degrees. However, they treat the consequences for cooperation differently (cf. Baldwin 1993: 5). While Liberal and Constructivist theories view the absence of a central authority as a lesser impediment to international cooperation, Realism sees it as a major hindrance. So why apply Realism at this point?

First, this book is about institutional decay. Realism's skepticism towards successful cooperation seems therefore only appropriate to assess the interests and the cooperation strategies of the United States and the Soviet Union/Russia. In short, the 'who-gets-what' from cooperation (Strange 1982: 496) gets better addressed by Realism. Also, Realism underscores the impediments to successful cooperation. Concentrating on these impediments might help to explain institutional decay. Further on, Realism is not very prone to any form of normative enthusiasm about cooperation as such, often found in Neoliberal or early Constructivist accounts.

Second, Russia's foreign and security policy has regularly been characterized as following Realist rationales (cf. Jonsson 2012: 450). Thorun (2009) describes Putin's first term as President as 'pragmatic geo-economic realism' and his second term as 'cultural geopolitical realism'. Jonsson (2012: 450) views Russia's foreign and security policy as 'pragmatic, geopolitically focused, [and] realist rather than value-based'. In conjunction with the Ukraine crisis, John Mearsheimer (2014) has argued that Putin acts like a Realist and that Western politicians do not understand his political provenance anymore. German Chancellor Angela Merkel's reported comment to U.S. President Obama that Putin was living 'in another world' (quoted from Packer 2014) has been used to underscore this assumption (cf. Charap and Shapiro 2014b). Realism could thus provide a valuable basis for better understanding and explaining contemporary Russian foreign and security policy.

Third, the ongoing conflict between the West and Russia over Ukraine has triggered a revival of the Neoliberal vs. Neorealist debate amongst some U.S. scholars (see Mearsheimer 2014; McFaul, Sestanovich, and Mearsheimer 2014; Charap and Shapiro 2014a, b; Lipman 2014) about which U.S. and/or Russian foreign policy orientation (Liberal vs. Realist) is to blame for the conflict. A Realist approach appears quite timely from that angle.

Fourth, the U.S.-Soviet/Russian security relationship has undergone recurring periods of competition and conflict. Realism's occupation with explaining the roots of conflict provides a valuable basis to analyze the reasons behind these two states' competitive relationship.

Fifth, the role of power remains central to understanding instances of international cooperation (cf. Müller 2013). The dominant actors in world affairs – states – are still highly unequal in terms of military, economic, technological, or cultural capabilities and will remain so for the foreseeable future. Even though international institutions have constraining effects on states' behavior (see Drezner 2008), particularly powerful states do not shy away from giving preference to the unilateral employment of power once critical interests are at stake. The United States and the Soviet Union/Russia are particularly powerful states. At the same time, particularly with regards to interests, the constraining effects of international institutions are indeed visible in the form of learning effects, adjustment of interests to the interests of others, and the implication of norms on states' behavior (cf. Finnemore and Sikkink 1998). To say that international institutions do not matter at all in the process of international cooperation would be a misrepresentation of reality; however, they matter less than usually assumed by Neoliberals (cf. Mearsheimer 1994/95).

2.2   Realism and the Problem of International Cooperation

The long history of Realism starts with Thucydides' depiction of the *Peloponnesian War* (431-411 B.C.), was expanded at the end of the Middle Age by Niccolo Machiavelli's *Il Principe* (1513) and Thomas Hobbes *Leviathan* (1651), and re-emerged as one of the principle schools of IR theorizing with the end of World War II (cf. exemplary Carr 1939; Morgenthau 1954). Particularly two scholars of IR have shaped modern Realism: Hans Joachim Morgenthau with his seminal work *Politics Among Nations* and Kenneth Neal Waltz with his opus magnum *Theory of International Politics*. The former gets equated with what is called *Classical Realism*, the latter with *Neorealism* or *Structural Realism* (cf. Pashakhanlou 2009). Both authors share significant views; at the same time, their works show important differences.

As all Realists, Morgenthau and Waltz attempt to see the world as what it is and not what it ought to be (cf. Carr 1939: 5). Their approaches are an empirical rather than a normative paradigm (cf. Morgenthau 1954: 4). They also agree that states are operating in an environment of *anarchy* (cf. Waltz 1959: 224 et seq; Hoffmann 1965: 54 et seq) which lacks any central authority. The state of anarchy has strong features of the Hobbesian state of nature of homo homini lupus (cf. Waltz 1979: 102). It should, however, not become confused with anarchy in the sense of complete political disorder and lawlessness. Rather, anarchy in international affairs means 'a lack of common government in world politics' (Axelrod and Keohane 1986: 226).[4] Morgen-

---

4   Art and Jervis (1992: 1) explain that 'international politics takes place in an arena that has no central governing body. No agency exists above individual states with authority and power to make laws and settle disputes. States can make commitments and treaties, but no sovereign power ensures compliance and punishes deviations. This – the absence of a supreme power – is what is meant by the anarchic environment of international politics.'

thau and Waltz concur that *states* are the principle actors in the environment of anarchy and that particularly powerful states have the most impact (Mearsheimer 2001: 17-8). Further on, it is the distribution of *power* which determines states' position in the environment of anarchy (cf. Morgenthau 1954: 31-7; Waltz 1979: 97-9). In addition, it is states' national *interest* and the constraining effects of anarchy which determine their behavior to act as *rational* egoists (cf. Morgenthau 1954: 5-12; Waltz 1979: 117). Realism assumes that it is rational for states to seek their individual advantage in an absolute and a relative understanding in order to avoid dependence on other states, or worst, their disappearance. Therewith, both agree that it is rational for states to seek *gains* (cf. ibid). However, they differ with regards to their definition of power and states' reasons for pursuing power.

For Morgenthau (1954: 5), 'international politics is the concept of interest defined in terms of power'. Power is 'anything that establishes and maintains the control of man over man.' (Ibid: 11) Aside from military power, Morgenthau also adds a moral stratum counting a nation's character, its morale, and the quality of governance as factors of power. (Ibid: 186) Waltz (1979: 131) infers that power derives from several factors which he summarizes under the term *capabilities*. Capabilities are the 'size of population and territory, resource endowment, economic capability, military strength, political stability and competence'. He adds that 'although power is a key concept in realist theory its proper definition remains a matter of controversy.' (Waltz 1986a: 333)

They also slightly differ with their reasoning why states seek power. According to Morgenthau (1954: 31), 'international politics, like all politics, is a struggle for power. Whatever the ultimate aims of international politics, power is always the immediate aim.' Morgenthau sees states' struggle for power primarily rooted in the nature of man (ibid: 4) and the inability of the anarchic system to constrain his, and thus states, desires. Morgenthau rests his theory on three images: the first image of the nature of man, the second image of the nature of nation states which he views as an extension to man's desires, and the third image of anarchy. Waltz puts greater emphasis on the third image and largely ignores the first. He sees primarily the structural causes of anarchy at work. Waltz (1979: 95) views states as 'the units whose interactions form the structure of international-political systems' and 'although capabilities are attributes of units, the distribution of capabilities across units is not. The distribution of capabilities is not a unit attribute, but rather a system-wide concept.' (Ibid: 98) The absence of a higher authority leads to a constant state of insecurity. In contrast to Morgenthau who sees a permanent struggle for power as states' prime interest, Waltz (1979: 126) views states as being less concerned with maximizing their power. 'States can seldom afford to make maximizing power their goal. International politics is too serious a business for that.' (Ibid: 127) Instead, 'states seek to ensure their survival.' (Ibid: 91; cf. also Mearsheimer 1994/95: 9) Since *sur-*

vival is the prime interest of states, *security* is posited as the principle goal in Waltz's theory (cf. Baldwin 1997: 11, footnote 33). He asserts, 'in anarchy, security is the highest end. Only if survival is assured can states safely seek such other goals as tranquility, profit, and power.' (Waltz 1979: 126) For Waltz, 'power is a means and not an end'. (Ibid)

Even though security and power considerably overlap from a conceptual point of view (cf. Buzan 1991: 7-11), the different emphases Waltz (survival/security as a more defensively-oriented approach) and Morgenthau (struggle for power as a more offensively-oriented approach) employ are probably the main features distinguishing their work and thus classical Realism from Neorealism (cf. Baldwin 1993; Powell 1994; Jervis 1999).

Interestingly though, Waltz does not provide a clear definition of security (cf. Baldwin 1997). This circumstance might have to do with the fact that Waltz was strongly influenced by Scientism and that security is extremely difficult to measure (cf. Buzan 1991). A host of international scholars have provided definitions of security (cf. exemplary Baldwin 1997: 8-9) but one of the most basic Realist definition comes from Wolfers (1952: 458): 'security in an objective sense, measures the absence of threats to acquired values, in a subjective sense, the absence of fear that such values will be attacked.' Correctly, Baldwin (1997: 13) adds that 'there is some ambiguity in the phrase "absence of threats"' if one thinks for instance about earthquakes. He offers to reformulate Wolfers' definition to describe security as 'a low probability of damage to acquired values' (ibid).

Realism's central tenets of power and security have been challenged very early by John H. Herz (1950: 157) who argues that groups and individuals are 'concerned about their security from being attacked, subjected, dominated, or annihilated by other groups and individuals. Striving to attain security from such attack, they are driven to acquire more and more power in order to escape the impact of the power of others. This, in turn, renders the others more insecure and compels them to prepare for the worst. Since none can ever feel entirely secure in such a world of competing units, power competition ensues, and the vicious circle of security and power accumulation is on.' (See also the conclusions of the Palme Commission; cf. Galtung 1983) This *security dilemma* renders the Realist assumption of the desirability of power and security at least questionable.

Aside from power and security, all Realists agree on the central role of the nation state and the constraining effects of anarchy which lead states to rely mostly on their own capabilities and which they employ for the pursuit of their interests (cf. Waltz 1959: 224 et seq; Hoffmann 1965: 54 et seq; Gilpin 1984: 304). In the realm of international security relations, Realism sees the effects of anarchy as particularly strong (cf. Jervis 1978; Gilpin 1984: 304) because security is inevitably connected to states' survival. While thus every state is in permanent *competition* with the others to secure its own survival (cf. Aron 1966: 5), cooperation offers states a chance to secure or enhance their position in the system (cf. Jervis 1999). Nevertheless, Realism is basically skeptical of states' chances to arrive at and uphold cooperation. Mearsheimer (1994/95: 12) explains: 'Although realism envisions a world that is fundamentally competitive, cooperation between states occur. It is sometimes difficult to achieve, however, and always difficult to sustain. Two factors inhibit cooperation: relative-gains considerations, and concern about cheating.'

2.2.1 States' Relative-Gains Concern

According to Realism, states have a very high sensitivity to their positionality (i.e. their power and thus their ability to survive) in the 'system of states' (Waltz 1979). States' position in the system is dependent on the distribution of power. Morgenthau (1954: 174) stresses that 'the concept of power is always a relative one.' Rousseau (1999: 3) adds that 'due to the anarchical nature of the international system any gain in power by one state represents an inherent threat to its neighbors.' Grieco (1988: 498) outlines that 'states fear that their partners will achieve relatively greater gains; that, as a result, the partners will surge ahead of them in relative capabilities; and, finally, that their increasingly powerful partners in the present could become all the more formidable foes at some point in the future.' (Ibid: 499) Waltz (1979: 105) adds: 'When faced with the possibility of cooperating for mutual gains, states that feel insecure must ask how the gain will be divided. They are compelled to ask not "Will both of us gain?" but "Who will gain more?" If an expected gain is to be divided, say, in the ratio of two to one, one state may use its disproportionate gain to implement a policy intended to damage or destroy the other.' The argument as such is fundamentally based on the third image of anarchy because 'states recognize that, in anarchy, there is no overarching authority to prevent others from using violence, or the threat of violence, to destroy or enslave them.' (Grieco 1988: 497-8)

States' relative-gains concern is directly linked to their positionality, their rationality, and their ambitions. Waltz (1979: 97) explains that 'changes in structure change expectations about how the units of the system will be-have and about the outcomes their interactions will produce.' Waltz thus points to changes in capabilities, to expectations, interests, and gains. With regards to *expectations*, Realism pleads to expect and prepare for the worst. In Morgenthau's words (1954: 52), 'history shows that nations active in in-ternational politics are continuously preparing for, actively involved in, or recovering from organized violence in the form of war.' (Cf. also Grieco 1988: 497-8) Waltz (1979: 99) takes a more materialistic view: 'We ask what range of expectations arises merely from looking at the type of order that prevails among [states] and at the distribution of capabilities within that or-der.' While the distribution of capabilities determines states' positionality, states' interests determine their policy and how states will perceive each other (ibid: 117).

Morgenthau (1954: 52-3) offers two basic patterns for identifying states' interests: 'A political policy seeks either to keep power [...] or to increase power'.[5] He thus identifies status quo and revisionist/expansionist[6] states which can be grouped around a defensive (status quo) and an offensive (revisionist/expansionist) orientation.

While classical Realism (cf. Morgenthau 1954) has put greater emphasis on states' *offensive* orientation (see for a debate Mearsheimer 1994/95; Schweller 1996; Jervis 1999), Structural Realism (cf. Waltz 1979: 126) stresses that 'the first concern of states is not to maximize power but to maintain their position in the system.' Accordingly, states rather have a *defensive* positionality. Grieco (1988: 498) adds, 'the fundamental goal of states in any relationship is to prevent others from achieving advances in their relative capabilities'. Mearsheimer (1994/95: 12) agrees but adds that 'not only that [states] look for opportunities to take advantage of one another, but also that they work to insure that other states do not take advantage of them. States are, in other words, both offensively-oriented and defensively-oriented.' The distinction between defensive and offensive Realism is an important one because it heavily influences states' chances to pursue cooperation.

Jervis (1999: 51) concludes that 'offensive realists see much less room for increasing cooperation [while] for defensive realists, much depends on the nature of the situation' and the strategies (ibid: 52) employed. In short, the probability of cooperation among status quo powers who aim at preserving the balance of power is much higher than between a status quo and a revisionist power with the latter aiming at changing the balance of power (ibid: 51-2).

Balance of power has basically two different meanings in conjunction with these observations: 'an approximately equal distribution of power' (as the state of near-perfect equilibrium between the United States and the Soviet Union during the Cold War) and 'any distribution of power' (Morgenthau

---

5   Morgenthau (1954: 52-3) actually offers a third basic pattern, namely 'to demonstrate power'. This third pattern is pursued by 'the policy of prestige' (ibid: chapter 6), which 'has two possible ultimate objectives: prestige for its own sake, or much more frequently, prestige in support of a policy of the status quo or imperialism.' For the sake of consistency with regards to the following argument about offensive and defensive positionality, the policy of prestige has been left out. Further on, as Morgenthau (ibid: 86) argues, 'the policy of prestige is one of the instrumentalities through which the policies of the status quo and of imperialism try to achieve their ends.'

6   Morgenthau (1954: chapter 5) originally speaks of 'imperialist states'. Since imperialism is a politically loaded term, Realists have used the more neutral terms 'revisionist' (cf. Schweller 1996) or 'expansionist' (cf. Jervis 1999) instead. Throughout this book, the terms revisionist and expansionist are used interchangeably and attached to the same basic meaning.

1954: 187, footnote 1).[7] Throughout this study, the concept of 'balance of power' is used to describe any distribution of power.

2.2.2 The Consequences of States' Relative-Gains Concern

How do states, according to Realism, deal with the consequences of their relative-gains concern? The important point Realist make by stressing states' relative-gains concern is that the relative gain-seeking mentality of states theoretically excludes *only* such cooperation which would relatively change the balance of power which existed before the act of cooperation (cf. Mearsheimer 1994/95: 12-3). Thus, the crucial aspect of relative gains is that they are always relative to the distribution of power. As long as gains distribution reflects the distribution of power, cooperation is possible. According to Grieco (1988: 501), 'states define balance and equity as distributions of gains that roughly maintain pre-cooperation balances of capabilities.' Accordingly, agreements which 'roughly reflect the [existing] distribution of power' (Mearsheimer 1994/95: 13) are tolerable for states (cf. Grieco 1988: 501). Only agreements which will not result in a gap in payoffs altering the distribution of power (ibid), or at least a mutual recognition of the tolerance of a gap, would be acceptable. The SALT and ABM agreements between the United States and the Soviet Union were extreme examples of that kind because they reflected the existing distribution of power of near-perfect equilibrium (cf. Bull 1973).

While the case of U.S.-Soviet cooperation on nuclear arms control was reflecting near-perfect equilibrium, *alliances* to preserve or alter the balance of power (cf. Morgenthau 1954: 192 et seq) or to line up against a threat (cf. Walt 1987) usually involve differently positioned states. In that case, cooperation among relatively weaker and stronger states would reflect their respective positionality. Morgenthau (1954: 205) explains that 'the distribution of benefits is [...] likely to reflect the distribution of power within an alliance'. Or, as Mattingly (1955: 163) puts it: 'the biggest dog gets the meatiest bone, and others help themselves in the order of size.'

Schweller (1996: 111) adds that 'who gets more through cooperation is often difficult to discern and may change over time.' He thus points to what Axelrod (1984) has termed poetically the *shadow of the future*, meaning that cooperation (under Axelrod's condition of repeated cooperation) can promise accumulated larger gains in the future if states continue to cooperate. A state might enter a cooperative arrangement believing that the gains from cooperation will relatively increase over time. However, the rationality of its cooper-

---

7   Morgenthau (1954: 187) explains: 'The aspiration for power on the part of several nations, each trying to maintain or overthrow the status quo, leads of necessity to a configuration that is called the balance of power and to politics that aim at preserving it.' In addition to the two meanings quoted above, Morgenthau (ibid: footnote 1) adds 'a policy aimed at a certain state of affairs' and 'an actual state of affairs'.

ation partner would, theoretically, not allow the former to gain relative increases. At the same time, cooperation might also tilt to the negative over time, thus leaving a state with relatively lesser gains than originally expected. Referring to firms as an equation for states' behavior, Waltz (1979: 106) infers that 'the relative strength of firms changes over time in ways that cannot be foreseen. Firms are constrained to strike a compromise between maximizing their profits and minimizing the danger of their own demise.' Since rationality calls for an ex post *evaluation of gains* from cooperation (cf. Schweller 1996: 111), states which find that over time gains turn out to be to their detriment will seek ways to address their dissatisfaction. For such cases, Grieco (1988: 487) finds that 'a state that is satisfied with a partner's compliance in a joint arrangement might nevertheless exit from it because the partner is achieving relatively greater gains.' Another way to address the problem would be for states to plead for a re-distribution of gains, for instance in the form of re-negotiating an existing agreement.

As explained before, power is relative and therewith hard to measure because of its abstract nature (cf. Morgenthau 1954: 9; see Waltz 1979: Chapter 7). What applies to the determining variable of power is also true for its distribution in a cooperative arrangement. Only in an ideal understanding do gains from cooperation reflect exactly the underlying distribution of power. Realists therefore agree that in order to moderate states' relative-gains concern, in reality, states expect to receive approximately equal *compensation* if gain allocation would favor one state and would work to change the balance of power (cf. Morgenthau 1954: 179; Grieco 1988: 501-2).

While gains distribution relative to the distribution of power is a precondition for Realists, compensation is a *strategy* to deal with states' relative-gains concern. Strategies and strategic thinking are inherent parts of Realist thinking and theorizing (cf. Kissinger 1957; Morgenthau 1954; Jervis 1999) and Snidal (1986: 37) defines strategy as 'a complete plan for action, covering all contingencies including random exogenous events as well as endogenous behavior by others.' In conjunction with cooperation, states employ different strategies in order to address the two basic problems of cooperation which Realism identifies. In addition to the strategy of compensation, the next paragraph will introduce strategies with regards to states' rationality to cheat.

Summing up, Realism is basically skeptical of states' chances to arrive at cooperation because states fear that cooperation might change the existing balance of power to their detriment and might therewith negatively affect their security and thus their chances to survive in the environment of anarchy. Since states are rational actors, they will not only seek to advance their gains from cooperation in an absolute way but also in a relative way. Cooperation amongst states is nevertheless possible if the gains from cooperation roughly reflect the underlying distribution of power.

According to Realism, the constraining effects of anarchy create a second problem for cooperative efforts. Not only works the absence of a world government to the detriment of states' security, it also creates undesired effects in conjunction with states acting as rational agents. Since Realism views states as behaving as unitary rational agents who are 'sensitive to costs' (Grieco 1988: 488; cf. also Waltz 1986b: 331) rational gain-seeking can lead states to forego cooperation even in cases where mutual cooperation would promise higher gains than mutual refusal. Different economic models have helped to illustrate that point.

Referring to Kahn (1966), Waltz outlines a 'collective action problem'. 'If shortage of a commodity is expected, all are collectively better off if they buy less of it in order to moderate price increases and to distribute shortages equitably. But because some will be better off if they lay in extra supplies quickly, all have a strong incentive to do so. If one expects others to make a run on a bank, one's prudent course is to run faster than they do even while knowing that if few others run, the bank will remain solvent, and if many run, it will fail.' (Waltz 1979: 107) The consequence is that the bank will go bankrupt even though no one desired so.

Another example comes from the security realm where the absence of a world government is particularly critical. As already referred, one state's intention to increase its security (through increased military spending or alliances) can result in another state's perception of diminished security which leads the latter to answer similarly. The resulting security dilemma (cf. Herz 1950; cf. Jervis 1978) is a spiral of policies with a heightened level of tensions that can lead to conflict – even though, none of the states really desired conflict. The arms races in the nuclear realm between the United States and the Soviet Union during the Cold War are examples of that kind (cf. Schelling and Halperin 1961).

The ideal type to illustrate the problem is the heuristic device of the payoff structure in a 2 x 2 matrix in the game-theoretical model of the Prisoners' Dilemma (PD). In a PD situation, two players are left with no information, no chance to communicate, and no superior enforcement mechanism (cf. McGinnis 1986: 162). They can choose between cooperation (C) and defection (D). Both have a higher incentive to defect (DC) even though both would prefer the gains from mutual cooperation (CC) over the gains from mutual defection (DD) because they fear exploitation (CD). For both, their preference ordering is DC>CC>DD>CD. Their dominant strategies lead them to defect which leaves both with a lower payoff than the possible payoff from cooperation in the end. Since both players act rational, meaning, they seek the highest guaranteed absolute payoff, which necessarily derives from the fact that they cannot assume that the other will not cheat, cooperation is, rationally, impossible even though both would desire it. Chart 1 illustrates the payoff structure and preference ordering in a single-shot PD.

CHART 1

SINGLE-SHOT PRISONERS' DILEMMA

PRISONER B

	B_1	B_2*
A₁ PRISONER A	2, 2	0, 3
A₂*	3, 0	1, 1**

For Chart 1: Cell numerals refer to ordinally ranked preferences with 3 = best, 0 = worst; the first number in each cell refers to A's preference and the second number in each cell refers to B's preference.
* Actor's dominant strategy ** Nash Equilibrium outcome

2.2.4   The Consequences of States' Rationality to Cheat

How do states, according to Realism, deal with the consequences of their rationality to cheat if cooperation is really desired? Realist scholars have first turned to the originally economic theorem of *hegemonic stability* (cf. Kindleberger 1973). Realist proponents of the theorem argued that international cooperation can be achieved if a dominant actor with a paramount interest in a given field of politics invests its capabilities to start and uphold cooperation while, at the same time, persuades and, if necessary, forces other states to cooperate (cf. Krasner 1976).

However, hegemonic stability might not be as stable as the term suggests because it encounters a 'public goods' problem (cf. Olson 1985; Waltz 1979: 196-7). Accordingly, the paramount interest of a certain actor can be sufficient to establish a public good – take for instance a free-of-charge museum established by a patron. As an example from international politics, the overriding interest of the United States to deter the Soviet Union was sufficient to uphold the long-term and costly U.S. military and nuclear assurance to European NATO allies throughout the Cold War. The downside of hegemonic stability is again its undesired consequences. Olson's analysis (1985) of 'privileged groups' shows that smaller states will exploit the dominant state as "free riders". Their unwillingness to pay for the public good, which gets provided anyways, can lead to continued losses for the dominant state. In turn, this behavior can lead the hegemon to lose power and/or interest in cooperation. The result is that cooperation breaks down (Haufler 1993).

An important contribution to address states' rationality to cheat comes from Neoliberal scholars. Even though their approach departs in significant points from the assumptions of Realism (see below for a debate; cf. Grieco 1988), they started by accepting a number of genuinely Realist tenets such as anarchy, the centrality of the nation state, and the rationality of states (cf. Baldwin 1993b). Their main points are that (1) cooperation under anarchy can be the rational choice even though states have an incentive to defect and (2) international institutions or regimes can provide frameworks for repeated cooperation, thus reducing states' transaction costs and increasing the accumulated gains from repeated cooperation (cf. Keohane 1984; Oye 1986). In order to prove their assumption, Neoliberals (cf. Axelrod 1984; Axelrod and Keohane 1986; Oye 1986) extended the PD situation through N rounds of iteration, arguing that 'in most instances the international environment is more akin to an iterated game' (Rousseau 1999: 4). Mutual cooperation 'can be rational because the sum of relatively small cooperative payoffs over time can be greater than the gain from a single attempt to exploit your opponent followed by an endless series of mutual defections.' (Ibid) This future discount parameter is what Axelrod (1984) terms the 'shadow of the future'. In his first computer tournament (1984), the conditional strategy of tit-for-tat (TFT) emerged as the most successful strategy. Under TFT (Axelrod 1984), one player (A) introduces a cooperative move and then subsequently replicates the other players' (B) previous action. If B was previously cooperative, A is cooperative. If B is not, A is not. If B returns to cooperation, A is "forgiving" and cooperates as well.

Axelrod et al tried to prove that cooperation can be rational; i.e. cooperation can maximize players' utility even under an artificial situation which has certain constraining features akin to the state of anarchy where the basic coordination problem would make defection (i.e. cheating) the rational choice for both players (cf. Axelrod 1984; Oye 1986). Neoliberals thus assume that states do not care whether other states gain from cooperation as long as they themselves gain from cooperation in an absolute understanding (cf. Axelrod 1984; Oye 1986). The prospect of maximizing one's own absolute gains provides the incentive to pursue cooperation if only both overcome the trust dilemma. Cooperation, which would benefit everyone, no matter how much each gains from cooperation, and leaving aside balance of power considerations, would thus be acceptable for states.

While the Neoliberal approach shows that cooperation can be rational it ignores states' relative-gains concern. Grieco (1988) argues that Neoliberals misconstrued the Realist understanding of anarchy. Accordingly, states are not primarily motivated by greed (i.e. maximizing absolute gains) but by fear (ibid: 498). He argues that the absence of a world government is not so much the problem because no higher institution would guarantee for the payoff from cooperation but because its absence fundamentally strips states of any higher guarantee of survival. States' sensitivity to costs makes them not only act as absolute gain-seekers (as Neoliberals assume) but more inclined to ascribe paramount importance to relative gains. Neoliberals could not falsify Grieco's argument (cf. Baldwin 1993b: 5-6; Schweller 1996; Keohane and Martin 1999). Their preoccupation with institutionalized cooperation on economic and environmental issues and their relative disinterest in the realm of security (cf. Jervis 1999: 51; for contrasting examples see Zürn, Efinger, Rittberger et al) only underscored Grieco's critique – because it is particularly the realm of international security where Realism sees a heightened importance of relative-gains concern (cf. Mearsheimer 1994/95: 13; Rousseau 1999: 3).

The Neoliberal regime debate and its emphasis on the benefits of international institutions had nevertheless left its marks on Realism. Accordingly, Waltz (1986: 81) conceded that 'supranational agents' (such as international institutions or regimes) do exist. Again referring to hegemonic stability, he assumed that in order to operate effectively, they have to acquire 'some of the attributes and capabilities of states' and ultimately need 'the support, or at least the acquiescence, of the principal states concerned with the matters at hand.' (Ibid) Neorealists therewith tried to integrate the tenets of hegemonic stability into the workings of international institutions. As Haufler (1993: 95) puts it: 'When power in the international system is concentrated in one state, that state, or hegemon, attempts to reduce the costs of its leadership by institutionalizing the framework for negotiation in particular issue areas. The hegemon establishes regimes in order to provide stability to the system as a whole.'

The downside of this argumentation is that it does not fully reflect reality. As Neoliberals such as Keohane (1984) have argued, international institutions might contain their own causal dynamics even in times of hegemonic decline. Following Neorealism, particularly in times of hegemonic decline a sharp decrease in the functioning of international institutions should become visible. However, this has not been the case in every issue-area. Take for instance the hegemonic decline of the United States in certain policy fields during the last 50 years (e.g. the economic crisis of the 1970s and the breakdown of the Bretton Woods system) which did not lead to a complete breakdown of international institutionalized cooperation (cf. Grieco 1988: 491-2; Müller 1993a: 18). Instead, other forms of international institutionalized cooperation such as the G6 (1975, Rambouillet) and later the G7, G8, and G20 Summits took over. In addition, international institutions have turned out to be much more persistent to changes in the general political climate (cf. Zangl 2010: 132) than expected by Realists (cf. Morgenthau 1954). However, in the realm of international multilateral security, the relative decline of American hegemony and the 'rise of the rest' (Kupchan 2012) parallel the increasingly weak performance of international institutions such as the NPT (cf. Müller 2009).

A second important aspect of the Neoliberal regime episteme was that the ensuing debate between Neoliberals and Neorealists (see Baldwin 1993b) shifted the focus towards cooperation, international institutions, and cooperative strategies – a field which Realism had previously often ignored; even though Realism has never denied the fact of states' potential interest in cooperation per se (cf. Carr 1939; Morgenthau 1954; Waltz 1979). Jervis summarizes:

> *[Neoliberals and Neorealists] agree that cooperation is more likely or can be made so if large transactions can be divided up into a series of smaller ones, if transparency can be increased, if both the gains from cheating and the costs of being cheated on are relatively low, if mutual cooperation is or can be made much more advantageous than mutual defection, and if each side employs strategies of reciprocity and believes that the interactions will continue over a long period of time.* (Jervis 1999: 52)

The 'slicing up' of certain policy issues into increments (cf. Oye 1986b: 17), the principle of reciprocity, and the believe that the gains from cooperation will increase over time if cooperation continues are basically all features or conclusions of the strategy of TFT which had emerged as the winner in Axelrod's (1984) first computer tournament. Translated into real-life politics, the separation of certain policy issues into segments, the reciprocity through repeated rounds of negotiation, and the expectation that cooperation would be more than a one-time encounter all point to the arms control strategy of *confidence-building* which basically aims at addressing states' trust deficit (cf. Kaiser 1983). Neoliberals have argued that confidence-building can lead to institutionalization if it continues over a longer period (cf. Oye 1986a). Jervis (1999: 52, footnote 27) infers that 'it is not true, however, that a long "shadow of the future" by itself increases cooperation.' Fearon (1998: 272) explains 'that though a long shadow of the future may make enforcing an international agreement easier, it can also give states an incentive to bargain harder, delaying agreement in hopes of getting a better deal.'

Beyond repeated TFT, Jervis' reference to increased transparency and to limiting the gains from cheating can be partially addressed by the strategy of employing *monitoring* mechanisms. Particularly in the security realm, cheating can quickly lead to changes to the balance of military power as modern arms technology develops in an increasingly rapid manner (cf. Jervis 1978). Mearsheimer (1994/95: 13) calls this effect a '"special peril of defection" in the military realm'. The gains from cheating in security relations are thus comparably higher than in most other issue-areas. Hence, the concrete monitoring instruments (e.g. inspections, notifications, data exchange) have to be extremely timely, intrusive, and reliable in order to decrease the possible break-out time and thus the gains from cheating. However, particularly in the realm of security, secrecy works against efforts to increase transparency (cf. Larsen and Wirtz 2009). States have to strike a balance between their own demand for transparency and their concern that too much transparency might advantage the other side. Monitoring instruments thus have to be carefully tailored. To be clear, monitoring cannot eliminate defection; it does not even directly address it. In a PD situation, non-transparency is not the problem because rational actors already know what to expect from each other (i.e. defection). However, in real life, monitoring can limit the losses one side will suffer once the other side cheats. In reaction, the betrayed side can faster return to its pre-cooperative policy (e.g. through arms deployment, development, or acquisition). Particularly international institutions can lessen the costly burdens associated with monitoring capabilities. Take for instance the sophisticated monitoring system of the CTBT which could not be technically and financially sustained on a single basis by most parties to the treaty. Nevertheless, also international institutions cannot eliminate the danger of cheating.

Contemporary Realism has largely accepted the role of international institutions (cf. exemplary Jervis 1999; Drezner 2009). However, today's Realists see the same forces (i.e. relative power distribution, competition, and states' rationality) at work within international institutions as in classical state-to-state relations. According to Mearsheimer (1994/95: 13), Realists 'recognize that states sometimes operate through institutions. However, they believe that those rules reflect state calculations of self-interest based primarily on the international distribution of power. The most powerful states in the system create and shape institutions so that they can maintain their share of world power, or even increase it.' Evans and Wilson (1992: 330) agree that institutions are 'arenas for acting out power relationships.'

Under the so called 'modified structural' approach, Schweller and Priess (1997) developed a model that combines traditional Realist state-to-state interactions on the sub-systemic level of international institutions with the structural notions of Neorealism, thus allowing international institutions to get integrated into what basically traditional Realist thinking is. Daniel Drezner (2007) takes this "Neo-Neo" Realist approach further by arguing that even in times of Multipolarity and globalization, states' regulatory power is not necessarily constrained by international institutions but that powerful states exert their power through international institutions in order to achieve their domestic interests. Following Drezner, "size matters" when looking at the politics employed and the goals pursued in international regimes. By means of their capabilities in specific issue-areas, states make strategic use of the various institutions of international cooperation (cf. Drezner 2009); particularly in the realm of security (cf. Thakur 2013).

While thus Realists have come to accept international institutions and even their potential role in international security, their assessment is that the operation of international institutions is essentially constrained by the same structural forces on a sub-systemic level. Their conclusion is that institutions 'have minimal influence on state behavior' (Mearsheimer 1994/95: 7) or, to carry the argument to the extreme, that they 'matter only on the margins' (ibid).

Summing up, Neorealists as well as Neoliberals have tried to address the problems of states' rationality to cheat. Both have provided arguments which speak for repeated cooperation (hegemonic stability, international institutions) and a reduced possibility that states will actually cheat (shadow of the future and to a lesser degree monitoring instruments). Nevertheless, none of their approaches can completely eliminate the problem that Realism assumes. Rational gain-seeking states in an environment of anarchy will still find it tempting to cheat on each other if they deem the short-term gains from cheating higher than the long-term gains from cooperation. International institutions provide stable frameworks for repeated cooperation. However, they too can neither eliminate cheating nor restrain states' ambitions.

2.3   A Realist Model of International Cooperation

In this paragraph, a Realist model for understanding international cooperation based on five variables (of which one is a composite variable) will be developed. The variables all derive from Realist theory and include reflections on power and security, interests, the central role of nation states, states' expectations, their related strategies, and their rational gain-seeking mentality.

2.3.1   Clarifying Realist Means and Ends

As already explained, classical Realism and Neorealism put different emphases on power. While for classical Realists, such as Morgenthau, power is the prime objective of states and their interest is defined in power, Neorealism sees power more as a means – though the *central* one – and not an end. The end is, according to Waltz, survival. In order to ultimately ensure survival, states strive for security. Herz's observations of security dilemmas have stressed the ambiguity of security. Glaser (1994/95) has therefore offered a different interpretation of security. He argues that 'if cooperation increases a country's security, then increases in the adversary's security are usually desirable, whether or not they exceed increases in the defender's security. In the security realm, instead of a relative-gains problem, we often have a mutual-gains benefit.' (Ibid: 76) Schweller (1996: 104) agrees: 'When security is the goal, as in the security dilemma, states will seek to succor, not sucker, their neighbors (the CC payoff).' Even though such viewpoints have remained a minority opinion among scholars of Realism, they should be taken into account in conjunction with the concept of cooperative security.

Baldwin correctly asks: 'Security for whom? And security for which values?' (Baldwin 1997: 13) This book examines security policies and institutionalization in a specific policy field of security between the United States and the Soviet Union/Russia. Hence, it is possible to answer Baldwin's first question: security for the United States and the Soviet Union/Russia. Defining, and particularly measuring security is indeed extremely hard (cf. Buzan 1991). Realism sometimes tends to equate security with military security (cf. Mearsheimer 1994/95). Such viewpoint is nevertheless too narrow for the purpose of this study. The analysis will show that particularly security considerations in the economic realm led the Soviet leadership under Gorbachev to forego certain military advantages vis-à-vis the United States and NATO (cf. Gorbachev 1996). Since this study analyzes the policies of the United States and the Soviet Union/Russia devoted to cooperative arms control in Europe, we can, partially, also answer Baldwin's second question: increased *mutual* security by means of reciprocity, inclusiveness, dialogue, a defensive orientation, transparency, confidence-building, and arms limitations. Waltz's Neorealism, emphasizing security, is closer to the analytical focus of this study. Therefore, his deliberations will provide the main, though not the exclusive, basis for the model.

Next, one should specify the gains from cooperation. Baldwin (1993b: 16) notes that Realists 'sometimes neglect to specify precisely what kinds of gains they have in mind. Usually the answer is gains in capabilities. This answer, however, begs yet another question, namely: "Capabilities to get whom to do what?"' Following Waltz (1979: 131), capabilities comprise various factors of power. Nagel (1975: 14) points out, 'anyone who employs a causal concept of power must specify domain and scope'. As explained before, the domain is security and the scope is achieving mutual security (i.e. cooperative security).

When assessing realms of security policy which include crucial military aspects, questions of military advantage and disadvantage come into play (cf. Mearsheimer 1994/95: 11-2). Mearsheimer (ibid: 12) summarizes that 'every state would like to be the most formidable military power in the system because this is the best way to guarantee survival in a world that can be very dangerous.' At the same time, the specific concept of cooperative security is inherently bound to a defensively-oriented approach, aimed at increased *mutual* security (cf. Zartman 1995: 892). Cooperative security thus tries to escape the security dilemma (cf. Herz 1950) by defining security not as unilateral national struggle but as concerted international effort (see also the arguments provided by Glaser 1994/95 and Schweller 1996). It thus breaks with the mainstream Realist definition of security which sees states competing for security. However, cooperative security and Realism are perfectly compatible as long as one assumes the gains from cooperation on cooperative security to reflect the balance of power. It follows that the gains from U.S.-

Soviet/Russian cooperation on cooperative arms control in Europe have to (1) reflect the balance of power and (2) increase mutual security.

A direct conclusion derives from this assumption: since the concept of cooperative security is inherently defensive, it has to involve at least two status quo-oriented powers (cf. Jervis 1999: 51-2). Since the United States and the Soviet Union/Russia have shaped, and continue to shape cooperative arms control in Europe (cf. McKenzie and Loedel 1998b: 8), their orientation in this specific realm of security has to be defensive (i.e. not geared towards changing the balance of power) in order to achieve cooperation. This assumption should help to distinguish cooperative from non-cooperative security policies.

Beyond these observations, the Realist model of international cooperation shall serve a central purpose in this book. Applying the model in the ensuing chapter shall help to assess potential reasons for cooperation, strategies of cooperation, and states' evaluation of gains from cooperation. Since the model is designed to take into account repeated instances of cooperation over a longer period, it shall highlight which factors may lead to repeated cooperation as well as the slowing-down or decay of cooperation. The model has five variables, which all reflect central Realist parameters as discussed previously: capabilities, interests, expectations, strategies, and the evaluation of gains. All variables depend on each other. Interests, expectations, strategies, and the evaluation of gains shall be understood as dependent in a sequential understanding, meaning that states' interests determine their expectations; then, interests and expectations trigger certain strategies. Finally, the composite variable of the evaluation of gains is the last stage in this sequence. The intervening variable of capabilities constantly interacts with the other four variables. Recalling Waltz (1979: 98): 'The distribution of capabilities is not a unit attribute, but rather a system-wide concept.' The model has been developed to describe bilateral international cooperation, and specifically cooperation on cooperative arms control in Europe between the United States and the Soviet Union/Russia during the last 41 years.

2.3.2   Capabilities

States' ability and willingness to engage in cooperative efforts is, in large parts, though not exclusively, shaped by their relative capabilities in the international arena (cf. Waltz 1979) – that is, their power. Different methods and factors allow for the comparison of states' capabilities (cf. Hart 1976). One method is to compare states' 'national material capabilities' (see COW 2014). Capabilities include, according to Waltz (1979: 131), the 'size of population and territory, resource endowment, economic capability, military strength, political stability and competence'. The Waltzian capabilities are a more materialistic definition of power than Morgenthau's is. From a methodological point of view, they are easier to quantify than for instance Morgenthau's factor of states' morality. They also take into account economic factors, which are important for the scope of this study.

For reasons of methodology, only three of the Waltzian factors are taken into account when assessing and comparing the capabilities of the United States and the Soviet Union/Russia. Those factors are: size of population and territory, economic capability, and military strength. The factor of resource endowment could, theoretically, comprise almost everything from natural resources over gender equality to intellectual capital. The political stability and competence of a given state is already hard to measure (see the Fund for Peace's Failed States Index 2014). It would be particularly burdensome to assess, in hindsight, the stability and competence of the closed Soviet system (cf. Cohen 2004). In addition, this book does not focus on Soviet or American domestic policies.

The remaining three factors make a straightforward comparison possible. Economic capabilities can be assessed by comparing the Gross Domestic Product (GDP in current US\$; see IISS 1973 and World Bank 1989-2013). The factor of economic capabilities of the United States and the Soviet Union/Russia was particularly important in relation to the end of the Cold War and the immediate post-Cold War period (cf. Gorbachev 1996). In addition, it pre-determines to a large degree both countries' performance in the military realm. Military strength can be assessed by counting total armed forces (not including reserve or paramilitary forces) and by comparing national defense budgets (see IISS 1973-2014). The factor of military strength is particularly important from a Realist point of view because some Realists assign military power a paramount role when determining states' national security (cf. Mearsheimer 1994/95). The size of population and territory can be assessed making use of official geographic (see CIA 1982-2014) and population geography data (see IISS 1973-2014).

Since the United States and the Soviet Union/Russia were/are part of military alliances (NATO and the Warsaw Pact, later also the CST), the combined forces of those countries, their combined defense budgets as well as their accumulated size of population and territory are included in the assessment as well. This procedure does not apply to the factor of economic capabilities. For those, the International Institute for Security Studies' *Military Balance* series (1973-2014), the *GDP Data Base* of the World Bank (1989-2013), and the CIA *World Factbook* series (1982-2014) are referenced. The respective data can be found in Annex I of this book.

Since capabilities can undergo changes in a quantitative and a qualitative understanding (cf. Morgenthau 1954: 11; Waltz 1979: 97), the variable of capabilities allows applying the model over a longer period of time that cover different instances of international cooperation.

2.3.3 Interests

According to Waltz, states' paramount interest is survival (1979: 91), and thus security (ibid: 126). Waltz views states' interest in securing their survival as fixed. According to this logic, every attempt at cooperation has to serve – in one way or another; directly or indirectly – the interest of securing survival. From now on, and throughout this study, this interest in securing survival is termed states' *general interest*. Below the level of general interest, states can rank their preferences in any order. Waltz (1979: 91) explains: 'Beyond the survival motive, the aims of states may be endlessly varied; they may range from the ambition to conquer the world to the desire merely to be left alone.' (Cf. also Morgenthau 1954: 31) Throughout this book, states' interests below the level of general interest are termed *issue-specific interests*. Issue-specific interests and the general interest may be extremely close connected, depending on which theoretical viewpoint is applied to which issue area. This might for instance be the case in the military realm. Realists, for example, view the military and respective policies as extremely close connected to states' security (cf. Morgenthau 1954; Mearsheimer 1994/95).

As a historic analogy, the general interest of the United States and the Soviet Union became particularly visible during the Cuban Missile Crisis. Their prime aim was to avoid the scenario of an all-out nuclear war. At the same time Washington had an issue-specific interest in the removal of Soviet nuclear arms from Cuba while Moscow had an issue-specific interest in challenging Washington through deployment of those weapons. If both would have remained on a collision course, the possibility of a nuclear exchange would have most likely become manifest reality (cf. Nathan and Allison 2012). Both issue-specific interests were thus closely connected to their general interest. The mutual general interest and the condition of MAD finally trumped the issue-specific interest of the Soviet Union (cf. Jervis 1978: 180). The Assistant to U.S. President Reagan for national security affairs, Robert C. McFarlane, explained in an interview in 1985 that albeit the 'expansionist' character of the Soviet Union, both countries 'share a fundamental interest in avoiding nuclear conflict and reducing tensions.' (Quoted from J. Stein 1985: 614)

States might seek cooperation when cooperation promises to serve states' general interest – notwithstanding states' relative-gains concern and the problem of cheating for a moment. In this case and when cooperation on an issue-specific subject is closely connected to states' general interest or states' perception of the interconnectedness, one can assume that states will bargain extremely hard in reaching a cooperative arrangement (cf. Jervis 1999). When issue-specific interests are convergent, achieving cooperation becomes either trivial (when interests are identical towards cooperation) or impossible (when interests are identical towards non-cooperation). When issue-specific interests are divergent, achieving cooperation gets complicated.

In that case, much will depend on states' expectations and the possible strategies they employ. Divergent issue-specific interests can nevertheless be overcome if they are closely connected to states' survival instinct, as was the case in the Cuban Missile Crisis. However, if one or both would see a chance to forge ahead of the other, the general interest in survival might become the driving force to forego cooperation on issue-specificity.

In the model, interests are classified as general interest and as issue-specific interests. The general interest is fixed. It does not change, according to Realism. Issue-specific interests however can change as a consequence of changes in capabilities, change in leadership, newly available information, technological developments and so forth. In the model, issue-specific interests are divided into convergent and divergent interests.

2.3.4   Expectations

While states' interests might be geared towards cooperation, states are nevertheless uncertain what to expect from their potential cooperation partner. Because states are uncertain, they are cautious. Therefore, they will assess cooperation ex ante according to their expectations. Their expectations are a form of ex ante assessment of the probability of cooperation.

Even though expectations are seldom referred to directly by Realists (cf. exemplary Waltz 1979), they are an indirect part of Realist theory because they derive logically from states' uncertainty (cf. Grieco 1988: 500; Glaser 1994/95: 56; Zakaria 1998: 20). According to Realism, all states act rational in the sense that they share a paramount concern for the balance of power and their own survival. At the same time, states have to come to terms with imperfect information and deviant behavior from this rule. Waltz (1979: 92) openly admits that his assumption of states' general interest 'allows for the fact that no state always acts exclusively to ensure its survival. It allows for the fact that some states may persistently seek goals that they value more highly than survival; they may, for example, prefer amalgamation with other states to their own survival in form. It allows for the fact that in pursuit of its security no state will act with perfect knowledge and wisdom'. States thus know only little about their opponents other than 'those who conform to accepted and successful practices [i.e. conforming to the consequences of anarchy] more often rise to the top and are likely to stay there.' (Waltz 1979: 92) At the same time, states' rationality demands assessing cooperation ex ante. Sebenius (1991) stresses that the actual existence of expectations is a precondition for the realization of interests. According to Realism, states assess each others' foreign and security policy in order to gain knowledge about what to expect from each other (cf. Morgenthau 1954: Part 2).

Three Realist expectations of the probability of cooperation exist. When a status quo power faces another status quo power, the possibility for cooperation exists because both have a defensive orientation (cf. Jervis 1999: 51-2) and because both states' relative-gains concern should become reflected in a cooperative arrangement which would roughly mirror the existing balance of power. When a status quo power faces an expansionist power, the probability of cooperation is very low because it would be irrational for the status quo power to accept relative losses (ibid).

In the model, the variable of expectations is divided into two possible ex ante expectations. The first expectation derives from a situation where two defensively-oriented states face each other. According to Realism, cooperation between the two is possible if it reflects their relative-gains concern and includes efforts to limit the consequences of cheating. This expectation is termed *defensive vs. defensive* in the model. The second expectation derives from a situation where a defensively-oriented state faces an offensively-oriented state. The chance to arrive at cooperation under this constellation is very low (cf. Jervis 1999: 51-2).[8] This expectation is termed *defensive vs. offensive* in the model.

2.3.5 Strategies

States have to employ strategies in order to ensure their relative-gains concern is met and to limit as much as possible the consequences of the rationality to cheat. States can make use of different strategies or a mix of strategies to cooperate (cf. Jervis 1999). The model contains three strategies, which derive from Realist and Neorealist/Neoliberal theory.

1. Compensation: States can choose a strategy of compensation if the distribution of gains does not roughly reflect the existing balance of power (cf. Morgenthau 1954: 179; Grieco 1988: 501-2). The strategy of compensation is in close vicinity to the concept of linkage (cf. McGinnis 1986) because states link the emerging gap in relative gains to a certain form of compensation in order to offset a result, which would alter the balance of power. Compensation often takes the form of a political quid pro quo. McGinnis (ibid: 161) notes that albeit official assurances about the separate nature of certain policy issues, nevertheless, tacit linkages between issues can be concluded. As another example from the Cuban Missile Crisis, during the thirteen days in October 1962, Kennedy agreed to withdraw nuclear weapons from Turkey as a political quid pro quo for Soviet withdrawal from Cuba while publicly denying any such deal (cf. Nathan and Allison 2012).

---

8   A third possible expectation is an offensively-oriented state facing another offensively-oriented state (offensive vs. offensive). In this situation, cooperation might be possible as the secret partition of Poland under the Molotov-Ribbentrop Pact (1939) shows. However, more often, instead of cooperating, expansionist powers wage war (cf. Morgenthau 1954: 67 et seq). Cooperation among the two would logically be at the expense of third states and is thus in contradiction to the concept of cooperative security which seeks to achieve mutual security for *all* (see Zartman 1995: 892). This expectation is therefore excluded from the cooperation model.

McGinnis (1986: 158) raises a caveat with regards political linkages in cooperative institutionalized arrangements. He notes that institutions of linkage-based cooperation 'may be very "brittle", in the sense that any disturbance can be quickly transmitted throughout the material, causing it to shatter into numerous pieces.' He concludes that particularly where cooperation is actually based on or achieved through a strategy of linkage, even minor changes can increase the already existing "brittleness" of the arrangement. While this assumption might pose a problem to international institutions, states might as well decide to adjust the consequences of change according to their preferences.

2. Confidence-building: Under the strategy of confidence-building, states aim at increasing trust in the actions of the other by: (1) slicing up the issue at stake into increments; (2) employing reciprocity; and (3) lengthening their levels of expectations through repeated engagement on the issue (cf. Jervis 1999: 52). Confidence-building is in close vicinity to the game-theoretical illustration of the strategy of TFT. If confidence-building continues successfully over a longer period of time, it can lead to institutionalization (cf. Oye 1986a).

However, confidence-building does not guarantee successful cooperation. Neoliberals such as Axelrod (1984) have only proven that under an artificial condition which resembles some of the constraining features of anarchy, a conditional strategy of cooperation emerges as the most successful, with "success" defined in purely economic terms of absolute gain-maximizing. TFT does neither eliminate the problem of cheating nor does it take into account states' relative-gains concern (cf. Grieco 1988). Jervis (1999) notes that the incentive which Axelrod's 'shadow of the future' (1988) promises does not increase the probability of cooperation – particularly not in the realms of security and arms control – because states will bargain even harder (cf. also Fearon 1998). It is not for nothing that politically binding CSBMs either preclude legally binding arms control treaties (as in the case of the Stockholm CDE stipulations preceding the CFE and INF treaties) or exist in issue areas where the most powerful states take a more relaxed stance towards possible cheating (take for instance most of the CSBMs of the C/OSCE). Even though confidence-building has proven that it can be a successful strategy in arms control negotiations (cf. Lachowski 2004), it cannot guarantee that the sides ultimately arrive at cooperation (see the failed MBFR talks; cf. Fearon 1998).

3. Monitoring: The strategy of employing monitoring mechanisms has proven to decrease the incentive to cheat in real-life cooperation (cf. Jervis 1999; Larsen and Wirtz 2009). Returning to the PD situation, Glaser (1994/95: 130) argues that 'improving a state's ability to monitor an agreement reduces the difference between an adversary getting a lead and starting an arms race at the same time, that is, it reduces CD-DD, thereby making cooperation more desirable.' Monitoring is particularly valuable for the realm of legally binding arms control agreements which is especially prone to cheating (cf. Mearsheimer 1994/95).

TABLE 2

COOPERATION STRATEGIES

Compensation	<ul><li>*addresses states' relative-gains concern*</li><li>*offsetting possible imbalance in the relative distribution of gains which would lead to changing the balance of power*</li><li>*form of political quid pro quo*</li><li>*close vicinity to the concept of political linkage, problem of increase of brittleness*</li><li>*problem of subjectivity of the value of compensation*</li><li>*does not eliminate the incentive to cheat*</li></ul>
Confidence-Building	<ul><li>*addresses states' trust deficit*</li><li>*allows states to engage in repeated interaction*</li><li>*tactics of slicing up policy issues into increments*</li><li>*principle of reciprocity*</li><li>*incentive of accumulated gains through lengthened shadow of the future*</li><li>*often employed ex ante to legally binding measures*</li><li>*can lead to institutionalization*</li><li>*does not eliminate the incentive to cheat*</li></ul>
Monitoring	<ul><li>*addresses the consequences of cheating*</li><li>*allows states to gain more transparency about implementation of cooperative arrangement*</li><li>*allows states to faster return to pre-cooperation policies in case of cheating*</li><li>*often employed in conjunction with legally binding measures in the "hard" sphere of security*</li><li>*problem of states' secrecy concern*</li><li>*possible forms: (on-site) inspections, data exchange, notifications, NTM, open source information, unilateral, bilateral, multilateral, or institutionalized basis*</li><li>*does not eliminate the incentive to cheat but limits the losses/gains from cheating*</li></ul>

In real life, however, monitoring does not eliminate the rationality to defect. It does not even address the problem of cheating in a direct way. Monitoring addresses the *consequences* of cheating because it limits the losses of the betrayed side and, at the same time, limits the gains that the cheating party achieves. Hence, the higher the possible losses from unilateral defection, the tighter the monitoring instruments states would seek. As explained above, states' monitoring requirements often clash with their secrecy concern which is particularly high in the military realm. Therefore, states seek to minimize the negative consequences of unwanted knowledge transfer by limiting the parties to those agreements which touch upon issues of high sensitivity and by insisting on strict reciprocity (cf. Larsen and Wirtz 2009). The U.S.-Soviet/Russian arms control agreements in the nuclear realm are examples of that kind. Monitoring can come in various forms such as (on-site) inspections, data exchange, notifications, national-technical means (including national intelligence), and open source information (e.g. crowd sourcing). It can be conducted unilaterally (if one state's independent national monitoring capabilities are already satisfactory), bilaterally, multilaterally, or on an institutionalized basis. The following table comprises the three cooperation strategies.

In the model, the three strategies of compensation, confidence-building, and monitoring are listed as 'and/or' options (see Chart 1 below). According to Realism, for successful cooperation to happen in policy areas which affect states' general interest, those strategies would most likely come in some form of combination.

2.3.6   Evaluation of Gains

The variable of the evaluation of gains is a composite variable because it combines reflections of states on the gains from cooperation (ex post to the act of cooperation) with their reflections on the variables of capabilities, interests, and expectations *over time*. In this understanding, states' evaluation of gains starts with Day One after cooperation has been agreed upon. Evaluation of gains is a form of ex post assessment of cooperation consequences, while states' expectations are a form of ex ante assessment of cooperation probability. This second form of assessment is important from a Realist point of view because states are initially uncertain about the consequences of cooperation (cf. Grieco 1988: 500; Glaser 1994/95: 56; Zakaria 1998: 20). Their ex post evaluation determines to a large degree whether to continue with cooperation or not. The composite variable shall help to analyze whether actors got what they wanted from cooperation and how changes to the variables of capabilities, interests, and expectations influence their assessment. The composite variable of the evaluation of gains allows application of the model over a longer period of time.

As argued above, power, security, gains, and gain allocation are all in the eye of the beholder (cf. Schweller 1996). States might differ in their ex post assessment of cooperation. In addition, states might value the long-term consequences of cooperation differently over time. Changes in capabilities, in leadership, with regards to issue-specific interests, technological innovations, or newly available information can all lead to changed assessments over time. States thus tend to conclude agreements with a rather long time horizon if crucial issues of national security are at stake (cf. Bull 1973). A longer time horizon allows for repeated rounds of re-evaluation of gains before possibly re-engaging on the issue. The 2011 U.S.-Russian New START agreement with its duration of ten years is an example of that kind. Yet, a longer time horizon also includes the possibility of critical changes which might be perceived by one side as to its detriment.

The ex post evaluation of gains from cooperation might be a difficult job for states against the background of subjectivity, longer time horizons, imperfect information, and possible changes. Particularly for agreements where strategies based on the concept of linkage (e.g. compensation), possibly involving more than one policy issue, have been employed, states might find it hard to assess gains, because linkage between different policy issues leads to more than a single assessment. As a consequence, evaluation of gains might produce mixed results, particularly where different national agencies with different interests are involved or where domestic opposition is challenging the administration's policy.

In the model, the composite variable of evaluation of gains concentrates on the relative gains that states achieve and their assessment of those gains over time. Their assessment leads states to pursue certain actions in response. In case of continued mutual satisfaction, continued cooperation between states might be the preferred option; renewed cooperation might be an additional choice. In case of mutual dissatisfaction, the chance for mutual exit increases and another round of cooperation becomes unlikely. In case where one side is satisfied and the other is (partially) not, states can either look for exit or plead for re-negotiation.[9] In the model, the composite variable is thus sub-divided into continued/renewed cooperation (i.e. satisfaction), re-negotiation (i.e. partial dissatisfaction), and exit (i.e. dissatisfaction). Chart 2 illustrates the Realist model for understanding international cooperation.

---

9   Even though these three options are akin to Hirschman's (1970) triad of 'exit, voice, and loyalty', there is no direct or intended correlation.

CHART 2

REALIST MODEL FOR UNDERSTANDING INTERNATIONAL COOPERATION

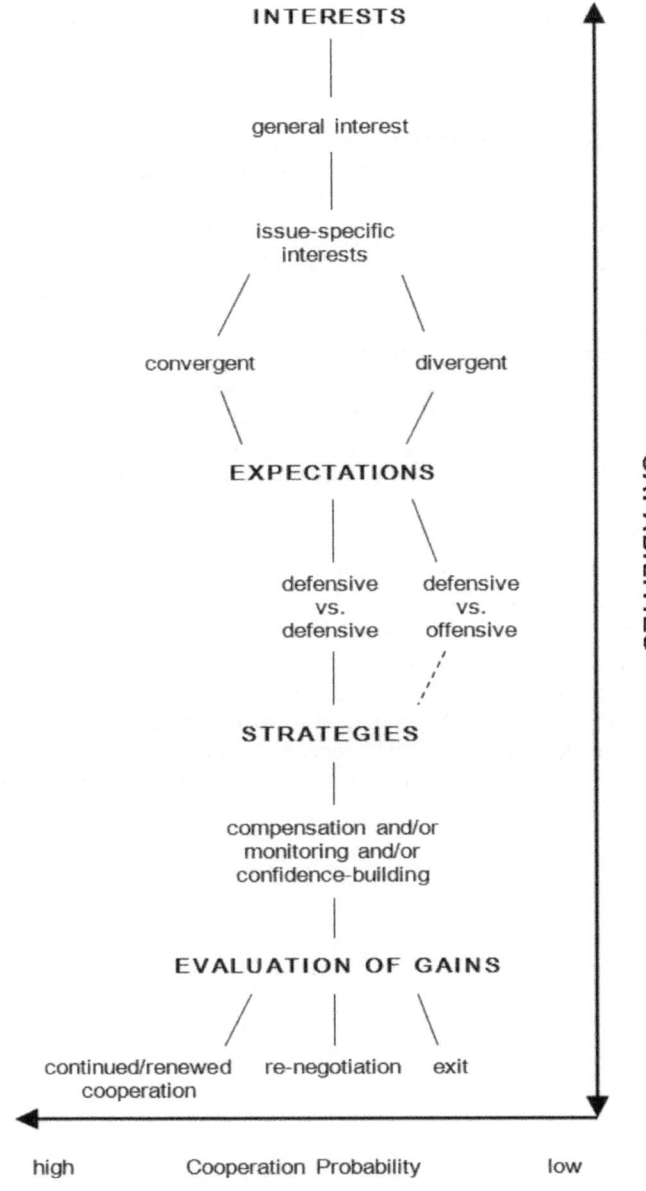

65

According to Realism, achieving international cooperation under anarchy faces certain barriers which can impede cooperation. The absence of a world government, a system of nation states in competition, the unequal distribution of power in the system of states, the survival concern of states, the primacy of security policies, states' relative-gains considerations, and the rationality to cheat are all factors complicating long-term, continued, and stable international cooperation, particularly in the realm of military security.

How do states, nevertheless, arrive at international cooperation? For successful cooperation to succeed, Realism assumes two basic prerequisites: the gains from cooperation have to roughly reflect the relative distribution of power and states have to limit the possible consequences of their rationality to cheat as much as possible. If those two prerequisites are met, international cooperation can take place. Nevertheless, it will still be hard to establish and even harder to maintain. International institutions have their role in this process. They can limit states' transaction costs, particularly in the realm of monitoring. By means of continuous interaction, they can help to build confidence. However, states employ their power in international institutions as much as they do in their state-to-state relations. These insights are particularly valuable for this study.

The model developed in this chapter shall help to understand international cooperation from a Realist point of view. Applying the model in the next chapter, its variables shall help to highlight what calculus led the United States and the Soviet Union/Russia to cooperate on cooperative arms control in Europe. What strategies did they employ? And, more importantly, did they get from cooperation what they wanted; and what were the consequences? In the next chapter, it will be important to focus on the different issue-specific interests of the two states, their cooperative or non-cooperative orientation, their strategies, and the 'who-gets-what' from cooperation (Strange 1982: 496).

3   Cooperative Arms Control in Europe, 1973-2014

This chapter is about the U.S.-Soviet/Russian policies towards cooperative arms control in Europe between 1973 and 2014. The guiding research questions of this chapter are: What calculus led the United States and the Soviet Union/Russia to cooperate on cooperative arms control in Europe, and did they get from cooperation what they wanted? Does the degree of institutionalization justify application of the regime episteme?

The aim of this chapter is to understand the respective policies of the United States and the Soviet Union/Russia, directed towards cooperative arms control in Europe along the lines of the Realist model of international cooperation. By focusing on their policies, also the degree of cooperation institutionalization shall be analyzed. A vast amount of literature has concentrated on issues of European and Euro-Atlantic security, U.S.-Soviet/Russian relations, the history of the Cold War, the C/OSCE, NATO, and related arms control policies. Those secondary as well as primary sources provide the empirical basis of this chapter, which is divided into six historical periods from 1973 to 2014. The model will be applied to each period.

3.1   Introductory Remarks

Cooperative arms control in Europe has undergone a number of fundamental shifts and changes during the last four decades. Those decades have seen the tentative rise of the paradigm of cooperative security including arms control policies between the two blocks during the 1970s, the establishment of a number of legally and politically binding arms control agreements during the late 1980s and early 1990s, the adaptation of these instruments during the mid- and late 1990s, eight years of stagnation and regress from 2000 to 2008, attempts to reset and repair cooperative arms control in Europe between 2009 and 2011, and the final breakdown with the confrontation in and over Ukraine. In terms of institutionalization, Europe has experienced an unparalleled growth in multilateral security institutions which include various types of agreements, actors, and overlapping organizations.

In this chapter, the empirical evidence of the policies of the United States and the Soviet Union/Russia is analyzed. Because of the rather long time span of 41 years, six specific periods are identified (1973-1989; 1990-1994; 1995-1999; 2000-2008; 2009-2011; 2012-2014). This periodization has been chosen because of a number of critical political events that serve as margins: (1) the start of the MBFR talks in 1973 and the start of CFE talks in 1989, (2) German reunification in 1990 and the conversion of the CSCE to the OSCE in 1994, (3) the start of the NATO enlargement debate in 1995 and the OSCE Istanbul Summit in 1999, (4) the beginning of George W. Bush's and Vladimir Putin's first presidency in 2000 and the Russian-Georgian war in 2008, (5) the beginning of Barack Obama's first presidency in 2009 and the end of the reset policy in 2011, and (6) Putin's third presidency in 2012 and the war in Ukraine in 2014. The account does not claim to be a complete historiographic portrayal but rather concentrates on the main institutional achievements and the respective U.S.-Soviet/Russian policies in the realm of cooperative arms control in Europe.[10]

An analysis of cooperation processes and policies is conducted at the end of each period based on the five variables of the Realist model. Since the composite variable of the evaluation of gains has been designed to cover the entire period of analysis, certain instances of analysis might refer to earlier periods of cooperation. As an example, the initial evaluation of the gains from cooperation on conventional forces in Europe produced a rather positive mutual feedback which changed over time to the negative.

The gains from U.S.-Soviet/Russian cooperation on cooperative arms control in Europe have to (1) reflect the balance of power and (2) increase mutual security. When the composite variable of the evaluation of gains is applied in the following paragraphs, this condition shall be tested. In each of the paragraphs below devoted to analysis, the composite variable shall help to assess whether this condition was met and to which degree. This is due to the problem that security is ultimately hard to measure (cf. Buzan 2011). However, in order to assess the gains from U.S.-Soviet/Russian cooperation, security has to be measured in either a qualitative and/or quantitative understanding. One way to address the problem could be to compare the initial claim of a state entering negotiation with the actual outcome. If the outcome would not be in line with the initial claim, one could assume that the state did not achieve the desired security. However, the initial claim could lead to the perception of insecurity on the other side (see the problem of the security dilemma). Also, states might employ maximal demands when entering negotiation for purely tactical reasons (cf. Kremenyuk 1991a). Another way to address the problem could be to measure certain capabilities (e.g. military manpower) before and after cooperation took place. Here the problem is that not every cooperative agreement in the military realm touches directly on specific capabilities (take for instance the monitoring agreement of Open Skies). Also, it is a question of perception whether increased or decreased specific capabilities increase or decrease security. To settle the problem, security in the realm of cooperative arms control in Europe shall be measured in a qualitative understanding, that is, the central tenets of the concept of cooperative security (i.e. reciprocity, inclusiveness, dialogue, a defensive

---

10 For an encompassing overview of the different historic stages of European security and arms control in general as well as the C/OSCE in particular see George (1988), Stares (1992), McKenzie and Loedel (1998), Ponsard (2007), Wenger, Nünlist, and Mastny (2008), Zellner, Schmidt, and Neuneck (2009), Villaume and Westad (2010), Alcaro and Jones (2011), Peter and Wentker (2012), or consult the annual IFSH OSCE Yearbook.

orientation, transparency, confidence-building, and arms limitations) shall be understood as increasing mutual security (cf. Mihalka 2005; Dewitt and Acharya 1996: 9-10; Nolan 1994b: 5; Zartman 1995: 892). Of course, this approach can be questioned as well for its per se interpretation of cooperative security leading to mutually increased security. However, the following paragraphs will show that the concept of cooperative security has helped to reduce the risk of open conflict. In addition, the initial U.S.-Soviet/Russian claims before cooperation and the actual outcomes of cooperation shall be addressed as well in order to get a more complete understanding.

3.2   Genesis and Change, 1973-1989

The genesis of cooperative arms control in Europe can be traced back to the late days of détente. In 1973, Moscow accepted the long-standing U.S. demand to enter into talks about conventional forces in Europe to address the imbalance in the conventional realm which was to the detriment of the United States and its NATO allies. The 'negotiations on mutual reduction of forces and armaments and associated measures in Central Europe'[11] – more commonly referred to as Mutual and Balanced Force Reductions (MBFR) talks – were the first institutionalized, formal, and (at least in official terms) multilateral arms control talks between the East and the West.[12] The talks continued for almost sixteen years without any concrete result and were finally replaced by the CFE negotiations in 1989. For the Soviet Union amongst the reasons to agree to MBFR was the start of formal negotiations on the mandate for a Conference on Security and Cooperation in Europe (CSCE) in 1972. Particularly at the beginning of the CSCE process, Washington showed a very low degree of interest (cf. Maresca 1988: 109, Morgan 2008) and was more inclined to view it as a bargaining chip in conjunction with conventional and nuclear arms control goals (cf. Morgan 2008). When MBFR gained shape, Washington gave its fiat to the Soviet prestige project (cf. Darilek 1987: 6).

According to Haftendorn (2008:237), MBFR and the CSCE are 'two sprouts from one bulb'. Even though the initial idea was to combine the two processes into one, NATO had difficulties to arrive at a common position with the United States pressing for separation of the two issues. In Haftendorn's (2008: 254) words, 'the U.S. benefited from its hegemonic position within the alliance and from its wealth of resources, including direct contacts with the USSR.' In the end, Washington prevailed and conventional arms control was handled separately and not formally integrated in the CSCE

---

11   Cited from Paragraph 2 of the Mutual Force Reductions in Europe - Communiqué of the Exploratory Talks, 28 June 1973.
12   For a good introduction to MBFR see Blacker (1988). For an encompassing account see Mutz (1983).

framework (cf. Schlotter 1999: 223). In July and August 1975, the CSCE process reached its first climax with the Helsinki accords.[13] As part of the accords, a non-binding declaration of intent in the realm of arms control, the 'Document on Confidence-Building Measures and Certain Aspects of Security and Disarmament' was agreed upon (cf. Ghébali 1989).

While the MBFR talks dragged on inconclusively until 1989, the deteriorating East-West climate led to two lengthy CSCE follow-on conferences in Belgrade (1977-1978) and Madrid (1980-1983). Particularly since the coming into office of the Carter administration, the United States used the CSCE mainly as a forum for charging the Soviet Union for continued violations of its human rights commitments under the 1975 Helsinki Charter (cf. Selvage 2012).

In January 1984, the Stockholm negotiations of the Conference on CSBMs and Disarmament in Europe (CDE) began with fundamentally divergent approaches taken by NATO and the WTO. The CDE was characterized by strong bipolarity and bilateralization of negotiations (cf. Ropers and Schlotter 1989: 320) and only arrived at a result in 1986 after a fundamental change in policy on the Soviet side began to loom with the advent of Gorbachev's 'new political thinking' (cf. Gorbachev 1996). Even though the CDE's stipulations were still of minor military relevance, the resulting CDE Document symbolizes the transition from the Cold War to a new European security order which started to take shape at the final days of the block confrontation (cf. Ghébali 1989; Alexander 2005). In 1987, Moscow and Washington concluded the INF Treaty. In 1988, Moscow announced the unilateral and unconditional withdrawal of 500,000 soldiers of the Red Army from Eastern Europe and thus relinquished an important part of its conventional superiority in the European theater (cf. Gorbachev 2011: 16). In early 1989, the Third CSCE Follow-up Conference in Vienna began. Shortly afterwards, in March 1989, MBFR talks were replaced by a novel conference on European force limitations (CFE).

3.2.1   Analysis of Cooperation

In this paragraph, three cooperation processes – MBFR, the Helsinki CSCE, and the Stockholm CDE – are analyzed using the Realist model of international cooperation. Before that, a closer look at the development of U.S./NATO-Soviet Union/WTO capabilities between 1973 and 1989 is taken.

Capabilities
The period from 1973 to 1989 saw the slowing-down and final collapse of the Soviet economic system and thus, a major change in the factor of eco-

---

13   The documents of the CSCE and the OSCE are accessible at www.osce.org.

nomic capabilities. During the Brezhnev era, economic growth first came to a halt (cf. Mazat and Serrano). From the mid-1980s onwards, the Soviet economy shrank (ibid). At the same time, the U.S. economy of the 1980s experienced a period of significant growth. These diverging trends were not so much influencing the relationship during the 1970s but more and more during the 1980s (cf. Leffler and Westad 2010). In 1989, the GDP of the United States (US\$ 5.6 trillion) was already ten times the GDP of the Soviet Union (US\$ 0.5 trillion). Chart 3 illustrates these diverging trends. With this huge increase in national GDP, Washington could devote relative more money to defense spending at a time when the Soviet Union was searching for ways to lift the financial burdens associated with its huge military apparatus.

CHART 3

COMPARISON OF U.S.-SOVIET ECONOMIC CAPABILITIES IN GNP/GDP[14], 1973-1989

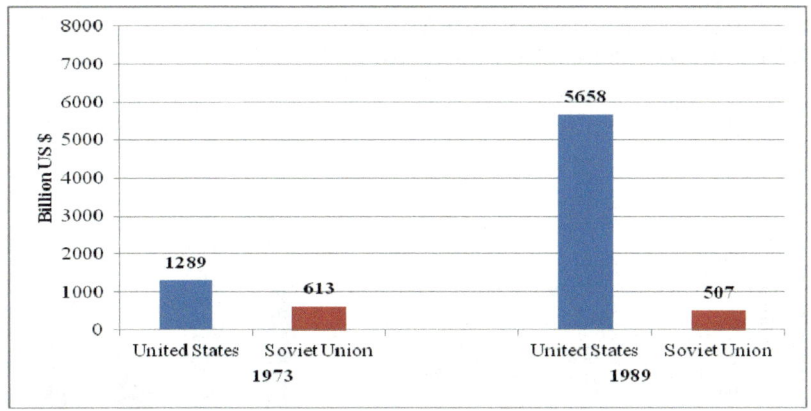

With regards the first capabilities factor of military strength, the development of national defense budgets of the United States and the Soviet Union and the combined defense budgets of NATO member states and WTO member states showed a similar trend. While in 1973, the combined defense budgets of NATO member states were only US\$ 30 billion ahead of WTO states, in 1989, the difference had grown to US\$ 300 billion. Chart 4 illustrates these diverging trends.

With regards the second capabilities factor of military strength, the number of total armed forces shows the military buildup of the Soviet Union

---

14   The World Bank GDP Data Base does only start with assessing the Soviet GDP from the year 1989 onwards. Therefore, data from the IISS Military Balance series (here issue 1973) has been taken for 1973. The IISS Military Balance series of 1973 only assesses the GNP.

during the late 1970s and early 1980s (see Military Balance 1977-1984). While in 1973, the combined total armed forces of NATO (5.2 million) exceeded the WTO forces (4.45 million) by 700,000 men, in 1989, the combined total armed forces of WTO states (5.42 million) and NATO (5.35 million) were almost equal. While the United States had roughly maintained its level of total armed forces and NATO allies had filled the gap (in 1982, Spain joined the alliance), on the Eastern side, the Soviet Union had increased its military commitment almost by one million soldiers. At the same time, the defense budget of the Soviet Union could not keep pace with the American one (see Chart 4). The economic effects of this additional military burden led the new Soviet leadership under Gorbachev to reconsider its military engagement from the mid-1980s onwards and to withdraw 500,000 soldiers from Eastern Europe. Chart 5 illustrates the Soviet military buildup in total armed forces between 1973 and 1989.

CHART 4

COMPARISON OF NATIONAL U.S.-SOVIET AND
NATO-WTO COMBINED DEFENSE BUDGETS, 1973-1989

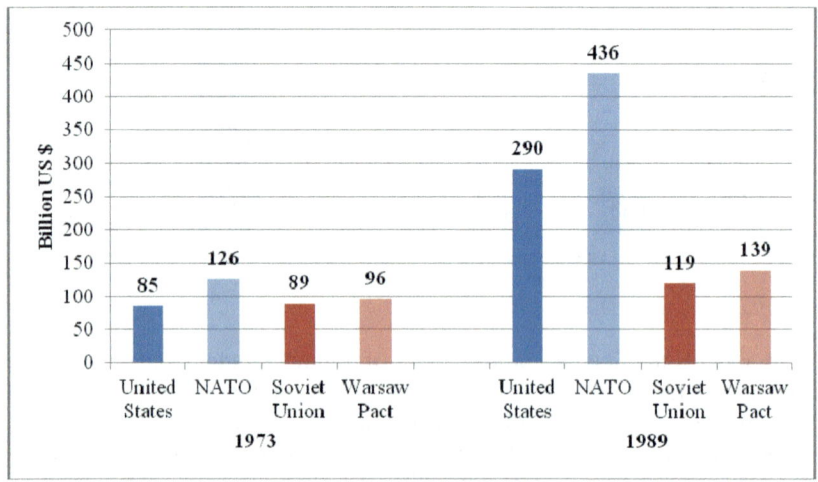

With regards the capabilities factor of the size of population, the existing relative difference between the Eastern and the Western bloc remained largely the same between 1973 and 1989. In 1973, the combined size of population of NATO member states was 0.54 billion. In comparison, WTO member states had 0.35 billion. In 1989, and after Spain had joined NATO in 1982, the alliance had 0.65 billion while the Eastern bloc had 0.4 billion. Chart 6 illustrates these figures. With regards the capabilities factor of the size of territory, the combined size of territory of WTO states was 32.3 million km² in 1973 and 1989. Only the combined size of territory of NATO member states increased between 1973 and 1989 due to the accession of Spain. In 1973, NATO member states had 22.2 million km² and in 1989 the figure was 22.7 million km². Chart 7 illustrates these figures.

CHART 5

COMPARISON OF NATIONAL U.S.-SOVIET AND
NATO-WTO COMBINED TOTAL ARMED FORCES[15], 1973-1989

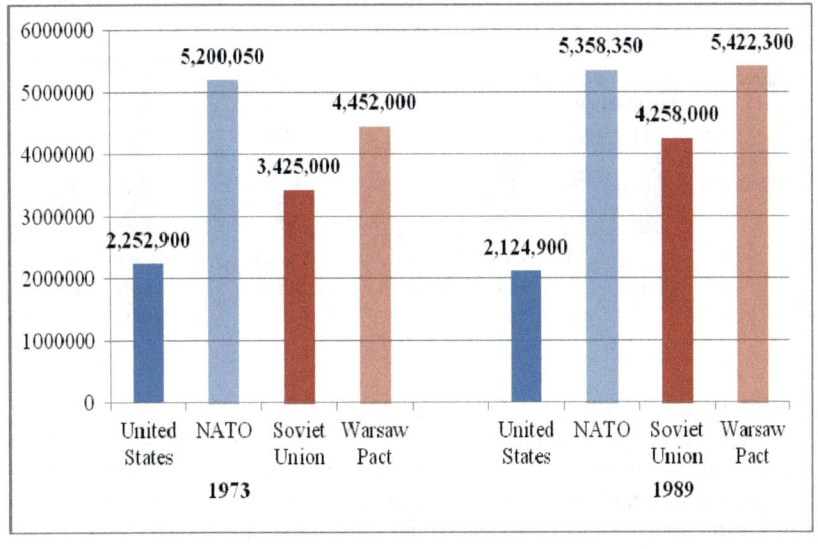

---

15   In this and the following charts on total armed forces, reserve and paramilitary forces are not included while forces assigned to WMD missions are included.

CHART 6

COMPARISON OF NATIONAL U.S.-SOVIET AND
NATO-WTO COMBINED SIZE OF POPULATION, 1973-1989

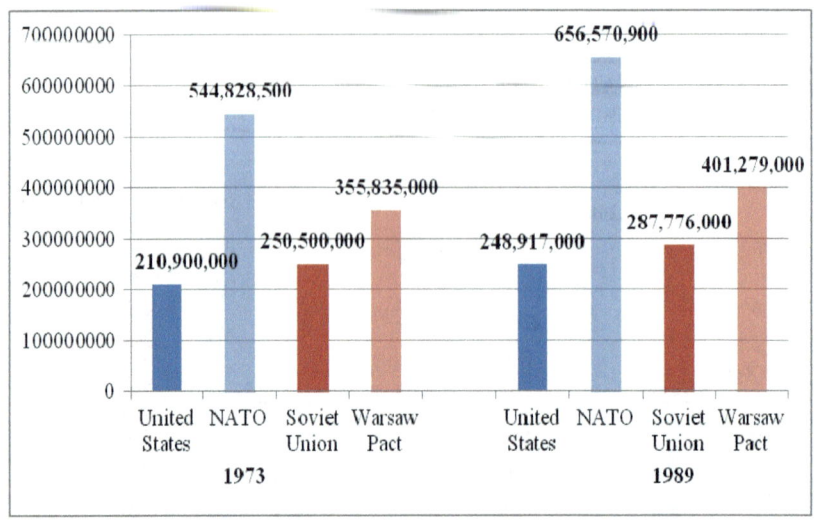

MBFR and the Helsinki CSCE
Interests: Throughout much of the Cold War the general interest of securing
survival of the United States and the Soviet Union was closely associated and
sometimes became even exclusively equated with aspects of military strength
(cf. Leffler and Westad 2010). Since the years 1962, their general interest had
led to a mutual interest in cooperation in order to avoid nuclear catastrophe.
The Cuban Missile Crisis of 1962 had underscored how real this worst case
scenario was and had triggered the Western policy of détente (cf. Hershberg
2010). Even though cooperation promised to enhance 'strategic stability' (see
Colby and Gerson 2013), the interrelationship between security and aspects
of military strength determined mutual policies. The SALT treaties with their
numerical parity were examples of that kind. With regards to Europe, the
issue-specific interests of the United States and the Soviet Union related to
détente were divergent (cf. Hershberg 2010). Washington had an issue-
specific interest in achieving a change to the imbalance in conventional forces in Europe, which was to NATO's detriment. Moscow was not interested in
relinquishing its conventional advantage (cf. Mutz 1983). On the Helsinki
CSCE, Moscow wanted a conference, which would cement the territorial
status quo in Europe (cf. Schlotter 1999). Washington was initially less interested in the CSCE (cf. Morgan 2008: 25 et seq).

CHART 7

COMPARISON OF NATIONAL U.S.-SOVIET AND
NATO-WTO COMBINED SIZE OF TERRITORY, 1973-1989

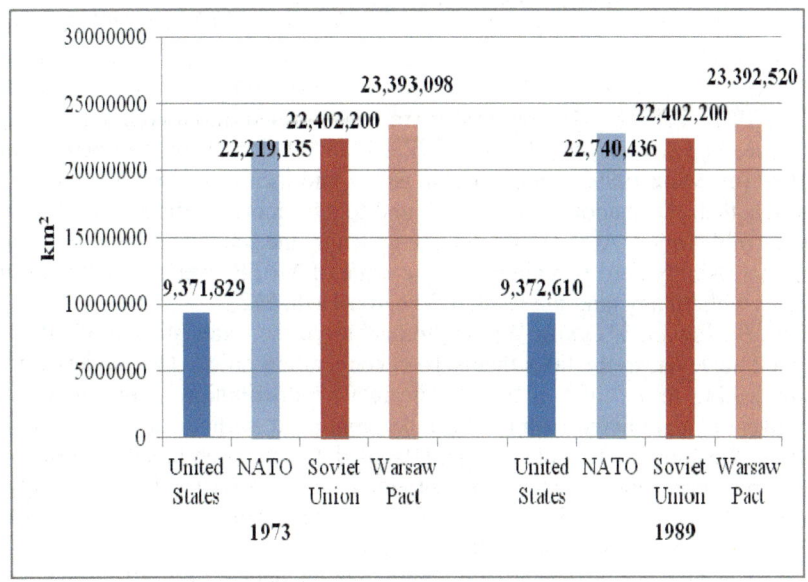

Expectations: With regards the MBFR talks, the setting was clear. Moscow wanted to avoid a change to the status quo through MBFR. Washington wanted to change the status quo to its advantage (cf. Blacker 1988; Mutz 1989). Washington acted as offensively-oriented power, Moscow as defensively-oriented. According to Realism, both could expect that cooperation on the issue would most likely fail. With regards the potential outcomes of the Helsinki CSCE, the setting was rather vague on the U.S. side. Moscow wanted to achieve an official recognition of the territorial status quo in Europe. It thus acted defensively-oriented. As referred to above, Washington did not show great interest or even enthusiasm for the CSCE and acted rather passively in the beginning, leaving the initiative in the initial negotiations to its allies and the non-aligned states (cf. Morgan 2008: 25 et seq). However, the closer the parties moved towards the 1975 Helsinki Summit, the more Washington pressed for an inclusion and official recognition of human rights commitments in the Final Act (cf. Schlotter 1999). Even though, Washington could not expect a somewhat binding declaration on human rights, its effort to press the East for declaratory commitments can be seen as an offensively-oriented undertaking at declaratory change. Washington thus acted as offensively-oriented as well as defensively-oriented power. According to Realism, both could expect that cooperation on the issue would be very hard to achieve, if at all.

Strategies: Both applied a strategy mix of (cross-policy) compensation and confidence-building. On the one hand, MBFR should compensate for the Helsinki CSCE and vice versa (cf. Haftendorn 2008).[16] Soviet cooperation on MBFR should thus secure U.S. cooperation on the Helsinki CSCE, which in turn should secure continued Soviet cooperation on MBFR (cf. Morgan 2008). On the other hand, both processes were sliced up into increments (cf. Oye 1986: 17). The Helsinki CSCE was transformed into a continuous conference and MBFR saw 47 negotiation rounds before it was suspended in 1989 (cf. Mutz 1989). Slicing up the issues into increments made it possible to lengthen the shadow of the future and to gain more confidence in the actions of the other. At the same time, lengthening the shadow of the future, led to increasingly hard bargaining on the issue of MBFR over the next sixteen years without any tangible result (cf. Fearon 1998: 272).

Evaluation of Gains: Washington achieved the establishment of MBFR talks; however, in the talks themselves, cooperation failed. The Soviets were not willing to accept a change to the relative distribution of power in the conventional military realm. The talks continued without any result until 1989. Washington did not get what it wanted. Cooperation failed because the different orientations (defensively-oriented on the Soviet side; offensively-oriented on the U.S. side) and the general interest, which was closely associated with aspects of military strength, did not allow for real cooperation on the issue. Hence, the evaluation of gains from cooperation on MBFR changed over time from initially positive assessment to increasing signs of U.S. and Western dissatisfaction (cf. Alexander 2005). The former Head of the United Kingdom's delegation to the talks, Michael Alexander (ibid: 172), later concluded: 'the MBFR talks were almost a metaphor for the Cold War itself – a negotiating confrontation for which there was no mutually acceptable outcome but whose infinitely tedious exchanges the participants were deter-

---

16   Ropers and Schlotter (1989: 325) argue that the Helsinki CSCE and MBFR were only part of a larger package deal of cross-issue linkages (cf. also Kremenyuk 1991: 34-5). MBFR and the Helsinki CSCE are, however, the only issues with direct reference to the subject of this book. Further on, Ropers and Schlotter claim that during the years 1972-1989 it was always the United States who acted as the 'linker' and the Soviet Union who acted as 'linkee'. (Ibid: 324) This assumption is supported by former Secretary of State Kissinger's portrayal of the U.S. foreign policy towards the Soviet Union during his time in office: 'We insisted that progress in superpower relations, to be real, had to be made on a broad front. Events in different parts of the world, in our view, were related to each other; even more so, Soviet conduct in different parts of the world. We proceeded from the premise that to separate issues into distinct compartments would encourage the Soviet leaders to believe that they could use cooperation in one area as a safety valve while striving for unilateral advantages elsewhere. This was unacceptable.' (Kissinger 1979: 129) Ulam (1983: 59) argues against a one-sided perspective on linkage policies: 'In fact, the Soviets, when it came to something they badly wanted, have themselves been strong believers in linkage'.

mined neither to abandon nor to allow to self-destruct.' In 1989, both exited from the MBFR format and shifted to the newly established CFE negotiations.

Moscow succeeded in convening the Helsinki CSCE and in writing down a number of status quo principles such as the 'indivisibility of security in Europe', 'sovereign equality, 'respect for the rights inherent in sovereignty', 'refraining from the threat or use of force', the 'inviolability of frontiers', the 'territorial integrity of States', and the 'non-intervention in internal affairs' – all of a declaratory and non-binding nature (see Helsinki Final Act 1975). At the same time, Washington, together with a number of other states, pressed for the inclusion of human rights commitments, the establishment of a first tentative approach at military CSBMs, and a continuation of the CSCE (cf. Schlotter 1999). Cooperation became possible because of this issue-specific form of compensation (human rights for status quo recognition) and because of an additional strategy of cross-policy compensation with Washington compensating Moscow for MBFR with the Helsinki CSCE and vice versa (cf. Haftendorn 2008).

While Moscow had achieved its preferred issue-specific interest on the Helsinki CSCE, the further processual character of the CSCE turned out to be to the Soviets' detriment over the years. On the one hand, the Carter and Reagan administrations increasingly used the CSCE to openly charging the Soviet Union for her human rights record (cf. Schlotter 1999). On the other hand, dissidents in the WTO states used the promises of the CSCE Charter to charge their own governments and to call for more personal freedoms (cf. Gorbachev 1996). Moscow initially gained and, over the long run, also lost from the CSCE. The evaluation of gains on the Soviet side (cf. Schlotter 1999) thus changed over time from an initially positive evaluation (shortly after 1975) over a period of negative evaluation (from the late 1970s onwards) back to a rather positive evaluation (towards the end of the 1980s). On the U.S. side, the initially rather negative evaluation of the gains from cooperation on the CSCE changed, over time, to positive evaluation. The actual gains from U.S.-Soviet cooperation on the Helsinki CSCE did reflect the balance of power inasmuch as the outcome of cooperation did not lead to a change in the relative distribution of military strength. The gains increased mutual security through confidence-building by repeated dialogue-based interaction and through declaratory commitments on human rights, military transparency, and the territorial status quo.

Stockholm CDE
Interests: The Stockholm CDE negotiations (1984-1986) displayed a slightly different setting. The mutual interest in cooperation had decreased since 1975 against the background of Moscow increasingly deploying SS-20 intermediate-range ballistic missiles, NATO's Double-Track Decision in 1979, the Soviet invasion in Afghanistan in the same year, and the proclamation of

martial law in Poland in 1981. The mutual close association of security with aspects of military strength only increased during those years (cf. Leffler and Westad 2010). When the CDE started in 1984, U.S. and Soviet issue-specific interests were divergent. Washington was interested in verifiable transparency on WTO conventional forces, suggesting intrusive on-site inspections (cf. Leatherman 2003: 171); Moscow was interested in disarmament measures in the realm of WMD (see ibid; Schlotter 1999: 230). At the same time, the INF and MBFR talks in Vienna had been suspended by Moscow as reaction to NATO's stationing of U.S. intermediate-range nuclear weapons to Europe in 1983. Therewith, a minimal convergent interest in establishing the CDE was apparent since no other forum for East-West arms control talks, aside from the United Nations, was available (see Alexander 2005). Negotiations dragged on without any concrete result until Gorbachev took office in March 1985.

With Gorbachev, the manifestations of the Soviet general interest in securing survival became much more influenced by economic considerations than in the past (cf. Gorbachev 1996). Increasingly since 1986, security aspects of military strength were not the prime variable determining Soviet security policy anymore (ibid). Instead, political-economic efforts to reform the Soviet command economy, which had come under increasing pressure since the end of the 1970s, became one of the prime interests of the Communist Party (cf. Gorbachev 1996). The foreign and security policy of the Soviet Union changed accordingly. Gorbachev sought closer relationship with the West in order to increase economic cooperation. In his own words, the Soviet Union needed, 'perhaps more than ever before, favorable external conditions so that we can cope with the revolutionary and broad task toward renewing Soviet society.' (Quoted from Baker 1991: 816)

The change in economic capabilities triggered a change in issue-specific interests and related policies (cf. Legvold 1991: 357 et seq). The survival-related interest in economic recovery led the new leaders of the Politburo to pursue the goal of economic cooperation with the West, which was dependent on efforts to lessen the costly effects of military competition through policies of arms control (ibid). As a consequence, Moscow started to act much more conciliatory on security aspects of military strength which were of interest to the West. The CDE was amongst these issues even though Washington's issue-specific interest in the conventional military realm was still geared towards reductions in the MBFR framework (cf. Alexander 2005). With regards to issue-specifity, Washington wanted to achieve more transparency on the conventional forces of the WTO through the CDE; Moscow wanted to make use of the CDE in order to pave the way for reductions in WMD and to achieve a lessening of expenditures associated with its costly military (cf. Leatherman 2003: 171). Even though for different reasons, their issue-specific interests in the CDE shifted towards convergence.

Expectations: Both states entered the CDE negotiations with a defen-sively-oriented approach which was not aimed at achieving a significant change to the balance of military power (i.e. the U.S. goal of conventional transparency; the Soviet goal of WMD reductions; cf. Schlotter 1999: 230). According to Realism, cooperation under this constellation was at least pos-sible. However, their initial and mutual close association of security with aspects of military strength and the general political climate at the early 1980s was not conducive to cooperation. As a consequence of Gorbachev's change in policy, Moscow's concern about military strength relatively de-creased and gave way to concerns related to issues of higher importance (i.e. economic recovery). Moscow could act cooperatively in the CDE because the promise of arms control was in line with the economic postulate of Gorba-chev (cf. Holloway 1988: 77-8). Since both states kept their defensive orien-tation, they could expect the possibility of successful cooperation.

Strategies: The processual character of the institution of the CSCE had allowed both sides to maintain cooperation at a low level since 1975 (cf. Schlotter 1999: 79, 227-33). On the CDE, they decided for continuation of the strategy of confidence-building and sliced up the issue into increments, thus, gaining more confidence in each other while at the same time allowing the process to remain inconclusive. The first cooperative Soviet move in the CDE was to accept on-site inspections on its territory in 1986. In parallel, Washington and Moscow opted for the strategy of cross-policy compensation by tacitly linking the talks to the nuclear realm (cf. Leatherman 2003: 171). Only one year after the CDE, Moscow achieved its aim of WMD reductions in the Vienna INF negotiations.

Evaluation of Gains: The evaluation of gains from cooperation on the CDE was positive on both sides (cf. Darilek 1987) because both got what they wanted in the end. Washington became the desired transparency on conventional Soviet forces and later serious negotiations on conventional forces (CFE) while Moscow achieved negotiations eliminating a whole cate-gory of nuclear weapons (INF) and, later, economic support by the West (cf. Baker 1991). Thus, both opted for renewed cooperation in other formats (i.e. CFE and INF). Falkenrath (1995a: 40) notes that 'the emphasis in Soviet policy toward Europe gradually shifted from scoring propaganda points to achieving meaningful results in serious negotiations'. The actual gains from U.S.-Soviet cooperation on the CDE did reflect the balance of power inas-much as the outcome of cooperation did not lead to a change in the relative distribution of military strength. The gains increased mutual security by achieving transparency through on-site inspections.

TABLE 3

U.S.-SOVIET COOPERATION ON MBFR, HELSINKI CSCE, AND CDE

INSTITUTION	ACTOR	ISSUE-SPECIFIC INTERESTS	EXPECTATIONS	STRATEGIES	EVALUATION OF GAINS
MBFR	USA	divergent	acting offensively-oriented	offering compensation through CSCE, confidence-building	continued cooperation, later exit
	USSR	divergent	acting defensively-oriented	confidence-building	continued cooperation, later exit
Helsinki CSCE	USA	divergent	acting offensively- as well as defen-sively-oriented	confidence-building	continued cooperation
	USSR	divergent	acting defensively-oriented	offering compensation through MBFR, confidence-building	continued cooperation
CDE	USA	initially divergent, later convergent	acting defensively-oriented	offering compensation through WMD reduc-tions, confi-dence-building	renewed cooperation in other fora
	USSR	initially divergent, later convergent	acting defensively-oriented	confidence-building	renewed cooperation in other fora

Institutionalization

The institutionalization in the realm of cooperative arms control between 1973 and 1989 developed on two parallel tracks. The CSCE became the mul-tilateral forum for CSBMs and military transparency, a sphere of arms con-trol where tentative results were comparably easier to reach than in the dis-puted sphere of bipolar force limitations under MBFR (cf. J. Stein 2003: 15).

80

Darilek (1987: 5) speaks of 'two competing approaches to arms control involving conventional military forces in Europe [...] a "structural" and an "operational"'. (Cf. also Auton 1998) The case of the early CDE shows that both sides were able to continue minimal cooperation on CSBMs within the wider framework of the CSCE over a longer period of deadlock in bilateral relations. The continuing process, even though inconclusive at that time, is a first sign of institutionalization in the realm of CSBMs.

3.3   Convergence and Realization, 1990-1994

The period between 1990 and 1994 marks the heyday of the politics of cooperative arms control in Europe. Spurred by the unraveling of the bloc confrontation, German unification, the demise of the Warsaw Pact and the Soviet Union, and the outburst of violent ethnic conflicts in South-East Europe and in a number of successor states to the USSR, institutionalization rapidly gained shape.

The politics of cooperative arms control in Europe were mainly grouped around and achieved within the CSCE framework, which also underwent a fundamental change in those years. Diverging interests about the future of the CSCE should characterize the discussion. The Soviet Union and, later, its main successor, the Russian Federation, saw NATO as obsolete and lobbied towards upgrading the role of the CSCE to become a pan-European security institution with primary responsibility for security in the whole region (cf. Krause 2003: 19). Then-Soviet Foreign Minister Eduard Shevardnadze (cited in Anstis 1994: 79) pledged in May 1990, 'the most important architectural element of the future Common European Home is the security system based on all-European cooperation.' What he meant was spelled out more clearly four years later by Foreign Minister of Russia Andrei Kozyrev in 1994 (65): 'The creation of a unified, non-bloc Europe can best be pursued by upgrading the Conference on Security and Cooperation in Europe into a broader and more universal organization.'

In contrast, strong voices in Washington called for not giving up the successful structures of NATO and preventing any form of subordination under a new pan-European structure (cf. Sloan 1990: 499-500). Out of 'long-held suspicions of the Soviet Union and the fact that the CSCE is seen as having resulted from a Soviet initiative, while NATO has been the main vehicle for U.S. influence in Europe' (ibid), Washington lobbied for adapting NATO to the new geopolitical changes while at the same time keeping the profile of the CSCE comparably low. As a result of these diverging interests and against the background of the CSCE's inability to stop the bloodshed in the former Yugoslavia, CSCE states agreed on adapting the structures of the CSCE; though, to a much lesser degree than envisioned by Moscow. At the CSCE's Budapest Summit in 1994, the Conference was re-named to the Organization for Security and Co-operation in Europe. Even though it was now officially named an organization, Washington lobbied successfully for not giving the OSCE an internationally recognized legal personality, privileges, and immunities.

In 1989, the new CFE negotiations took off. Like MBFR, negotiations took formally place outside the CSCE and between the two blocks with their respective hegemons, of which one, the USSR, was already in rapid decline. The resultant CFE Treaty is a classic dyadic East-West agreement achieved at a time where its design already became anachronistic because of the rapid changes the Eastern bloc underwent. CFE is based on the idea of perfect equilibrium of balance of forces between two 'groups of states' (meaning NATO and WTO). The treaty led to the destruction of approximately 70,000 pieces of treaty-limited equipment (TLE) in five categories[17], eliminated the two blocs' ability to launch large-scale surprise attacks on one another, and established a hitherto unmatched level of military transparency. Even though the treaty has been hailed as the 'cornerstone of European security', much of its relevance already vanished shortly before and during the negotiation process and even more so in the following years (cf. Coker 1992). The basic Western goal in the negotiations was to achieve that Western Europe is no longer threatened by a numerically superior force which could rapidly attack through coordinated pincer movements from the north and the south (cf. Zellner 1994). With Gorbachev's 1988 announcement at the UN General Assembly to unilaterally withdraw Soviet forces and military equipment from Eastern Europe (cf. Gorbachev 2011: 16), together with the subsequent signs of disintegration of the USSR, this goal was already partly achieved (cf. Falkenrath 1995a: 242). One of the main Soviet interests was to release the USSR from the economic burdens associated with its troop deployments in Eastern Europe (cf. Horelick 1991: 627) and to back up its unilateral withdrawal announced in 1988 with mutual legally-binding commitments. Therefore, Moscow was willing to make large-scale concessions to accommodate the West on the central questions of conventional arms control in the run-up to and during the negotiations (cf. Gorbachev 1996: 502; Horelick 1991).

Meanwhile, the CSCE's role in arms control was debated as well between Moscow and Washington but also between Washington and the states of the European Community (EC) (cf. Schlotter 1999: 90 et seq). The Paris CSCE Summit in 1990 established the Conflict Prevention Center (CPC) in Vienna to deal with arms control issues. Because of Washington's concerns that it might undermine the work of NATO (ibid), its role was limited to tasks related to the implementation of politically-binding or purely voluntary CSBMs. The United States became the prime leader of minimalist solutions,

---

17   The five CFE weapons categories are battle tanks, armored combat vehicles, artillery, combat aircraft, and attack helicopters. For a comprehensive overview of CFE see Croft 1994, Kelleher, Sharp, and Freedman 1996, Sharp 2006, Zellner, Schmidt, and Neuneck 2009.

cautiously resisting the evolution of the CSCE into a pan-European security institution (cf. Anstis 1994: 102). As a result of this blockade policy, the new arms control framework envisaged by the Berlin Council in July 1991 did not result in a forum that would somehow upgrade the role of the CPC. Instead, it was established in parallel. The resultant Forum for Security Cooperation's (FSC) tasks were arms control, disarmament, and CSBMs, security cooperation, and conflict prevention.[18] As Anstis predicted in 1994 (103) 'the lack of concrete proposals for "hard security" seems to confirm limited prospects for traditional arms control negotiations in the foreseeable future.' Nevertheless, the C/OSCE produced an extensive amount of multilateral CSBM agreements during these years. Examples are the Vienna Documents of 1990 and 1992 and the eight stipulations of the 'Programme for Immediate Action Series'.

The increasing institutionalization was not limited to the C/OSCE. NATO as well began to adjust its political structures and strategy to the new geopolitical landscape. It 'emerged as the most promising security organization' (Kelleher 1994: 314), at least in the view of many U.S. analysts and politicians. As Kelleher predicted in 1994, it could even 'extend its presence into central and eastern Europe and ultimately over the entire CSCE area.' (Ibid) A first step in this direction – also meant as political reassurance to the new eastern democracies that NATO would not be indifferent to those states' security concerns – was a U.S.-German initiative which led to the establishment of the North Atlantic Cooperation Council (NACC) in late 1991. In January 1994, the U.S.-led Partnership for Peace (PfP) was launched to establish closer ties with the former WTO states and the newly emerging CIS states and to enhance European security. The program also served the function of preparing for the possibility of enlarging NATO to the east (cf. U.S. State Department 1995), as predicted by Kelleher in 1994. Moscow saw its participation in PfP mainly as a chance to derail such development (cf. Ponsard 2007: 68).

The debate about possible NATO enlargement accelerated in 1994 (cf. Pradetto 2004). Moscow's first negative reactions already showed the high degree of sensitivity on the Russian side towards the issue (cf. Talbott 2003: 96). The larger historical background to this debate are the talks, which led to German reunification, the withdrawal of Soviet forces from East Germany, and full NATO membership of then-unified Germany. Two interpretations of historical narratives compete. On the one side, particularly the current Russian leadership under Vladimir Putin claims that Washington had promised Gorbachev not to enlarge NATO further to the East as a political quid pro quo for German unification and NATO membership of unified Germany (cf. Putin 2007). According to this view, Gorbachev had been tricked by the Americans and had failed to get a written commitment from Washington. In

---

18   See Section V 'CSCE Forum for Security Cooperation', Helsinki Document 1992.

an interview of 2014, Gorbachev has denied that any such commitment was ever expressed by the Americans (quotes from Gorbachev in Korshunov 2014). On the other side, U.S. policy analysts have long argued that the mainstream Russian view on the issue is wrong (see Zelikow 1995; Kramer 2009; Pifer 2014b). According to this viewpoint, the U.S. leadership of 1989/90 never made any promises related to NATO in conjunction with German unification other than not to enlarge its military structure to the territory of the former East Germany. Three extensive studies by Mary Elise Sarotte (see 2010a, b; 2014) based on newly available primary sources contests the mainstream U.S. viewpoint. According to Sarotte, U.S. and West German leaders implicitly signaled Gorbachev and Shevardnadze not to enlarge NATO's borders further to the east. The hectic environment of the talks and the turbulent developments within the Soviet political apparatus made any written agreement impossible (Sarotte 2014). Whatever viewpoint one takes on the issue, the contested interpretations of the events are only a minor aspect of the larger East-West divide that NATO enlargement should produce in the post-Cold War order. Even though the Clinton administration recognized the Russian concern (cf. Talbott 2003), in 1994, Western expectations towards enlargement were rather positive (ibid).

As an additional development, in 1992, one year after the official dissolution of the Warsaw Pact, six former Soviet Republics[19] signed the Treaty on Collective Security (CST). In substance and partially in terms of terminology, the CST mirrors the 1949 North Atlantic Treaty – an indication of Moscow's objective of consolidating its geopolitical environment in light of possible NATO enlargement (see Rozanov and Dovgan 2010).

3.3.1 Analysis of Cooperation

In this paragraph, four cooperation processes – CFE, adaptation of the CSCE, adaptation of NATO, and CSBMs under the auspices of the C/OSCE – are analyzed along the lines of the Realist model of international cooperation. Before, a closer look at the development of U.S./NATO-Soviet Union/Russian/WTO/CST capabilities between 1990 and 1994 is taken.
Capabilities

With the end of the Cold War, the capabilities of the Soviet Union and the Warsaw Pact underwent a fundamental change in political, geographic, economic, and military terms (cf. Garthoff 1994). In 1992, the Soviet Union dissolved and the Soviet command economy was replaced by a market economy (cf. Gorbachev quoted in Breslauer 2002: 98). The same year, the Warsaw Pact fell apart. As a result of the revolutionary developments, the Soviet/Russian economy tanked. According to the World Bank (2014), the Soviet/Russian GDP fell from US$ 517 billion in 1989 to US$ 395 billion in

---

19   Armenia, Kazakhstan, Kyrgyzstan, Russia, Tajikistan, and Uzbekistan were the initial
      Parties to the Treaty (see Treaty on Collective Security 1992).

1994. At the same time, the United States' GDP rose from $ 5.6 trillion to $ 7.3 trillion. In 1994, the U.S. GDP was already 18 times the GDP of Russia. Chart 8 illustrates these diverging trends.

CHART 8

COMPARISON OF U.S.-SOVIET/RUSSIAN ECONOMIC CAPABILITIES IN GDP, 1990-1994

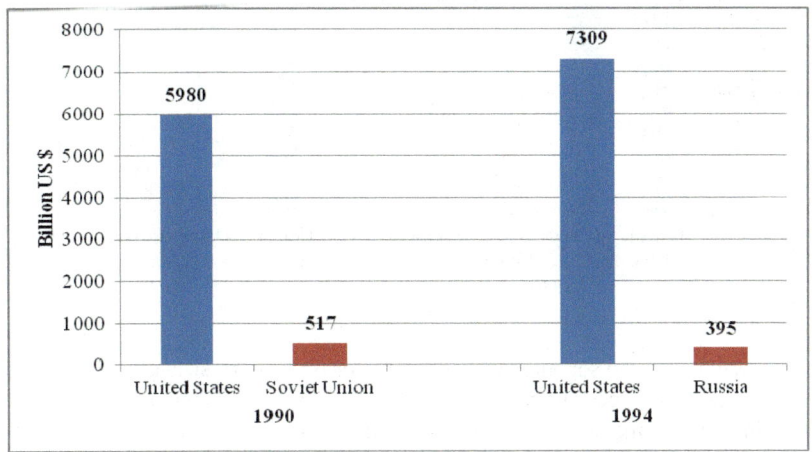

With regards the first capabilities factor of military strength, the development of national and combined defense budgets showed two trends. On the one hand, in 1991, the Warsaw Pact dissolved and was replaced the same year by the newly founded CST. On the other hand, the end of the Cold War and the decrease in military manpower (see Chart 10) affected national defense budgets. In addition, the 1990 concluded CFE Treaty had led to the destruction of ~70,000 costly heavy conventional weapons systems over the next years (cf. Hartmann, Heydrich, and Meyer-Landrut 1994). The result was a parallel decrease in national defense budgets. While in 1990, the combined defense budget of NATO allies was US$ 451 billion and the combined defense budget of WTO states was US$ 137 billion, already in 1994, the combined defense budget of NATO allies was US$ 387 billion and the combined defense budget of CST states was US$ 81 billion. The figures also suggest that the CST was in no way a substitute for the WTO since the financial commitment of the other CST states (besides Russia) is only marginal (~US$ 2 billion) compared to the financial commitment of the other WTO states (~US$ 20 billion). Chart 9 illustrates these trends.

CHART 9

COMPARISON OF NATIONAL U.S.-SOVIET/RUSSIAN AND
NATO-WTO/CST COMBINED DEFENSE BUDGETS, 1990-1994

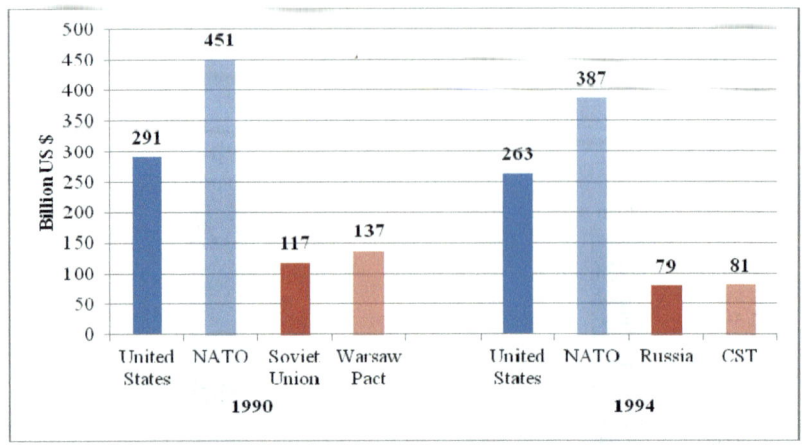

With regards to the second capabilities factor of military strength, the number of total armed forces shows the remarkable drop in Russian and CST forces. Again, the reasons behind this development are the dissolution of the Warsaw Pact and the Soviet Union and the downsizing of forces in conjunction with the CFE-1A agreement. While in 1990, the combined total armed forces of the WTO were 5.02 million soldiers, in 1994, the combined total armed forces of the CST were 1.99 million soldiers. In parallel, also the number of NATO forces decreased from 5.24 million in 1990 to 4.19 in 1994. Chart 10 illustrates these trends.

CHART 10

COMPARISON OF NATIONAL U.S.-SOVIET/RUSSIAN AND
NATO-WTO/CST COMBINED TOTAL ARMED FORCES, 1990-1994

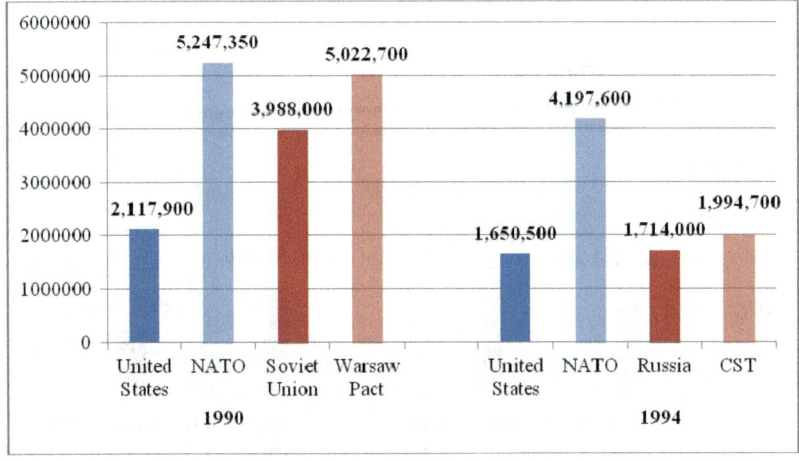

With regards the capabilities factors of the size of population and territory, the breakup of the Eastern bloc and the Soviet Union led to a significant drop in the size of population and territory of the Russian Federation. While the Soviet Union had ~288 million inhabitants and a territory of 22,4 million km² in 1990, the Russian Federation had ~148 million inhabitants and a territory of ~17 million km² in 1994. With regards to the Eastern military alliance, the Warsaw Pact had ~402 million inhabitants and a territory of ~23.3 million km² in 1990, the newly established CST had ~226 million inhabitants and a combined territory of ~20.9 million km². In contrast, the territory of NATO remained the same size and the number of inhabitants increased by ~40 million. Charts 11 and 12 illustrate these trends.

CHART 11

COMPARISON OF NATIONAL U.S.-SOVIET/RUSSIAN AND
NATO-WTO/CST COMBINED SIZE OF POPULATION, 1990-1994

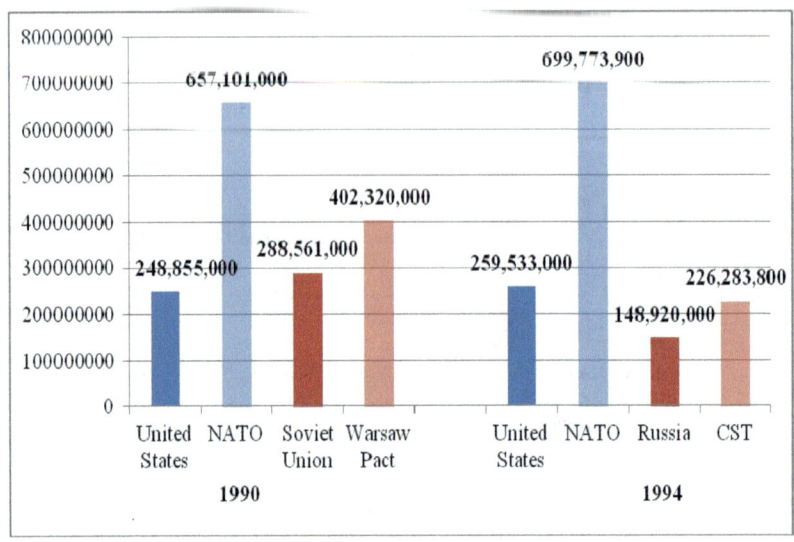

CHART 12

COMPARISON OF NATIONAL U.S.-SOVIET/RUSSIAN AND
NATO-WTO/CST COMBINED SIZE OF TERRITORY, 1990-1994

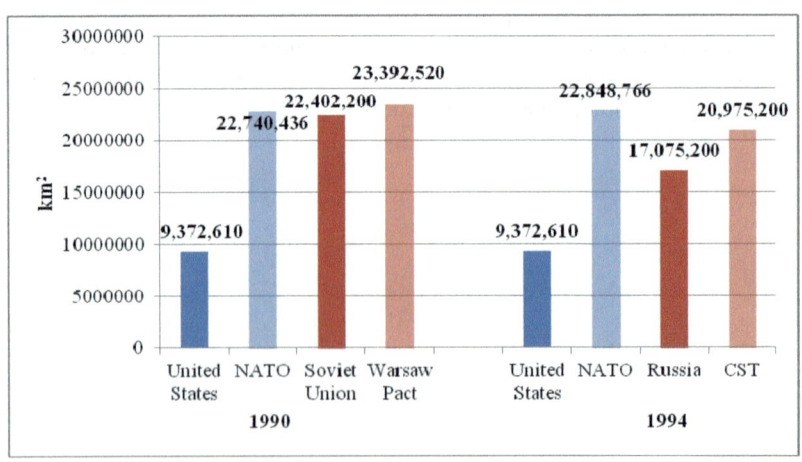

CFE

Interests: The Soviet general interest in securing survival became more and more influenced by economic considerations towards the end of the Cold War. Gorbachev wanted to reform the USSR while at the same time preserving the state's unity (cf. Gorbachev 1996). In order to succeed with that policy goal, his foreign and security policy focused, amongst other policy objectives, on ending the bloc confrontation and lessening the financial burden of the Soviet Union associated with its huge military apparatus (cf. Baker 1991; Legvold 1991; Gorbachev 1996). A first important step was the unilateral withdrawal of 500,000 men from Eastern Europe, announced in 1988 (cf. Gorbachev 2011: 16). Against this background, Washington's general interest in securing survival triggered a cooperative stance towards Moscow. Supporting Gorbachev was not an altruistic move by Washington but out of fear that he could become replaced by a less cooperative leader (cf. Baker 1991). Washington thus responded by giving preference to cooperation and by quickly locking in the Soviets in the security realm by a number of legally and politically-binding arms control and risk-reduction agreements (ibid). On CFE, both had a convergent issue-specific interest in cooperation – though for different reasons. Washington wanted to quickly lock in the Soviets (cf. Baker 1991) and finally achieve what sixteen years of MBFR talks could not. In the U.S. view, CFE should codify the relative distribution of military strength in the conventional realm which was already in flux since 1988 (cf. Gorbachev 2011). The Pentagon wanted reductions in conventional forces with the aim of equal ceilings for the two blocs in order to offset the numerical advantage of WTO forces and geographical limitations to prevent large-scale surprise attack (cf. Zellner 1994). Moscow had a critical interest in economic cooperation with the West and was willing to make large-scale concessions on CFE in exchange (cf. Gorbachev 1996: 502).

Expectations: Since 1988, the relative distribution of military strength in the conventional realm was undergoing changes due to the Soviet decision to significantly downsize its military deployments in the other Warsaw Pact countries. Moscow thus acted defensively-oriented. Washington wanted to seize the moment and aimed at codifying the new state of affairs (cf. Baker 1991). Its goal was an equilibrium state of balance of heavy military equipment between the two blocs (cf. Zellner 1994). Even though the Soviet withdrawal announcement had already changed the balance of military strength, the U.S. aim of equilibrium was a significant step further. One could therefore argue that Washington acted offensively-oriented because it sought a further change to the balance of forces. Nevertheless, Washington did not act against the Soviet will but in unison with the Gorbachev postulate to reduce the Red Army's military size and commitments and Washington and Bonn signaled to pay compensation. Washington's orientation could thus as well be described as defensive in nature. According to Realism, both could expect that cooperation on the issue was possible as long as the gap in relative gains was adjusted by compensation.

Strategies: Both employed a strategy mix of compensation, confidence-building, and monitoring. First, Washington engaged on compensation in the form of side-payments because of the wide-ranging concessions Russia was willing to make on CFE (cf. Gorbachev 1996: 502). At the Malta Summit in 1989, George H.W. Bush promised Gorbachev various arms control proposals in order to end the pressure on the Soviet economy stemming from the U.S.-Soviet arms races (cf. Grogin 2001: 338-9). In addition, West Germany agreed to shoulder major economic and financial commitments in return for German unification and the removal of Soviet forces from East Germany (ibid: 339). This policy was in line with Moscow pleading for compensation in the economic realm (cf. Gorbachev 1996: 502). All issues were dealt with separately but tacitly linked (cf. Grogin 2001). Second, both opted for confidence-building through slicing up the issue into increments. Negotiations concentrated on five different categories of heavy conventional armaments (cf. Zellner 1994). In order to limit the possible consequences from cheating, CFE was equipped with a wide-ranging monitoring system inside and outside of the treaty. To the inside, CFE came with monitoring provisions such as regular and challenge on-site inspections, regular consultations in the JCG, and data exchange (cf. Hartmann, Heydrich, and Meyer-Landrut 1994). To the outside, the later agreed upon Treaty on Open Skies served as supplementary monitoring instrument (cf. Spitzer 2011). As a result of these successful strategies and because of the immense time pressure, both came to an agreement within a few months only (cf. Zellner 1994).

Evaluation of Gains: The evaluation of gains from cooperation on CFE was positive on both sides (cf. Feinstein 1990) because both got what they wanted. Washington received codifying the drawback and downsizing of Soviet and Warsaw Pact conventional forces, resulting in a state of equilibrium between the two 'groups of states' (CFE 1990); Moscow could lift some of its military-economic burdens and received large-scale credits in return, particularly from Germany. During the next nine years the evaluation of gains from cooperation on CFE should change. Even though initially positive on both sides, particularly on the Russian side evaluation changed to the negative, visible through continued calls for re-negotiation. The actual gains from U.S.-Soviet cooperation on CFE in 1989/90 did reflect the balance of power inasmuch as the outcome of cooperation was rather a codification of the already existing reality than real change. Where the agreement produced change (i.e. the new state of equilibrium), compensation was paid. The gains increased mutual security by providing the Soviets with financial aid and the European NATO allies with security against large-scale surprise attack. In addition, both sides achieved significantly lower levels of conventional equipment and transparency through intrusive on-site inspections.

Adapting NATO and the CSCE

Interests: The crumbling of the Warsaw Pact as well as the impact of the war in the former Yugoslavia and in a number of newly emerging CIS states had underscored the need for a new post-Cold War security order for Europe (see US.-Russia 1992; cf. Flynn and Farrell 1999: 506). The general interest of the United States and Russia in securing survival by means of cooperation was thus put to a test. Both had directly related issue-specific interests. For Moscow it was: (1) preserving the territorial integrity of Russia; (2) restructuring the Russian economy with the help of the West; (3) establishing an all-inclusive European security architecture replacing the old alliance structure and readily addressing secessionist conflicts in Europe (cf. Breslauer 2002; Yeltsin 2001). Washington had a continued interest in stabilizing the new Russian government under Boris Yeltsin. In the words of George H.W. Bush: 'Our support for Russia is unshakable because it is in our interest.' (The White House 1992b) In addition, Washington wanted to avoid any subordination of NATO under any form of multilateral European security governance. Secretary of State James Baker advised President George H.W. Bush that the 'real risk to NATO is CSCE.' (Quoted from Sarotte 2010: 112) Instead, Washington focused on preserving Western unity (cf. Schlotter 1999: 90 et seq) by adapting and, from early 1994 onwards, possibly enlarging NATO (cf. Holbrooke 1995), and, similar to Russia, avoiding further scenarios of civil war in Europe. One of the main U.S. reasons behind NATO maintenance and adaptation was uncertainty about the future development of Russia in particular and European security in general (cf. Cohen 1995). U.S. and Russian issue-specific interests were partially overlapping but also significantly divergent. Particularly with regards to the basic design of the new European security order, divergence in interest prevailed. Moscow lobbied for an upgrade of the CSCE and the dissolution of NATO. Foreign Minister of Russia, Kozyrev (1994: 65) argued: 'After all, it was the democratic principles of the 56-member CSCE that won the Cold War – not the NATO military machine.' Washington did not seek a greatly expanded role for the CSCE and instead remained firmly committed to the structures of NATO. 'In no way can the OSCE be made "superior" to NATO', U.S. Assistant Secretary for European and Canadian Affairs, Richard Holbrooke (1995), declared shortly after both organizations had been adapted. The OSCE, he continued, 'will not become the umbrella organization for European security, nor will it oversee the work of the NATO alliance.'

Expectations: Both states could expect a difficult setting with regards cooperation on NATO and CSCE. On NATO, Russia acted offensively-oriented since it sought changes to the existing relative distribution of power (i.e. NATO dissolution). Washington wanted the maintenance of the balance of power, which was already to its advantage after the dissolution of the WTO. Washington thus acted defensively-oriented (i.e. maintaining and adapting NATO). According to Realism, chances of cooperation were small as long as Russia would neither compensate Washington for the losses from potential NATO dissolution nor give up its offensive orientation. On the CSCE, again, Russia acted offensively-oriented, for Moscow lobbied for an upgrade of the CSCE to an all-inclusive European security institution over-looking all other security institutions including NATO (cf. Tscharner and Castelmur 1997). Washington wanted to keep the status quo of the CSCE as much as possible (ibid). According to Realism, the chance for cooperation on the CSCE was small, would Russia stick to its orientation.

Strategies: Both applied a strategy of confidence-building on the issues of NATO and the CSCE. However, the strategy of confidence-building alone would have most likely failed if Moscow would not have changed its orientation (nevertheless, without evidence, this is speculation). When Moscow realized that it was not in the position to either change Washington's interest or to pay enough compensation, the Russians gave in on both issues and accepted the U.S. position (cf. Anstis 1994: 102). Moscow thus shifted from an initially offensive orientation to a defensive one. In turn, Washington compensated Moscow by including Russia in the new structures of the adapted NATO (i.e. the PfP and the NACC) and allowing for an upgrade of the CSCE – even though conditional to its preferred option. Cooperation in both frameworks was secured by lengthening the shadow of the future by formally institutionalizing the processes.

Evaluation of Gains: In the end, both gained on both issues but Washington gained comparably more. The United States could achieve the further maintenance and adaptation of NATO while the CSCE remained inferior to NATO. Moscow did not achieve its preferred interest, neither on NATO nor on the CSCE. By changing its orientation, Moscow not only accepted the results but also took account of the relative distribution of power. It accepted that it was in no position to challenge the U.S. interest. On the question of the new design of Europe's security architecture Russia was simply not capable of following through with its preferred option. At the same time, Moscow also gained from cooperation because it was formally included in the new NATO cooperation frameworks and it achieved an upgrade of the CSCE, even though to a much lesser degree than hoped for. The evaluation of gains, though initially positive on Moscow's side soon gave way to increasing signs of dissatisfaction and continued calls for re-negotiating the principal institutionalized security design of post-Cold War Europe (cf. Kozyrev 1994: 65). Nevertheless, Russia continued cooperation on both issues. Having achieved all preferred interests, Washington's evaluation was almost completely positive. In the understanding of some U.S. analysts, the successful handling of the end of the Cold War marked the 'end of history' (Fukuyama 1992) and the beginning of America's 'unipolar moment' (Krauthammer 1991). The actual gains from U.S.-Russian cooperation on NATO adaptation and CSCE upgrade did reflect the balance of power. At the same time, the gains increased mutual security by achieving a continued and institutionalized exchange on issues of military and non-military security.

CSBMs under the Auspices of the C/OSCE

Interests: As explained above, both Washington and Moscow had an overlapping convergent issue-specific interest in containing secessionist ethnical conflicts in Yugoslavia and the entire CSCE area (cf. Kaufman 2002). The envisioned establishment of number of CSBMs under the auspices of the C/OSCE should address the new challenges emerging from civil war and ethnic strife. With regards to the concrete design of CSBMs, issue-specific interests were also rather convergent and geared towards achieving stability and increasing military transparency and predictability (cf. Auton 1998).

Expectations: Since the direct focus of most of the CSBMs of that period was not on U.S. and Russian forces, both could expect that no change affecting the relative distribution of power in the sphere of military strength would result. Both orientations were defensive in nature. According to Realism, cooperation was possible if both would agree on a successful strategy.

Strategies: Both employed a mix of strategies. On the one hand, the strategy of confidence-building within the successful-proven CSCE framework was maintained also in the new institution of the OSCE. On the other hand, monitoring mechanisms were attached to a number of CSBMs such as the Vienna Document.

Evaluation of Gains: On CSBMs, both got what they wanted from cooperation. The evaluation of gains was positive in both capitals. Both opted for continued and renewed cooperation on the issue. The actual gains from U.S.-Russian cooperation on CSBMs under the auspices of the C/OSCE did reflect the balance of power. At the same time, the gains increased mutual security by devising arms control measures to increase transparency, predictability, and stability.

Institutionalization

The institutionalization in the realm of cooperative arms control between 1990 and 1994 developed on three parallel tracks. On the first track, the signing of CFE cemented the MBFR legacy inasmuch as conventional arms control was maintained as an exclusive NATO-WTO issue with strong bilateral U.S.-Soviet characteristics (cf. Zellner 1994). The complementing treaties from 1992 on Personnel Strength of Conventional Armed Forces in Europe (CFE-1A) and on Open Skies (OS) underscored this development. On the second track, the C/OSCE emerged as the principal gatekeeper of various kinds of CSBMs and benefited from past experiences, which made realization easier to achieve. On the third track, NATO adapted its structures to the new post-Cold War Europe by setting up institutions for military and political cooperation with the former WTO states and the newly emerging states of the CIS.

TABLE 4

U.S.-SOVIET/RUSSIAN COOPERATION ON CFE, CSCE, NATO, AND CSBMS

INSTITUTION	ACTOR	ISSUE-SPECIFIC INTERESTS	EXPECTATIONS	STRATEGIES	EVALUATION OF GAINS
CFE	USA	convergent	acting defensively- as well as offensively-oriented	offering compensation through economic aid, confidence-building, monitoring	continued cooperation
	USSR	convergent	acting defensively-oriented	confidence-building, monitoring	continued cooperation, calls for re-negotiation
CSCE Adaptation	USA	divergent	acting defensively-oriented	offering compensation through CSCE up-grade, confidence-building	continued cooperation
	USSR/ Russia	divergent	initially acting offensively-oriented, later defensively-oriented	confidence-building	continued cooperation, calls for re-negotiation
NATO Adaptation	USA	divergent	acting defensively-oriented	offering compensation through including Russia, confidence-building	continued cooperation
	Russia	divergent	initially acting offensively-oriented, later defensively-oriented	confidence-building	continued cooperation, calls for re-negotiation
CSBMs	USA	convergent	acting defensively-oriented	confidence-building, partially monitoring	continued cooperation, renewed cooperation
	USSR/ Russia	convergent	acting defensively-oriented	confidence-building, partially monitoring	continued cooperation, renewed cooperation

Table 4 comprises the four cooperative processes of CFE, adapting the CSCE, adapting NATO, and establishing CSBMs under the auspices of the C/OSCE and assesses them in short according to the Realist cooperation model.

3.4   Adaptation and Re-Adjustment, 1995-1999

Four major institutional processes happened during the years 1995-1999. The first was the process of adapting CFE. In late 1994, fighting in Chechnya escalated to open civil war which led Russia to exceed specific CFE limitations in the so called southern flank region – a geographical remnant of the old bloc-to-bloc arrangement of CFE (cf. Falkenrath 1995b). The flank issue had military priority for the Kremlin (ibid). Aside from that, Russian demand re-negotiating CFE because of the changed political realities. Already during the late CFE negotiations in 1990, some WTO states were tacitly contemplating the option of leaving the Pact (cf. Zellner 1994). Therefore, the treaty does not speak of NATO and the WTO but refers to two general 'groups of States Parties' (Article II, 1(A), CFE 1990), meaning the two alliances. While the treaty's rationale of bloc-to-bloc parity had vanished with the end of the Warsaw Pact in 1991, particularly the prospect of NATO enlargement would further change the balance of power and gave Russia an additional argument to request re-negotiation. While the Clinton administration officially denounced any connection between CFE adaptation and the flank issue on the one hand and NATO enlargement on the other, Washington's policy was tacitly steered towards compensating Moscow for its unease with enlargement (cf. Kühn 2009). A first Russian attempt demanding compensation from Washington made Russia's accession to the PfP framework conditional on changes in the flank (cf. Deni 1994: 28). As a commentary concluded in 1997, 'revising the CFE Treaty is likely to be the key to reducing Moscow's concerns with NATO enlargement.' (IISS 1997b: 2). Washington agreed to a first round of re-negotiation which resulted in the Flank Document of 1997 (cf. Kühn 2009).

The ensuing ratification process of the flank agreement revealed strongly diverging political approaches in the U.S. Senate (ibid: 2 et seq). The domestic chasm was not only caused by partisan politics but more generally by disagreement between those who favored a more cooperative Russia policy and those who argued for a more confrontational approach. The latter saw the Russian Federation as the undemocratic and neo-imperialistic revenant of the Soviet Union (ibid). Their "antidote" was a policy mix of fast NATO enlargement, cuts to financial aid, and rigorous support of the independence of former Soviet Republics, amongst them particularly Azerbaijan, Georgia, Moldova, and Ukraine. In the words of Republican Congressman Gerald Solomon (1996: E80): 'there can be no doubt that Russia will attempt at least to "Finlandize" the former Warsaw Pact countries. It is silly to oppose NATO enlargement with talk of drawing lines in Europe. There already is a line, and because of it, stability has been fostered in those countries west of it. Quite frankly, the farther east that line is, the better.'

The consequence of this approach, which went along with a general dismissal of the Clinton administration's arms control policy (cf. Rosner 1995), were fourteen conditions attached to the resolution of ratification of the Flank Document. Amongst them was the condition 'to achieve the immediate and complete withdrawal of any armed forces and military equipment under the control of the Russian Federation that arc deployed on the territories of the independent states of the former Soviet Union [...] without the full and complete agreement of those states.' (U.S. Senate Committee on Foreign Relations 1997: 28) This condition binds the U.S. administration to promote the withdrawal of remaining Russian forces from secessionist entities in Georgia and Moldova. Also the second round of re-negotiating CFE turned out to be successful (cf. Dunay and Zellner 2000). On November 19, 1999 the Adapted CFE Treaty (ACFE) was signed in Istanbul. In a number of accompanying politically binding commitments – the so called Istanbul commitments – Russia agreed to withdraw excess military equipment and personnel from Georgia and Moldova (see OSCE 1999).

The second important development was the handling of NATO enlargement. From late 1994 onwards, the White House followed a double-track policy. It advanced continuously on the enlargement track while filing measures aimed at alleviating Russian concern (cf. Kaufman 2002: 45). Besides the hard-fought Flank Document and the ensuing negotiations on ACFE, a third measure in the realm of cooperative security was the signing of the NATO-Russia Founding Act in 1997 (cf. Kupchan 2000: 132). Established in parallel to the new cooperation structure of the Euro-Atlantic Partnership Council (EAPC), the successor framework to the NACC, the Founding Act gave Russia a prominent and visible role in its future dealings with the alliance. In the words of the Founding Act, this development 'marks the beginning of a fundamentally new relationship between NATO and Russia.' Both sides 'intend to develop, on the basis of common interest, reciprocity and transparency a strong, stable and enduring partnership.' (NATO and Russia 1997) In addition, the NATO-Russia Permanent Joint Council (PJC) was established. While Russia had pledged for a legally binding agreement and a say in NATO's decision-making (cf. Ponsard 2007), the Founding Act was as a politically binding agreement with the PJC based on the formula of 16+1 instead. Besides compensation in the realm of cooperative security and arms control, the White House offered a number of other rewards such as Russian accession to the G7 (cf. Aggarwal 2000:77).

The third development of that period saw Russia still promoting her idea of the OSCE as an all-encompassing security organization for Europe (cf. Ghébali 2005). In September 1996, the Russian leadership took up the proposal of elaborating a 'new security system', encompassing all international organizations active in Europe (cf. Primakov 1996). Central to the Russian proposal was the claim that no state should ensure its own security at the expense of others (cf. Kühn 2010b). The discussion continued for years and was finally watered down to become the 1999 OSCE's Charter for European Security – a politically binding declaration of intent, signed at the 1999 Istanbul Summit and '*empty* by Russian standards' (Ghébali 2005: 378) Even according to the former British OSCE Ambassador, the Charter 'lacked substance' (Cliff 2012: 65). Besides the Charter, the Summit agreed on an updated version of the Vienna Document and on the Platform for Cooperative Security to enhance inter-organizational division of labor.

The fourth development was an answer to the civil wars on the Balkans. With the Dayton peace accords of 1995 (General Framework Agreement for Peace in Bosnia and Herzegovina) all sides had agreed on an encompassing framework to guarantee for peace and stability. In the realm of cooperative arms control, two agreements on CSBMs and disarmament[20] were negotiated and agreed upon. In both cases, previous experiences under the auspices of the C/OSCE served as the basis for institutionalization and led to a close modeling of the two agreements along the lines of the OSCE's Vienna Document on CSBMs and the CFE Treaty (cf. Vetschera 2009). The stipulations represent the first sub-regional arms control arrangements in Europe after the Cold War and were later extended in 2001.[21]

Aside from these cooperative approaches, in 1999, NATO member states launched a 78-days air campaign to end the Kosovo War. Afraid of a Russian veto, Washington decided for circumventing the UN Security Council (cf. Kaufman 2002). 'Deeply angered' about the air campaign, President Yeltsin (quoted in Hoffman 1999) ordered a suspension of NATO-Russian institutionalized cooperation. Aside from rhetorical condemnation of 'NATO's aggression' (Yeltsin 1999), Moscow exercised restraint, mainly because the Kremlin was interested in a renewed loan from the International Monetary Fund (IMF) to stop the increasing downward spiral, the Russian economy was facing since 1998 (see Chart 13 and cf. Hoffman 1999). NATO air strikes against Yugoslavia had a decisive impact on the European security setting. Freedman (2014: 15) argues that 'this was a key moment in Russia's disenchantment with post-Cold War security arrangements, especially in the context of the wider restructuring of the European state system, which had already begun and led to many post-communist states joining NATO and then the EU. This was largely beneficial to those countries, in terms of governance and economics as well as security, but was viewed from Moscow with increasing misgivings.' Aside from the structural implications the

---

20   Agreement on Confidence- and Security-Building Measures in Bosnia and Herzegovina, 1996, Agreement on Sub-Regional Arms Control, Article IV, 1996.
21   Concluding Document of the Negotiations Under Article V of Annex 1-B of the General Framework Agreement for Peace in Bosnia and Herzegovina.

NATO air campaign had, the campaign also demonstrated to Moscow the significant gap that had opened up between U.S. and Russian military capabilities since the end of the Cold War (cf. Renz 2014). In the coming years, Russia would invest in modernizing its conventional forces, trying to narrow the gap (cf. McDermott 2011).

3.4.1   Analysis of Cooperation

In this paragraph, four cooperation processes – re-negotiating CFE, establishing the NATO-Russia Founding Act, further adapting the OSCE, and establishing a sub-regional arms control framework for the Balkans – are analyzed along the lines of the Realist model of international cooperation. The first three cooperation processes are closely intertwined and dependent on the issue of NATO enlargement. Before, a closer look at the development of U.S./NATO-Russian/CST capabilities between 1995 and 1999 is taken.
Capabilities
    Between 1995 and 1999 the capabilities gap between the United States and Russia further increased. The Russian GDP fell from US$ 396 billion in 1995 to US$ 196 billion in 1999 while the U.S. GDP increased from US$ 7.6 trillion to US$ 9.6 trillion. In 1999, the GDP of the United States had ~50 times the size of the Russian GDP. The year 1998 brought the ruble crisis and resulted in the Russian Central Bank devaluing the ruble and defaulting on its debt (see Government of Russia 1998). Chart 13 illustrates these diverging trends.

CHART 13

COMPARISON OF U.S.-RUSSIAN ECONOMIC CAPABILITIES IN GDP, 1995-1999

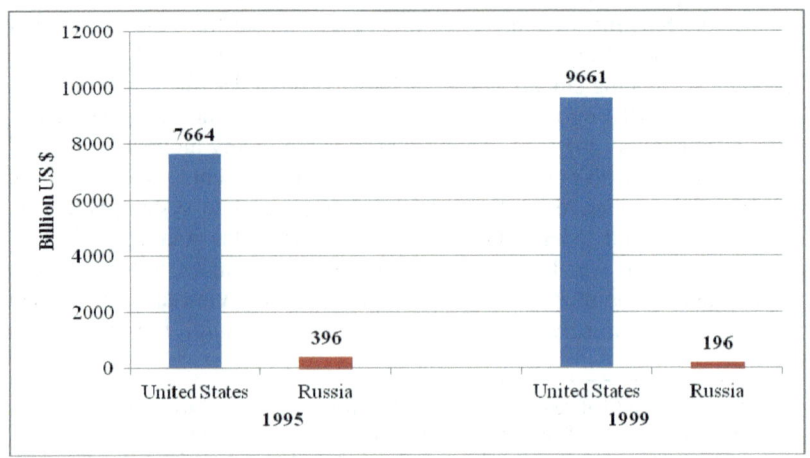

With regards the first capabilities factor of military strength, the development of national defense budgets of the United States and Russia and the combined defense budgets of NATO member states and CST member states also show diverging trends. While the Russian/CST defense budgets were halved, the U.S and NATO budgets started to grow for the first time since the end of the Cold War. On the side of NATO, this development was also due to Poland, Hungary, and the Czech Republic joining NATO officially in April 1999. All in all, in 1999, the combined defense budget of NATO was 14.4 times the combined defense budget of the CST. While Washington could pursue a policy of financial burden-sharing, the national defense budget of Russia and the combined budget of the CST are almost identical. Chart 14 illustrates these diverging trends.

CHART 14

COMPARISON OF NATIONAL U.S.-RUSSIAN AND
NATO-CST COMBINED DEFENSE BUDGETS, 1995-1999

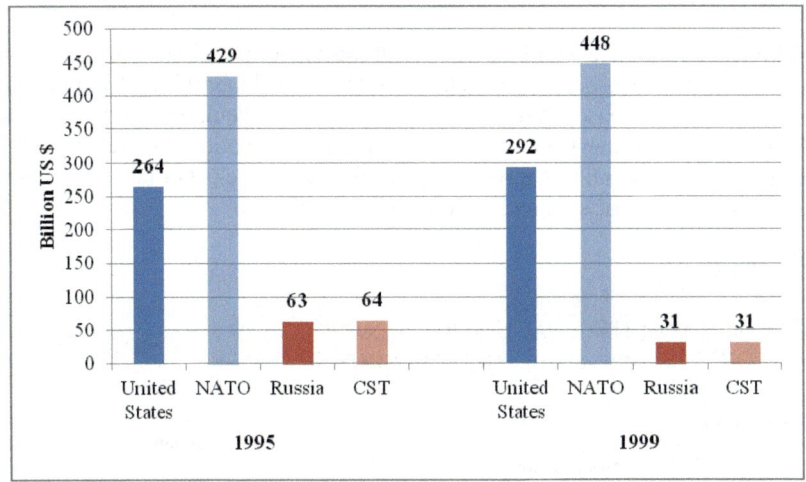

With regards to the second capabilities factor of military strength, the number of total armed forces shows a slight increase in NATO's combined total armed forces (due to the accession of Poland, Hungary, and the Czech Republic), a considerable drop in U.S. national total armed forces, and a significant drop in Russian and CST total armed forces. Therewith, the trend since the end of the Cold War towards smaller national armies continued; however, much more pronounced on the Russian/CST side. Chart 15 illustrates these parallel trends.

CHART 15

COMPARISON OF NATIONAL U.S.-RUSSIAN AND
NATO-CST COMBINED TOTAL ARMED FORCES, 1995-1999

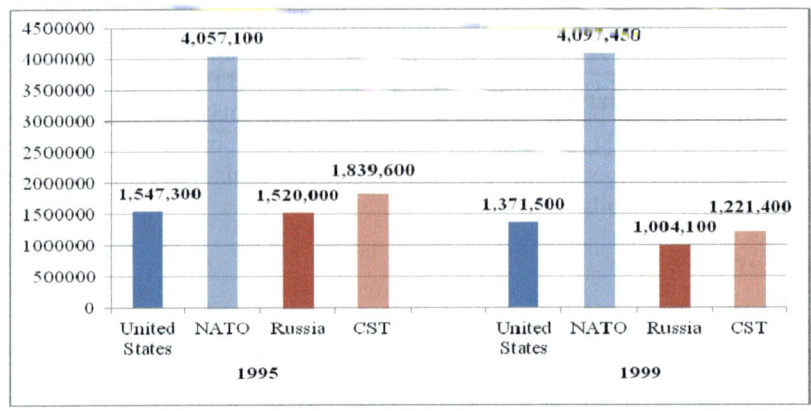

With regards to the capabilities factors of the size of population and territory, the trends are also divergent. While NATO's combined size of population and territory increased due to the accession of Poland, Hungary, and the Czech Republic, the CST's combined size of population and territory decreased, partly because Azerbaijan, Georgia, and Uzbekistan left the organization in 1999. Charts 16 and 17 illustrate these trends.

CHART 16

COMPARISON OF NATIONAL U.S.-RUSSIAN AND
NATO-CST COMBINED SIZE OF POPULATION, 1995-1999

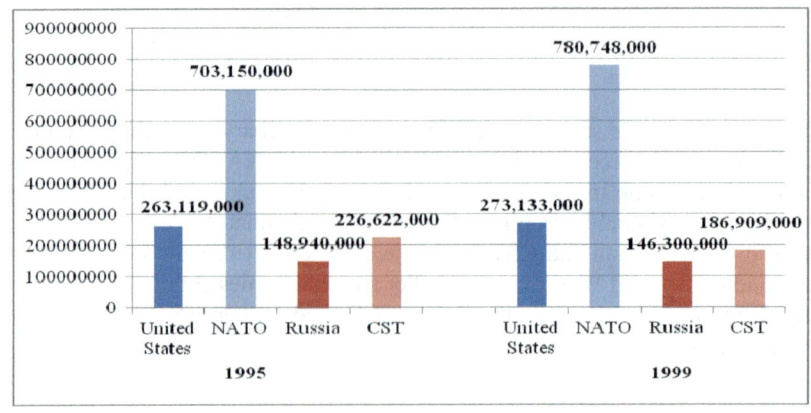

100

CHART 17

COMPARISON OF NATIONAL U.S.-RUSSIAN AND
NATO-CST COMBINED SIZE OF TERRITORY, 1995-1999

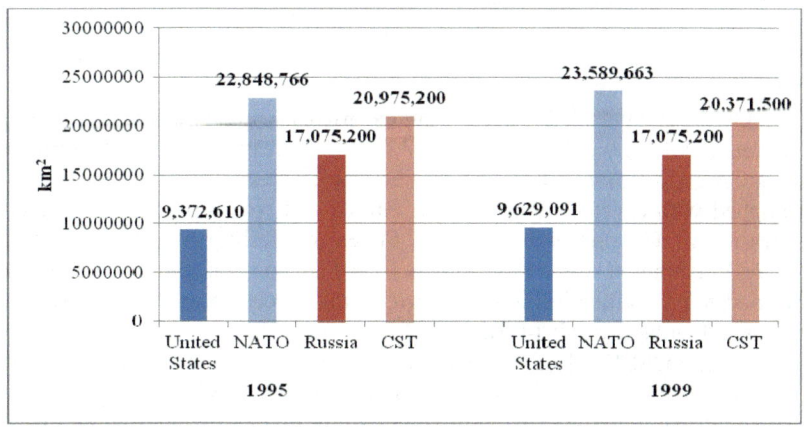

Re-Negotiating CFE, Establishing the NATO-Russia Founding Act, and Further Adapting the OSCE
Interests: From 1995-1999, the general interest of the United States and Russia in securing survival remained bound to the concept of cooperation; though, for different reasons. Washington had an issue-specific interest in continuing its support for the Yeltsin administration while the Kremlin had a continued issue-specific interest in halting and reversing economic recession with the help of the United States and its allies (cf. Lippman 1997). On the further design of Europe's security architecture, again divergence prevailed. In 1995, Washington had finally decided to enlarge NATO (ibid). Because of the well-known Russian resentment towards the issue, Washington sought the consent of Moscow (ibid). The Russian leadership found itself in a dilemma. On the one hand, it was Moscow's interest to avert NATO enlargement. According to Russian President Yeltsin, 'the eastward expansion of NATO is a mistake and a serious one at that.' (Quoted in Lippman 1997) The problem was that Moscow had no pivotal leverage against the inevitable and a continued interest in a cooperative relationship with the West. (Cf. Aggarwal 2000: 73) While facing the inevitable, at least, the Kremlin wanted to receive compensation (cf. Kaufman 2002: 45). For Moscow, compensation could include one or more of the following policy objectives: re-negotiating CFE, establishing a treaty regulating NATO-Russian relations, and/or significantly upgrading the OSCE (cf. Truscott 1997: 54; Tscharner and Castelmur 1997; Sharp 1995).

On CFE, Moscow wanted a change to the old bloc system and more freedom of military movement in the Russian southern flank where the First

Chechen War was raging (cf. Kühn 2009). In addition, the prospect of a potential future accession of the Baltic States to NATO forced Russia to press for re-negotiation (cf. Sharp 1995). Washington was divided on the issue. The Clinton administration did not attach huge military value to CFE anymore and was willing to meet the Russian concerns (ibid). The GOP-dominated Congress wanted to make use of CFE to press Russia on withdrawing her remaining forces from secessionist entities in Georgia and Moldova (cf. Kühn 2009).

On a potential NATO-Russia treaty, Moscow aimed at legally binding assurances which would prevent the Alliance from moving military installations closer to Russia's borders. At best, such agreement would have to be equipped with a veto mechanism for Russia and would preclude the future accession of Ukraine and the Baltic States (cf. Kahl 1998: 24-5; Ponsard 2007). Washington wanted to avert such far-reaching concessions and instead pleaded for a politically binding charter with no veto power for Russia (cf. Lugar and Nuland 1997: 14-5).

On the OSCE, Moscow continued to lobby for a 'new security system' under the auspices of the OSCE (cf. Borawski 1996: 384). Part of such system should be a charter for the organization in order to transform the OSCE into a legal entity with a possible European Security Council overseeing the work of all other security institutions (i.e. NATO) in the area (cf. Tscharner and Castelmur 1997). Washington was open to declaratory adjustments but declared to remain steadfast in resisting any attempts to give the OSCE a legal capacity (cf. Dean 1998).

Expectations: On the issue of NATO enlargement, Washington acted offensively-oriented and aimed at changing the existing distribution of power. Moscow acted defensively-oriented and wanted to keep the status quo. According to Realism, cooperation on the issue was almost impossible if Washington would not compensate Russia for her losses. On CFE, Russia wanted the codified recognition of the changes that had occurred since 1990. Russia thus acted defensively-oriented. Washington – at least the Democratic government – showed the same stance. According to Realism, cooperation on the issue was possible if the strategies would ensure cooperation. On the issue of establishing a NATO-Russia agreement, Moscow acted defensively-oriented. Pleading for legally binding assurances that NATO would not enlarge further east (i.e. the Baltics and Ukraine) and a veto mechanism which could, theoretically, block any future NATO decision-making underscored that Moscow was interested in options cementing the status quo. Washington also acted defensively-oriented; aiming at a politically binding document which would reflect the balance of power. However, since Washington was against a Russian veto and against a no-further-enlargement pledge it aimed at keeping the option of further changing the balance of power in the future. According to Realism, cooperation on the issue was possible if the strategies would ensure cooperation. On the issue of further adapting the OSCE, Russia entered the talks again with an offensive orientation aimed at changing the balance of power (i.e. making NATO subject to OSCE decision-making). Washington acted defensively-oriented and tried to stick with the status quo as much as possible. According to Realism, cooperation on the issue was rather unlikely as long as Moscow was not changing its orientation or paying compensation to Washington.

Strategies: Direct cooperation between Russia and the United States on NATO enlargement did not take place because their issue-specific interest was too divergent and because of their different orientations (Washington offensively, Moscow defensively). In addition, NATO enlargement was formally an intra-alliance decision not dependent on U.S.-Russian cooperation and the Clinton administration was already facing domestic criticism from the GOP for being too soft on Russia (cf. Kühn 2009). However, Aggarwal (2000: 68) is correct to note that enlargement 'can be seen as a game primarily between the U.S. and Russia'. In order to alleviate Russian concern and to back the Yeltsin administration against domestic opposition, Washington tacitly offered compensation (cf. Talbott 2003). Moscow openly linked the establishment of the NATO-Russia Founding Act as well as re-negotiating CFE to the issue of NATO enlargement (cf. Solomon 1997: 219, Wilcox 2011) while avoiding portraying the issues as being of equal value. Washington cautiously avoided any official linkage and instead continued its strategy of tacit compensation. Bill Clinton (1997: 9) insisted: 'The NATO-Russia Founding Act was not an effort to buy Russian acquiescence to enlargement.' Russian opposition to enlargement were 'an issue on which we have decided to disagree, while working together to manage that disagreement.' The management of disagreement took the form of a complex bundle of compensating deals, including in the economic realm (see Aggarwal 2000: 76 et seq). As Pipes (1997: 77) suggested, 'the situation calls for a subtle policy that mixes toughness with understanding of Russian sensitivities.'

The first compensation would be to negotiate with Russia the NATO-Russia Founding Act (cf. Lippman 1997). In the words of the Joint U.S.-Russian Statement on European Security of 1997: 'In order to minimize the potential consequences of [NATO enlargement], the Presidents agreed that they should work, both together and with others, on a document that will establish cooperation between NATO and Russia as an important element of a new comprehensive European security system.' (U.S.-Russia 1997) In the words of Boris Yeltsin (quoted in Lippman 1997): 'in order to minimize the negative consequences [of NATO enlargement] for Russia, we decided to sign an agreement with NATO.' Beyond compensation, both employed the strategy of confidence-building through institutionalization. Therefore, the Founding Act includes the establishment of the PJC.

The second compensation would emerge from CFE adaptation in 1999. Adapting CFE was, according to Sharp (1995: 21), 'the quid pro quo for Russian acceptance of NATO's expansion'. In the process of negotiating

ACFE, both employed a strategy mix of confidence-building and monitoring. On the one hand, the process was sliced up into increments so that negotiations continued for almost three years (cf. Hartmann and Heydrich 2002). Negotiators could build on the already established CFE institution of the JCG. On the other hand, ACFE was equipped with stricter monitoring clauses to minimize possible cheating consequences (ibid).

The third compensation would result from further adapting the OSCE at the 1999 Istanbul Summit while simultaneously resisting Russian claims for a legal upgrade of the organization (cf. Dean 1998). When Moscow changed its offensive orientation towards a defensive orientation, thus recognized the distribution of power, cooperation became possible. The U.S. degree of attention to the OSCE, Dean (ibid: 39) concluded, 'evidences an energetic United States effort to meet – or to appear to meet – [the Russian interest and] was part of the vigorous effort to bring President Yeltsin to acquiesce in at least the first stage of NATO enlargement.' Here, both could build on existing OSCE institutions to continue the successfully proven strategy of confidence-building.

A fourth compensation was paid in the economic realm. In 1998, Russia was given access to the G7 and the Asia-Pacific Economic Cooperation (APEC) in order to open up new economic possibilities for the Yeltsin administration (cf. Aggarwal 2000: 76 et seq).

Evaluation of Gains: The evaluation of gains from this complex deal is as difficult as the deal itself. In general, Washington got what it wanted from cooperation. It achieved NATO enlargement and could "buy" Russian acquiescence. It achieved adapting CFE and could include the Senate's demand for Russian forces withdrawal from Moldova and Georgia in the form of politically binding pledges by Russia (i.e. the Istanbul commitments). In addition, Washington achieved the Founding Act and the PJC, both operating on the formula of "16+1" without a Russian veto and based on politically binding mechanisms. A plead not to enlarge NATO further eastwards was not included. On the OSCE, Washington achieved keeping the status quo and endowing the organization with additional declaratory instruments (i.e. the 1999 Charter for European Security). The evaluation of gains was mostly positive on the U.S. side. The Founding Act and the results of the 1999 OSCE Istanbul Summit were positively welcomed by the administration (cf. The White House 1999). At the same time, members of the GOP criticized the administration for their soft handling of Russia in conjunction with CFE (cf. Kühn 2009: 14-5). Washington continued cooperation on the OSCE and even allowed for renewed NATO-Russia cooperation (i.e. setting up the NRC in 2002) when the PJC showed signs of dysfunctionality in conjunction with the Kosovo crisis (cf. Ponsard 2007). After George W. Bush had taken over, the new Republican administration continued cooperation on CFE but made the ratification of ACFE conditional on Russia fulfilling her Istanbul commitments (cf. Kühn 2009).

Moscow did mostly not get what it wanted from cooperation. NATO enlargement took place without an official cooperation process. The distribution of power allowed the United States to move forward on the issue and to change the balance of power. Moscow did not have the means and/or will to thwart the issue (cf. Yeltsin quoted in Lippman 1997). In addition, the Russian leadership did not achieve a legal personality for the OSCE. On the Founding Act it failed to meet its goal of a legally binding treaty based on an inclusive framework "at 17" with full veto power for the Kremlin and a guarantee that NATO would not include former Soviet states at a later stage. In the case of CFE, the 1997 Flank Document met the initial Russian claim for greater freedom of movement for her troops in the southern flank (cf. Kühn 2009). However, the 1999 adaptation agreement came at the price of signing political commitments to withdraw Russian forces from Moldova and Georgia. The evaluation of gains on the Russian side soon turned from positive to negative. For Moscow, the OSCE Istanbul Summit was rather disappointing, not only for reasons of Western criticism with regards to Russian actions in Chechnya (cf. BBC 1999). Nevertheless, Russia continued cooperation but increasingly voiced its disenchantment with the organization over the following years. ACFE was positively received until NATO's decision to withhold ratification (cf. Putin quoted in Wilcox 2011: 571). In 2007, Russia partially exited from the agreement. The evaluation of gains from cooperation on the Founding Act and the PJC (later the NRC) soon turned from positive to negative in the context of the Kosovo crisis. Even though both continued cooperation based on the Founding Act, Russia soon called for re-negotiating the PJC. Therefore, renewed cooperation took place in 2002 with the establishment of the NRC (cf. Ponsard 2007).

The actual gains from U.S.-Russian cooperation on these issues did reflect the balance of power. Where the balance of power was changed (i.e. NATO enlargement) official cooperation did not take place. The gains increased mutual security to differing degrees. The Flank Document and the adaptation of CFE provided Russia with more security by lifting the regulations in the southern flank and led to further downsizing of conventional forces of all parties to the treaty. However, since ACFE never entered into force, the security gains from cooperation largely remained in the declaratory realm. The NATO-Russia Founding Act provided Russia with politically binding assurances that NATO member states 'have no intention, no plan and no reason to deploy nuclear weapons on the territory of new members' (NATO-Russia 1997). In addition, the alliance committed itself to 'carry out its collective defense and other missions by ensuring the necessary interoperability, integration, and capability for reinforcement rather than by additional permanent stationing of substantial combat forces.' (Ibid) In turn, Russia pleaded to 'exercise similar restraint in its conventional force deployments in Europe.' (Ibid) The establishment of the PJC increased security in the sense of confidence through institutionalized dialogue-based interaction.

Establishing a Sub-Regional Arms Control Framework for the Balkans

Interests: In contrast to the above analyzed setting, the establishment of a sub-regional arms control framework for the Balkans was built on issue-specific convergent interests between the United States and Russia. Both had an issue-specific interest in peace and stability in the region (cf. Hartmann 1997). Washington was the first member of the Contact Group to press for measures of disarmament and CSBMs in the Dayton negotiations (ibid: 256). Even though negotiations within the Contact Group were divisive at times (cf. Camisar et al 2005: 12), with regards to the issue-specific measures devised to ensure stability, also convergence prevailed that they should be modeled along the lines of the CFE Treaty and the Vienna Document (cf. Hartmann 1997). Both were able to devise cooperative measures for the war-torn region in a top-down approach.

Expectations: Since the direct focus of the stipulations of the sub-regional arms control framework for the Balkans was not on U.S. and Russian forces, both could expect that no change affecting the relative distribution of power in the sphere of U.S.-Russian military strength would result. Both orientations were defensive in nature. In addition, the force levels foreseen in the agreements reflected the relative distribution of power in the sphere of military strength of the Balkan states (ibid). According to Realism, cooperation was possible if both would agree on a successful strategy.

Strategies: Washington and Moscow pursued a mix of strategies. On the one hand, the strategy of confidence-building through slicing up issues into increments (i.e. different categories of weapons) proved successful. On the other hand, the strategy of monitoring limited the possible consequences from cheating. Monitoring mechanisms could build on earlier C/OSCE experiences and were designed along the lines of the CFE Treaty and the Vienna Document.

Evaluation of Gains: On the issue of establishing a sub-regional arms control framework for the Balkans, both got what they wanted from cooperation. The evaluation of gains was positive in Moscow and Washington (cf. Jopp 2000: 346-7). Both opted for continued and renewed cooperation on the issue in 2001. The actual gains from U.S.-Russian cooperation on sub-regional arms control for the Balkans did reflect the balance of power. At the same time, the gains increased mutual security by devising reciprocal measures increasing transparency, predictability, and stability as well as limiting conventional military equipment in the region. In addition, the dialogue-based process was institutionalized by setting up the JCC and the Sub-Regional Consultative Commission.

TABLE 5

U.S.-RUSSIAN COOPERATION ON CFE ADAPTATION, FURTHER OSCE ADAPTATION, NATO-RUSSIA FOUNDING ACT, AND BALKANS ARMS CONTROL FRAMEWORK

INSTITUTION	ACTOR	ISSUE-SPECIFIC INTERESTS	EXPECTATIONS	STRATEGIES	EVALUATION OF GAINS
CFE Adaptation	USA	convergent	acting defensively-oriented	confidence-building, monitoring	continued cooperation conditional on Istanbul commitments
	Russia	convergent	acting defensively-oriented	demanding compensation for NATO enlargement, confidence-building, monitoring	continued cooperation, partial exit
Further OSCE Adaptation	USA	divergent	acting defensively-oriented	confidence-building	continued cooperation
	Russia	divergent	initially acting offensively-later defensively-oriented	demanding compensation for NATO enlargement, confidence-building	continued cooperation, calls for re-negotiation
NATO-Russia Founding Act (Including the PJC)	USA	divergent	acting defensively-oriented	confidence-building	continued cooperation, renewed cooperation
	Russia	divergent	initially acting offensively-later defensively-oriented	demanding compensation for NATO enlargement, confidence-building	continued cooperation, calls for re-negotiation, renewed cooperation
Sub-Regional Arms Control Framework for the Balkans	USA	convergent	defensively-oriented	confidence-building, monitoring	renewed cooperation
	Russia	convergent	defensively-oriented	confidence-building, monitoring	renewed cooperation

Institutionalization

During the years 1995-1999, the institutional fragmentation of cooperative arms control in Europe solidified. Institutional "winners" and "losers" emerged (cf. Hækkerup 2005: 371). While NATO broadened its political-military portfolio through the NATO-Russia Founding Act, the PJC, and the EAPC, the OSCE's pace of institutional achievements slowed down. With the first round of NATO enlargement in 1999, the OSCE's fate as a secondary or even tertiary security organization was being cemented. The OSCE became the forum for debate, NATO the framework for action. This development was illustrated by the painstaking evolution of the Istanbul Charter (cf. Ghébali 2005: 378). 'It was not the OSCE but NATO that emerged as the decisive security and defence organisation in Europe', Hækkerup (2005: 371) concluded. In addition, a new institutional framework which concentrated on sub-regional arms control at the Balkans was added to the realm of cooperative arms control in Europe.

Table 5 comprises the four cooperative processes of CFE adaptation, establishment of the NATO-Russia Founding Act (including the PJC), further adaptation of the OSCE, and establishment of a sub-regional arms control framework for the Balkans and assesses them according to the Realist cooperation model.

3.5   Stagnation and Regress, 2000-2008

The years between 2000 and 2008 were heavily influenced by the 9/11 attacks on U.S. homeland. The period saw the mutual departure from the essentials of cooperative security in Moscow and Washington. Consequently, only one major new institution in the realm of cooperative arms control in Europe was created.

With the coming into office of the new Russian President Vladimir Putin in 2000, Moscow changed its policy towards the OSCE and the West (cf. Ghébali 2005: 379 et seq). Dissatisfied with the role and work of the OSCE, the Kremlin launched a verbal attack on the organization, arguing that it could no longer accept seeing the OSCE being assigned 'a kind of maid-servant's role, carrying out the orders and implementing the decisions of other organizations' (2001 Russian statement to the OSCE, quoted from Ghébali 2002: 36). Moscow's warnings that 'the pan-European process will be doomed to extinction' (ibid) turned into an active policy substantially blocking the organization's work (see Ghébali 2005: 379 et seq). Washington's OSCE policy under the new George W. Bush administration was twofold. One the one hand, efforts to strengthen the politico-military dimension of arms control were rejected (cf. Ghébali 2002: 36). On the other hand, the United States increasingly promoted human rights standards in conjunction with continued critique about Moscow's politics in this realm. Hopmann

(2009: 89) analyzed that 'human rights has been virtually the sole focus of the United States within the OSCE for many years, especially since 2001.' Consequentially, new institutional cooperative efforts under the OSCE's auspices were rare in this period.

On conventional arms control, NATO made the fulfillment of the Russian Istanbul commitments a precondition to ratifying ACFE at the Alliance's 2002 Summit in Prague; a policy decision which was harshly criticized by Moscow (cf. Kühn 2009: 15-6). In response, Russia significantly slowed down the pace of withdrawing military equipment from Moldova and Georgia (cf. Boese 2002: 22). The following years were characterized by mutual recriminations which side was responsible for the deadlock (cf. Zellner, Schmidt, and Neuneck 2009). Frustrated with the ongoing standstill and after having launched a series of political warning signals (see Kulebyakin 2009), Moscow unilaterally suspended the CFE Treaty in 2007 – an action not in accordance with the formal stipulations of the treaty.

Meanwhile, NATO enlargement advanced with two further rounds in 2004 and 2009 against previous warnings from Moscow (cf. Pradetto 2004; Umbach 2004). The Russian National Security Concept of 2000 had explicitly named 'NATO's eastward expansion [a] fundamental threat [to] the Russian Federation's national security'. (Russian Security Council 2000) With Estonia, Latvia, and Lithuania, for the first time three countries that were previously part of the Soviet Union joined the Alliance. In addition, Bulgaria, Romania, Slovakia, and Slovenia joined. In 2008, NATO member states agreed after heavy pressure from Washington (cf. Erlanger and Myers 2008) that Georgia and Ukraine 'will become members of NATO' (NATO 2008). In contrast to the Clinton years, the U.S. administration under George W. Bush sought not to compensate Moscow by means of cooperative arms control measures. While the Clinton administration for instance had viewed CFE as an important bargaining chip in the game about the first round of NATO enlargement (cf. Aggarwal 2000), the new Republican-led policy establishment in Washington did not anymore. A study by the influential RAND Corporation of 2000 illustrated that 'it is not CFE but rather NATO that must play a leading role in managing contemporary European crises and local wars.' (Peters 2000: 2) In September 2002, U.S. Secretary of Defense, Rumsfeld declared: 'I don't see any linkage between NATO enlargement and CFE, and I don't know any NATO countries that do.' (Quoted from Disarmament Diplomacy 2002: 63)

The only major institutional achievement was the establishment of the NATO-Russia Council (NRC) in conjunction with the signing of the Rome Declaration in 2002. In contrast to the U.S. policy during the 1990s, the NRC was not an attempt at compensating Russia for further enlargement. It was the product of two factors. First, the structures of the PJC had failed the test of the Kosovo crisis when cooperation in this format was suspended. Both sides wished for a fresh start (cf. Ponsard 2007: 77 et seq). Second, President

Putin's support for Washington after the 9/11 attacks and the initially convergent interests of Moscow and Washington in the war on terrorism had laid the basis for a new understanding. The new structures should readily address, amongst others, the threat of international terrorism and should compensate Russia for opening her airspace to coalition forces fighting in Afghanistan (ibid: 78-84). Even though the NRC operates on the principle of consensus and holds meetings on the principle of equality, it still deprives Russia of a veto on security issues. 'At best, Russia will still be a junior partner in the increasingly important Alliance', Mlyn (2003: 52) concluded.

In addition, substantially diverging national policies in Washington and Moscow negatively affected U.S.-Russian arms control relations. Under George W. Bush, the U.S. administration pursued a foreign policy which rejected the essentials of cooperative security (cf. Luongo 2001). Consequently, Washington departed from the legacy of bilateral arms control accords from the Cold War. In 2002, the United States withdrew from the Anti-Ballistic Missile Treaty (ABM) and started to promote a missile defense system for the protection of its European NATO allies – an effort which provoked strong negative reactions from Moscow (see Becher and Zagorski 2007). The revival of missile defense produced 'a cataclysmic break in U.S.-Russian relations' (Goldgeier and McFaul 2003: 312). Nevertheless, Washington did not perceive its policy as problematic. 'The Russian government has bet it will not lose as much from a world without the Anti-Ballistic Missile Treaty as it will gain from a United States willing to cooperate', the current Deputy Assistant Secretary of Defense for Russia, Ukraine, and Eurasia, Celeste A. Wallander, observed in 2002 (Wallander 2002: 4). The subsequent U.S. Ambassador to Russia, Michael McFaul noted: 'Bush could threaten to withdraw unilaterally from the ABM Treaty [...] because Russia was too weak to do anything about it.' (Goldgeier and McFaul 2003: 312) In addition, the newly concluded bilateral Strategic Offensive Reductions Treaty (SORT) could not live up to the intrusive quality of its predecessors in the realms of verification and transparency (cf. Kimball 2002). The new U.S. understanding of arms control culminated in the perception that 'the philosophy and practice of traditional arms control are no longer contributing effectively to the goal of reducing threats to U.S. national security.' (Sokolsky 2001: 4)

Beyond arms control, the U.S.-Russian relationship experienced a significant downturn during those eight years. With the 9/11 attacks and the subsequent wars in Afghanistan and Iraq, Washington increasingly followed a "go-it-alone" approach which centered on unilateralism and coalitions of the willing (cf. Kelleher 2012: 16-7). On the one hand, for Washington, Russia did not matter a great deal anymore. 'Beyond its nuclear weapons', Kelleher (ibid: 17) assessed, 'Russia, in the view of some neo-conservative members of the Bush administration, was simply no longer relevant to the new American strategic and political preeminence.' On the other hand, the relationship vis-à-vis Moscow centered on criticism of Russia's human rights record. In that regard, the U.S. policy mirrored the Russia-critic stance which a number of GOP representatives had already shown during the late 1990s (cf. Solomon 1996). Collective security, in the form of NATO enlargement or missile defense was deemed more important than cooperative security (see Kelleher 2012).

Russia, under its new President Putin, answered with a similar departure from cooperative security. Kelleher (ibid: 17) explained, 'just like traditional European allies, Russia in the end had no other choice but to deal with the United States on its own terms and within the framework of the American global agenda.' Particularly at the highest echelon of Russian leadership, dissatisfaction with the new American administration gained the upper hand. 'Putin has come to the conclusion that a gentlemen's agreement is not possible with the United States', Lukyanov (2012) concluded. 'He thinks Bush responded with base ingratitude to Moscow's positive gestures more than once – from its support during 9/11 and the subsequent war on terror, to its voluntary closing of military facilities in Vietnam and Cuba. Putin believes that these gestures were met with aggressive efforts of the United States to bolster its presence in the post-Soviet space, expand NATO, and deploy missile defense systems on Polish and Czech territory, to name a few.'

Clandestine U.S. support through state-sponsored NGOs and intelligence for the Georgian Rose Revolution in 2003 and the Ukrainian Orange Revolution in 2004 (cf. McFaul quoted in Remnick 2014) further increased the tensions between Russia and the United States. In 2002, the members to the CST established the collective defense organization of the Collective Security Treaty Organization (CSTO) and thus gave the CST an institutional framework for continuous cooperation (see Kurtov 2008). At the 2007 Munich Conference on Security Policy, President Putin accused the United States of overstepping 'its national borders in every way' and condemned 'an almost uncontained hyper use of force – military force – in international relations' (President of Russia 2007).

Only a few months later, in August 2008, Russia used military force to advance into Georgian territory. The triggering events were increasing skirmishes between pro-Russian fighters in the Georgian breakaway region of South Ossetia and official Georgian forces through the first half of 2008, followed by a ground offensive of Georgian forces (cf. Independent International Fact-Finding Mission on the Conflict in Georgia 2009). In response, Russian official forces crossed the border to Georgia and drove back the Georgian military, basically occupying South Ossetia and the second breakaway region of Abkhazia (see Asmus 2010). The background of the conflict was strong vocal support by the U.S. administration of the Georgian Saakashvili administration which had culminated in the April 2008 NATO announcement that Georgia will became an alliance member (ibid). The Saakashvili administration had apparently hoped for active U.S. military support should fighting escalate – a possible option that a minority of U.S.

government officials seriously pondered (ibid). As reaction, NATO member states condemned Russian actions and suspended the NRC. On 25 August 2008, the Russian State Duma unanimously urged President Dmitry Medvedev to recognize Abkhazia and South Ossetia as independent states. A consequence of Russia's mixed military performance in Georgia was a comprehensive reform of the Russian military, launched in late 2008 (see McDermott 2011).

3.5.1   Analysis of Cooperation

In this paragraph, the cooperation process of the establishment of the NRC is analyzed along the lines of the Realist model of international cooperation. Before, a closer look at the development of U.S./NATO-Russian/CST capabilities between 2000 and 2008 is taken.

Capabilities
For the first time since the end of the Cold War, the economic capabilities gap between the United States and Russia decreased between 2000 and 2008. According to the World Bank (2014), the Russian GDP grew from US$ 260 billion in 2000 to US$ 1.6 trillion in 2008. Under the new Russian President Vladimir Putin, the Russian economy recovered relatively and registered strong annual growth rates (ibid). At the same time, the U.S. GDP further increased from $10.2 trillion to $14.7 trillion. In 2008, the U.S. GDP was eight times the size of the Russian GDP. Chart 18 illustrates these trends.

CHART 18

COMPARISON OF U.S.-RUSSIAN ECONOMIC CAPABILITIES IN GDP, 2000-2008

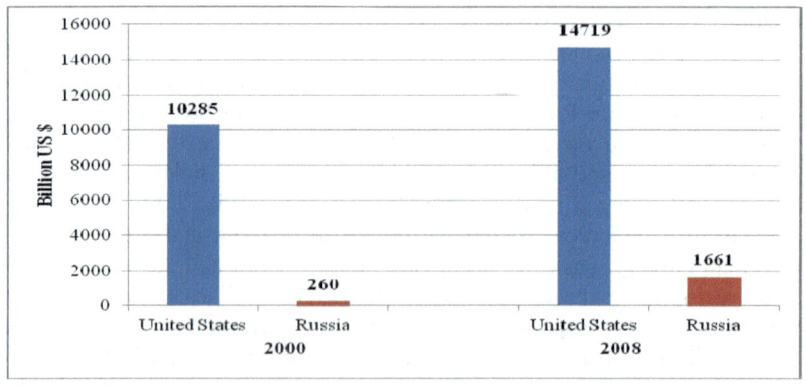

On the first capabilities factor of military strength, comparison of the development of national defense budgets of the United States and Russia and the combined defense budgets of NATO and CST member states shows a re-markable increase on the side of the United States and NATO. Between 2000 and 2008, the national defense budget of the United States more than doubled in size and reached an unprecedented high of US$ 693 billion in 2008. The reason behind this significant jump was the U.S.-led War on Terror in Afghanistan and the war in Iraq (cf. Thompson 2011). The combined defense budget of the other NATO member states also increased by ~US$ 100 billion, in parts due to the accession of Bulgaria, Estonia, Latvia, Lithuania, Roma-nia, Slovakia, and Slovenia in 2004. At the same time, Russia and the CST increased their defense budgets as well. In comparison, the 2008 combined defense budget of NATO has ~24 times the size of the combined defense budget of the CST. Chart 19 illustrates these trends.

CHART 19

COMPARISON OF NATIONAL U.S.-RUSSIAN AND
NATO-CST COMBINED DEFENSE BUDGETS, 2000-2008

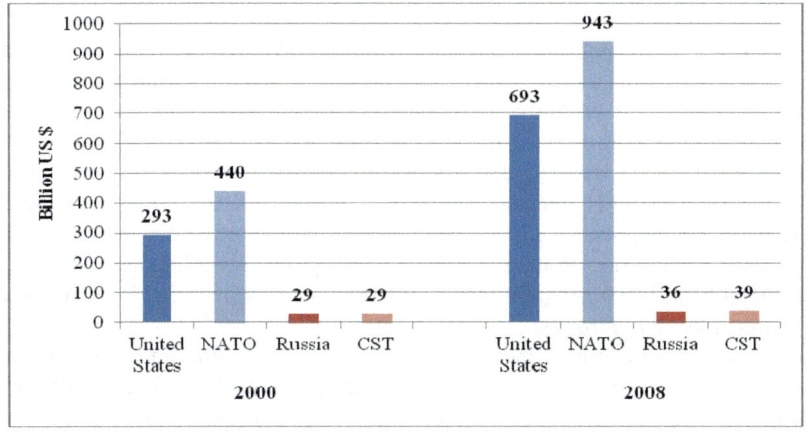

CHART 20

COMPARISON OF NATIONAL U.S.-RUSSIAN AND
NATO-CST COMBINED TOTAL ARMED FORCES, 2000-2008

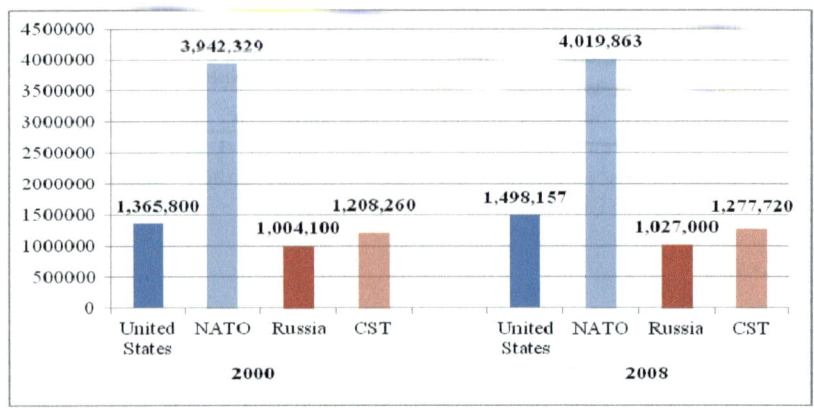

On the second capabilities factor of military strength, the number of total armed forces shows only a relatively modest increase in Russian and CST forces. NATO shows only a relatively slight increase, even though seven countries joined the alliance in 2004. Washington increased the number of its total armed forces by ~135,000 soldiers. In comparison to the strong increase in the U.S. national defense budget (see Chart 19), the relatively modest increase in manpower leads to conclude that the United States ramped up its military capabilities from a qualitative viewpoint, including new military-technological R&D programs (cf. U.S. Army War College 2012: 140). Chart 20 illustrates these trends.

On the capabilities factors of the size of population and territory, the combined size of CST population increased by ~25 million while the Russian population decreased. The combined size of population of NATO member states increased by ~85 million. The size of the U.S. population increased as well. With regards to territory, NATO's territory increased due to the 2004 round of enlargement and the territory of the CST increased by the re-entry of Uzbekistan in 2006. By 2008, the combined size of population of NATO was more than four times the combined size of population of the CST. Charts 21 and 22 illustrate these trends.

CHART 21

COMPARISON OF NATIONAL U.S.-RUSSIAN AND
NATO-CST COMBINED SIZE OF POPULATION, 2000-2008

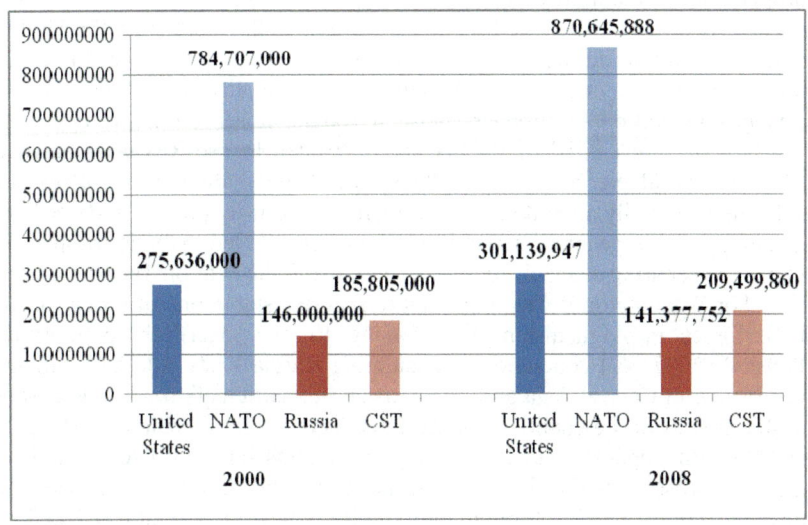

CHART 22

COMPARISON OF NATIONAL U.S.-RUSSIAN AND
NATO-CST COMBINED SIZE OF TERRITORY, 2000-2008

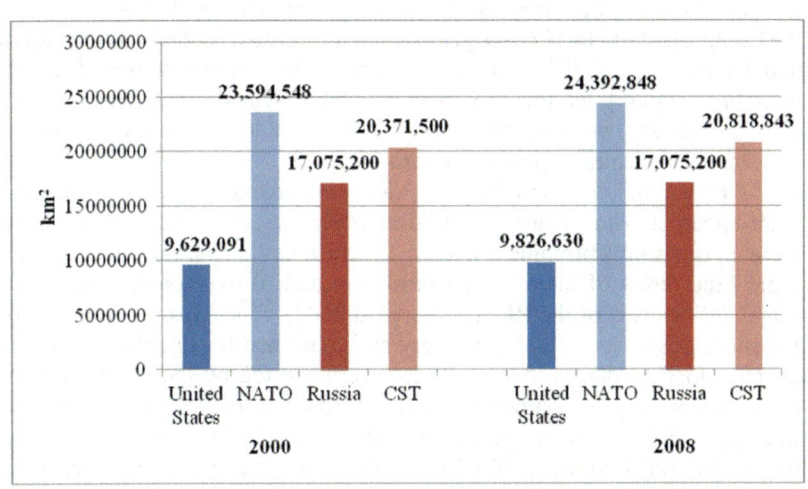

Establishment of the NATO-Russia Council

Interests: With the 9/11 attacks the U.S. general interest in securing survival led Washington to focus on fighting terrorism and to heavily increase its defense budget. Hence, the Islamic World came into focus and Russia dropped out of the immediate focus (Daalder and Lindsay 2005). The consequence was that for the first time since the end of the Cold War, the United States and Russia did not share an interest in cooperation in order to secure mutual survival anymore. Even though both had initially issue-specific interests in cooperation – Russia because it sought closer economic ties with Washington; the United States because it wanted to use Russia to balance China (cf. Goldgeier and McFaul 2003: 312 et seq) – the terrorist attacks of 9/11 fundamentally altered the U.S. foreign and security policy (ibid). Subsequently, the U.S. general interest in securing survival led to the issue-specific interest in securing as much support as possible in the War on Terror.

For Washington it was important to secure a stable line of ordnance for U.S. forces in Afghanistan; thus having Russian overflight permission. Ponsard (2007: 77) concludes: 'Considering Russia's key role and military experience in Central Asia and Afghanistan, its participation was paramount to the success of the coalition against terrorism'. As initial reaction, Moscow stated its full support, linked to the hope for a fresh start in bilateral relations after the Kosovo crisis (ibid). Given the increasing dissatisfaction with the development of the U.S. foreign and security policy, the Kremlin reduced its engagement with Washington (cf. Kelleher 2012: 16-7).

With a short delay of almost two years, also the Russian general interest in securing survival through means of U.S.-Russian cooperation decreased (cf. Charap and Shapiro 2014b). Instead, the Russian general interest shifted towards consolidating its geopolitical neighborhood in the so called Near Abroad (meaning the former Soviet Republics, excluding the Baltics) against the background of NATO enlargement and the colored revolutions in Georgia and Ukraine (cf. Kelleher 2012: 30 et seq). As a direct consequence, the Kremlin's support for the U.S. war in Afghanistan decreased because the Russian military was concerned about a possible long-term engagement of U.S. forces in Central Asia (cf. Ponsard 2007: 78).

On the issue of establishing the NRC, convergent issue-specific interests were apparent with regards to political objectives. The political objectives were: a) devising a prominent institution which could address, amongst other issues, the threat of international terrorism; and b) overcoming the institutional deficiencies of the PJC (cf. Ponsard 2007). Since Washington benefitted enormously from Russian military assistance and the opening of Russian airspace to U.S. planes, the White House, pressured by the British government, was willing to compensate Russia through a new cooperation mechanism (the NRC) which would remove some of the institutional inefficiencies of the PJC (cf. Ponsard 2007: 78-84). The NRC was thus a product of the Kosovo crisis and 9/11. It was never seen as compensating Moscow for the looming second round of NATO enlargement in 2004 (ibid). With regards to the concrete design of the NRC, issue-specific divergence prevailed. Moscow pleaded again for an institution based on equality and including the right to veto NATO policies. The Pentagon's concern was that Russia would 'sneak in by NATO's back door, split the allies and veto military decisions' (quoted from ibid: 82). Therefore, Washington was only willing to give the Kremlin an enhanced "voice but not a veto" in NATO decision-making (ibid: 81-3).

Expectations: The setting resembled some of the features of U.S.-Russian cooperation on the 1997 Founding Act. Again, a compensation deal loomed in the background (i.e. in 1997 the Founding Act compensated Russia, amongst other deals, for NATO enlargement; in 2002 the NRC should compensate Russian for her support of the U.S. war on terror). Again, both acted defensively-oriented. Russia sought a legal codification of the status quo by means of a veto on future NATO decision (i.e. blocking further enlargement). Washington sought a politically binding institution which would reflect the status quo but which would not exclude the possibility to change the status quo in the future (i.e. therefore not giving Moscow a veto). According to Realism, cooperation was possible if both would agree on a successful strategy.

Strategies: The convergent issue-specific interest in establishing the NRC led both to pursue a strategy of confidence-building through institutionalization. Such effort could build on and continue their previous cooperation experiences in the NATO-Russia framework (i.e. PfP, the NATO-Russia Founding Act, and the PJC).

Evaluation of Gains: The actual gains from U.S.-Russian cooperation on establishing the NRC did reflect the balance of power. Washington fully got from cooperation what it wanted. It succeeded in tailoring the new cooperation mechanism according to its preferred interest of giving Russia "a voice but not a veto". The Kremlin did only partially get what it wanted. It achieved a new institutionalized cooperation mechanism. It did not get a veto mechanism. Even though Vladimir Putin faced considerable criticism for his initially positive attitude towards NATO (Ponsard 2007: 83), the Kremlin's interest in an agreement was too high and Russia's position relative to NATO too weak (cf. Mlyn 2003: 53; Mankoff 2009: 22) to insist on a veto. The result was that 'the NRC does resemble the PJC in many ways' (ibid: 82). and the cooperation in the NRC framework did not prevent the further enlargement of NATO or plans for the deployment of European missile defense. The evaluation of gains was initially positive in Washington but changed over time to dissatisfaction the more that the NRC became the forum for Russian discontent with NATO's and the United States' security policy (cf. U.S. Mission NATO 2009). On the Russian side, the evaluation of gains over time turned into the negative the more the working format of the NRC impeded proportionate influence for Russia (cf. Kelleher 2012: 50). Both have continued cooperation on the NRC but NATO has partially suspended the institution in reaction to the Russian-Georgian war in 2008 and the 2014 Ukraine conflict and Russia has increasingly voiced its dissatisfaction with the institution (cf. U.S. Mission NATO 2009). The establishment of the NRC increased security in the sense of confidence through institutionalized, dialogue based interaction.

Institutionalization

In terms of institutionalization, the years between 2000 and 2008 brought a slowing down in the establishment of new institutions of cooperative arms control in Europe. Existing institutions came under political stress; most notably the CFE Treaty, the OSCE, but also the NRC in conjunction with the Russian-Georgian war of 2008. The derailment of the CFE process was to a lesser degree a sign of the treaty's dysfunctionality in particular but more the result of a mutual U.S.-Russian neglect of cooperative security in general (cf. Zellner, Schmidt, and Neuneck 2009). The institutionalization of conventional arms control itself did not prevent both actors from pursuing policies that were in contradiction with cooperative security (i.e. unilateralism, non-cooperation, and warfare). At the same time, Moscow did not give up completely on CFE, for the act of "suspension" allows Russia to return to implementation – albeit conditional on institutional changes to Moscow's advantage (cf. Russian Statement of 12 June 2007 in OSCE 2007a). Table 6 assesses U.S.-Russian cooperation on the establishment of the NRC according to the Realist cooperation model.

TABLE 6

U.S.-RUSSIAN COOPERATION ON THE ESTABLISHMENT OF THE NRC

INSTITUTION	ACTOR	ISSUE-SPECIFIC INTERESTS	EXPECTATIONS	STRATEGIES	EVALUATION OF GAINS
NRC Establishment	USA	divergent	acting defensively-oriented	offering compensation for Russian support in the war on terror, confidence-building	continued cooperation, later partial exit
	Russia	divergent	acting defensively-oriented	confidence-building	continued cooperation, calls for re-negotiation

118

With the first presidential term of Barack Obama, the pendulum of America's foreign and security policy swung again towards a more cooperative approach (cf. Brzezinski 2010). Under the catchphrase of "Reset" Washington re-engaged with its Russian counterparts in order to repair the strained relationship (see The White House 2010). A result of this policy was a revival of bilateral arms control policies, most notably the conclusion of the New START agreement, tentative talks about negotiating cuts to non-strategic nuclear weapons (NSNW), and the U.S.-led initiative to involve Russia in the newly designed missile defense approach for Europe, the European Phased Adaptive Approach (EPAA).

However, Washington's cooperative approach did not result in successfully repairing the institutions of cooperative arms control in Europe. On the one hand, Moscow continued to show a deep-seated frustration with the existing European security architecture. A leaked U.S. cable summarizes well Russian dissatisfaction: 'Russia's frustration with its declining influence in European affairs has been magnified by waves of NATO and EU enlargement, the abandonment of the ABM Treaty and subsequent development of new missile defense plans on European soil, the stalemate in progress toward an adapted CFE agreement on conventional arms control, NATO's refusal to engage on Russia's other proposals for confidence-building measures, Western actions in Kosovo, and increasingly close NATO, EU, and bilateral relations with Russia's immediate neighbors', the U.S. cable concludes (Mission U.S. OSCE 2009). On the other hand, the Russian administrative apparatus was split between divergent opinions of the Ministry of Foreign Affairs and the Ministry of Defense. These internal Russian quarrels blocked for instance a reform of the NRC (see Mission U.S. NATO 2009).

In the realm of conventional arms control, a last effort led by Washington in order to revive the CFE Treaty at informal talks "at 36" (meaning CFE parties to the treaty and new NATO members not part to the treaty) failed in 2011, mainly due to Russian disengagement.[22] As a consequence, Washington announced that it would not accept Russian inspections of U.S. bases under CFE any longer and that it would not provide Russia with the annual December exchange notifications and military data called for in the treaty (cf. United States State Department 2011). A few days later, NATO allies and Georgia followed the example. In addition, the Treaty on Open Skies temporarily became hostage to disputes between Turkey and Greece as well as between Georgia and Russia (cf. Spitzer 2011). The treaty's operation was therewith partially affected as well (cf. Delawie 2013).

For the OSCE, the change in office in Washington initially brought along a wave of optimism, which was even more propelled by an initiative by

---

22   This information was passed on to the author by German officials; cf. also Kühn 2013.

then-President Dmitry Medvedev for an overhaul of Europe's security structures (cf. Voronkov 2011). In November 2009, Medvedev publicly put forward the draft of a European Security Treaty (EST) to OSCE participating States. At the same time, a second draft for an agreement between Russia and NATO was introduced to the NRC (cf. Mission U.S. NATO 2009). This second draft, suggesting a concretization of the Founding Act's formula of 'substantial combat forces' (NATO-Russia 1997), was more or less an attempt to re-negotiate the Founding Act in light of the Russian non-attendance of CFE (cf. Mission U.S. NATO 2009c). Even though both drafts were in large parts duplicating Russian initiatives from the 1990s for an all-encompassing European security order (cf. Kühn 2010b), the initiative showed certain re-engagement of Russia after almost eight years of stone-walling. The main drawback of the initiative was again its more or less hidden attempt to subordinate NATO to an inclusive legally binding treaty mechanism based on the consensus rule. NATO states therefore rejected the idea and suggested transferring the debate to the OSCE instead (see Embassy U.S. Moscow 2009b).

The result was the so called Corfu Process of the OSCE which was launched in June 2009 at an informal meeting of OSCE foreign ministers on the Greek island of Corfu. Its stated aim was to 'restore confidence and take forward dialogue on wider European security' (OSCE 2014). The Corfu Process turned out to become a shortened version of the OSCE's Security Model exercise of the late 1990s (cf. IFSH 2010). The initial optimism of 2009 vanished soon (ibid). The more it turned out that NATO member states would not accept either one of Medvedev's drafts, the faster Moscow lost interest in the project (cf. Mission U.S. NATO 2009). With the OSCE Astana Summit in 2010 – the first summit since eleven years – the short period of optimism and re-engagement came to an end. Participating States could not decide on a concrete Framework for Action due to substantially divergent views on the OSCE's political role (cf. Zagorski 2011). Instead, participating States decided for a declaratory document, the Astana Commemorative Declaration, which outlined the vague idea of a Security Community for the OSCE space (cf. Mützenich and Karádi 2013). From Astana on, the political climate in the OSCE deteriorated gradually. The long-awaited update of the Vienna Document resulted in merely technical and procedural changes, agreed upon in 2011 (see Schmidt and Zellner 2012). With overt disappointment, 36 parties to the VD stated, 'in contrast to the strategic update of the Vienna Document on Confidence and Security-Building Measures that we believed was required, [the VD2011] is clearly less ambitious than we expected.' (OSCE 2011)

With regards to NATO-Russian relations, the first term of the Obama administration brought a certain level of re-engagement albeit both sides were unable to forge new institutions of cooperation. At the 2010 Lisbon Summit, NATO member states invited Russia to cooperate on the development of the EPAA. Divergent interests about the system's concrete design and operation prevented Washington and Moscow from reaching a preliminary understanding (cf. Zadra 2014). At the same time, Washington's aim of reducing NSNW with Russia rather led to increase tensions, both within the alliance and vis-à-vis Russia (cf. Chalmers, Chalmers, and Berger 2012). Meanwhile, further enlargement plans took a back seat due to political frictions within the alliance, cost considerations, non-readiness of potential candidates, and, though not officially voiced, also because of Moscow's military intervention in Georgia (cf. Freedman 2014: 17).

3.6.1 Analysis of Cooperation

In this paragraph, two cooperation processes – the CFE talks 'at 36', and the Corfu Process – are analyzed along the lines of the Realist model of international cooperation. The two cooperation processes are closely intertwined and dependent on the discussion about the Medvedev EST proposals. Before, a closer look at the development of U.S./NATO-Russian/CST capabilities between 2009 and 2011 is taken.

Capabilities
With regards to economic capabilities, between 2009 and 2011 both countries struggled economically because of the effects of the 2008 global financial crisis. Nevertheless, both national economies continued to grow between 2009 and 2011. According to the World Bank (2014), the Russian GDP grew from US$ 1.2 trillion in 2009 to US$ 1.9 trillion in 2011. At the same time, the U.S. GDP increased from US$ 14.4 trillion to US$ 15.5 trillion. By 2011, the U.S. GDP had 8.1 times the size of the Russian GDP. Chart 23 illustrates these trends.

CHART 23

COMPARISON OF U.S.-RUSSIAN ECONOMIC CAPABILITIES IN GDP, 2009-2011

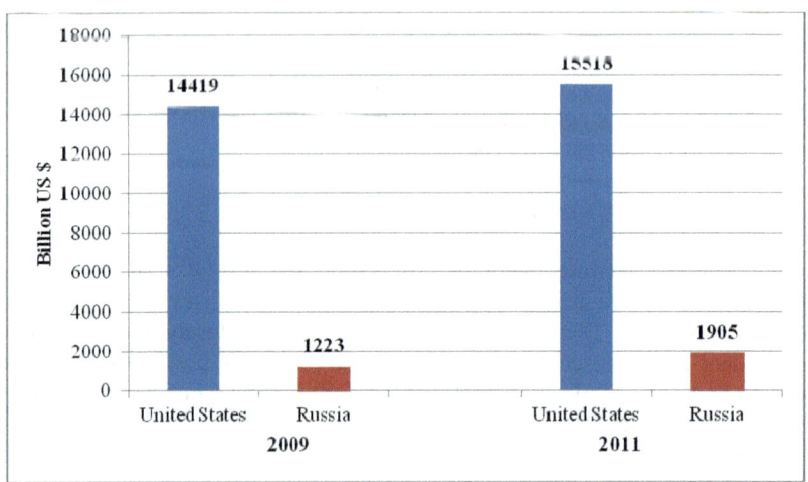

With regards the first capabilities factor of military strength, the development of national defense budgets of the United States and Russia and the combined defense budgets of NATO member states and CST member states show a further comparably stronger increase on the side of the United States/NATO. By 2011, the combined defense budget of NATO was 14.3 times the size of the combined defense budget of CST states. Chart 24 illustrates these trends.

With regards the second capabilities factor of military strength, the number of total armed forces shows a significant decrease on the side of NATO (minus ~270,000) even though two further countries (Albania and Croatia) joined the alliance in 2009. For the first time since the end of the Cold War, Russia increased the number of total armed forces. Chart 25 illustrates these trends.

CHART 24

COMPARISON OF NATIONAL U.S.-RUSSIAN AND
NATO-CST COMBINED DEFENSE BUDGETS, 2009-2011

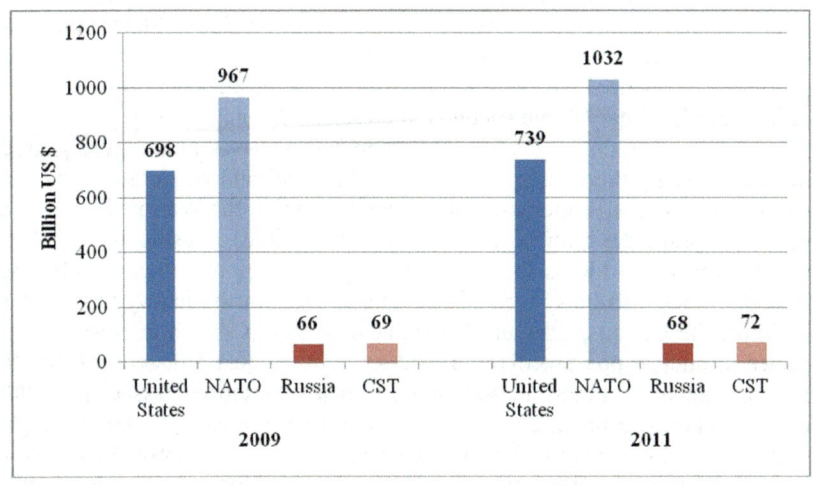

CHART 25

COMPARISON OF NATIONAL U.S.-RUSSIAN AND
NATO-CST COMBINED TOTAL ARMED FORCES, 2009-2011

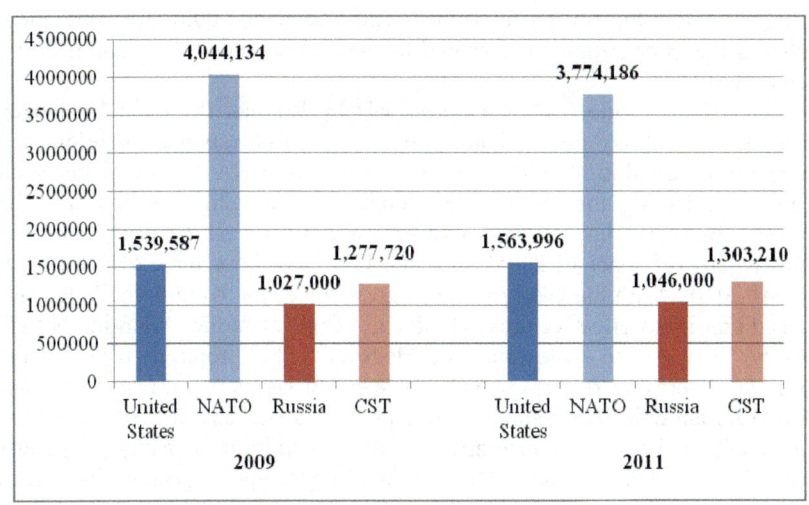

With regards the capabilities factor of the size of population and territory, no significant changes occurred during this period (see years 2009 and 2011 in Annex I).

CFE Talks "at 36" and the Corfu Process
Interests: Like during the George W. Bush years, the United States and Russia did not share an interest in cooperation in order to secure mutual survival (cf. Indyk, Lieberthal, and O'Hanlon 2012: 12 et seq). Rather, both had partially complementary issue-specific interests in different policy fields. The Obama administration's general interest in survival was much more geared towards fighting the consequences of the financial and economic crisis, restoring Washington's international reputation, ending the War on Terror, and hedging against the growing influence of China (ibid). Washington's policy towards Europe and Russia was only one objective amongst many (ibid). The "Reset" policy was thus more of a pragmatic attempt to identify those areas in which the United States and Russia actually had a shared interest, for instance in nuclear non-proliferation and strategic nuclear arms control (ibid). Russia's general interest in securing survival was closely associated with consolidating its economic growth and its influence in Russia's direct neighborhood. In 2006, Dmitri Trenin observed that 'until recently, Russia saw itself as Pluto in the Western solar system, very far from the center but still fundamentally a part of it. Now it has left that orbit entirely: Russia's leaders have given up on becoming part of the West and have started creating their own Moscow-centered system.' (Trenin 2006: 87) Selective cooperation with the West and the United States was thus seen as means of preserving the status quo and preventing any changes to the detriment of Russia and the Russian leadership (cf. Lyne, Talbott, and Watanabe 2006). All subsequent attempts at cooperation were geared towards these ends (cf. Mankoff 2009: 16 et seq).

Particularly the two treaty proposals by Russian President Medvedev tried to prevent any future changes to Russia's disadvantage. Therefore, the Kremlin returned to the older idea of subordinating NATO to a higher legal authority. During the 1990s, the vehicle for achieving this end was the OSCE. Because Moscow had more or less given up on the organization in this regard (cf. Ghébali 2005), now the EST was the vehicle of choice (cf. IFSH 2010). With the Georgia campaign in 2008, the Kremlin had also signaled that it has effective means to thwart efforts at further enlarging NATO to the East. At the same time, the Medvedev EST proposals reflected the Russian interest to re-engage with the West on issues of European security. The Russian objective behind the two proposals was obvious: subordination of NATO under a new cooperative mechanism and thus a change to the distribution of power (cf. Kühn 2010b). Washington had a genuine interest in preventing such scenario (see Embassy U.S. Moscow 2009b). Instead, Washington sought to make use of the Medvedev proposals to advance on the deadlocked cooperation processes of CFE and the OSCE. A leaked U.S. cable from 2009 concludes: 'an effective response to Medvedev's proposal should acknowledge Russia's apprehensions about the status quo and European security and accept the possibility of building incrementally on existing structures without compromising the centrality of NATO and OSCE.' (Ibid) Consequently, the United States did neither dismiss nor agree to the proposals but instead transferred the Russian initiative to the existing institutions of CFE and the OSCE. 'With skillful diplomacy, we can use Medvedev's proposal to try to overcome deadlocks on CFE and A/CFE as well as enhancing transparency measures', the same cable suggested. (Ibid) While thus both had a convergent issue-specific interest in cooperation on European security, the objectives behind that interest were fundamentally divergent. Divergence was further elevated by issue-specific divergent interests with regards to CFE and the OSCE.

On CFE, Moscow's issue-specific interest was still NATO ratification of ACFE (cf. Collina 2011) together with additional demands such as CFE accession of the Baltic States (cf. Kühn 2010a). Washington had still an issue-specific interest in Russia fulfilling her Istanbul commitments related to Moldova and Georgia as a precondition to ACFE ratification (ibid). Meanwhile, the Russian recognition of sovereignty of South Ossetia and Abkhazia and the additional Russian forces stationed in the two Georgian breakaway regions had further complicated the setting. Also, the Russian issue-specific interest in a clear definition of 'substantial combat forces' (NATO-Russia 1997) had already been transferred by Moscow to NATO member states as part of the second Medvedev treaty draft. Therewith, Moscow had tied an additional demand in conjunction with CFE to the signing of the second draft (cf. Mission U.S. NATO 2009c). In an exchange between then-Russian Prime Minister Putin and NATO Secretary General Rasmussen, Putin explained 'that lack of progress on the CFE front had forced Moscow to table the proposed treaty on European Security' (ibid).

On the OSCE and the subsequent Corfu Process, Russia had an issue-specific interest in making the signing of the first Medvedev treaty draft the outcome of the Corfu Process. 'Russia did not have any timeframe to deliver a treaty, but [...] Russia would seek a legally binding instrument as the outcome', a leaked U.S. cable explained (Embassy U.S. Moscow 2009b). In addition, Russia lobbied again for strengthening the politico-military dimension (cf. Zagorski 2010). Already before the start of the Corfu Process, a U.S. guidance demarche had outlined the U.S. issue-specific interest: 'The Corfu Ministerial presents an opportunity for the U.S. to channel discussion in a productive direction, locating the security dialogue firmly within the OSCE framework, and basing it on the OSCE's comprehensive concept of security.' (Secretary of State 2009) Hence, Washington's issue-specific interest was geared towards the comprehensive security approach of the OSCE, stressing "soft" security issues, for instance in the realm of human rights (ibid).

Expectations: Both could expect a difficult setting with different policy issues and institutions in close interaction. On the EST and the Corfu Process, Moscow acted offensively-oriented. The EST was an attempt at changing the existing distribution of power by subordinating NATO to the treaty's mechanisms. With regards to the Corfu Process, Russia again showed an offensive orientation; insisting on a legally binding outcome which would echo the tenets of the EST (i.e. subordinating NATO). Washington tried to keep the status quo and acted defensively-oriented; hoping that Moscow would change its orientation in the Corfu Process as it did during the 1990s (see Embassy U.S. Moscow 2009b). According to Realism, cooperation on the issues would be impossible as long as Russia was not either changing her orientation or compensating Washington for its anticipated losses. On CFE, both continued with their respective orientations from the previous years. Washington acted offensively-oriented, trying to change the balance of power by insisting on Russian forces withdrawal from Moldova and Georgia (cf. Kühn 2013). Moscow acted defensively-oriented, demanding ratification of ACFE (ibid). Again, cooperation was almost impossible, according to Realism, as long as Washington was not either compensating Moscow for the anticipated losses or changing its offensive orientation.

Strategies: On the issue of the EST proposals, Washington decided, backed by its allies, not to engage directly and to transfer the initiative to the CFE consultations "at 36" and the OSCE Corfu Process instead (cf. Secretary of State 2009). In both institutional frameworks, the United States and Russia agreed on the strategy of confidence-building by slicing up issues into increments. In the CFE case, consultations happened in twelve rounds of talks over almost a year. For the Corfu Process, a leaked U.S. cable explained the strategy: 'Ensure that this process remains open-ended. At least at the outset, this dialogue would have no fixed timeline and no fixed outcome; rather, the results of the discussions would determine whether additional security arrangements, or adjustments to current arrangements, might be necessary.' (Secretary of State 2009) The strategy of confidence-building had the additional advantage of building on previous experiences in the JCG of the CFE Treaty and the FSC of the OSCE. No strategies of compensation were employed.

Evaluation of Gains: The two cooperation processes of CFE talks "at 36" and the Corfu Process failed. In the end, no side got what it wanted. The only real (non-cooperative) success for Washington was that it succeeded in rejecting the EST proposals. Basically, Washington repeated its stance from the 1990s, blocking all attempts at relegating existing institutions, and particularly NATO, to any higher mechanism. The downturn of that approach was that Washington failed to achieve a serious long-term involvement of Russia in a comprehensive discussion on European security. Neither the CFE Treaty nor the OSCE were seriously revived despite all atmospheric optimism. In the CFE case, the talks "at 36" were a continuation of the policies of the previous ten years (cf. Kühn 2013). No side was willing to make a first cooperative move (ibid). The talks were abandoned without any concrete result after twelve rounds of consultations. After the end of the talks, NATO allies partially exited from the treaty by suspending data exchange with Russia and Russian inspections on-site inspections on NATO soil while officially remaining bound by the treaty (cf. Collina 2011). Russia continues her partial exit strategy of "suspension" of CFE.

For Russia, the whole process of short-term engagement was disappointing (cf. IFSH 2010). Most prominently, Moscow failed on the EST proposals. From a Realist point of view, both treaty drafts were either hopelessly naïve or blatantly over-estimating Russian capabilities. Moscow did also not get what it wanted in the CFE and the OSCE frameworks. On CFE, Russia did not get the ratification of ACFE. Moscow's additional demands only helped to overburden the already fragile agenda (cf. Schmidt 2013). The Corfu Process ran basically into the same old problems that earlier Russian efforts at OSCE reform had displayed (cf. Zagorski 2011). The difference to the 1990s was that this time Moscow was not interested in achieving its issue-specific interest through multilateral negotiations within the organization but instead relied on a unilateral course of action, confronting OSCE and (in parallel) NATO countries with a ready to sign treaty coupled with the demand for separate discussions in different institutional frameworks (cf. Mission U.S. OSCE 2010). The further the Corfu Process evolved, the more serious the Russian disappointment got (cf. Zagorski 2011). The ensuing OSCE Summit in Astana, the first since 1999, did not only mark the inconclusive end of the Corfu Process, the Summit itself was a disappointment (cf. Kühn 2010a). Even though Russia and the United States have quietly exited from the Corfu Process, they continue minimal cooperation in the OSCE format.

In all three cases, cooperation either failed (CFE and Corfu Process) or did not take place (in the case of the EST) because of the non-conducive orientations (Moscow offensive on EST and Corfu Process; Washington offensive on CFE) and the mutual reluctance to either change orientations towards a defensive approach or to pay compensation. The strategy of confidence-building was not enough to ensure cooperation.

Institutionalization
In terms of institutionalization, two developments stick out during the years 2009-2011. First, like during the previous eight years of the George W. Bush administration, the unraveling of certain institutions of cooperative arms control in Europe (i.e. CFE and the OSCE) continued. Second, in contrast to all other previous periods, neither the United States nor Russia employed the strategy of compensation in order to possibly mitigate the consequences of their respective offensive orientation. Table 7 assesses U.S.-Russian coopera-

tion on the CFE Talks "at 36" and the Corfu Process according to the Realist cooperation model.

Between 2012 and 2014, West-Russian relations deteriorated to an unprecedented state of confrontation. With the start of Vladimir Putin's third term as President of Russia in May 2012, relations quickly turned sour. Already in 2009, Mikhail Gorbachev had openly criticized Putin's intention of a hand-over of power from Medvedev. 'Questions of modernization - in the economy, in the social sphere, and in culture - cannot be decided without the involvement of the people, and without increasing civil liberties. And this cannot be done through pressure, commands, and administrative methods, but only through the further development of democracy. The people must be involved in this', Gorbachev (RIA Novosti 2009) urged. With the municipal elections in March 2012, mass protests throughout the big cities of Russia started and increased towards the Presidential election which saw Putin's re-election. The Kremlin reacted with a clamp down on civil liberties, considerable pressure on critical media, rhetorical demonization of 'the West', and politically motivated trials against unpleasant opponents such as the punk band Pussy Riot or political activist Alexei Nawalny (cf. Freedman 2014: 16).

TABLE 7

U.S.-RUSSIAN COOPERATION ON CFE TALKS "AT 36" AND THE CORFU PROCESS

INSTITUTION	ACTOR	ISSUE-SPECIFIC INTERESTS	EXPECTATIONS	STRATEGIES	EVALUATION OF GAINS
CFE Talks "at 36"	USA	divergent	acting offensively-oriented	confidence-building	partial exit
	Russia	divergent	acting defensively-oriented	confidence-building	continued partial exit
Corfu Process	USA	divergent	acting defensively-oriented	confidence-building	exit, continued minimal cooperation in OSCE
	Russia	Divergent	acting offensively-oriented	confidence-building	exit, continued minimal cooperation in OSCE

Inner-Russian developments increasingly affected the bilateral U.S.-Russian relationship, most visibly in acts of open intimidations against the newly appointed U.S. Ambassador to Russia, Michael McFaul, whom the Kremlin viewed as an active supporter of Russian opposition groups (see Remnick 2014). In late 2012, the U.S. Senate passed a law punishing Russian officials assumed to be responsible for the death of Russian lawyer Sergei Magnitsky attached to a wider act normalizing bilateral trade relations more than 20 years after the end of the Cold War. The State Duma reacted with a ban on the international adoption of Russian children into the United States.

Tensions quickly spilled over to the multilateral and bilateral levels of security policy. With its inherent focus on human rights, particularly the OSCE was affected. Already shortly after the OSCE's Astana Summit, Zagorski (2011: 32) had commented: 'When we talk about old or new dividing lines that may occur because of this or that decision, we need to keep in mind that this dividing line already exists, and it clearly manifested itself during the Corfu Process and at the Summit Meeting in Astana.' The 2012 OSCE Ministerial Council in Dublin underscored that assessment as participating States could not even agree on the language of non-binding declarations of intent anymore. Herd (2013: 395-6) concluded: 'Over the past year, we have witnessed multilateralism becoming less effective, efficient, and legitimate on account of institutional and organizational weaknesses. Solidarity and shared responsibility are less in evidence – states prefer to act according to their own immediate interests and priorities, giving these precedence over the longer-term interests of preserving peace in the system. When we survey the strategic landscape through 2011 and 2012, a crisis of governance - with governments being overwhelmed - manifests itself at the level of leading states and international organizations within the OSCE area.'

What pertained to the OSCE continued at other levels of institutionalized cooperation. Efforts to reach an understanding about the EPAA in the working groups of the NRC ran ashore due to diverging views about the system's capabilities and scope (cf. Zadra 2014). A last-ditch effort by the Obama administration to open discussions with Russia about a follow-on agreement to New START (see The White House 2013) did not receive an answer from the Kremlin. Without further rounds of engagement, the CFE Treaty remained blocked with Armenia, Azerbaijan, and Russia in non-compliance with specific force and geographical limitations (see United States Department of State 2014: 7).

What started as domestic Russian crisis with already severe repercussions at the international level turned into open confrontation with escalating events in Ukraine. When then-Ukrainian President Victor Yanukovych turned down the Ukraine-European Union Association Agreement in November 2013 and instead sought closer political and economic ties with Russia, pro-Western protests started in Kyiv and culminated in the ousting of Yanukovych and his cabinet in February 2014. Russia, viewing the protests as illegal overthrow of an elected government by 'fascist elements' actively supported by the United States and the EU (Trenin 2014), employed special forces without national insignia and local activists to take over institutions in Crimea on February 27 (cf. Freedman 2014: 8-9). A hastily arranged referendum resulted in the de facto annexation of Crimea on March 18.

This totally unexpected turn of events led NATO and EU states to punish Russia for her 'illegal activities' (Burke-White 2014) with economic sanctions. The situation worsened when fighting between the Russian minority of the Eastern-Ukrainian Donbas region and official as well as unofficial Ukrainian forces escalated to open civil war. Between April and December, 4,707 people were killed and 10,322 wounded in the conflict-affected areas of eastern Ukraine, according to the UN Human Rights Office (cf. United Nations in Ukraine 2014). More than 200,000 IDPs have registered in Ukraine (ibid), not counting those that fled to Russia. Pro-Russian militias backed by the Russian military and forces without national insignia are fighting in South-Eastern Ukraine (cf. MacFarquhar and Gordon 2014).

In response to Russia repeatedly violating Ukrainian borders and sovereignty, NATO member states came close to revoking the Founding Act and partially suspended the NRC which is only theoretically functioning at the level of ambassadorial meetings while all working groups have been suspended. Against the background of the Russian belligerence, member states decided at the Newport Summit to gear up their collective defense capabilities through enhanced military engagement in the Baltic States and Poland on a rotational basis (see NATO 2014b). While NATO Deputy Secretary General Ambassador Alexander Vershbow (NATO 2014a) concluded that the alliance 'will be forced to consider Russia less of a partner and more of an adversary', President Putin allegedly threatened to be able to quickly deploy Russian forces to Kyiv, Riga, Vilnius, Tallinn, Warsaw, and Bucharest (Brössler 2014).

In December 2014, the low price of crude oil and the Western sanctions, which had been concluded in response to the annexation of Crimea, plunged the Russian ruble to experience its steepest intraday low since the Russian financial crisis in 1998 (cf. Winning and Abramov 2014). Increasingly, some Western policy-makers saw the consequences of the economic confrontation with concern. In an interview from December 19, German Minister of Foreign Affairs, Steinmeier issued a warning: Whoever tries to bring Russia to her knees is terribly wrong to conclude that this would lead to increased security in Europe, Steinmeier insisted (quoted in Spiegel on-line 2014). I can only warn against such perception, he added (ibid). Already in August 2014 Vladimir Putin had flexed his muscles by stressing that "it is better not to come against Russia as regards a possible armed conflict." "I want to remind you that Russia is one of the most powerful nuclear nations," he added (Putin quoted in Botelho and Smith-Spark 2014). At the December 4 Basel Ministerial, OSCE participating States voted for Germany as OSCE Chairman in 2016.

3.7.1   Analysis of Policies

The years 2012-2014 and particularly the Ukraine conflict mark a watershed for cooperative arms control in Europe – to a lesser degree in institutional terms but more with a view to the principles that had guided policies and institutional development since the end of the Cold War. Those three years did not bring any new cooperation on cooperative arms control in Europe, let alone any new institutions. Therefore, this paragraph will concentrate on analysis of U.S.-Russian policies in conjunction with the Ukraine conflict and the tenets of cooperative security. The Realist model for understanding international cooperation cannot be applied in its entirety. However, some of the variables of the model will be used in this paragraph to assess U.S.-Russian policies.

Comparison of Capabilities, Interests, and Orientations
Capabilities: Between 2012 and 2013 the economic capabilities of Russia stagnated in terms of GDP (see Chart 26).

CHART 26

COMPARISON OF U.S.-RUSSIAN ECONOMIC CAPABILITIES IN GDP, 2012-2013

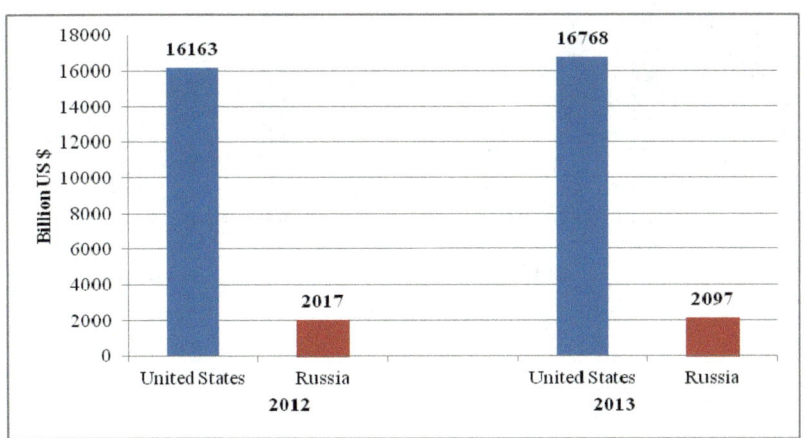

According to the World Bank (2014), the Russian GDP roughly remained at US$ 2 trillion. In comparison, the U.S. GDP showed a relatively stronger increase from US$ 16.1 trillion in 2011 to US$ 16.7 trillion in 2013. For

2014, analysts by the World Bank (2014b) expect a further increase in U.S. GDP and a decrease in Russian GDP.

With regards the first capabilities factor of military strength, the development of national defense budgets from the previous period continued. Between 2012 and 2013, the combined defense budget of NATO, and this time also of the United States decreased. The reason behind this development was the decision by the White House to significantly downsize its military engagement in Afghanistan and Iraq (cf. Walker 2014). In contrast, Russia's and the combined CST defense budget increased. Chart 27 illustrates these divergent trends.

With regards the second capabilities factor of military strength, the number of total armed forces all decreased between 2012 and 2014. This is only the second period since the end of the Cold War where a parallel decrease happened. Chart 28 illustrates these parallel trends.

CHART 27

COMPARISON OF NATIONAL U.S.-RUSSIAN AND
NATO-CST COMBINED DEFENSE BUDGETS, 2012-2013

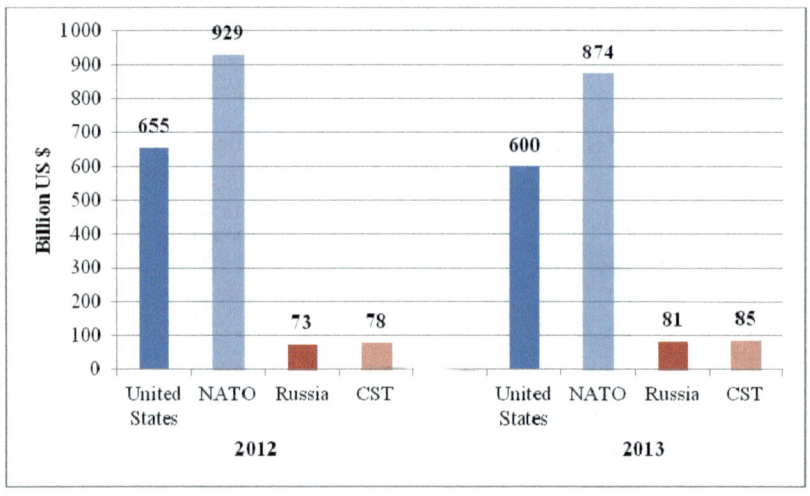

CHART 28

COMPARISON OF NATIONAL U.S.-RUSSIAN AND
NATO-CST COMBINED TOTAL ARMED FORCES, 2012-2014

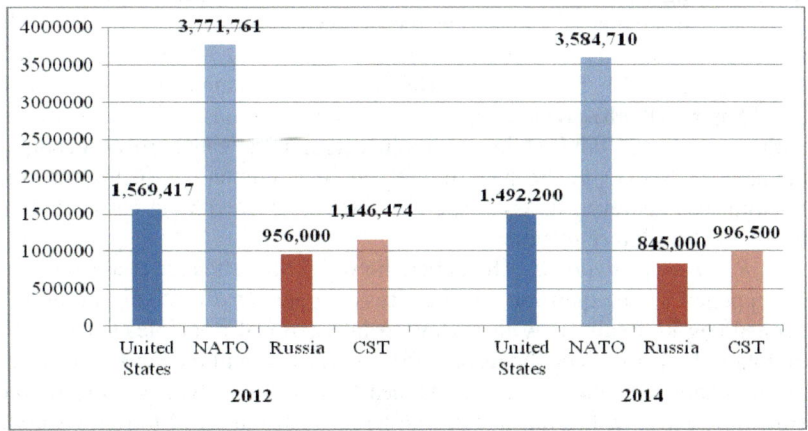

With regards the capabilities factor of the size of population and territory, no significant changes occurred during this period (see years 2012 and 2014 in Annex I).

Russian Interests: Since the beginning of the millennium, the Russian general interest in securing survival was much closer associated with consolidating Russian influence in the so called Near Abroad (cf. Jonsson 2012: 450). Therewith, the Russian leadership saw NATO enlargement and colored revolutions as prime concerns (cf. Erickson 2013) for two reasons. On the one hand, further NATO (and also EU) enlargement to the east was seen as moving the Western military geopolitically closer to the Russian border (cf. President of Russia 2007; 2014b). Already since the Napoleonic wars, the Russian military highly values the enormous geographic depth of the Russian homeland and has continuously tried to assemble additional territories (i.e. buffer states) around the Russian territory in order to increase geographical depth (cf. Erickson 2013). On the other hand, the colored revolutions in neighboring states were a possible precedent for Russia itself – a scenario which touched upon the Russian leadership's general interest in its own personal survival. That was the reason why the Putin government reacted so harshly to the protests throughout Russia in the first half of 2012.

Hence, in the Kremlin's understanding, the situation in and around Ukraine was somewhat the "perfect storm". The new Kyiv leadership was willing to sign an association agreement with the EU which includes, amongst many other stipulations, also aspects of continuous military cooperation (see Title II in EU-Ukraine 2013). Ukrainian membership in the EU and, possibly, later NATO was not excluded. In conjunction, the large Russian naval bases of the Black Sea Fleet in the Crimea port of Sevastopol would be at stake in such a scenario. At the same time, the ousting of Yanukovych was just another example of the swift toppling of an autocratic leadership. The debate amongst scholars of IR, which of those two factors (preventing further NATO enlargement vs. preventing the domestic loss of power) are mainly responsible for Russia's policies in Ukraine is only about to start (cf. Mearsheimer 2014; Sestanovich, McFaul, and Mearsheimer 2014; Charap and Shapiro 2014b). What seems obvious for the moment is that Ukraine, with a protracted conflict in its south-eastern part, can hardly become a member of NATO in the near future. For the moment, it seems that the Kremlin has achieved its issue-specific interest of preventing Ukraine from becoming an alliance member.

Russian Orientations: The debate between Mearsheimer et al (ibid) has also opened up the question whether Russia is acting offensively in the understanding of Realism. With a view to international principles such as the inviolability of frontiers, the respect for sovereignty, and the non-use of force in international relations, Russia has clearly shown an offensive orientation. However, Moscow has not altered the larger distribution of power vis-à-vis the West since Ukraine was neither a NATO member nor an immediate candidate to join the alliance (albeit the 2008 NATO Bucharest promise). Moscow has rather prevented a possible future change to the balance of power which was perceived in Moscow as being to Russia's detriment. Vladimir Putin has explained the situation in a recent interview: 'I will reiterate: where are the guarantees that the coup d'état, this second color revolution that happened in Ukraine, won't be followed by NATO's arrival in Ukraine? Nobody has ever discussed this issue with us in the past two decades. I'd like to emphasize that nobody has conducted a meaningful dialogue with us on this. All we heard was the same reply, like a broken record: Every nation has the right to determine the security system it wants to live in and this has nothing to do with you.' (Putin quoted in Charap and Shapiro 2014a) Given Russian occupation with keeping the status quo, one can argue from a Realist viewpoint that the Kremlin acted defensively-oriented. Again, the debate about this question is only about to unfold and it is too early to give a sound and compelling answer.

U.S. Interests: Since the end of the 20th Century, the U.S. general interest in survival is not closely associated with Russia anymore; neither with a view to an interest in containment (as during the Cold War) nor with a view to cooperate for the sake of mutual survival (as during détente and in conjunction with the end of the Cold War). Therewith, other objectives have entered center stage. Amongst them was the U.S. issue-specific interest in promoting the Liberal Western model based on free markets, Capitalism, individual human rights, and democracy worldwide (cf. Lagon 2011). The autocratic design of most post-Soviet states (including Russia) was an apparent challenge to these rationales. Therewith, Washington supported civil movements in those states wherever it was seen to enhance Liberal values (cf. Remnick 2014). These policies started already during the mid-1990s – at that time, mostly promoted by the Republican-led Congress (cf. Kühn 2009) – and became a central tenet of U.S. foreign and security policy under George W. Bush (cf. Lagon 2011). At the same time, policies of multilateralism, particularly in the realm of arms control, took a back seat (cf. Luongo 2001). The two Obama administrations returned to the policies of multilateralism and arms control; however, democracy promotion remained a central U.S. objective, seemingly confirmed by the Arab Spring (cf. Lagon 2011). From this point of view, the events in Ukraine were only another confirmation of the U.S. objective. It was and is therefore in the interest of the United States to support the democracy, freedom, and territorial integrity of Ukraine (cf. The White House 2014a).

A second issue-specific interest, which has remained a central tenet of U.S. foreign and security policy since a very long time, is the maintenance and (possible) further enlargement of NATO (cf. Pradetto 2004). The policy of "open door" continues to allow other states to enter NATO as long as the state wishes so and as long as membership would enhance the alliance's security (cf. NATO 2014a). Because Washington views NATO enlargement as increasing the stability of new democratic states and therewith European security as a whole, the policy tool of enlargement is in close relation to the objective of democracy promotion. Even though, Moscow has since long expressed its concern with NATO enlargement, Washington continues to officially denounce Russian concerns as unfounded. At the recent Wales Summit, Heads of State and Government reiterated that "the Alliance does not seek confrontation and poses no threat to Russia." (NATO 2014b) From this angle, Russia has no reason to deny Ukraine alliance membership; both from a normative point of view (i.e. Ukraine's sovereign decision) and from a security point of view (because Ukraine's possible membership would not be directed against Russia and because NATO enlargement is to the security advantage of all states, including Russia).

U.S. Orientations: From a Realist viewpoint, both U.S. issue-specific interests – democracy promotion abroad and NATO's open door policy – show strong features of an offensive orientation. Both approaches aim at changing the distribution of power. Realists do not ask whether the policy objective behind an offensive orientation – be it stabilizing the new European democracies after the end of the Cold War – is morally just or not. Realism concentrates primarily on the resultant changes to capabilities and who benefits from those changes. To assume that Washington engages on democracy promotion and the open door policy because of altruistic motives as some U.S. comments might imply (cf. McFaul in Sestanovich, McFaul, and Mearsheimer 2014) is irrelevant from a Realist viewpoint. Assuming that democracy promotion and the open door policy would really lead to the desired U.S. outcome of increased international stability; at the same time, they do increase U.S. influence and power.

Taken together, both U.S. interests clash with the Russian interest of keeping the status quo. According to Realism, because of the offensive orientation of the U.S.-led policies of NATO enlargement and democracy promotion, they make real cooperation on the issues themselves almost impossible. The consequences of this incompatibility have partially contributed to the conflict in and over Ukraine (see Mearsheimer 2014). They might also have contributed to the decay of the institutions of cooperative arms control in Europe.

Consequences for Institutions

With the ongoing war in the Donbas region, its military involvement, its continued ignorance of international law, and its openly belligerent stance towards the West, Russia has departed from the idea of cooperative security. Even though Russian policy shows some remains of respect for institutional constraints – its continued participation in the OSCE, its acceptance of the OSCE as an interlocutor in the bargaining process for a ceasefire agreement (Protocol on the results of consultations of the Trilateral Contact Group of September 5, 2014), its only clandestine military involvement in contrast to the possibility of open invasion, and the continued application and observation of the Vienna Document (cf. Richter 2014)[23] – Moscow has openly declared an end to the European security order of the post-Cold War era (cf. Legvold 2014). Putin's continued reference to international law (cf. Burke-White 2014) and the alleged transgressions of the West, most vividly brought forward in his March 18 speech following the annexation of Crimea (President of Russia 2014a), extrapolate two important aspects.

On the one hand, Russian policy has not gone completely off the beaten track but feels internationally pressured to justify her actions (cf. Burke-White 2014). On the other hand, the current situation provides the Kremlin with an opportunity to paint a picture which resembles all the Russian dissatisfactions associated with the development of the European security order after the collapse of the Soviet Union. Amongst those are institutional developments such as NATO enlargement, the degradation of the OSCE, and the standstill and regress in arms control matters; but also significant instances of Western power projections such as the Yugoslavia bombing in 1999 or the Iraq War in 2003 (President of Russia 2014b). Following the Kremlin's rationale, this sequence of Western "wrong doings" led to and culminated in a last resort to self-help. Since the way back is not imaginable for the moment and also not desired, as the rhetorical Russian campaign against 'Western values' (cf. Lukin 2014) underscores, Russia seems to see its future in Asia (cf. Meister 2014). The continued push for a Eurasian Union – though for the

---

23   Nevertheless, Russia successfully used existing loopholes in the VD to cloak its troop concentrations at the Ukrainian border. (Cf. Richter 2014: 3-4)

foreseeable time without Ukraine – coupled with stronger economic ties with China (see Luhn and Macalister 2014) and the development of a somewhat alternative values model as compared to the 'Western model' (cf. Lukin 2014) start to crystallize as essentials of a possible new orientation of Russia in the international arena.

For the West, events in Ukraine came as a big surprise (cf. Freedman 2014) and were interpreted as the possible dawning of a 'New Cold War' (Legvold 2014). Its reactions – mainly condemnation and economic sanctions – revealed a certain degree of helplessness and a lack of policy conceptions on how to re-engage with Russia (cf. Charap and Shapiro 2014). Some commentators even suggested reviving elements of cooperative security (cf. Brocking 2014).

3.8 Conclusions

The years 1973 to 2014 saw the rise and fall of cooperative arms control in Europe. The United States and the Soviet Union/Russia were the two main driving forces behind institutionalization. During the last two decades, these institutions came under increasing duress. Some institutions are experiencing signs of decay, though to varying degrees. In the following, the main conclusions with regards the variables of the Realist model, with regards institutionalization, and institutional decay are summarized. Then, the two guiding research questions of this chapter are answered.

3.8.1 Capabilities

In the years between 1973 and 2014, the capabilities of the United States and the Soviet Union/Russia developed completely different. In economic terms, the United States experienced an almost steady growth with only short periods of stagnation (see Chart 29). In contrast, the Soviet/Russian economy more or less stagnated. The collapse of the Soviet Union, the fast transformation to Capitalism, and the subsequent years of internal turbulence left their marks on the Russian economy. Between 1989 and 1999, the Russian GDP shrank by half. Only with the coming into office of Vladimir Putin in 2000 and the rise in international crude oil and gas prices did the Russian economy again experience significant growth rates – shortly interrupted by the 2008 international financial crisis (cf. Gill and Young 2012). Since early 2014, reform gridlock, the drop in oil and gas prices, and the Western sanctions have all pushed the Russian economy towards recession (cf. World Bank 2014). All in all, the current economic capabilities of the United States in terms of GDP outnumber the Russian economic capabilities by a factor of eight. In economic capabilities in terms of GDP, Russia is far from being a peer competitor to the United States.

CHART 29

TREND ANALYSIS OF U.S.-SOVIET/RUSSIAN ECONOMIC CAPABILITIES IN GDP[24] DEVELOPMENT, 1973-2013

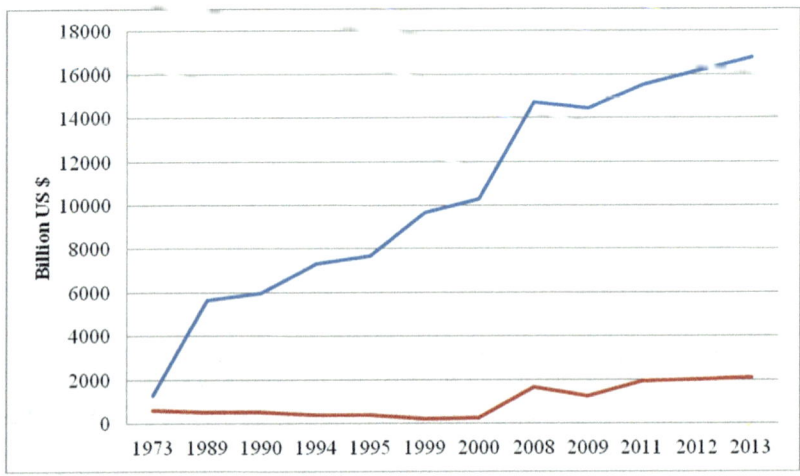

With regards the first capabilities factor of military strength (national defense budget), the diverging trends are even more obvious (see Chart 30). During the early and mid-1970s, Moscow and Washington were equal competitors in this realm. In 1973, the national defense budgets of the United States (US$ 85 billion) and the Soviet Union (US$ 89 billion) were almost equal. With the coming into office of Gorbachev, the Soviet defense budget fell behind the American. The breakup of the Soviet Union led to a drop from US$ 117 billion in 1990 to US$ 31 billion in 1999. Only since 2001, the Russian defense budget has increased and is US$ 81 billion in 2013. In contrast, the U.S. defense budget has skyrocket during the eight George W. Bush years. Between 2000 and 2008, the national defense budget grew from US$ 293 billion to US$ 693 billion. In terms of comparing the defense budgets, Russia is far from being a peer competitor to the United States.

---

24 For the respective data underlying the following five charts, please see Annex I. The basis for assessing economic capabilities is a comparison of GDP in the years of periodization, except for 2014 (there had not yet been data available for 2014 when this study was concluded). For some years, the basis was comparison of GNP. This is due to the alternating methods applied in the IISS Military Balance series (see Annex I). For this and all following charts: Blue line = United States; red line = Soviet Union/Russia.

CHART 30

TREND ANALYSIS OF NATIONAL U.S.-SOVIET/RUSSIAN AND NATO-WTO/CST
COMBINED DEFENSE BUDGET DEVELOPMENT[25], 1973-2013

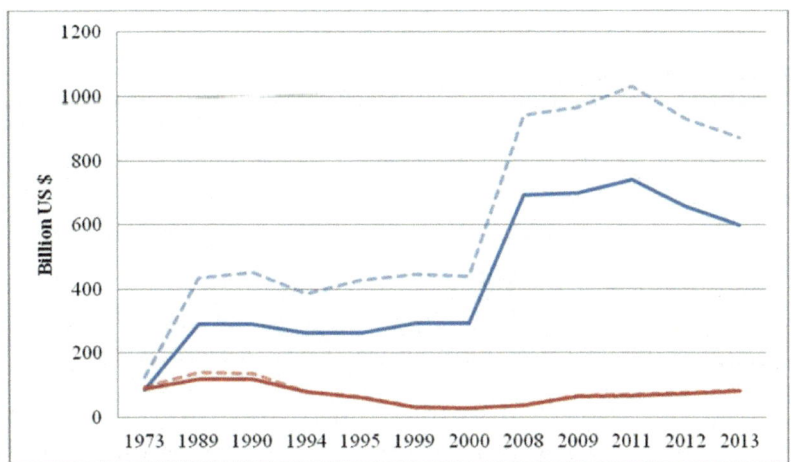

In terms of the second capabilities factor of military strength (total armed forces), trend analysis shows a different development (see Chart 31). During the Cold War, the total armed forces of the Soviet Union were superior to the United States in the European theatre in a quantitative understanding (cf. Neuneck 1995). At the end of the Cold War in 1989, the number of combined forces of the Warsaw Pact (5.4 million) and the combined forces of NATO (5.3 million) was almost the same. With the end of the Cold War, the drop in defense spending, the huge reductions in military manpower (including through arms control agreements), and the breakup of the WTO and the Soviet Union, a massive change in the number of total armed forces occurred. Since 1989, the overall trend in numbers is going down. Even though, NATO has enlarged three times since 1989, the current overall number of total armed forces of the alliance (3.5 million) is still below the number at the end of the Cold War. In comparison, the United States (1.49 million) has almost double the number of the total armed forces of Russia (0.8 million) in 2014. The difference in numbers of the combined total armed forces of NATO (3.58 million) and the CST (0.99) is much greater. NATO exceeds the CST forces by a factor of more than three. Again, in this realm, Russia and the CST are far from being peer competitors to the United States and NATO.

---

25   The figures for the year 2014 were not yet available at the time of writing.

CHART 31

TREND ANALYSIS OF NATIONAL U.S.-SOVIET/RUSSIAN AND NATO-WTO/CST
COMBINED TOTAL ARMED FORCES DEVELOPMENT[26], 1973-2014

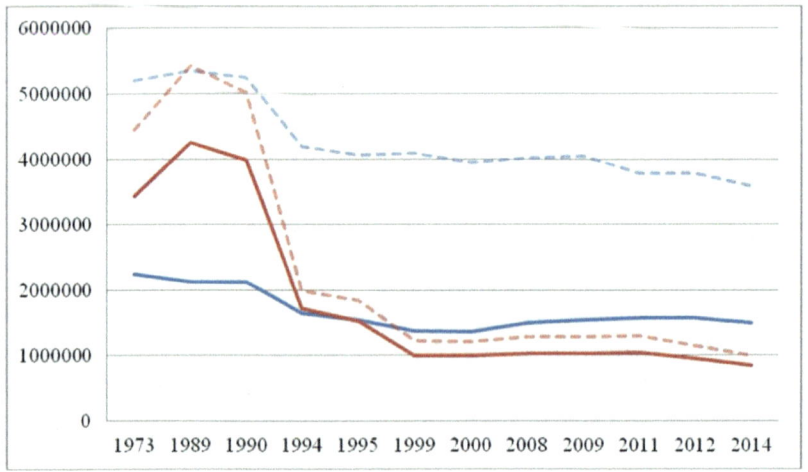

In terms of the capabilities factor of size of population, the trends are again diverging (see Chart 32). The United States show slow but steady growth rates while the Russian population has largely remained at the same level since the end of the Cold War. Today, Russia has a population of about 142 million; the United States has a population of about 316 million. The size of population of combined NATO member states has continuously gone up; particularly due to the fact of three rounds of enlargement. In comparison, the combined size of population of NATO member states (921 million) outnumbers the combined size of population of CST member states (186 million) roughly by the factor of five. Again, in this realm of capabilities, Russia and the CST are far from being peer competitors to the United States and NATO.

26   For this and all following charts: Blue dotted line = combined capabilities of United States and NATO; red dotted line = combined capabilities of Soviet Union/WTO resp. Russia/CST.

CHART 32

TREND ANALYSIS OF NATIONAL U.S.-SOVIET/RUSSIAN AND NATO-WTO/CST
COMBINED SIZE OF POPULATION DEVELOPMENT, 1973-2014

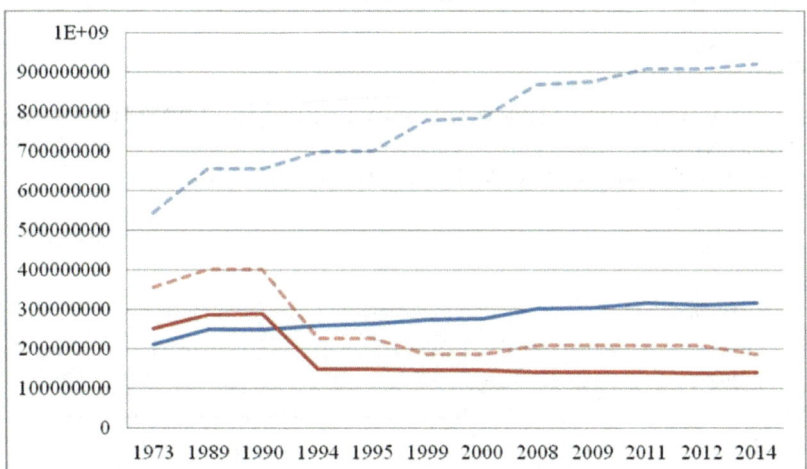

In terms of the capabilities factor of size of territories, the trends mirror the political developments of the breakup of the Soviet Union and the Warsaw Pact as well as the three rounds of NATO enlargement (see Chart 33). While in 1990, the combined territories of NATO member states (22.7 million km²) were almost the same size compared to the combined territories of Warsaw Pact member states (22.4 million km²), today, the combined territories of NATO member states are about 24 million km² and the combined territories of CST member states are about 20 million km² - not including overseas territories. In this specific realm of capabilities, the combined territory of NATO member states outnumbers the combined territory of CST states by almost a fifth.

What were/are the consequences of the significant decline of Soviet/Russian capabilities relative to the United States? While during the Cold War, Moscow could act as an equal competitor to Washington, with the breakup of the Soviet Union and the WTO and the parallel loss in power, Moscow lost its ability to challenge Washington on an equal basis. The consequences of this relative decline in power can be seen in the design of the post-Cold War European security architecture and its institutionalization. While Washington could follow through with its preferred issue-specific interests, Moscow could not. The most vivid examples are the design of the OSCE and the enlargement of NATO. Particularly with regards to NATO, Russia could not prevent enlargement but could only 'minimize the negative consequences' (Yeltsin quoted in Lippman 1997). In contrast, Washington, the winner of the Cold War (see The White House 1992a), was not only in a stronger position, it could even enhance its capabilities, for instance by enlarging NATO. According to Realism, the change in relative capabilities determined to a large degree the two states' abilities to pursue their respective issue-specific interests. The change favored the United States.

CHART 33

TREND ANALYSIS OF NATIONAL U.S. -SOVIET/RUSSIAN AND NATO-WTO/CST
COMBINED SIZE OF TERRITORY DEVELOPMENT, 1973-2014

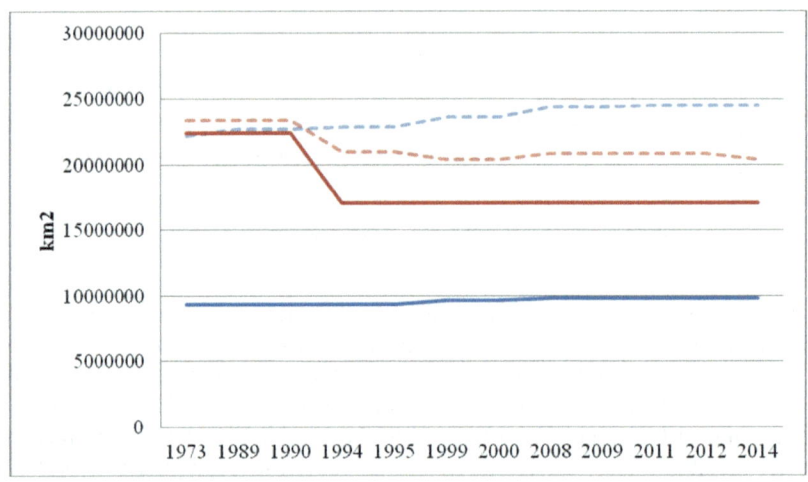

From a Realist viewpoint (cf. Grieco 1988; Mearsheimer 1994/95), the huge difference in relative capabilities between the United States and Russia should lead Moscow to worry with regards to securing Russian survival in the future. In purely power-political terms, Washington is a giant compared to Russia. Barack Obama's talk of Russia as a 'regional power' (quoted in Blake 2014) might not have been very wise under the current conditions, it is nevertheless the truth. The only realm where Russia can threaten U.S. survival is the nuclear (cf. Deep Cuts Commission 2014). Not surprisingly, it is this realm where Vladimir Putin has issued indirect threats to Washington and its allies in conjunction with the Ukraine conflict (cf. Botelho and Smith-Spark 2014). If Putin really thinks and acts like a Realist (cf. Mearsheimer 2014), he should know that possible cooperation with the United States would almost always roughly reflect the underlying balance of power. And the balance is to Russia's detriment (see charts above). He should thus be interested in either securing the status quo while possibly waiting for a relative decrease in U.S. capabilities, or forging an alliance with a potent partner to balance the United States (cf. Walt 1987). At the same time, Washington's continuing increase in capabilities and its ability to act offensively-oriented in the sense of changing the balance of power makes it even more threatening the closer U.S. military installations are moving towards Russia's borders. This second aspect should, from a Realist viewpoint, increase pressure on Russia to seek a strong alliance partner in the future.

3.8.2 Interests

According to Realism, states share an equally strong interest in securing survival. With regards each other, this general interest of the United States and the Soviet Union/Russia underwent two crucial changes between 1973 and 2014. During the times of the Cold War, the general interest of the United States and the Soviet Union was pointed at each other. Because of a state of constant competition, sometimes narrowly below the level of open warfare (see the 1958 Berlin Crisis and the 1962 Cuban Missile Crisis), the general interest was almost always closely associated with questions of military strength (cf. Leffler and Westad 2010). Given the omnipresent scenario of nuclear Armageddon, the mutual interest in cooperation to prevent such scenario became an integral part of the survival motive. Cooperation, even though to strongly varying degrees, remained a central tenet of the relationship until the end of the Cold War.

The first significant shift occurred with Gorbachev's new political thinking and the Soviet turn towards economic survival aspects. The relative decline in the general interest to secure survival almost exclusively by military means led to the end of the military standoff and to a significant asymmetric reduction of military capabilities (most vividly through the CFE Treaty) in exchange for economic and financial aid. Washington answered the Soviet shift in interest by giving preference to the politics of cooperative security in general and cooperative arms control in Europe in particular. It continued this policy throughout the 1990s.

The second important shift occurred with the coming into offices of George W. Bush and Vladimir Putin and the subsequent attacks of September 11, 2001. The terrorist attacks had the consequence that the U.S. interest in survival focused on the War on Terror and a major increase of the U.S. defense budget. Cooperation with Russia was not one of the central survival motives anymore. At the same time, the Russian interest in survival shifted away from cooperation towards consolidating the Russian economy and the Russian influence in its direct geopolitical neighborhood. Even though the Obama administration recalibrated the U.S. foreign and security policy, cooperation with Russia remained outside of any immediate survival interest. In contrast, Moscow' interest in securing its influence in the so called Near

Abroad increasingly clashed with the U.S. policy of further enlarging NATO to the east.

Taken together, the combined survival interest had tied the two states together during and shortly after the end of the Cold War. They managed this interest – though only partially during the Cold War – through means of enhancing security through cooperation. With the end of the Cold War, they managed their security concern increasingly through enhancing *mutual* security. The policies of cooperative security and cooperative arms control in Europe were the results of this combined interest. With the fading confrontation and the massively increasing gap in relative capabilities, this interest got lost. The attacks of 9/11 were only the triggering events for the United States to finally shift their attention to other areas of immediate survival concern. Since the late 1990s, the two states have not found a mutually compelling rationale for aligning their mutual survival concern beyond the realm of strategic nuclear arms control. From a Realist viewpoint, the reason for this circumstance lies in the weak state of Russian capabilities, relative to the United States. Accordingly, Moscow is simply not perceived as a serious challenge in Washington anymore. In the words of U.S. President Obama, Russia is just a 'regional power' (quoted in Blake 2014).

Below the level of general interest in survival, U.S.-Soviet/Russian issue-specific interests were largely divergent throughout the period of analysis. This pertains particularly to issues such as the C/OSCE or NATO enlargement. Here, Washington followed its general interest in securing survival through cooperation while, at the same time, furthered its issue-specific interest of maintaining and later enlarging NATO while keeping the OSCE's profile comparably low. Even where both shared an issue-specific interest in cooperation (take the establishment of the CFE Treaty), their objectives behind cooperation where mostly divergent. Because of the weak Russian position throughout the 1990s, Russia often changed its issue-specific interest during the course of negotiations. In contrast, Washington remained firm to its issue-specific interests. The last time that this form of cooperation took place was the signing of the Rome Declaration and the establishment of the NRC in 2002. Since then, divergence in issue-specific interests has prevented relevant cooperation. One can argue whether this is due to the Russian relative increase in economic capabilities since the year 2000 (see Chart 29), whether it is due to the Russian survival concern with regards NATO enlargement (cf. Mearsheimer 2014), whether it is due to the Russian leadership's survival concern in response to Washington's promoting democracy abroad (cf. McFaul in Sestanovich, McFaul, and Mearsheimer 2014), or whether it is due to a difficult to distinguish combination of all three factors.

3.8.3   Expectations

According to Realists, cooperation between an offensively-oriented and a defensively-oriented power is ultimately hard to achieve, if at all (cf. Jervis 1999). This assumption holds true for most of the empirical evidence of this chapter. As long as the United States and the Soviet Union/Russia acted both defensively-oriented, they were able to cooperate. In the case of MBFR, cooperation failed because of the offensive U.S. orientation which was geared towards changing the balance of power to the advantage of Washington. In the case of the first round of NATO enlargement, cooperation did not even take place (directly) because of the offensive orientation of the United States. The same is true with regards the failed CFE talks "at 36" and the Russian EST proposals.

However, a significant difference to the assumption of Realists exists in relation to CFE and NATO enlargement. In the case of CFE, the treaty did change the distribution of power to the detriment of Moscow. The Soviet Union nevertheless agreed to the treaty. This was mostly due to the shift of interest at the level of general interest (towards giving preference to economic considerations) and because Washington, and particularly Bonn, paid large compensation. In the case of the first round of NATO enlargement, Washington could have proceeded without considering the Russian concern at all – according to a Realist view, simply because Moscow was too weak. However, Washington did pay compensation in the form of the Founding Act, further OSCE adaptation, ACFE, and Russian accession to the G7 and APEC. One could therefore argue that cooperation on NATO enlargement actually did take place (albeit tacitly; cf. Aggarval 2000) and that Washington acted not exclusively offensively-oriented on the issue.

Two important differences exist between the Cold War years, the 1990s, and the new millennium. First, offensive orientations did not lead to a change in the relative distribution of power during the Cold War. During the 1990s, they did lead to a relative change in the distribution of power (i.e. NATO enlargement) and were accompanied by cooperative processes. Second, offensive orientations continued to lead to changes to the relative distribution of power in the new millennium (i.e. the second and third round of NATO enlargement). However, they were not accompanied by successful cooperation processes anymore. It is thus also possible to distinguish between cooperative and non-cooperative policies. In a narrow sense, NATO enlargement was a non-cooperative process in three stages (1999, 2004, and 2009). In a wider sense, the Clinton administration acted both offensively- and defensively-oriented on the issue by making use of the policies of cooperative arms control in Europe. In contrast, the George W. Bush administration did exclusively act offensively-oriented on the issue and did not make efforts to engage cooperatively with Moscow. As explained above, the establishment of the NRC had no political links to the second and third round of enlargement.

3.8.4   Strategies

An important insight of the analysis of this chapter is that issue-specific divergence and even different orientations were often overcome by policy changes at the level of issue-specificity and the employment of the strategy of compensation. Compensation was a prominent strategy tool throughout much of the Cold War and during the 1990s. Compensation was paid in conjunction with the MBFR/CSCE deal (in a mutual way), the CFE Treaty (United States/West Germany to the Soviet Union), the first round of NATO enlargement (United States to Russia), and in conjunction with the War on Terror (NRC establishment; United States to Russia). Every time crucial aspects of national survival and power were dealt with cooperatively (A/CFE), the strategy of monitoring was added to the strategy of compensation. Where issues of military security were dealt with on a politically binding level which was not directly affecting the relative distribution of military strength (CSBMs under the auspices of the C/OSCE), the strategy of confidence-building was sufficient – however, only after the end of the Cold War. The strong institutionalization in the sphere of cooperative arms control in Europe during the period of analysis is a clear evidence of the success of the strategy of confidence-building through repeated interaction. Both, the United States and the Soviet Union/Russia have recurrently sliced up contentious policy issues into increments (cf. Oye 1986b: 17). In some cases (take MBFR and CFE after 1999), this strategy has resulted in continued deadlock.

3.8.5   Evaluation of Gains

Today, only a few institutions and cooperative processes of cooperative arms control in Europe enjoy positive feedback in both capitals. The CSBMs under the auspices of the C/OSCE still generate mostly positive feedback (cf. Richter 2014). The OSCE's role in conjunction with the Ukraine conflict has been strengthened (cf. President of Russia 2014b). On the other institutions, the mainstream opinion in contemporary Russia (cf. President of Russia 2007) is that Moscow was tricked by the West at the end of the Cold War (cf. Sarotte 2014), that NATO distorts the European security architecture, that NATO-Russia cooperation has failed, that the OSCE does not live up to its mandate, and that conventional arms control is dead. Russian officials often argue from a Realist point of view and infer that Russia was too weak during the 1990s and that Washington exploited that weakness (cf. Mearsheimer 2014). A quote from U.S. President George H.W. Bush from 1991 only underscores this view: 'We [the United States] prevailed, they didn't. We can't let the Soviets clutch victory from the jaws of defeat.' (Quoted from Sarotte 2014: 94) In the Russian understanding, Moscow did not get what it wanted from cooperation. In the words of Vladimir Putin: 'The Cold War ended, but it did not end with the signing of a peace treaty with clear and transparent agreements on respecting existing rules or creating new rules and standards. This created the impression that the so-called "victors" in the Cold War had decided to pressure events and reshape the world to suit their own needs and interests.' (President of Russia 2014b) In contrast, Washington continues to value the gains from cooperation, particularly on the C/OSCE. The positive American evaluation of gains implies that Washington got what it wanted from cooperation (see Sarotte 2014: 97).

Against the current one-sided and negative assessment in Russia, it becomes increasingly hard to argue in hindsight that the gains from cooperation on cooperative arms control in Europe only increased mutual security. However, it would be false to argue exactly the other way around. No-one knows what the European security landscape would look like today without the gains achieved from cooperation on cooperative arms control in Europe in conjunction with the end of the Cold War. It is questionable whether the breakup of the Warsaw Pact and the Soviet Union would have happened in a largely peaceful way without these cooperative policies. It is also questionable whether the parallel decrease of military capabilities after the direct end of the Cold War would have happened without the policies of cooperative arms control in Europe.

From a Realist viewpoint, the gains from cooperation on cooperative arms control did almost always roughly reflect the underlying balance of power (in parts except for the 1990 CFE Treaty). Where the balance of power was changed (i.e. through NATO enlargement), the respective policies cannot be characterized as being fully in line with the concept of cooperative security (even though the Clinton administration made use of the instruments of cooperative security in order to cushion Russian unease with enlargement).

Therefore, it seems adequate to explain the negative Russian evaluation of gains by distinguishing between two broader strands of policy. The first strand of policy does mostly resemble the central tenets of the concept of cooperative security and has resulted in the creation of the C/OSCE, agreements in the realm of conventional arms control, CSBMs under the auspices of the OSCE, and a sub-regional arms control framework for the Balkans. The second strand of policy is hybrid in nature. On the one hand, it has resulted in the enlargement of NATO. On the other hand, it has partially been endowed with political-military cooperation measures from the realm of cooperative security (i.e. NACC, PfP, Founding Act, PJC, EAPC, and NRC) and has been achieved through cooperation strategies that have linked this second strand to other institutions of cooperative security from the first strand (e.g. A/CFE). According to its basic nature of an offensive orientation (thus changing the balance of power), this second strand does not comply with the concept of cooperative security. While it had been softened by policies of cooperative security during the 1990s (cf. Lipman 2014), since the year 2000, its offensive orientation has not been mitigated anymore. According to the Russian complaints (cf. President of Russia 2007), it is this hybrid strand of policy that the Russian leadership has a principle problem with and which led to the Russian perception of dissatisfaction with the European security structures. To quote again Vladimir Putin: 'But the United States, having declared itself the winner of the Cold War, saw no need for [checks and balances]. Instead of establishing a new balance of power, essential for maintaining order and stability, they took steps that threw the system into sharp and deep imbalance.' (President of Russia 2014b)

The first guiding research questions of this chapter can now be answered. What calculus led the United States and the Soviet Union/Russia to cooperate on cooperative arms control in Europe, and did they get from cooperation what they wanted? The mutual U.S.-Soviet interest in securing survival led them to seek cooperation on security issues during the Cold War, even though cooperation was largely constrained by considerations of military strength. After the Cold War, both sought to increase mutual security by means of cooperative arms control in Europe. According to the evaluation of gains, the United States got what it wanted from cooperation. It achieved the reciprocal downsizing of forces, supporting the Russian leadership throughout the 1990s, a network of CSBMs to help stabilizing post-Cold War Europe, and a low profile role for the OSCE with a strong impetus on the so called third basket. At the same time, Washington could maintain and enlarge NATO. As explained above, Moscow claims that it has not achieved what it wanted, particularly not with a view to NATO and the role of the OSCE in the European security architecture.

3.8.6   Institutionalization

In terms of institutionalization, the empirical evidence collated in this chapter leads to the preliminary conclusion that four cooperation clusters have evolved under the broad rubric of cooperative arms control in Europe.

The first cooperation cluster evolved around conventional arms control (see Table 8). MBFR kick-started a difficult cooperation process on the issue which was informed by strong divergence in issue-specific interests. After MBFR had been put to rest, a meaningful cooperation process evolved around the central elements of CFE, CFE-1A, ACFE, and the supporting monitoring instrument of the Treaty on Open Skies under the auspices of the C/OSCE. From the onset of the process until today the cooperation cluster displays strong bilateral U.S.-Soviet/Russian elements. As a byproduct of the strategy of compensation, conventional arms control has been linked to a number of significant political decisions, foremost NATO enlargement. The United States employed the strategy of compensation in the MBFR/CSCE context and particularly during the years of the Clinton administration. After the signing of ACFE, divergent issue-specific interests prevented further cooperation. Today, the cooperation cluster of conventional arms control is technically highly outdated, politically deadlocked, and disputed (cf. Kühn

2013). The cooperation cluster is based on reciprocity, dialogue, transparency, confidence-building, and arms limitations. It resembles central tenets of the concept of cooperative security. However, its political links to NATO enlargement have put it in close political vicinity to a policy which does not resemble the tenets of the concept of cooperative security.

TABLE 8

COOPERATION CLUSTER OF CONVENTIONAL ARMS CONTROL

- *MBFR (1973-1989 inconclusive)*

- *CFE (1990 in force, partially suspended)*

- *CFE-1A (1992 in force, partially suspended)*

- *Flank Agreement (1997 in force, partially suspended)*

- *ACFE (1999 not in force)*

- *Treaty on Open Skies (1992 in force since 2002)*

- *Talks "at 36" (2010-2011 inconclusive)*

The second cooperation cluster developed in the realm of confidence- and security-building measures (see Table 9). It is the oldest of the four cooperation clusters and has its roots in the Helsinki accords. It evolved through the CDE and gained its full shape during the early 1990s with the elaboration of a number of politically binding agreements. While the early CSBMs developed as part of a larger compensation deal between MBFR and the CSCE, convergence in issue-specific interests stood behind the instruments achieved during the early 1990s. Their realization took place in the multilateral C/OSCE framework. The continued strategy of confidence-building, most vividly in the form of institutionalization, made realization easier to achieve. Today, this cooperation cluster is still functioning from a technical point of view. From a political point of view, some of the instruments, such as the VD, are in need of a timely update in order to better address contemporary security challenges (cf. Richter 2014). The cooperation cluster is based on reciprocity, inclusiveness, dialogue, a defensive orientation, transparency, and confidence-building. It resembles central tenets of the concept of cooperative security.

The third cooperation cluster developed in the realm of political and military cooperation under the auspices of NATO (see Table 10). It includes cooperation mechanisms such as the PfP framework, the EAPC (the former NACC), the NATO-Russia Founding Act, and the NRC (the former NATO-Russia PJC). Issue-specific divergent interests were present at all times between the United States and Russia. Early on, Washington linked the cluster to the issue of NATO enlargement. Today, the cluster is functioning where military and political cooperation mechanisms are concerned involving third states. In NATO's political and military dealings with Russia, the cluster is dysfunctional and politically deadlocked. The cluster is hybrid in nature because it combines tenets of cooperative security (e.g. dialogue-based, confidence-building, declaratory limitations in the case of the Founding Act) with elements of inequality and partial non-transparency (e.g. the information- and decision-making design of the NRC). It did not develop through an inclusive negotiation process but by exclusive means of invitation and qualification.

TABLE 9

COOPERATION CLUSTER OF CSBMS UNDER THE AUSPICES OF THE C/OSCE

• *Helsinki CBMs (1975-1986)*
• *Stockholm CDE stipulations (1986-1990)*
• *Vienna Document (versions 1990-2011 in force, in need of update)*
• *Forum for Security Cooperation (1997 in force)*
• *Programme for Immediate Action Series (1992-1994 in force, in need of update)*
• *OSCE Framework for Arms Control (1996 in force)*
• *OSCE Document on SALW (2000 in force)*
• *OSCE Document on Stockpiles of Conventional Ammunition (2003 in force)*

TABLE 10

COOPERATION CLUSTER OF POLITICAL-MILITARY COOPERATION UNDER THE AUSPICES OF NATO

• *NACC (1991-1997)*
• *PfP (1994 in force)*
• *NATO-Russia Founding Act (1997 in force)*
• *PJC (1997-2002)*
• *EAPC (1997 in force)*
• *NRC (2002 in force, partially suspended)*

The fourth cooperation cluster emerged out of the need to achieve sub-regional stability for the war-torn countries of the Balkans (see Table 11). Based on the experiences of the CSBM enterprise of the C/OSCE and the framing of conventional arms control, a top-down approach was pursued. Moscow and Washington basically shared an issue-specific interest on the issue. Today, the cluster is still functioning. It is based on reciprocity, dialogue, inclusiveness (in a regional sense), transparency, confidence-building, and arms limitations. It resembles central principles of the concept of cooperative security.

TABLE 11

COOPERATION CLUSTER OF SUB-REGIONAL ARMS CONTROL FOR THE BALKANS

- *Agreement on Confidence- and Security-Building Measures in Bosnia and Herzegovina (1996 in force)*

- *Agreement on Sub-Regional Arms Control, Article IV (1996 in force)*

- *Concluding Document of the Negotiations Under Article V of Annex 1-B of the General Framework Agreement for Peace in Bosnia and Herzegovina (2001 in force)*

With these observations, also the second guiding research questions of this chapter can be answered. Does the degree of institutionalization justify application of the regime episteme? To answer the question, the preceding definition of regimes should be recalled. Accordingly, regimes are 'sets of implicit or explicit principles, norms, rules, and decision-making procedures around which actors' expectations converge in a given area of international relations.' (Krasner 1982: 2) Departing from this definition, the degree of institutionalization justifies application of the regime episteme because cooperative 'sets' in the form of political agreements accompanied by and achieved under the auspices of certain organizations are omnipresent in the realm of cooperative arms control in Europe. The incomplete analysis of the previous paragraphs suggests four cooperation clusters under the rubric of cooperative arms control in Europe. Those four clusters might turn out to represent regimes. More specific analysis is needed to prove this assumption and to clearly define what their respective 'principles, norms, rules, and decision-making procedures' are.

Together, these findings allow for a first, though incomplete, take on explaining the rise and fall of cooperative arms control in Europe. The empirical evidence suggests that the forms of institutions of cooperative arms control in Europe might well be captured by the regime episteme. Of the four cooperation clusters identified, three show serious signs of decay.

Even though the search for the reasons behind decay continues, three significant findings with regards to decay derive from the analysis of this chapter. First, Washington and Moscow are not equals in terms of capabilities anymore. Washington leads on all five factors assessed above. On four of the five factors, Washington outnumbers Russia considerably. The massive shift in capabilities after the Cold War has heavily influenced cooperation between the United States and the Soviet Union/Russia on cooperative arms control in Europe. On a number of important occasions (take the adaptation of the C/OSCE), Moscow could not get from cooperation what it wanted. From the viewpoint of Realism, cooperation among relatively different powers results in the relative distribution of gains (cf. Mattingly 1955: 163). In reality, this circumstance seems to have created a perception of grievance in Russia (see Sarotte 2014: 97). On other occasions, issue-specific interests were divergent to such a degree that cooperation was impossible (take NATO enlargement). In those cases, Russia could only but accept the change to the balance of power and take the compensation Washington offered during the 1990s. This circumstance seems to have exacerbated grievances in conjunction with the survival instinct of Russia.

Second, the change in cooperation interest on the U.S. side has had a significant impact on the policies based on the concept of cooperative security. In a basic understanding (cf. Mihalka 2005), cooperative security either helps to stabilize an adversarial relationship (as during the Cold War) or it helps to transform the relationship to a non-adversarial state (as in conjunction with the end of the Cold War). Cooperative security becomes meaningless when the relationship has not been adversarial for a long time (take for instance the EU) or if one side does not perceive the relationship to be adversarial. If one side (United States) has no direct survival concern with respect to the other side (Russia), instruments of cooperative security become somewhat obsolete. This might explain why the United States turned away from cooperation with Russia and cooperative arms control in Europe in the new millennium. Against the background of the obviously existing and continuously communicated Russian grievance (see Sarotte 2014: 97), this finding would imply a lack of political foresight on the U.S. side and could partially explain the unpleasant surprises the Russian-Georgian war of 2008 and the Ukraine conflict have caused in Washington (cf. Asmus 2010; Charap and Shapiro 2014b).

Third, policies of linkage might have contributed to decay. Issue linkages in the form of compensation were established between the cooperation clusters of conventional arms control and the NATO political and military cooperation cluster (and therewith NATO enlargement) as well as between the development of the C/OSCE (and therewith the CSBM cluster) and the NATO political and military cooperation cluster (and therewith NATO enlargement). As a consequence of linkage, negative developments such as the CFE deadlock could potentially spill over to other cooperation clusters more easily (cf. McGinnis 1986). Table 12 lists the preliminary findings related to decay.

TABLE 12

PRELIMINARY FINDINGS PERTAINING TO DECAY

- *massive shifts in capabilities*
- *Russian perception of grievance*
- *divergent issue-specific interests*
- *diminished U.S. interest in cooperation*
- *issue linkage*

In the next chapter, the theoretical concept of regime is introduced and scrutinized against the background of the empirical evidence collated in this chapter.

4   Regime Theory and the Empirical Evidence

This chapter connects the concept of regime to the empirical evidence. The guiding research question is: What findings and assumptions of regime theory are relevant for cooperative arms control in Europe?

The aim of this chapter is to analyze the concept of regime in order to highlight approaches applicable to the empirical evidence collated in the previous chapter. From the mid-1970s onwards Anglophone and later European scholars of IR developed the theoretical concept of regime in an effort to explain patterns of institutionalized cooperation between states in an increasingly interconnected world of political and socio-economic interaction. The fast evolving debate drew attention from all strands of IR theory (for a good overview see Rittberger 1993a and Hasenclever, Mayer, and Rittberger 1997). While particularly the early works of regime analysts focused mainly on economic and environmental issues, research on security regimes gained certain prominence in conjunction with the bipolar constellation and with respect to regional security regimes. Empirically, the study of security regimes was, and still is, underrepresented and regime analysis of the subject of this book has held a niche existence, even during Cold War times. Today, regime research on cooperative arms control in Europe is more or less nonexistent. Another underrepresented issue in the study of regimes is regime decay.

4.1   Introductory Remarks

In this chapter, regime theory is being applied due to three reasons. The main reason is that previous research on cooperative arms control has employed the terminology of regime without providing sound and convincing empirical evidence that the forms of institutions of cooperative arms control in Europe actually *are* regimes.

Second, Realism provides a good basis for focusing on the *decay* of international cooperation because Realism underscores the hurdles to arrive at and uphold international cooperation. However, Realism is too biased when it comes to international institutions. Even though contemporary Realists have accepted the role of international institutions, they view them as a mere subordinate level of engagement below the level of classical state-to-state relations in an environment of anarchy. Therewith, Realism is still in opposition to Neoliberal and particularly Constructivist accounts, which ascribe international institutions a life of their own. Realism has also a problem explaining the persistence of international institutions, particularly in times of fundamental change of states' interests and capabilities and in the case of continued dissatisfaction of major states. Following Realist logic, Russian exit from the OSCE is long overdue. In the case of CFE, despite Russian dissatisfaction, it took Moscow ten years to exit from the treaty. There are probably additional factors at work when it comes to the staying power of institutions. Realism misses to address these factors.

Third, regime theory was an effort by Neoliberal scholars to bring the Neorealists on board in their effort to explain international institutions and to make Neorealists accept the role of international institutions. Regime theory thus builds upon a number of distinct Realist assumptions and can be viewed as the Neoliberal "extension" to Neorealism (cf. Crawford 1996). It is thus well-suited to build upon the previous Realist approach and to complement it. The discussion in the following paragraphs will mainly focus on Neoliberal and Constructivist approaches to the concept of regime, for Chapter 2 saw already a detailed discussion of international cooperation from a Realist angle.

4.2   The Concept of Regime

Today, regime theory is considered a recognized approach, amongst others, to the study of institutionalized international cooperation (cf. Zangl 2010). Through the concept of regime, Neoliberal scholars tried to take Neorealists on board in their analysis of international cooperation (cf. Nye 1987: 372-4). Neoliberal regime scholars accepted a number of distinct Neorealist assumptions such as states as the prime actors in the international arena, states' rationality, and certain constraining effects of the environment of anarchy (particularly states' rationality to cheat). At the same time, Neoliberal proponents of regime remained committed to John Locke's vision of mankind's common interest in cooperation (Locke 1689). Neoliberal regime scholars took the rapidly increasing phenomenon of institutionalized international cooperative after World War II as a fact in need of analysis and explanation. They viewed it as a clear challenge to the classical Realist assumption of the limited role of international institutions and the constraining effects of anarchy. Making use of microeconomic models of rational choice, they tried to prove that cooperation under anarchy can be rational, and that international institutions significantly increase trust and reduce states' transaction costs. Realist scholars had to respond to the Neoliberal regime challenge in order to preserve Realism's explanatory credibility. The ensuing debate between Neoliberals and Neorealists, later extended to include Constructivists, was one of the most fruitful IR debates and helped to shift the focus towards international cooperation, international institutions, and cooperative strategies (cf. Oye 1986; Baldwin 1993).

The Anglo-American domination of IR theory (cf. Hollis and Smith 1990: 16; Waever 1998; Crawford and Jarvis 2000; Acharya and Buzan 2007) was mirrored in the concept-building process of international regimes

(Crawford 1996: 4-7). By its very promotion, regime theory increased vice versa the perception of conceptual dominance.[27] If Cox's argument (1981: 128) is right that 'theory is always *for* someone and *for* some purpose than regime theory was, at least in its juvenile stage, an exclusive American intellectual reflex to a perceived decline of hegemony during the Carter presidency (cf. Strange 1982: 480-4; Russett 1985; Müller 1993a; Yoshimatsu 1998) American regime scholars addressed the perceived decline through means of enhanced and institutionalized cooperative efforts in the international arena. Such attempt should not be mistaken with the intellectual development of a purely egoistic American national agenda, particularly not since a large number of Liberal American regime theorists might have come to view increased cooperation less as a national prerogative but more as a common moral good (cf. Hurrell 1993: 67). Rather, the concept of regime reflected the Realist-Idealist dichotomy of IR theory in general as 'the science not only of what is, but of what ought to be' (Carr 1939: 5). Hence, regime theory took into account the steadily growing phenomenon of international institutionalized cooperation and sought to prescribe ways and means of how to address and shape it – though, mostly from a U.S. perspective and for a U.S. audience.

A general sense of dissatisfaction with the works of formal International Organizations (IOs) such as the UN during the late 1970s triggered a shift in the focus of IR away from formal IOs towards broader forms of international institutionalized cooperation (cf. Kratochwil and Ruggie 1986). Scholars started to look for more fruitful research areas, which promised more positive results; the underlying reasoning being the principle question of IR scholars of how the international community (should) govern(s) itself. The resulting focus on regimes pushed research on IOs to the sidelines, up until the mid-1990s.

The occurrence of the regime episteme correlates with the ascent of Scientism, which challenged the traditional humanities methods of political theory, history of diplomacy, and international law (cf. exemplary the classical English School). Particularly Waltz's seminal work *Theory of International Politics* triggered the use of analytical methods endemic to economics also in IR. Methods such as analysis of market failure or Game Theory allowed Neorealists but also Neoliberals to assess international cooperation along the lines of scientific models, based on the assumption that states act as rational gain seekers in an environment of anarchy. Methodological Scientism thus fertilized the works of scholars of regime theory, most notably visible in the works of Robert Keohane (1984).

---

27 However, regime theory soon became more internationalized, particularly through contributions of German (e.g. the Tübingen group) and Scandinavian scholars (cf. Rittberger 1993b: 3-22).

4.2.1 Definitions of Regimes

Defining regimes in a stringent, precise, and commonly agreed way has always been difficult and disputed (cf. A. Stein 1982: 299; Rochester 1986: 800; 1989a: 9). The regime concept by its very nature entails a certain vagueness (cf. Crawford 1996: 55). Robert Keohane and Joseph Nye were the first to make the term 'international regime' popular in IR study through their usage in *Power and Independence*. They argue that 'by creating or accepting procedures, rules, or institutions for certain kinds of activity, governments regulate and control transnational and interstate relations. We refer to these governing arrangements as *international regimes*.' (Keohane and Nye 1977: 5) From a purely formalistic point of view, no clear and commonly agreed definition of what regimes are exists. However, most IR scholars (Rittberger 1993a: xii; Zangl 2010) rely on the widely accepted definition by Stephen Krasner:

> *Regimes can be defined as sets of implicit or explicit principles, norms, rules, and decision-making procedures around which actors' expectations converge in a given area of international relations. Principles are beliefs of fact, causation, and rectitude. Norms are standards of behavior defined in terms of rights and obligations. Rules are specific prescriptions or proscriptions for action. Decision-making procedures are prevailing practices for making and implementing collective choice.* (Krasner 1982: 2)

Haufler (1993: 96-7) provides a simplified declination of Krasner's definition: 'principles are beliefs of fact, cause, and right. Norms are standards of behavior. Rules tell the actors what to do or not to do under specified conditions. Decision-making procedures refer to practice and implementation.' According to Hurrell (1993: 68), 'the term 'norm' is mostly used in regime theory to describe generalized rules of cooperative social behavior.'

A fundamental problem arises from Krasner's definition when linking regimes to and demarcating them from more classical institutions of international cooperation, such as agreements or international organizations (cf. Young 1989a: 195; Crawford 1996: 83). According to Keohane (1982: 337), regimes 'facilitate the making of substantive agreements by providing a framework of rules, norms, principles, and procedures for negotiation.' Their main function is thus to *facilitate* cooperation by providing states with information and thus reducing transaction costs. Regimes limit uncertainty (Keohane 1984: 97, 245). This assumption nevertheless leads to two questions: If regimes facilitate cooperation, for instance in the form of agreements, what upstream cooperative endeavors and possible frameworks facilitate the establishment of regimes? And what distinguishes this exercise from mere agreement-making?

As an example, the Vienna Document is an agreement within the wider cooperation cluster of CSBMs under the auspices of the OSCE. The CSBM cooperation cluster (which some scholars label a 'regime'; see Ropers and Schlotter 1989: 333) emerged as an outcome of the CSCE process, which other authors view as a regime itself (Nye 1987; Chung 2005). If the CSCE is indeed a regime than it came into being through the 1975 Helsinki Final Act, which, on the other hand, is an agreement made possible through the politics of détente. Most likely, one could also find relevant evidence that already the politics of détente displayed certain regime characteristics. Not ending up in a "chicken and egg" paradox of what came first, the question as such is not trivial, particularly not since Keohane and Young, who most vividly shaped the regime debate, disagree when it comes to distinguishing regimes from agreements. While for Young (1982: 283) regimes *are* agreements, or 'negotiated orders', for Keohane (1982: 334) regimes *facilitate* agreements.

The same problems arise when distinguishing regimes from international organizations. Young (1982: 277) argues that 'as with other social institutions, regimes may be more or less formally articulated, and they may or may not be accompanied by explicit organizational arrangements.' Ropers and Schlotter (1989: 317) point to the fact that international organizations or 'negotiation systems' such as the CSCE are important for regime creation and maintenance, particularly with a view to regime evolution. Müller (1993b: 135-6) and Cirincione (2000b: 3) share this view for the realm of multilateral nuclear non-proliferation and arms control. Thus, regimes might lead to the creation of international organizations. They might also be accompanied by IOs. A number of additional indicators for defining regimes have been stressed by regime scholars. Amongst them are what Young (1982: 278) calls 'the impact of time' and effectiveness. These two factors also give evidence about the persistence of regimes. According to Young (1982: 337):

> *A set of rules need not be 'effective' to qualify as a regime, but it must be recognized as continuing to exist. Using this definition, regimes can be identified by the existence of explicit rules that are referred to in an affirmative manner by governments, even if they are not necessarily scrupulously observed. (Young 1982: 337)*

That way, regimes display 'a form of cooperation that is more than the following of short-run self-interest.' (Jervis 1982: 357) Krasner (1982: 186) complements: 'Regimes must be understood as something more than temporary arrangements that change with every shift in power or interests.'

The behavioral dimension influences regime persistence as well. Following Zacher (1987: 174) the 'effectiveness of behavioral guidelines' is a very part of the nature of regimes. While 'deviance or nonconforming behavior is a common occurrence in connection with most social institutions' (Young 1982: 278), 'occurrences of major or long-term noncompliance, particularly involving participation of or support by major actors in the system, bring into question the efficacy of regime injunctions' (Zacher 1987: 174). Thus compliance in its various forms seems to be an indicator for identifying regimes. Nevertheless, again the definitional opacity stands in the way of assessing compliance as a clear-cut variable since compliance equals seldom (in)action limited to a single regime aspect. It is often hard to assess whether compliance pertains to the whole of the regime, to the normative level (principles, norms), or to the action level (rules, procedures), and what the interplay between those levels of analysis is.

As an example from the empirical evidence, longstanding Russian non-compliance with the Istanbul commitments is a violation of rules whereas NATO's refusal to ratify ACFE could as well be judged as a rejection of general principles of conventional arms control. Is the violation of rules as severe as the negation of shared principles in a regime? Keohane stresses the wider policy space and points to the fact that violation or 'cheating' becomes also limited by the often broader framework regimes are nested in. In this way regimes produce issue linkages (cf. Keohane 1984: 89 et seq; Axelrod and Keohane 1986: 234).

A noteworthy approach comes from Aggarwal (1985). Addressing the dichotomist nature of Krasner's definition (principles/norms and rules/decision-making procedures) and the problem of demarcating regimes from agreements, he pleads for a distinction between 'meta-regimes' (principles and norms) and 'regimes' (rules and procedures). (Ibid: 18-20) 'By distinguishing between rules and procedures […] and norms and principles […]', he argues, 'we can proceed to systematically analyze changes that take place in both of these areas.' (Ibid: 18) His approach makes it also possible to reconcile Young's and Keohane's positions on the relation between regimes and agreements. Regimes, in Aggarwal's understanding, would equal agreements (cf. Young 1982: 283) and meta-regimes would underlie, and thus facilitate, in Keohane's words, the making of regimes/agreements.

4.2.2   Security Regimes

Research on security regimes has particularly benefitted from early works of German scholars on East-West security regimes in conjunction with the end of the Cold War (cf. Wolf and Zürn 1986; Efinger, Rittberger, and Zürn 1988; Efinger 1989; Efinger 1990; Efinger and Zürn 1990; Rittberger and Zürn 1990). A number of authors have stressed the special role of security regimes and argued that the issue-area of international security is generally less propitious to regime establishment because of its severe nature, compared to areas such as trade or telecommunication (cf. Jervis 1982; Lipson 1984). Nye (1987: 374-5) concludes that 'the difficulty of ascertaining intentions and the large stakes at risk in case of defection may be higher in most security issues than it is in most economic issues'. However, if security regimes involve 'timely warning' mechanisms, 'states are not totally vulnerable to defection'. (Ibid: 375; cf. also J. Stein 1985) Nye thus points to the cooperation strategy of monitoring.

Jervis (1982: 360-1) outlines four conditions for the establishment of a security regime which can be circumscribed with shared interests, shared expectations, shared convictions, and cost-benefit considerations in favor of cooperation. Furthermore, he stresses reciprocity as a pattern of interaction likely to strengthen the operation of a security regime. Janice Stein (1985: 607) concludes that 'new [security] regimes are often created in the aftermath of an important change in the distribution of power, especially after a major war.' This hypothesis is in accordance with the empirical evidence that at least two of the cooperation clusters of cooperative arms control in Europe (conventional arms control and the political-military cooperation under the auspices of NATO) took off in conjunction with, and shortly after, the end of the Cold War. Stein (ibid: 609) goes on to argue that regimes continue to exist even in cases where the distribution of power and interest shifts.

Focusing on the bipolar security constellation, Jervis (1982: 371-2) denounces successful regime establishment. Nye (1987: 376) objects, arguing that rather 'than focusing on whether the overall U.S.-Soviet relationship can be categorized as a security regime, we should more fruitfully consider it as a patchwork quilt or a mosaic of sub-issues in the security area, some characterized by rules and institutions we would call a regime and others not.' Janice Stein (2003: 7) sees an early version of a U.S.-Soviet security regime emerging in the 1960s, which 'certainly did not transform their relationship until the collapse of the Soviet Union in 1991.' In an earlier article, she highlights 'the difference between bargaining over principles and norms where no consensus exists and bargaining over the distribution of benefits within the framework of agreed principles. Most of bargaining theory concentrates on the latter, but much of the conflict over security takes place precisely when principles and norms are not shared.' (J. Stein 1985: 626) With regards to the empirical evidence, it would be important to scrutinize the qualitative degree of sharing of principles.

Peter Jones (2011: 11) concentrates on regional security regimes and infers that 'the key is the adoption of a set of agreed norms within a given region which best expresses the local traditions and desires'. He goes on to argue that regional security regimes must be inclusive, membership must be voluntary, and the regime 'must be able to adapt and develop in response to new concerns and issues.' Beyond that, he stresses the factor of perceptions. '[A]ctor's perceptions are shaped over time by […] the evolutionary *process* of developing a regional security regime'. Thus, perceptions function as a result of the complex interplay of the variables outlined in the above cooperation model.

4.2.3   Regime Complexes

Oran Young (1996) concluded in the mid-1990s that rather often international institutions interact closely (cf. Young 1996). Describing institutional linkages, he differentiated between 'embedded', 'nested', 'clustered', and 'overlapping' institutions. When referring to nested institutions, Young primarily described efforts to build on existing institutions, e.g. in the form of protocols, to translate international institutional obligations into national law, and to extend the reach of international institutions through means of regional arrangements. Aggarwal (1998) then advanced the term of 'nested regimes' and described their architecture as telescoped like the different pieces of a 'Russian doll'.

In the 2000s, a new generation of regime scholars sought to refine the incipient stages of research on regime interaction. Rosendal (2001) differentiated between compatibility and divergence of both rules and norms, thus referring to overlapping regimes. Raustiala and Victor (2004) took regime analysis to the next level by providing for a more encompassing approach to regime interaction which avoided Young's four-type classification: 'The rising density of international institutions', they concluded 'make[s] it increasingly difficult to isolate and "decompose" individual international institutions for study.' (Ibid: 278) In order to take account of institutional interaction, they coined the term of 'regime complex' as an 'array of partially overlapping and non-hierarchical institutions governing a particular issue-area.' (Ibid: 279)

During recent years, regime scholars have increasingly paid attention to the issue. Keohane and Victor (2011: 7) see nested regimes and regime complexes as located 'between comprehensive international regulatory institutions, which are usually focused on a single integral legal instrument, at one end of a spectrum and highly fragmented arrangements at the other.' They infer that 'regime complexes are marked by connections between the specific and relatively narrow regimes but the absence of an overall architecture or hierarchy that structures the whole set.' (Ibid: 8; cf. also Alter and Meunier 2009: 13)

Orsini, Morin, and Young (2013: 29) offer a more detailed taxonomy of a regime complex 'as a network of three or more international regimes that relate to a common subject matter; exhibit overlapping membership; and generate substantive, normative, or operative interactions recognized as potentially problematic whether or not they are managed effectively.' In their understanding, single regimes are the constitutive elements of a regime complex. Their respective principles, norms, and rules can, to some degree, diverge or converge. To achieve network quality, at least three regimes have to form a complex. In accordance to Keohane (1984: 61), they argue that 're-gime complexes focus on a specific subject matter, often narrower in scope than an issue area.' (Orsini, Morin, and Young 2013: 30) As another requirement for a regime complex, membership has to partially overlap, but seldom entirely. Interaction between the elemental regimes is a key component of their definition with every distinct regime interacting at least with one other regime of the complex. Finally, they claim that 'policymakers and stakeholders must see the simultaneous existence of elemental regimes as being actually or at least potentially problematic for a regime complex to exist.' (Ibid: 31) To enable comparison between regime complexes, the authors stress 'the conflictual or synergetic nature of its links.' (Ibid: 32) Employing network analysis, they offer three modes of regime interaction (links): (1) dense networks where all nodes (the elemental regimes) are connected to one another, (2) centralized networks with one node having relatively more ties with other nodes than the remaining ones, and (3) fragmented networks where both centrality and density are low.

4.3   Regime Creation and Maintenance

In this paragraph, explanations by Neoliberal and Constructivist scholars towards the creation and maintenance of regimes are introduced in order to get a better understanding of the multiple factors that lead states to engage in regularized patterns of cooperative behavior. Such factors might, in an inverse understanding, also hint at possible factors to disengage. Neorealist explanations towards the creation of regimes are rare. They mainly refer to the paradigm of hegemonic stability (see Krasner 1976).

Before entering the life cycle of regimes, we should ask why states create regimes. First, it will be important to get rid of any misleading notion of cooperation as a moral good per se, as sometimes brought forwards by Neoliberal scholars of regime (cf. Hurrell 1993: 67). Cooperation as such has no moral value or origin. Soviet-Nazi Germany cooperation on the partition of Poland is just one example. Keohane consequently admonishes that 'although international regimes may be valuable to their creators, *they do not necessarily improve world welfare*. They are not *ipso facto* "good".' (Keohane 1984: 73) A number of authors have demonstrated that regimes might serve only the interests of a single state – in most cases a hegemon – with this state pressuring other reluctant states to comply with the regime (cf. Krasner 1993: 152-5). The propensity of certain regime scholars to view cooperation as a moral good is actually more of a reflection of regime theory's inherent liberal nature than a distinct research program. Regime creation by virtue of altruistic or, more general, moral motives should thus be discarded. Also, states do not engage in cooperative endeavors for the very sake of cooperation. Instead, regime scholars agree that states seek certain gains from cooperation (cf. Keohane 1984; Oye 1986). Cooperation thus needs to be understood as a purely neutral and unbiased term.

4.3.1   Neoliberal Approaches

One of the most influential substantiations of the Neoliberal regime episteme comes from Robert Keohane. His main argument for the creation of regimes is based on rational choice assumptions. In *After Hegemony* (1984) he applies various situation-structural approaches to prove that stable cooperation can emerge even if the contracting parties find themselves in anarchy-like situations where it is rational for both to defect. Keohane departs from the repeated Prisoners' Dilemma and concentrates on other coordination games as well (cf. Keohane 1984: 75-8). Regimes, he concludes, can provide a stable framework for facilitating agreements because of their repetitive character, the information that regimes provide, the accumulated gains over time (Axelrod's 1984 'shadow of the future'), and the reduced transaction costs for states.

As the title of Keohane's seminal work (1984) implies, institutionalized international cooperation can emerge and persist even in times of hegemonic decline. Having said that, Keohane did not dismiss hegemony as a positive foundation for the emergence of regimes (cf. Hasenclever, Mayer, and Rittberger 1997: 87) but underlined that even in cases of declining satisfaction by the hegemon or other regime participants, regimes can persist because of the difficulty – that is costliness – of creating a regime in the first place (Keohane 1988: 386 et seq). Following this approach, maintaining the regime even in times of dissatisfaction is more cost-effective than rather 'letting it die' (cf. Keohane 1984: 103). Regime maintenance thus rests also on cost-benefit considerations.

The value of Neoliberal explanations for the creation of regimes based on models of rational choice is limited insofar as they suppose purely rational gain seekers – concerned with absolute and not relative gains; a criticism most vividly brought forward by Grieco (1988). Also, Neoliberals did not eradicate the basic problem of states rationality to cheat. Furthermore, they have favored two-party games, which miss to take into account complex multi-preference settings. Last but not least, Nye has argued that states' preferences are not stable over time but could be influenced by the regime framework (cf. Nye 1987: 400). Such understanding is already in close vicinity to Ernst Haas's Constructivist understanding of learning (cf. E. Haas 1990: 23 et seq.). Taken together, rational choice approaches have received criticism for their rigid and unrealistic postures (cf. Hopmann and Druckman 1991: 273). Nevertheless, Neoliberal explanations make their cogent points when stressing cost concerns as an argument for regime maintenance.

Another important, though different, Neoliberal contribution comes from Young. In his account of 'institutional bargaining' (Young 1989b: 359-66), he affiliates himself with the skeptics of game theory and argues that 'the analytic literature on bargaining exhibits a marked tendency to abstract itself from a number of real-world factors that are important in the context of international regime formation, for example, incomplete information or unstable preferences.' (Young 1982: 284) In Young's model, 'uncertainty' is the major variable as actors are uncertain about their opponents' strategies as well as to their own strategies, and with respect to possible outcomes. Uncertainty about the time and the unpredictability of the future creates, what Young terms, a 'veil of uncertainty' regarding the future positions and interests of the parties involved. As those interests can change over time – the established regime nevertheless cannot be changed easily – states opt for institutional arrangements that can produce acceptable results for states in quite different positions. (Cf. Young 1989a. Chapter 3) Besides the influence of uncertainty, Young presents six factors responsible for successful regime formation which are 'contractual environment', 'exogenous shocks or crises', 'availability of equitable solutions', 'existence of salient solutions', 'compliance mechanisms', and 'leadership' (Young 1989b: 366-74). By 'capturing some of the essential features of the processes involved in the formation of international regimes', Young (1989b: 374) both augments the regime approach with concrete variables and rejects 'mainstream utilitarian' as well as classical 'power theorists[']' accounts of regime formation. With a view to regime maintenance, Young (cf. 1989a: 62-70) is mostly in line with Keohane's argument (cf. 1984; 1988) of regime persistence as a result of cost considerations.

George (1980: 248) approaches uncertainty from a different angle. He points to the impact of uncertainty in leaders' calculations and suggests that leaders are generally uncertain about consequences of potential new arrangements. Furthermore they are uncertain about how to secure domestic support for a new regime. In light of these uncertainties, leaders tend to give preference to already established forms of cooperation instead of striving for new ones. This form of explaining regime maintenance could be labeled "leadership conservatism".

A third approach under the rubric of Neoliberalism comes from German scholars of international regimes. The so called 'problem-structural approach' (cf. Hasenclever et al 1997: 59-68) is located between the attributes of the actors and the characteristics of the international system as a whole. Thus the nature of the issue-area enters the limelight. According to Efinger and Zürn (1990: 68) 'issue-areas […] consist of one or more, in the perception of the actors inseparably connected objects of contention and of the behavior directed to them. The boundaries of issue-areas are determined by the perception of the participating actors.' Thereby 'objects of contention' equate conflict and 'the behavior directed to them' equates conflict management. Thus conflict equates positional differences (cf. Czempiel 1981: 198-203) and conflict management equates cooperation, which, theoretically, ranges from total war to stable peace. In opposition to Keohane, problem-structuralists highlight the conflictual background of regime-based cooperation (cf. Hasenclever et al 1997: 61-2). They classify the policy space in which regimes might occur, with 'security' included in their typology. In order to allow for a classification of the conflictual background, problem-structuralists scrutinize the issue-area and the type of conflict under consideration. Their classification of issue-areas departs from Czempiel (1981: 198) and rates security as medium positioned in terms of regime-conduciveness (cf. Efinger and Zürn 1990: 75). Following their conflict typology, conflicts can be categorized into dissensual and consensual conflicts with the former divided into conflicts about values (very low regime-conduciveness) and conflicts about means (medium regime-conduciveness) and the latter divided into conflicts about relatively assessed goods (low regime-conduciveness) and conflicts about absolutely assessed goods (high regime-conduciveness). (Cf. Rittberger and Zürn 1990: 31 et seq.)

The problem-structural approach can be questioned on grounds of its overt formalism. Issue-areas often comprise more than one subject of contention. Further on, different stages of negotiation might cover different types of conflicts and the conflictual issue at stake might change its nature over time. These objections highlight the artificial rigidity inherent to the problem-structural account and contest its value for comprehensively explaining regime maintenance.

4.3.2 Constructivist Approaches

Cognitivist or (social) Constructivist[28] explanations for the emergence of regimes highlight the impact of norms, ideas, knowledge, and epistemic communities. In an attempt to further develop the rational interest-based model of states as utility-maximizers, Constructivists sought to focus not only on fixed interests but particularly on the impact and emergence of changed interests. Ernst Haas (1990: 7) asserts 'that the knowledge actors carry in their heads and project in their international encounters significantly shapes their behavior and expectations'. Following Constructivist assumptions, knowledge can change over time, which in turn can lead to a change in preferences. Also under conditions where power relations are in flux, new 'ideas serve the purpose of guiding behavior' (Goldstein and Keohane 1993a: 8-24).

According to the Constructivist approach, uncertainty claims a prominent role. Uncertainty in a Constructivist sense should not be confused with uncertainty as in Young's model. Rather the term serves the function of a more fundamental understanding of uncertainty in the sense of 'what do I know?' Particularly in an ever more interconnected world of specific technicalities decision-makers cannot be certain to make the right choices without seeking advice from experts who supply the desired knowledge (cf. Adler and Haas 1992: 375 et seq). Such knowledge becomes available through like-minded and well-informed peer groups, so called *epistemic communities*. 'Scientific knowledge may be best operationalized in terms of epistemic communities. Consensual knowledge does not emerge in isolation, but rather is created and spread by transnational networks of specialists. [...] Epistemic

---

28 For a discussion of the two closely interlinked concepts see Hasenclever et al (1997: Chapter 5) and Ulbert (2010). For reasons of consistency the term 'Constructivism' is used when referring to the two concepts.

communities are networks of knowledge-based communities with an authoritative claim to policy-relevant knowledge within their domain of expertise […]'.[29] (P. Haas 1993: 179) Adler and Haas (1992: 372-85) see the influence of epistemic communities during both stages of regime creation and maintenance.

During the 1990s, the Constructivist research agenda gained further prominence through the so called normative debate. Scholars such as Finnemore and Sikkink (1998) criticized behavioral approaches for their economics-induced fascination with measurements of all kinds, therewith leaving ideational or social phenomena outside of IR. In their understanding, the effects of ideas and knowledge only constitute interests, reality, and therewith, actors themselves. According to such understanding, even anarchy is only 'what states make of it' (Wendt 1992).

Constructivists have not only added valuable explanatory variables to the first two stages of the regime life cycle, they have also helped to question the rigidity of the Neorealist, the situation-structural and, in a form of actors' disentanglement from the causal regularity of the issue-area, also the problem-structural approach. Their merit is the substantiation of the idea that regimes can assume a life of their own through providing a framework for the exchange of ideas, through the effects of learning in changed and complex constellations, and through the input of epistemic communities. Obviously, Constructivism places an important emphasis on change as an integral dynamic element of regimes. It could thus provide explanatory variables for the decay of regimes if change is to be understood as a continuum of possibilities. Particularly changing norms, more precisely understood in terms of a changed understanding about norms, could have a serious impact on the survivability of a regime (cf. Krasner 1982: 4). A caveat should be raised with regards to the influence of epistemic communities. It is questionable whether their influence is as vital and verifiable when it comes to the realm of "hard" security (see Mutschler 2013).

4.4   Regime Decay: In Search of Indicators

It becomes important to think about the developmental patterns or life cycles of regimes. How can we account for the emergence of any given regime? What factors determine whether an existing regime will remain operative over time? Can we shed light on the rise of new regimes by analyzing the decline of their predecessors? Are there discernible patterns in these dynamic processes? Is it feasible to formulate nontrivial generalizations dealing with the dynamics of international regimes? (Young, 1982: 278)

---

29   For a defining set of characteristics of epistemic communities, see Peter Haas (1993: 180).

What reads like a research agenda for scholars of regime has in practice not resulted in a consequent study of the life cycle of regimes. Peter Haas (1993: 168-201) observes that 'in general, international scholars of regime have been mainly occupied with regime creation, persistence and change'. Even though change is basically neutral, change towards the unraveling of a regime – more precisely, regime decay – is still underrepresented in regime analysis.[30] In the following, regime scholars' approaches to indicators of decay are highlighted.

4.4.1   Signs of Decay

Before turning to a number of potential reasons for regime decay, signs of decay shall be highlighted first. Ernst Haas (1983: 192) defines regime decay as 'the gradual disintegration of a previously routinized pattern of conduct.' All proponents of regime agree that regime decay is a function of change. Differences exist mainly with regards to the reasons for and the consequences of change. Krasner (1982: 4) asserts: '*Changes in principles and norms are changes of the regime itself.* When norms and principles are abandoned, there is either a change to a new regime or a disappearance of regimes from a given issue-area.' His proposition highlights a crucial sign of decay: changes in principles and norms. He admits that 'assessments of whether principles and norms have changed [...] are never easy because they cannot be based on objective behavioral observations.' However, 'if actual practice is increasingly inconsistent with principles, norms, rules, and procedures, then a regime has weakened'. (Ibid: 5) Another sign of decay highlights protracted negotiations compared to earlier periods of swift and successful negotiations as potential indicators for decay (Aggarwal 1985: 143-82). In contrast to the very few signs of regime decay identified by IR scholars, the likely reasons for decay have gained comparably more attention.

4.4.2   Reasons for Decay

As already explained, Neorealists have ascribed regime decay mainly to the more general problem of upholding international cooperation over a longer period. According to Neorealism, the consequences of states' rationality to cheat, which is particularly high in the security realm, can be limited, particularly through monitoring agreements (cf. Jervis 1999). But the rationality to cheat can never be completely eliminated (ibid). In addition, a state which might come to the assessment that the cooperating state receives relatively more gains from an agreement over time, thus altering the distribution of power, will exit from the agreement. Further on, Neorealists have set decay

---

30   For a good treatment of the phenomenon of decay see Ernst Haas 1983. His account of global and regional conflict management nevertheless lacks the identification of general indicators of regime decay, applicable to other issue-areas.

in relation to the decay of hegemonic stability. 'When the hegemon loses its power, […] regimes will weaken and fail' (Haufler 1993: 95).

Neoliberal and Constructivist scholars of regime stress the ambiguity of change. Focusing on the power variable, Young's assessment is already in close vicinity of the paradigm of hegemonic decline. He observes that 'it should come as no surprise that shifts in the distribution of power will be reflected, sometimes gradually rather than abruptly, in changes in social institutions like international regimes.' (Young 1982: 293)

While regimes can disintegrate, more often they are being adapted in the wake of technological changes, learning effects related to new problem areas, shifts in power and capabilities, or changing domestic preferences (Müller 1993a: 48). 'Situations sometimes arise (for example, as a result of the collapse of some pre-existing order) in which it is difficult to avoid conscious efforts to create or reform specific regimes.' (Young 1982: 281) In such situations 'planned changes in regimes require not only the destruction of existing institutions but also the coordination of expectations around new focal points.' (Ibid: 280) As a result of this difficulty, 'deliberate efforts to modify or reform international regimes can easily produce disruptive consequences neither foreseen nor intended by those promoting specific changes, so that there is always some risk that ventures in social engineering will ultimately do more harm than good.'

Hasenclever, Mayer, and Rittberger (2004) put forward the hypothesis that distributive justice is a necessary condition for a high level of regime robustness. 'Inequity in the allocation of benefits and burdens among regime members', they assume, 'guarantees a low degree of "staying power" in the face of exogenous shocks.' (Ibid: 184)

Müller (1993a: 49) stresses the need for converging interests. Regimes' further existence, he argues, is in danger when actors' divergent interests forestall regime adaptation to external changes.

Jervis (1982: 366) takes into account cognitive repercussions of negative expectations: 'If an actor thinks the regime will disintegrate – or thinks others hold this view – he will be more likely to defect from the cooperative coalition himself. On the other hand, if he believes the regime is likely to last, he will be more willing to "invest" in it (in the sense of accepting larger short-run risks and sacrifices) in the expectation of reaping larger gains in the future.'

Janice Stein (2003: 13) helps to broaden the picture and emphasizes positive aspects of regime decay. 'The European experience suggests that regimes tend to be created after the kind of behavior they are prescribing is already becoming politically taboo, but participants are not confident that the taboo is deeply enough embedded so that it will be universally observed. Once confidence grows that the taboo is universally accepted, regimes tend to fade away as they evolve into security communities.' A differentiation of Stein's approach comes from McGinnis (1986: 165): 'cooperation that comes to be seen as routine may lose its relative appeal, as the costs of defection recede from memory. Thus, a disquieting substantive interpretation of this sensitivity problem is that a linkage-based international regime of cooperation may be unstable in the presence of changes in actor interests, even though the very existence of such a regime may stimulate exactly such changes.'

Issue linkage can further threaten the stability of regimes if conflicts from other issue-areas penetrate the regime or other closely connected regimes. It can also hamper regime evolution if connected to progress in an already stagnating issue-area. (Müller 1993a: 43) Amongst the most precarious implications of issue linkage are attempts to increase actor-specific gains through the inclusion of other, not directly related issue-areas. Müller (ibid: 48) argues that such forms of issue linkage signal that the issue-introducing actor is not satisfied with the conventional gains from cooperation. 'Although some linkage-based regimes of cooperation are resilient to perturbations, others are particularly brittle and subject to dissolution should one of the players attempt to add other, especially highly contentious, issues to that regime.' (McGinnis 1986: 165) Sebenius (1983: 315) adds: 'In some cases, the combination of individually resolvable issues may wreck the chances of settling any of them.' McGinnis (1986: 158) thus pleads 'to be at best guardedly optimistic in our assessment of the potential contributions of linkage to the establishment of stable patterns of international cooperation.'

Further on, possible 'birth defects' can erode a regime over time. 'The development of an international regime frequently involves intense bargaining that leads to critical compromises among the interested parties.' (Young 1989: 22) As a consequence, 'some regimes harbor internal contradictions that eventually lead to serious failures and mounting pressure for major alterations. Such contradictions may take the form of irreconcilable conflicts among the constituent elements of a regime.' (Ibid: 96) Müller (1993a: 50-1) argues that particularly old regimes with a long history of evolution might display a high degree of internal dissent.

4.4.3   Complexity Decay

Scholars of regime complexity are paying comparably more attention to decay than the classical school of regime analysis has done over the years. Alter and Meunier (2009: 20) collected possible consequences of regime complexity and found 'that changes within one institution could reverberate across parallel institutions. [...] Events in one area', they conclude, 'can reverberate in ways that states cannot fully anticipate or control.' Such changes include for instance negative spill-over effects. (Ibid: 19) Further on, they summarize that 'international regime complexity facilitates exit via non-compliance, regime shifting, or withdrawal from IOs.' Hafner-Burton (2009: 35) notes a tendency 'for actors to use one institution to escape or invalidate a legal obligation in another institution. Regime complexity makes this à la carte behavior more likely by reducing the clarity of legal obligations and by producing opportunities to forum shop.' Betts (2009) finds that states tend to use the environment of regime complexity to escape existing legal obligations by creating new institutional structures.

For the area of regime complexity in international security, Hofmann (2009) detects a number of strategies and effects that might have a negative influence on questions such as persistence and performance. Hostage taking and turf battles are just two strategies states employ to assert their interest. Besides competition, reverberation occurs in the form of institutional inefficiencies such as duplicated structures.

All in all, scholars of regime complexity have identified a number of negative effects that might arise from institutional density. In general, interdependent institutions seem to increase the likelihood of "negative" behavior of actors towards specific institutions. This is also true with respect to "positive" behavior such as compliance. However, the question and consequences of decay (e.g. negative spill-over and ripple effects) in relationship to the evolution of regime complexes remain an unexplored matter (cf. Morin and Orsini 2013).

4.5   Of Dragons and Fireflies: Regime Critique ... and Apologia

Amongst the earliest but still most profound critics of regime analysis Susan Strange (1982) vividly revealed the concept's inherent weaknesses. To quote from her terminology, five 'dragons' inhabit the arcane waters that surround the concept. While Strange reveals where the dragons lurk on the epistemological map of regimes, she does, however, not explain where the creatures came from.

4.5.1   Five Dragons

Dragon number one: 'The study of regimes is, for the most part a fad, one of those shifts of fashion not too difficult to explain as a temporary reaction to events in the real world but in itself making little in the way of a long-term contribution to knowledge.' (Strange, 1982: 479) Adding to the first dragon, Palan (2012), a scholar of Strange, asserts that 'regime theory supposedly tells us about the impact of coordination, but has little to say about the substance of the regime as such.' Crawford (1996: 86) asks 'whether regimes provide order and stability in international politics so much as they reflect it.' The underlying reproach is that form prevails over substance in the study of regimes. Such critique of regime theory as being almost apolitical and a fashionable l'art pour l'art exercise over-estimates its theoretical explanatory power. As will be discussed further below, regime theory was never made to arrive at a fundamental understanding of *why* regimes come about but rather *how*.

Dragon number two: 'It is imprecise and woolly.' (Strange, 1982: 479) Indeed, as already discussed above, the very concept of regimes is imprecise and even prone to cause what Blaise Pascal (1909-14: Para. 34) denoted a 'confusion of controversies'. Instead of following a classical 'spirit of precision' (ibid) in scientific discourse, confusion is partially apparent in Keohane's, Krasner's, and Young's definitions. Strange is therefore generally right in criticizing regime theory's imprecision but misses to scrutinize it from a systemic point of view. Her critique lingers at the surface of the regime debate.

Dragon number three: 'It is value-biased, as dangerous as loaded dice.' (Strange, 1982: 479) Strange exemplifies that regime theory helps to solidify existing divergences, particularly in the global North-South divide. (1982: 487-8) The blame is that regime theorists have fallen too deeply in love with their subject and lost critical distance. While Keohane rightfully raises caveats to a value-laden treatment of cooperation in general (1988: 380) and regimes in particular (1984: 73), Keeley (1990: 84) argues that Liberal regime theory even encourages IR scholars 'to regard regimes as benevolent, voluntary, cooperative, and thus legitimate associations.' Strange's critique might be too rigid inasmuch international institutions generally tend to 'reflect and sustain the existing political order and distribution of power', as Schachter (1982: 28) notes with recourse to international law. However, she is right to point to regime theory's propensity to elevate cooperation into a moral sphere (cf. Hurrell 1993: 67) without elaborating on what kind of cooperative endeavor is morally just and worthwhile pursuing.

Dragon number four: 'It distorts by overemphasizing the static and underemphasizing the dynamic element of change in world politics.' (Strange, 1982: 479) Strange's critique of the static weltanschauung of regime theorists is incomplete as she misses to take on IR theory's generally increasing occupation with positivist designs, which gained speed through the regime debate. As Judt (2010: 38-9) noted in his final lecture, the rationalist economic contributions of Anglo-American scholars of IR during the last decades tend to generally over-emphasize static suppositions. Regime theory, propelled by approaches of Scientism such as rational choice projections, reflected and amplified this process during the 1980s.

Dragon number five: 'It is narrow minded, rooted in a state-centric paradigm that limits vision of a wider reality.' (Strange, 1982: 479) At the time of her critique Strange was right to find fault with regime theory's almost exclusive concentration on international issues dealt with by the nation state. However, later analyses have displayed the impact of non-state actors on regimes (cf. Haufler 1993) and the emergence of private corporate regimes (cf. Cutler et al 1999). Even in the security realm, non-state actors have gained a certain impact level, for instance in the realm of humanitarian arms control (cf. Wisotzki 2010). The important but incompletely elaborated aspect of Strange's critique points to the systemic vicinity of regime theory to Neorealism. This kinship can be either questioned or lamented; it should, however, and in hindsight, rather lead to a debate about the general value of state-centric epistemes for theories of IR in the 21st century than to a justified dismissal of the concept of regime.

4.5.2   Where the Dragons Came From

Strange's critique of the concept of regime addresses a range of shortcomings of which most can be explained by an inherent conceptual contradiction. As Crawford (1996) proves convincingly, the regime concept is means and ends in itself. It is both the result of a paradigm which partially tries to reconcile Realist and Idealist/Liberal suppositions and the intellectual vehicle leading to the desired outcome. Accordingly, Krasner (1982: 1-2) has coined the term of 'modified structural' approach to regimes, based on the 'analytic assumptions of structural realist approaches'. This modified structural or, more pronounced, modified Realist approach derives from the assumption that Neorealists can explain the creation of regimes but are unable to provide convincing reasons for their growth into autonomous or semi-autonomous actors in international politics. Most regime proponents start from Waltzian structural suppositions about the state as both producer and product of the system of states and modify them to include Liberal assumptions that extend the international structure to include (semi)-autonomous supranational agents. The beauty of this idea lies in its attempt of a transformative reconciliation of the two oldest schools of theory in IR. It can thus partially explain the wide reception the regime episteme has gained (cf. Crawford 1996: 4).

Regime theory's origin, located between structural Realist and Liberal idealist suppositions about international institutionalized cooperation, explains for its imprecision, its value-biased affirmation of cooperation, its obsession with static models, and the centrality of the nation state. Regime theory elevates form so much over substance because of the concept's close vicinity to Neorealism. As Palan (2012) puts it: 'Regime theories are theories about the coordination problems that states are facing with no particular reasons or cause for coordination besides some vague notion that those states join regimes have a reason for doing so.'

In its essence, Palan's critique (ibid) questions regime theory's explanatory value. Its descriptive value, even though challenged by its very own definitional vagueness, was not so much put into question, not even by its harshest critics (cf. Crawford 1996: 3). It was regime theory that acknowledged the increasing interdependence of states and recognized the growing number of cooperative efforts in various international institutions of all policy areas. Its main added value derives from the attempts of scholars of regime to map the complex space of convergence towards cooperation and coordination. To put it simple: regime theorists gave the policies of complex interdependence (Keohane and Nye 1977) a form. Beyond that, Constructivist regime theory allowed institutionalized international cooperation a life of its own. Nevertheless, both merits cannot hide the facts that regime theory remained in parts at the descriptive level. There is thus reason to assume that regime theory is less of a *theory* but more of a praxeologic *description*.[31] Regime theory would be ipso facto an analytical tool of methodology (cf. Donnelly 1986: 640; Ropers and Schlotter 1989: 316; Hasenclever, Mayer, and Rittberger 1997: 11) that was never apt to arrive at a fundamental understanding of *why* regimes come about but rather *how* (cf. Thompson and Snidal 2000: 705). If one accepts this assumption, regime theory can be used as what it is: nothing more and nothing less than a methodology, helpful in identifying institutionalized patterns of cooperative behavior. From this perspective, Strange's dragons would lose much of their threatening posture when being dwarfed to the size of small but, in their entirety, highly illuminating fireflies.

4.6   Regime Theory and the Empirical Evidence

In the previous paragraphs, definitions of and theoretical approaches towards the concept of regime, its establishment, maintenance, and decay have been introduced, analyzed, and critically questioned. In the following, regime scholars' approaches will be shortly summarized and put into relation to the empirical evidence.

4.6.1   Definitions of Regimes and the Empirical Evidence

Various definitions of regimes and regime complexes exist in the literature. Before those definitions are put in relation to the empirical evidence, Table 13 will list scholars' key definitions of regimes and regime complexes.

---

31   Note that Strange constantly employs the term of regime 'analysis' instead of 'theory'.

TABLE 13

DEFINITIONS OF REGIME (AND REGIME COMPLEXES)

Aggarwal (1985)	• distinction between meta-regimes and regimes
Jervis (1982)	• a form of cooperation that is more than the following of short-run self-interest • reciprocity strengthens the operation of security regimes
Jones (2011)	• norms of security regimes express regional traditions and desires, regional security regimes should be inclusive, voluntary, and able to adapt
Keohane (1982, 1984)	• regimes facilitate cooperation in the form of agreements • regimes limit uncertainty and reduce costs • existence of explicit rules that are referred to in an affirmative manner • regimes are often nested in broader frameworks, they produce issue linkages
Keohane, Victor (2011)	• regime complexes are marked by connections between the specific and relatively narrow regimes • absence of an overall architecture or hierarchy that structures the whole set (of a regime complex)
Krasner (1982)	• principles, norms, rules, and decision-making procedures around which actors' expectations converge • more than temporary arrangements
Kratochwil (1993)	• regimes trigger domestic procedures
Orsini, Morin, Young (2013)	• regime complex: a network of three or more international regimes that relate to a common subject matter • a regime complex exhibits overlapping membership • a regime complex generates substantive, normative, or operative interactions recognized as potentially problematic whether or not they are managed effectively • regime complexes focus on a specific subject matter, often narrower in scope than an issue-area • interaction between the elemental regimes (every distinct regime interacting at least with one other regime) • three modes of regime interaction: dense, centralized, fragmented
J. Stein (1985, 2003)	• security regimes include detection and defection mechanisms • security regimes are often created after a major shift in power • regimes endure significant changes in power and interest
Young (1982, 1986, 1989)	• regimes as the product of conjunction of convergent expectations and patterns of behavior or practice • regimes are agreements and may be accompanied by organizations
Zacher (1987)	• effectiveness of behavioral guidelines • compliance of major actors

174

Krasner's set of regime characteristics (1982: 2) is a useful starting point for an inductive approach testing the empirical evidence. Keohane's assumption that regimes facilitate cooperation in the form of agreements (1982: 337) is supported by the empirical evidence of various agreements in the realm of cooperative arms control in Europe. The persistence of the majority of agreements in the realm of cooperative arms control in Europe points to the likely existence of explicit rules referred to in an affirmative manner (Keohane 1982: 337). Jervis' assumption that regimes are a form of cooperation that is more than the following of short-run self-interest (Jervis 1982: 357; cf. also Krasner 1982) is also supported by the persistence of some of the agreements of cooperative arms control in Europe which continue to (formally) exist since almost 40 years, such as the Helsinki Final Act. Jones' (2011: 11) reference to security regimes, which ought to be inclusive, voluntary, and able to adapt, is underscored by the empirics in the C/OSCE's CSBM cooperation cluster. All of those agreements are inclusive, voluntary, and some have been successfully adapted, such as the VD 2011.

Young's proposition that regimes may be accompanied by organizations (Young 1982: 277) is in line with the empirical evidence of two major European security organizations – NATO and the C/OSCE) – which are in very close vicinity to the agreements of cooperative arms control in Europe. Janice Stein's hypothesis about security regime creation after the occurrence of significant shifts in capabilities (J. Stein 1985: 607) concurs with the empirical evidence since two of the cooperation clusters emerged either in conjunction with the end of the Cold War or shortly thereafter. Her finding that security regimes include detection and defection mechanisms concurs with a number of C/OSCE CSBMs (e.g. the VD) and the A/CFE Treaties. Stein's assumption that regimes endure significant changes in power and interest (1985: 609) is nevertheless questionable with regards to the empirical evidence. Zacher's observation that major instances of long-term non-compliance, involving major actors, weaken regimes (1987: 174) is supported by acts of Russian non-compliance in the cooperation cluster on conventional arms control (cf. Kühn 2009).

Keohane's argument of the wider framework regimes are nested in (1984: 89 et seq) is crucial inasmuch as the empirical evidence shows that political linkages in the form of the strategy of compensation have been established between the four cooperation clusters and have led to close relationship between the four. Particularly the adjoining concept of regime complexity (see Thakur 2013) might turn out to best characterize the relationship of institutions of cooperative arms control in Europe.

Aggarwal's differentiation between 'regimes and meta-regimes' (1985: 18-20) could be applied towards the empirical evidence in order to clarify the question of the relationship between those four cooperation clusters, particularly as the historical provenance and the political linkages between these clusters might hint at a common origin. If the cooperation clusters were to share specific principles and norms, the likelihood for the existence of an "Aggarwalian meta-regime" would increase. Deriving from such hypothesis, the relationship between institutional decay and potential repercussions to the meta-level would come into focus.

Taken together, definitions of regime and regime complexes provide a sound basis for a regime analytical approach towards the empirical evidence because they mirror important institutional developments in the area of cooperative arms control in Europe.

4.6.2   *Regime Creation and Maintenance and the Empirical Evidence*

Beyond defining regimes, IR scholars have collated a number of explanations for regime creation and maintenance. Table 14 lists explanations according to their theoretical origin.

TABLE 14

EXPLANATIONS FOR REGIME CREATION AND MAINTENANCE

Neoliberalism	• hegemony a positive but not necessary foundation
	• cooperation can be rational even under anarchy
	• states strive to reduce transaction costs
	• regimes limit the incentive to defect; particularly through monitoring mechanisms
	• costliness of disbanding regimes even in times of hegemonic decline
	• regimes provide a stable framework for facilitating agreements; they lengthen the 'shadow of the future'
	• states opt for institutional arrangements that limit the 'veil of uncertainty'
	• leadership conservatism
	• contractual environment and equitable solutions
	• regime creation dependent on the conflictual background
Constructivism	• regime members learn and exchange ideas
	• regimes can assume a life of their own
	• politicians are uncertain about the issues at stake; influence of epistemic communities

Neoliberals' assumption that states maintain regimes in order to limit transaction costs (Keohane 1984; 1988) could be in line with the transformation of the CSCE to the OSCE. Cost considerations with regards to institutional dissolution, uncertainty about the future, and leadership conservatism (cf. George 1980: 248) could have explanatory power with a view to the (formal) maintenance of the cooperation cluster on conventional arms control. Neoliberals' proposition that regimes limit the incentive to defect, particularly through monitoring mechanisms (cf. Nye 1987: 374-5) gets underscored by the employment of monitoring instruments in two of the four cooperation clusters (CSBMs and conventional arms control) and might explain in parts for the maintenance of the CSBM cooperation cluster. Young's regime-conducive factor of the 'availability of equitable solutions' (1989b: 366-74) is on the one hand in line with the Realist tenet which sees the distribution of gains roughly reflecting the relative distribution of power; at least as long as equity is understood in terms of reflecting the Realist tenet of the relative distribution of power. On the other hand, this factor might prove valuable for addressing the Russian frustration with the gains from cooperation on cooperative arms control in Europe which Russia perceives as inequitable (cf. President of Russia 2007; cf. Sarotte 2014: 79).

Constructivists' impetus on learning effects and change has direct value for the empirical evidence. In the context of the changed Soviet attitudes towards the evolving CSBM and conventional arms control cooperation clusters (cf. Falkenrath 1995a: 40), the effect of learning through repeated interaction is clearly visible. The argument that regimes can assume a life of their own can claim validity concerning the evolution of the C/OSCE against continuous diverging issue-specific interests in Washington and Moscow. The likely influence of epistemic communities (see Adler and Haas 1992: 372-85) is nevertheless hard to assess, particularly in the realm of security, which is often constrained by secrecy concerns.

Not all Neoliberal and Constructivist assumptions and approaches have explanatory power in relation to the empirical evidence. Neoliberal scholars of regime have emphasized that cooperation can be rational even under the constraining effects of anarchy (cf. Axelrod 1984). Aside from the Neorealist critique that Neoliberals have not fully understood the constraining effects of anarchy (see Grieco 1988), that Neoliberals miss to take into account states' relative-gains concern, and that international institutions cannot fully eliminate the problem of states' rationality to defect (particularly not in the security realm), their methodology of rational choice has received criticism for its rigid, static, unrealistic, and one-dimensional approach (see exemplary Strange 1982). A possible game-theoretic model applicable to all instances of repeated cooperation in the realm of cooperative arms control in Europe would be hard to apply without ending up with one-dimensional explanations.

Scholars of regime have collated a number of indicators of regime decay, which are highlighted in the following and set in relation to preliminary findings from the empirical evidence.

According to Realism, states' rationality to cheat can undermine and terminate institutionalized cooperation. What Krasner (1982: 5) has termed 'inconsistent practice' would thus equal non-compliance. An example from the empirical evidence would be Russian non-compliance with the Istanbul commitments (cf. Kühn 2009) as well as non-compliance with a number of political commitments stemming from the Helsinki Final Act in conjunction with the war in Eastern Ukraine.

According to Young (1982: 293), shifts in the distribution of power can weaken regimes. His assumption is in close vicinity to Realist assumptions that states' relative-gains concern can lead them to exit from an agreement if they evaluate that the gains from cooperation do not roughly reflect the underlying distribution of power anymore (cf. Grieco 1988: 487). One example from the empirical evidence would be Russia's slow withdrawal from cooperative security in parallel to the reemergence of the Russian economy after the year 2000. In addition, his assumption is particularly valuable because of the strong shifts in capabilities as assessed in Chapter 3. The indicator will be summarized under the previously applied headline of "shifts in relative capabilities".

States' possible perception of the inequitable distribution of gains is in close vicinity to notions of justice and injustice (cf. Hasenclever, Mayer, and Rittberger 2004: 184) According to Realism, the distribution of gains is neither just nor unjust; it is simply relative to the distribution of power (cf. Grieco 1988: 501). However, the argument of the *perception* of inequity might have explanatory power when it comes to explaining the long-term dissatisfaction the Russian leadership continues to nurture with regards to the gains from cooperation on cooperative arms control in Europe after the end of the Cold War (cf. President of Russia 2007) and which seems to have created feelings of grievance on the Russian side. The indicator will be summarized under the headline of "Russian perception of the inequitable distribution of gains".

The decline of hegemonic stability (cf. Krasner 1976) is not directly applicable to cooperative arms control in Europe for three reasons. First, the United States never held a hegemonic role towards Russia. Second, it is questionable whether the United States is actually in hegemonic decline since the end of the 1990s (cf. Kupchan 2012). Third, if all four cooperation clusters would have been established during the Cold War and between the two hegemons, hegemonic decline would be a possible partial argument because of the decline of the Eastern hegemon, the Soviet Union; however only the cooperation cluster of CSBMs under the auspices of the C/OSCE has already been established during the Cold War. Aside from the decline of hegemonic stability, the large capabilities of the United States relative to Russia leads to the question whether the possibly negative influence of U.S. hegemonic *practices* could be an argument relevant for explaining decay. This indicator will be addressed in Chapter 8. The indicator will be summarized under the headline of "hegemonic practices".

The indicator of negative adaptation consequences (Young 1982: 281) could have explanatory power concerning the adaptation of the CFE Treaty and the concomitant Istanbul commitments. Looking at the other cooperation clusters, the empirical evidence does not suggest that adaptation had directly negative repercussions. Rather, adaptation reflected the issue-specific interest of the more powerful cooperation partner, as in the case of C/OSCE adaptation.

The indicator of divergent interests (Müller 1993a: 49) is only partially in line with the empirical evidence. On the one hand, divergent issue-specific interests have informed the U.S.-Soviet/Russian policies of cooperative arms control in Europe throughout the whole of the evaluation period. On the other hand, divergence has not blocked the main actors from achieving cooperation. It seems appropriate to continue to follow the approach taken so far, and to distinguish between issue-specific interests and a general interest in cooperation rooted in the Realist survival motive; the latter will be addressed shortly below. The indicator as such will be summarized under the previously applied headline of "divergent issue-specific interests".

The indicators of regime success, routine, and fading memories (cf. Janice Stein 2003: 13; McGinnis 1986: 165) might be worthwhile exploring in conjunction with the shift in general interest on the U.S. side away from European security and cooperation with Russia after 9/11. In order to define success in conjunction with cooperation on cooperative arms control in Europe it is useful to return to the definition of the gains from U.S.-Soviet/Russian cooperation on cooperative arms control in Europe as used above. Accordingly, the gains have to reflect the balance of power and to increase mutual security, in the sense of reflecting the canon of cooperative security. Analysis of the empirical evidence in Chapter 3 has shown that the gains have mostly met those two conditions. However, a second parallel strand of U.S. policy – NATO enlargement – was not in line with cooperative security and made use of the gains from cooperative arms control in Europe in order to compensate Russia. The combination of these two policies has led to an overall negative assessment on the Russian side. Hence, to speak of success and fading memories would be counterfactual with a view to continuing Russian dissatisfaction and grievance (cf. President of Russia 2007; 2014b). However, if one takes account of Washington's positive evaluation of the gains from cooperation one can assume that Washington viewed cooperation as successful and did thus not see an immediate need to re-engage on the issue. The conclusion would be that Washington showed a somewhat diminished interest in cooperation with Russia. Therefore, the indicators of regime success, routine, and fading memories will be summarized under the previously applied headline of "diminished U.S. interest in cooperation" in order to better address the question of decay of cooperative arms control in Europe.

The indicator of negative expectations (Jervis 1982: 366) is particularly visible on the Russian side from the late 1990s onwards. However, it should not become confused with the variable of 'expectations' from the Realist model used above.

The indicator of protracted negotiations (Aggarwal 1985: 143-82) has its merits because protracted negotiations are apparent with regards to the CFE negotiations after the 1999 OSCE Istanbul Summit and the stalled development of the cooperation cluster on CSBMs under the auspices of the OSCE (cf. OSCE 2011).

The indicator of the possible negative consequences of issue linkage (cf. Müller 1993a: 43-8; McGinnis 1986: 165; Sebenius 1983: 315) has already been shortly addressed. Issue linkage has certainly influenced the establishment and maintenance of the four cooperation clusters; particularly by employment of the linkage strategy of compensation, for instance in conjunction with the first round of NATO enlargement.

Because of linkages between several cooperation clusters, the indicator of negative spill-over effects (Meunier 2009: 19) comes into the picture. However, since the formal relationship of the cooperation clusters has not been fully analyzed at this stage of research, it is too early to make statements about negative spillover.

The same applies to the indicator of regime-internal contradictions (cf. Young 1989: 96; Müller 1993: 50-1). Without having assessed the agreements of cooperative arms control in Europe using a regime-methodological approach, it is too early to assess the likely impact of regime-internal contradictions. Krasner (1982: 4) argues that changes in principles and norms can be indicators of decay. Again, such possible changes can only be assessed after the principles and norms of the four cooperation clusters have been clearly identified. Table 15 lists the thirteen indicators of regime decay.

TABLE 15

THIRTEEN INDICATORS OF REGIME DECAY

- *protracted negotiations*

- *changes in principles and norms*

- *non-compliance*

- *hegemonic practices*

- *shifts in relative capabilities*

- *Russian perception of the inequitable distribution of gains*

- *negative adaptation consequences*

- *divergent issue-specific interests*

- *negative expectations*

- *diminished U.S. interest in cooperation*

- *issue linkage*

- *negative spill-over*

- *regime-internal contradictions*

Proponents of regime complexity have highlighted a number of additional negative effects of the systemic interrelationship in regime complexes. While the question whether the institutions of cooperative arms control in Europe might form a regime complex remains unanswered at this point, some of the negative implications of complexity correlate with the empirics. Table 16 lists possible negative effects of complexity.

TABLE 16

NEGATIVE EFFECTS OF COMPLEXITY

•   competition
•   reverberation
•   inefficiencies
•   regime shifting
•   non-compliance

Particularly the effects of reverberation might turn out to have explanatory value. Even though negative spill-over effects are observed by scholars of complexity, their real impact has so far not been linked to decay in complex institutionalized systems (cf. Thakur 2013). With regards to cooperative arms control in Europe, contradictory issue-specific interests were often overcome through strategies of linkage. These linkages might serve the function of a "negative bridge" that helps proliferate ripple effects, which reverberate throughout the whole system. If such inverse logic might turn out to be true, the dysfunctionality of specific sub-systems such as CFE could spill over into other sub-systemic units to negatively influence the system as a whole. To proof such hypothesis, an inductive test, which tests whether the politics of cooperative arms control in Europe have resulted in the formation of a regime complex, will be conducted in the following two chapters.

4.7   Conclusions

The Neoliberal, and later Constructivist, regime episteme provides a number of compelling reasons how international institutions such as regimes can help establish and uphold international cooperation. Regimes fulfil an important role, particularly with regards confidence-building and monitoring. However, from a Realist point of view, international institutions can neither fully elimi-nate the cheating problem nor can they really constrain states' interest and power (cf. Mearsheimer 1994/95).

What findings and assumptions of regime theory are relevant for the rise and fall of cooperative arms control in Europe? Answering the guiding re-search question of this chapter, the majority, of the findings and assumptions about regime establishment, maintenance, and decay are relevant for coopera-tive arms control in Europe. The four different cooperation clusters identified in Chapter 3 resemble a broad range of regime characteristics. However, this correlation does not yet allow concluding that the institutions of cooperative arms control in Europe *are* regimes. First, clear evidence should verify or falsify the regime assumption. Indeed, regime scholars have collated a number of important indicators of institutional decay that will be included in the further analysis. At this stage of research, it is yet premature to make convincing statements about the origins of decay without having classified the empirical evidence by means of a regime test.

Steven Krasner's regime typology has become almost equated with the regime episteme itself. It provides a well-recognized tool for identifying regimes. In order to provide sound regime evidence, the different institutions that form the four cooperation clusters will undergo a rigorous regime test according to Krasner's typology in the next chapter.

5   A First Abductive Test

So far, the empirical evidence points to a densely institutionalized policy space under the rubric of cooperative arms control in Europe. Assessed through the Realist model of international cooperation, four cooperation clusters are traceable. Of the four, three clusters exhibit signs of decay, though to different degrees. The ensuing qualitative review of various works of regime scholars has helped to gather possible theoretic and methodological approaches.

In this chapter, a regime-methodological approach is applied. By means of an abductive test, 36 agreements with direct relevance for cooperative arms control in Europe are qualitatively assessed. The 36 agreements are listed under Annex II. In order to classify the provisions of these agreements, Krasner's regime typology of 'principles', 'norms', 'rules', and 'decision-making procedures' is applied as methodological framework. The aim of the test is to either verify or falsify whether the institutions of cooperative arms control in Europe are regimes and, if so, which institutions are part of which regime.

The guiding research questions of this chapter are: Is there clear evidence that the four cooperation clusters under the rubric of cooperative arms control in Europe are actually four regimes? If so, do those four regimes form a regime complex? Which indicators of decay are present, and to what degree?

5.1   Introductory Remarks

In the following four paragraphs, 36 agreements with relevance to cooperative arms control in Europe are classified and assessed continually from 1975 to 2014 in four historical periods, depending on their date of signature and not entry into force.[31] In contrast to Chapter 3, four instead of six historical periods are applied as breakdown. This is owed to the fact that the years between 2000 and 2014 have only produced a total of six relevant agreements. The assessment will proceed as follows.

---

31   Only successfully concluded agreements are taken into account. This leaves out the unsuccessful MBFR talks. Some agreements, particularly from the C/OSCE, entail a wide range of political provisions going beyond the scope of this book. In order to avoid recalibrating the focus, only those principles, norms, rules, and decision-making procedures are taken into account with direct relevance for cooperative arms control in Europe. For all agreements, preambular paragraphs are treated as an integral part of the respective agreement and are thus assessed as well. Reaffirmations of conformity with the UN Charter and/or relevant UN conventions are not taken into account.

First, each agreement is shortly introduced with respect to its regulations and its historical background and attributed to its corresponding cooperation cluster on conventional arms control (CAC), CSBMs under the C/OSCE, NATO political-military (pol-mil) cooperation, or the Balkans subregional arms control stipulations. Attribution follows the insights gained from assessment of the empirical evidence in Chapter 3. A number of agreements cannot be attributed to one of the four cooperation clusters. A discussion regarding this fact will follow below.

Second, departing from a qualitative assessment, the agreements' main provisions are listed and matched to the corresponding regime framework of Krasner (1982: 2). To allow for a more focused application of Krasner's typology, agreements are not scrupulously assessed on a paragraph-by-paragraph analysis of their respective injunctions. Instead, attention is being paid to its central provisions. As an example, the CFE Treaty lists an extensive range of specific verification and counting rules for conventional weaponry. These rules are not taken into account. Rather, central rules of a general character, such as CFE's "sufficiency rule" (Article VI, CFE 1990), are listed.

Third, the current state of each agreement and of its provisions is shortly observed with respect to indicators of regime decay. All thirteen indicators of regime decay, as collated in Chapter 4, are applied to the agreements. Also indicators of decay are listed that do not exclusively pertain to U.S.-Russian political decisions. The thirteen indicators of regime decay are again listed below.

13 INDICATORS OF REGIME DECAY

- *protracted negotiations*
- *changes in principles and norms*
- *non-compliance*
- *hegemonic practices*
- *shifts in relative capabilities*
- *Russian perception of the inequitable distribution of gains*
- *negative adaptation consequences*
- *divergent issue-specific interests*
- *negative expectations*
- *diminished U.S. interest in cooperation*
- *issue linkage*
- *negative spill-over*
- *regime-internal contradictions*

Each of the four historical periods is assessed at the end of each paragraph in a specific table. The goal of this assessment is to highlight the number of indicators of regime decay in each specific period and with regards to agreements concluded before that period. As some of the indicators of regime decay are not bound to the act of conclusion of a given agreement but can occur sometime after the agreement's conclusion, it will be important to highlight also such indicators of decay that pertain to already concluded agreements.[32]

The test is abductive since it combines the inductive process of extrapolating from potentially shared principles and norms to a general regime quality with the deductive process of extrapolating from general findings of regime scholars about decay to the specific state of certain institutions.

In the following paragraphs, the respective 36 agreements from the realm of cooperative arms control in Europe are assessed.

5.2   Agreements, Period 1975-1989

TABLE 17

CSCE, QUESTIONS RELATING TO SECURITY IN EUROPE, DECLARATION ON PRINCIPLES GUIDING RELATIONS BETWEEN PARTICIPATING STATES, 1975

Agreement	**Agreement 1: Conference on Security and Co-operation in Europe Final Act, Helsinki 1975: Questions relating to Security in Europe, Declaration on Principles Guiding Relations between Participating States**
Attribution	--
Description	The Helsinki Decalogue is at the heart of the 1975 CSCE and the nucleus of the further C/OSCE process. It was the prestige project of the Kremlin and only came into being in conjunction with MBFR and the West's insistence on the inclusion of human rights standards. The central aim of Moscow was the recognition of the territorial status quo in Europe.
Principles	• indivisibility of security in Europe • commitment to peace, security, and justice • sovereign equality, respect for the rights inherent in sovereignty

---

32   For instance: Agreement X might have been established in Period Y and did not show any signs of decay during that period. However, in the following Period Z, Agreement X was violated by Actor P. In such a case, the corresponding indicator of regime decay will be counted in the respective assessment at the end of the paragraph that deals with Period Z.

	• refraining from the threat or use of force • inviolability of frontiers • territorial integrity of States • peaceful settlement of disputes • non-intervention in internal affairs • cooperation among States • fulfillment in good faith of obligations under int. law
Norms	• taking effective measures for disarmament
Rules	• - -
Decision-Making Procedures	• exchange of views on implementation of provisions • multilateral meetings of representatives in Belgrade in 1977 • possibility of a new conference • meetings held in participating States in rotation • technical secretariat provided by the host country
Indicators of Regime Decay, Period 1973-1989	non-compliance, protracted negotiations, divergent issue-specific interests, negative expectations, issue linkage, internal contradictions
Evidence for Regime Decay, Period 1973-1989	During the period 1973-1989, non-compliance with principles and norms appeared on a regular basis until the mid-1980s because effective measures for disarmament were not pursued at least until the Soviet announcement of unilateral partial withdrawal of forces from Eastern Europe in 1988 and because the Solidarity movement in Poland was suppressed by the declaration of martial law – a violation of the principle of 'peaceful settlement of disputes'. Protracted negotiations, divergent issue-specific interests, and negative expectations characterized the CSCE process between 1977-1985/86 (cf. Schlotter 1999). Issue linkage with MBFR was the force behind the genesis of the CSCE (cf. Haftendorn 2008). Internal contradictions are apparent as the principle of the 'indivisibility of security' clashes with the principle of 'sovereign equality'. Theoretically, every state under the CSCE could follow any sovereign policy which in turn could be interpreted by any other state as a violation of the 'indivisibility of security'. Bonn's decision to implement NATO's dual track policy is a good example.

TABLE 18

CSCE, QUESTIONS RELATING TO SECURITY IN EUROPE, DOCUMENT ON CON-
FIDENCE-BUILDING MEASURES AND CERTAIN ASPECTS OF SECURITY AND DIS-
ARMAMENT, 1975

Agreement	**Agreement 2: Conference on Security and Co-operation in Europe Final Act, Helsinki 1975: Questions relating to Security in Europe, Document on confidence-building measures and certain aspects of security and disarmament**
Attribution	CSBM cooperation cluster
Description	The Document on CBMs marks the starting point of the cooperation cluster on CSBMs of the C/OSCE. It is part of the CSCE Final Act and reflected the West's desire for more transparency in military relations. As regards its substance, the Document contains only a limited set of non-binding transparency rules.
Principles	<ul><li>strengthening of peace and security</li><li>strengthening of confidence</li><li>increasing stability in Europe</li><li>territorial integrity of States</li><li>sovereign equality</li><li>complementary nature of the political and military aspects of security</li><li>indivisibility of security in Europe</li><li>reciprocal measures</li></ul>
Norms	<ul><li>reducing the dangers of armed conflict</li><li>promoting disarmament</li><li>promoting military exchanges</li><li>further developing measures</li></ul>
Rules	<ul><li>voluntary stipulations</li><li>prior notification of major military maneuvers (>25,000)</li><li>territory of Europe plus adjoining sea area and air space</li><li>exchange of observers by invitation at military maneuvers at a voluntary basis</li><li>prior notification of major military movements</li><li>provide negotiations information to CSCE third parties</li></ul>
Decision-Making Procedures	<ul><li>see CSCE Final Act</li></ul>

Indicators of Regime Decay, Period 1973-1989	non-compliance, protracted negotiations, negative expectations, divergent issue-specific interests, internal contradictions
Evidence for Regime Decay, Period 1973-1989	During the period 1973-1989, non-compliance occurred with regards to the non-promotion of disarmament until the end of the Stockholm CDE in 1986. Protracted negotiations with partially negative expectations and divergent issue-specific interests characterized the CBM process until 1986 (cf. Ropers and Schlotter 1989: 320). Internal contradictions are present with the 'sovereign equality vs. indivisibility of security' contradiction.

TABLE 19

CSCE, STOCKHOLM DOCUMENT, 1986

Agreement	**Agreement 3: Document of the Stockholm Conference on CSBMs and Disarmament in Europe Convened in Accordance With the Relevant Provisions of the Concluding Document of the Madrid Meeting of the CSCE, 1984-1986**
Attribution	CSBM cooperation cluster
Description	The 1986 Stockholm Document builds on the stipulations of the 1975 Helsinki CBM Document. Its central aim was extending and further concretizing the Helsinki provisions, particularly through means of intrusive inspections. It marks the transition from the phase of erratic CBMs of small scale to a full-fledged cooperation cluster with complementary provisions and came into being by a fundamental change in survival-related interest on the Soviet side towards more cooperation with the West.
Principles	• strengthening peace, security, and confidence • territorial integrity of States • refraining from the threat or use of force • sovereign equality • peaceful settlement of disputes • prevent and combat terrorism • compliance • reciprocal measures

Norms	• reducing the dangers of armed conflict • promoting disarmament • further developing measures • compliance
Rules	• politically binding • territory of Europe plus adjoining sea area and air space • prior notification of military activities (>13,000 troops and further specific provisions) • specification of information given • observation of military activities (>7,000) through observers • provide prior specific information to observers • exchange of annual calendars of military activities • constraining military activities (>40,000) • national technical means allowed for monitoring • specification of inspections
Decision-Making Procedures	• reference to Vienna CSCE Follow-up Meeting • consideration of all topics deemed relevant
Indicators of Regime Decay, Period 1973-1989	--
Evidence for Regime Decay, Period 1973-1989	--

TABLE 20

EVALUATION OF PERIOD 1973-1989

Number of Agreements	Indicators of Regime Decay Pertaining to Agreements Concluded in 1975-1989	Ratio of Indicators of Regime Decay Per Agreement Concluded in 1975-1989	Indicators of Regime Decay Pertaining to Agreements Concluded Before 1975	Overall Number of Indicators of Decay in 1975-1989
3	11	3.66	--	11

Evidence for Indicators of Regime Decay Pertaining to Agreements Concluded Before 1975	There is no evidence for indicators of regime decay pertaining to agreements concluded before the period of 1975-1989.

Of the three agreements concluded in 1975-1989, two can be easily attributed to one of the four cooperation clusters identified above. The 1975 Document on confidence-building measures and the 1986 Stockholm Document kick-start the cooperation cluster on CSBMs. The 1975 Helsinki Final Act cannot be clearly attributed to one of the four cooperation clusters. All agreements show a high ratio of indicators of regime decay per agreement (3.66), with the specific indicator of inconsistent behavior sticking out.

TABLE 21

CSCE, CHARTER OF PARIS, 1990

Agreement	**Agreement 4: Charter of Paris for a New Europe**
Attribution	--
Description	The 1990 Charter of Paris recalls and renews the Helsinki Decalogue. It formally ends the Cold War and states the goal of a Europe free from dividing lines. Its aim is to set the standards of security and cooperation after the bloc confrontation. Besides its reaffirmation of principles and norms, the Charter contains a large amount of concrete decision-making procedures for the further CSCE process.
Principles	• refraining from the threat or use of force • territorial integrity of States • sovereign equality • peaceful settlement of disputes • indivisibility of security • commitment to peace, security, and justice • cooperation among States
Norms	• promoting arms control and disarmament • developing mechanisms for the prevention and resolution of conflicts
Rules	--
Decision-Making Procedures	• CSCE Follow-up Meeting in 1992, then every two years • annual Council meeting of Ministers of Foreign Affairs • establishment of Committee of Senior Officials • establishment of a Secretariat in Prague • creation of Conflict Prevention Centre (CPC) in Vienna • establishment of an Office for Free Elections in Warsaw • intended creation of a CSCE parliamentary assembly • financial arrangements
Indicators of Regime Decay, Period 1990-1994	non-compliance, issue linkage, shifts in relative capabilities, inequitable distribution of gains, divergent issue-specific interests, internal contradictions

Evidence for Regime Decay, Period 1990-1994	During the period 1990-1994, non-compliance occurred during the First Chechen War and the Balkan Wars as both cases were instances of the violation of the principle of 'peaceful settlement of disputes'. Shifts in relative capabilities and the Russian perception of the inequitable distribution of gains shaped the CSCE process during those years (cf. Ghébali 2005). Divergent issue-specific interests between the United States and Russia prevailed with a view to the further role and the institutional framework of the CSCE process. Issue linkage was apparent in the evolution and the subsequent organizational upgrade of the CSCE being linked by Washington to maintaining NATO. Internal contradictions are apparent in the 'sovereign equality vs. indivisibility of security' contradiction.

TABLE 22

CSCE, VIENNA DOCUMENT, 1990

Agreement	**Agreement 5: Vienna Document 1990 of the Negotiations on Confidence- and Security-Building Measures Convened in Accordance with the Relevant Provisions of the Concluding Document of the Vienna Meeting of the CSCE**
Attribution	CSBM cooperation cluster
Description	The Vienna Document 1990 takes significantly forward and broadens CSBM stipulations of the Helsinki and Stockholm Documents. Its aim is to strengthen transparency and predictability after the end of the Cold War.
Principles	• strengthening confidence and security • achieving disarmament • refraining from the threat or use of force
Norms	• further developing measures
Rules	• politically binding • annual exchange of military information, annual calendars • information on the plans for the deployment of major weapon and equipment systems • information on military budgets • mechanism for consultation and cooperation as regards unusual military activities • cooperation on hazardous incidents of a military nature • rules for military contacts

	• prior notification of certain military activities • observation of certain military activities • specific constraining provisions • compliance and verification rules • evaluations and communications rules
Decision-Making Procedures	• annual implementation assessment meeting (AIAM)
Indicators of Regime Decay, Period 1990-1994	--
Evidence for Regime Decay, Period 1990-1994	--

TABLE 23

TREATY ON CONVENTIONAL ARMED FORCES IN EUROPE, 1990

Agreement	**Agreement 6: Treaty on Conventional Armed Forces in Europe**
Attribution	CAC cooperation cluster
Description	The CFE Treaty of 1990 establishes parity in conventional armed forces on significantly lower levels between the two blocs. It is built on a zonal system of concentric circles aimed at disentangling the troop concentrations in Central Europe. Established in five categories of conventional armaments, special limitation zones to the very North and South deprive the former antagonists of their ability to launch large-scale offensive action and surprise attacks. After the unsuccessful MBFR experience, CFE marks the laying of the foundation stone of the cooperation cluster on conventional arms control in Europe. During the following years, the cluster gained its full shape through the supporting agreements of CFE-1A, the Treaty on Open Skies, and the Adapted CFE Treaty of 1999.
Principles	• territorial integrity of States • refraining from the threat or use of force • prevent military conflict • strengthen stability and security in Europe

194

	• peaceful cooperation • balance of forces at lower levels • eliminating the capability for launching surprise attack and for initiating large-scale offensive action in Europe • sovereign equality • indivisibility of security
Norms	• further developing measures
Rules	• legally binding • specification of treaty-limited equipment (TLE) • TLE not to exceed 40,000 battle tanks, 60,000 armored combat vehicles, 40,000 pieces of artillery, 13,600 combat aircraft, and 4,000 attack helicopters • Protocol on Existing Types • sufficiency rule • NATO-WTO balance of forces • ATTU area, concentric regional zones, TUR exclusion zone • specific rules of holdings, flank rule • host nation consent rule • verification, notification, destruction, and storage rules
Decision-Making Procedures	• establishment of a Joint Consultative Group • consensus rule • review conferences every five years
Indicators of Regime Decay, Period 1990-1994	non-compliance, issue linkage, internal contradictions
Evidence for Regime Decay, Period 1990-1994	During the period 1990-1994, non-compliance occurred with Russia violating CFE ceilings in the so called Southern Flank (cf. Kühn 2009: 4). Those violations were nevertheless openly communicated by the Russian government in conjunction with the First Chechen War (see Letter of President Yeltsin to German Chancellor Kohl from September 17, 1993, in Hartmann et al 2002: 701-4). Issue linkage shaped CFE's genesis with economic aid to the Soviet Union being linked to Russian forces withdrawal from Eastern Europe (cf. Gorbachev 1996: 502). The deal resulted in the inequitable distribution of gains (see Table 10). Internal contradictions are apparent in the 'sovereign equality vs. indivisibility of security' contradiction.

TABLE 24

NATO, NORTH ATLANTIC COOPERATION COUNCIL, 1991

Agreement	**Agreement 7: North Atlantic Cooperation Council Statement on Dialogue, Partnership and Cooperation, 1991**
Attribution	NATO pol-mil cooperation cluster
Description	The establishment of the NACC in 1991 marks the beginning of NATO's adaptation to the post-Cold War era after the 1990 NATO London Summit. It provided NATO with an institutionalized framework for political-military cooperation with the countries of Central and Eastern Europe. The NACC depicts the nucleus of the evolving cooperation cluster of political and military cooperation under the auspices of NATO.
Principles	• strengthening peace and security in Europe • promoting stability in Central and Eastern Europe • indivisibility of security • sovereign equality • principle of sufficiency in arms
Norms	• building partnership among the North Atlantic Alliance and the countries of Central and Eastern Europe • strengthening the role of the CSCE, recalling CSCE principles • strengthening non-proliferation
Rules	• focus of consultations and cooperation on defense planning, conceptual approaches to arms control, democratic concepts of civilian-military relations, civil-military coordination of air traffic management, and conversion of defense production to civilian purposes
Decision-Making Procedures	• establishment of NACC • annual meetings with the North Atlantic Council at Ministerial level • bi-monthly meetings of the North Atlantic Council with liaison partners at the Ambassadorial level • additional NACC meetings at Ministerial level or of the North Atlantic Council in permanent session with Ambassadors of liaison partners • meetings at regular intervals of NATO subordinate committees with representatives of liaison partners

Indicators of Regime Decay, Period 1990-1994	shifts in relative capabilities, divergent issue-specific interests, issue linkage, inequitable distribution of gains, internal contradictions,
Evidence for Regime Decay, Period 1990-1994	During the period 1990-1994, indicators of regime decay are apparent in shifts in relative capabilities and the subsequent Russian perception of the inequitable distribution of gains in conjunction to issue linkage. As explained above, NATO's further maintenance was linked to an upgrade of the CSCE with Washington securing its preferred issue-specific interest. Divergent issue-specific interests between Moscow and Washington were thus present. Internal contradictions apply to the 'sovereign equality vs. indivisibility of security' contradiction.

TABLE 25

CSCE, VIENNA DOCUMENT, 1992

Agreement	**Agreement 8: Vienna Document 1992 of the Negotiations on Confidence- and Security-Building Measures Convened in Accordance with the Relevant Provisions of the Concluding Document of the Vienna Meeting of the CSCE, 1992**
Attribution	CSBM cooperation cluster
Description	The Vienna Document 1992 enhances and deepens the provisions of its predecessor. It contains a number of new regulations such as the voluntary hosting of visits to dispel concerns about military activities and the demonstration of new types of major weapon and equipment systems.
Principles	• strengthening confidence and security • achieving disarmament • refraining from the threat or use of force
Norms	• further developing measures
Rules	• politically binding • annual exchange of military information, annual calendars • information on the plans for the deployment of major weapon and equipment systems • information on military budgets • mechanism for consultation and cooperation as regards unusual military activities

197

	• cooperation on hazardous incidents of a military nature • voluntary hosting of visits to dispel concerns about military activities • rules for military contacts • demonstration of new types of major weapon and equipment systems • prior notification of certain military activities • observation of certain military activities • specific constraining provisions • compliance and verification rules • evaluations and communications rules
Decision-Making Procedures	• AIAM • CPC serves as the forum for meetings
Indicators of Regime Decay, Period 1990-1994	--
Evidence for Regime Decay, Period 1990-1994	--

TABLE 26

TREATY ON OPEN SKIES, 1992

Agreement	**Agreement 9: Treaty on Open Skies, 1992**
Attribution	CAC cooperation cluster
Description	The 1992 Treaty on Open Skies establishes a system of unarmed aerial observation flights over the states parties' entire territory. It is designed to gather information about military forces and activities and is mainly being used for monitoring states' compliance with the provisions of the CFE Treaty. The treaty came into effect in 2002.
Principles	• promoting openness and transparency in military activities • enhancing stability • sovereign equality
Norms	• enhancing security by means of CSBMs

198

	• facilitating the monitoring of compliance with existing or future arms control agreements • strengthening the capacity for conflict prevention and crisis management
Rules	• legally binding • establishment of observation quotas • specification of sensors • designation of aircraft • provisions for the conduct of observation flights • requirements for mission planning • specific flight provisions • designation of personnel
Decision-Making Procedures	• establishment of the OSCC • consensus rule • review conferences every five years
Indicators of Regime Decay, Period 1990-1994	--
Evidence for Regime Decay, Period 1990-1994	--

TABLE 27

CFE-1A, 1992

Agreement	**Agreement 10: Concluding Act of the Negotiation on Personnel Strength of Conventional Armed Forces in Europe, 1992**
Attribution	CAC cooperation cluster
Description	The so called CFE-1A agreement originates in the stipulations of Article XVIII of the CFE Treaty 'to conclude an agreement […] to limit the personnel strength of [States Parties] conventional armed forces within the area of application.' Its stipulations are closely connected to those contained in CFE. As distinct from the 1989-90 CFE negotiations, the number of signatories to CFE-1A had increased significantly through the break-up of the Soviet Union. The agreement is of a politically binding nature and was initiated by Germany in

order to avoid being singularized as the only state with limits on military personnel through the stipulations of the so called Two Plus Four Agreement (Treaty on the Final Settlement With Respect to Germany). In contrast to CFE, the agreement was not adapted in 1999. The CFE suspensions by Russia (2007) and NATO (2012) are also pertaining to CFE-1A since the agreement's verification measures were carried out as parts of regular CFE inspections. The agreement is nevertheless formally in force.

Principles	• strengthening stability and security in Europe • sovereign equality
Norms	• further developing measures
Rules	• politically binding • sufficiency rule • specific national personnel limits • specific information exchange • specific stabilizing measures such as notification of increases • specific verification and evaluation measures
Decision-Making Procedures	• responsibility of the CFE Joint Consultative Group • review conferences every five years
Indicators of Regime Decay, Period 1990-1994	--
Evidence for Regime Decay, Period 1990-1994	--

TABLE 28

CSCE, SECTION V OF THE HELSINKI DOCUMENT, 1992

Agreement	**Agreement 11: Section V 'CSCE Forum for Security Cooperation', Helsinki Document 1992**
Attribution	CSBM cooperation cluster
Description	Section V of the 1992 CSCE Helsinki Document establishes the Forum for Security Cooperation (FSC) as the main responsible body for dealings with disarmament and CSBMs. The establishment of the FSC marks the beginning of the institutional adaptation process of the CSCE in the realm of cooperative arms control in Europe as a result of the end of the Cold War and the Balkan wars. A significant number of CSBMs were concluded in the FSC since its inception.
Principles	<ul><li>strengthening stability and security in Europe</li><li>sovereign equality</li><li>indivisibility of security</li><li>principle of sufficiency</li></ul>
Norms	<ul><li>establishing new negotiations on disarmament and confidence- and security-building</li><li>giving new impetus to conflict prevention</li><li>designing specific regional measures (border areas)</li><li>enhancing transparency</li><li>increasing predictability</li><li>supporting measures for non-proliferation and arms transfers</li><li>enhancing military contacts</li><li>enhancing verification measures</li><li>strengthening the CPC</li><li>further developing measures</li></ul>
Rules	--
Decision-Making Procedures	<ul><li>establishment of the FSC</li><li>establishment of a Special Committee and a Consultative Committee</li><li>an Executive Secretary will provide conference services to the two Committees</li></ul>
Indicators of Regime Decay, Period 1990-1994	internal contradictions

Evidence for Regime Decay, Period 1990-1994	Regime-internal contradictions are apparent in the 'sovereign equality vs. indivisibility of security' contradiction.

TABLE 29

CSCE, PROGRAMME FOR IMMEDIATE ACTION, 1992

Agreement	**Agreement 12: Programme for immediate action, Helsinki Document 1992**
Attribution	CSBM cooperation cluster
Description	The Programme for immediate action is an annex to Section V of the 1992 CSCE Helsinki Document. It complements the provisions of Section V and can be understood as a working program for the newly established FSC. It contains the rules that Section V did not outline. In the further CSCE process, it led to the establishment of eight CSBM agreements. The Programme was strongly influenced by the war in the former Yugoslavia.
Principles	--
Norms	--
Rules	<ul><li>harmonization of obligations concerning arms control, disarmament and confidence- and security-building</li><li>further development of the Vienna Document 1992</li><li>further enhancement of stability and confidence</li><li>global exchange of military information</li><li>enhancing cooperation on non-proliferation</li><li>developing regional measures</li><li>transparency about force planning</li><li>cooperation in defense conversion</li><li>further developing provisions on military cooperation and contacts</li><li>enhancing security consultations</li><li>encouraging verification cooperation</li></ul>
Decision-Making Procedures	--

Indicators of Regime Decay, Period 1990-1994	--
Evidence for Regime Decay, Period 1990-1994	--

TABLE 30

CSCE, PROGRAMME OF MILITARY CONTACTS AND CO-OPERATION, 1993

Agreement	**Agreement 13: Programme for Immediate Action Series, No. 1: Programme of Military Contacts and Co-operation, 1993**
Attribution	CSBM cooperation cluster
Description	The 1993 Programme of Military Contacts and Co-operation was the first agreement to develop from the 1992 CSCE Programme for Immediate Action. It governs military contacts with the aim of enhancing mutual knowledge and transparency about national forces on a voluntary basis.
Principles	--
Norms	--
Rules	<ul><li>politically binding</li><li>specific provisions to enhance military contacts at all levels</li><li>joint military exercises and training</li><li>visits to military facilities and to military formations</li><li>observation visits</li><li>provision of experts</li><li>seminars on cooperation in the military field</li><li>exchange of information on agreements on military contacts and cooperation</li></ul>
Decision-Making Procedures	<ul><li>Programme implementation assessed at AIAM</li></ul>

Indicators of Regime Decay, Period 1990-1994	--
Evidence for Regime Decay, Period 1990-1994	--

TABLE 31

CSCE, STABILIZING MEASURES FOR LOCALIZED CRISIS SITUATIONS, 1993

Agreement	**Agreement 14: Programme for Immediate Action Series, No. 2: Stabilizing Measures for Localized Crisis Situations, 1993**
Attribution	CSBM cooperation cluster
Description	The 1993 Stabilizing Measures for Localized Crisis Situations were amongst the responses of CSCE participating States to sub-regional conflicts on the Balkans and in the newly emerging CIS. The agreement establishes a catalogue of de-escalating rules of engagement for the military in localized crisis situations.
Principles	--
Norms	--
Rules	<ul><li>voluntary</li><li>identification of parties involved in a particular crisis situation does not affect their status</li><li>extraordinary information exchange</li><li>notification, constraints, and observation of certain military activities</li><li>notification of plans for acquisition and deployment of major weapon and equipment systems</li><li>introduction and support of a cease-fire</li><li>establishment of demilitarized zones</li><li>cessation of specific military flights</li><li>deactivation of certain weapon systems</li><li>specific treatment of irregular forces</li><li>handling of public statements</li><li>specific communications and experts measures</li></ul>

	• specific measures for monitoring of compliance and evaluation
Decision-Making Procedures	• specific selection of measures and their specific application based on the decision of the appropriate CSCE body and on the consensus rule • application requires prior consent and active support of the parties involved in a particular crisis situation
Indicators of Regime Decay, Period 1990-1994	--
Evidence for Regime Decay, Period 1990-1994	--

TABLE 32

CSCE, PRINCIPLES GOVERNING CONVENTIONAL ARMS TRANSFERS, 1993

Agreement	**Agreement 15: Programme for Immediate Action Series, No. 3: Principles Governing Conventional Arms Transfers, 1993**
Attribution	CSBM cooperation cluster
Description	The 1993 Principles Governing Conventional Arms Transfers focus on streamlining the different national approaches to the control of weapons and equipment transfer and CSCE participating States' cooperation in the field of export controls of conventional weapons.
Principles	• promoting peace and security with the least diversion for armaments of human and economic resources • recognition of the peace dividend
Norms	• adherence to transparency • restraint • prevention of excessive arms build-ups • streamlining national policies with CSCE criteria
Rules	• provision of national mechanisms

	• principled criteria for arms transfers
Decision-Making Procedures	• exchange of information in the FSC
Indicators of Regime Decay, Period 1990-1994	Adherence to the agreement's principles and norms itself is hard to judge as there is no clear and commonly agreed criteria to what 'the least diversion for armaments of human and economic resources' really means. The same pertains to the extent and the effects of the peace dividend. Particularly with respect to the peace dividend, the large military budgets of the United States and Russia (see Annex I) as well as the amount of arms exports of a number of C/OSCE partici- pating States (e.g. United States, Russia, Germany, and France) seem to collide with the agreement's reaffirmation 'that the reduction of world military expenditures could have a significant positive impact for the social and economic development of all peoples'.
Evidence for Regime Decay, Period 1990-1994	--

TABLE 33

CSCE, DEFENCE PLANNING, 1993

Agreement	**Agreement 16: Programme for Immediate Action Series, No. 4: Defence Planning, 1993**
Attribution	CSBM cooperation cluster
Description	The 1993 Defence Planning agreement addresses information ex- change of CSCE participating States' respective national defense planning and military doctrines.
Principles	--
Norms	--
Rules	• politically binding • provide annual information about defense policy, doctrine, force planning, previous expenditures, budgets • specific provisions for clarification, review, dialogue

Decision-Making Procedures	--
Indicators of Regime Decay, Period 1990-1994	--
Evidence for Regime Decay, Period 1990-1994	--

TABLE 34

CSCE, GLOBAL EXCHANGE OF MILITARY INFORMATION, 1994

Agreement	**Agreement 17: Programme for Immediate Action Series, No. 5: Global Exchange of Military Information, 1994**
Attribution	CSBM cooperation cluster
Description	The 1994 Global Exchange of Military Information regulates the annual exchange of information about CSCE participating States' major weapons and equipment systems and personnel in their conventional armed forces, on their territory as well as worldwide. The agreement is not subject to limitations, constraints, or verification.
Principles	--
Norms	--
Rules	<ul><li>politically binding</li><li>annual exchange of specific information about command structure and personnel with specific levels of disaggregation</li><li>annual exchange of specific information about holdings of major weapon and equipment systems and those newly entered into service</li><li>specific provisions for clarification</li><li>communications made in accordance with the VD 1994</li></ul>
Decision-Making Procedures	--

207

Indicators of Regime Decay, Period 1990-1994	--
Evidence for Regime Decay, Period 1990-1994	--

TABLE 35

CSCE, VIENNA DOCUMENT, 1994

Agreement	**Agreement 18: Programme for Immediate Action Series, No. 6: Vienna Document 1994 of the Negotiations on Confidence- and Security-Building Measures, 1994**
Attribution	CSBM cooperation cluster
Description	The VD 1994 takes forward stipulations of its predecessors and contains new regulations such as specific information on military forces, exchange of specific major weapons data, and a regular exchange of information on defense planning.
Principles	• strengthening confidence and security • achieving disarmament • refraining from the threat or use of force
Norms	--
Rules	• politically binding • annual exchange of military information, annual calendars • specific information on military forces • exchange of specific data relating to major weapon and equipment systems • information on the plans for the deployment of major weapon and equipment systems • exchange of information on defense planning • clarification, review, and dialogue on defense planning • mechanism for consultation and cooperation as regards unusual military activities • cooperation on hazardous incidents of a military nature • voluntary hosting of visits to dispel concerns about military activities

	• specific rules for military contacts • specific program on military contacts and cooperation • demonstration of new types of major weapon and equipment systems • prior notification of certain military activities • observation of certain military activities • specific constraining provisions • compliance and verification rules • evaluations and communications rules
Decision-Making Procedures	• AIAM and annual meeting on defense planning • establishment of a Communications Group • the Special Committee of the FSC will hold preparatory meetings for the AIAM
Indicators of Regime Decay, Period 1990-1994	--
Evidence for Regime Decay, Period 1990-1994	--

TABLE 36

CSCE, CODE OF CONDUCT ON POLITICO-MILITARY ASPECTS OF SECURITY, 1994

Agreement	**Agreement 19: Programme for Immediate Action Series, No. 7: Code of Conduct on Politico-Military Aspects of Security, 1994**
Attribution	CSBM cooperation cluster
Description	The 1994 Code of Conduct on Politico-Military Aspects of Security sets rules for national forces in relation to human rights and democracy. It combines various political and military aspects of inter- and intra-state security and proscribes principles for good conduct. It marks the peak in CSCE efforts to set common norms for the regulation and control of the national military.
Principles	• enhancing security cooperation

	• indivisibility of security • strengthening security and stability • sovereign equality • principle of sufficiency
Norms	• responsible and cooperative behavior in the field of security • further developing measures and institutions • act in solidarity if norms are violated • prevent and combat terrorism • commitment to conflict prevention • determining military capabilities on the basis of national democratic procedures • denial of imposition of military domination of one state over any other state • implementation and further pursuit of arms control, disarmament, and CSBMs • democratic political control of military, paramilitary, internal security forces, intelligence services, and the police • consistency of armed forces, defense policies, and doctrines with international legal provisions
Rules	• politically binding • host nation consent rule • early identification and effective cessation of hostilities • rules for the democratic conduct of military and other forces
Decision-Making Procedures	• if requested, a participating State will provide appropriate clarification regarding its implementation of the Code
Indicators of Regime Decay, Period 1990-1994	--
Evidence for Regime Decay, Period 1990-1994	--

TABLE 37

CSCE, PRINCIPLES GOVERNING NON-PROLIFERATION, 1994

Agreement	**Agreement 20: Programme for Immediate Action Series, No. 8: Principles Governing Non-Proliferation, 1994**
Attribution	CSBM cooperation cluster
Description	The 1994 Principles Governing Non-Proliferation focus on the prevention of the proliferation of weapons of mass destruction (WMD), the related control of the spread of missile technology, and other sensitive goods and technologies.
Principles	• proliferation of WMD and missiles poses a threat to international peace, security, and stability
Norms	• strengthen existing norms • full implementation of existing international obligations
Rules	• streamline national legislation with international commitments • promote international co-operative efforts to provide peaceful opportunities for weapons scientists and engineers • exchange information about national laws, regulations and practical measures
Decision-Making Procedures	• security dialogue within the FSC (including through seminars and working parties)
Indicators of Regime Decay, Period 1990-1994	--
Evidence for Regime Decay, Period 1990-1994	--

TABLE 38

NATO, PFP FRAMEWORK AGREEMENT AND INVITATION AGREEMENT, 1994

Agreement	**Agreement 21: Partnership for Peace: Framework Agreement and Invitation Agreement, 1994**
Attribution	NATO pol-mil cooperation cluster
Description	The 1994 Partnership for Peace (PfP) was the first far-reaching NATO initiative towards the East since the NACC in 1991. Its aim was keeping NATO at the center of European security issues and, at the same time, introducing a concrete cooperation framework for states interested in NATO membership. Furthermore, PfP helped to alleviate Russian concerns about NATO enlargement. The Framework Agreement and Invitation Agreement were amended by the Individual Partnership Programme.
Principles	<ul><li>enhancing security and stability in Europe</li><li>strengthening ties with the democratic states to the East</li><li>deepening political and military ties</li><li>refrain from the threat or use of force</li></ul>
Norms	<ul><li>commitment to the CSCE acquis</li><li>fulfillment of disarmament and arms control obligations</li><li>active participation in PfP as an important role in the process of NATO expansion</li><li>transparency in national defense planning and budgeting processes; exchange of information</li><li>ensuring democratic control of defense forces</li><li>maintenance of the capability and readiness to contribute to operations under UN and/or CSCE authority</li><li>development of cooperative military relations with NATO for specific purposes</li><li>long-term development of forces able to operate with NATO</li></ul>
Rules	<ul><li>provision of a country-specific Presentation Agreement, followed by a program of partnership exercises and the development of an individual Partnership Programme and a corresponding liaison office with NATO Headquarters</li><li>specific funding provisions</li><li>access to NATO technical data</li><li>review, evaluation, direction, and guidance processes</li></ul>

Decision-Making Procedures	--
Indicators of Regime Decay, Period 1990-1994	shifts in relative capabilities, divergent issue-specific interests, inequitable distribution of gains, issue linkage
Evidence for Regime Decay, Period 1990-1994	During the period 1990-1994, indicators of regime decay are apparent: shifts in relative capabilities, divergent issue-specific interests, and the Russian perception of the inequitable distribution of gains shaped the genesis of the PfP initiative as Washington pushed through its preferred issue-specific interest of NATO maintenance and enlargement against the Russian issue-specific interest to derail enlargement (cf. Ponsard 2007: 68). Issue linkage occurred in conjunction to the upgrade of the CSCE and its instruments.

TABLE 39

EVALUATION OF PERIOD 1990-1994

Number of Agreements	Indicators of Regime Decay Pertaining to Agreements Concluded in 1990-1994	Ratio of Indicators of Regime Decay Per Agreement Concluded in 1990-1994	Indicators of Regime Decay Pertaining to Agreements Concluded Before 1990	Overall Number of Indicators of Decay in 1990-1994
18	18	1.0	--	18

Evidence for Indicators of Regime Decay Pertaining to Agreements Concluded Before 1990	There is no evidence for indicators of regime decay pertaining to agreements concluded before the period of 1990-1994.

The short period of 1990-1994 produced an impressive number of 18 agreements. Most of the agreements in that period pertain to the CSBM cooperation cluster. The CAC cooperation cluster took off in 1990 with the conclusion of CFE; further supporting instruments followed in the ensuing years. With the 1991 North Atlantic Cooperation Council Statement on Dialogue, Partnership and Cooperation, also the NATO pol-mil cooperation cluster started to gain shape. The ratio of indicators of regime decay per agreement (1.05) is comparably low in the period of 1990-1994, particularly when compared to the previous period. Indicators of regime decay are rather diverse and pertain to a lesser degree to instances of non-compliance. This fact is, however, also owed to the circumstance that a critical number of agreements were only concluded at the end of this period. Possible instances of non-compliance before the agreements' conclusion can thus not be counted. A certain consistency between the two periods can be traced, as there are no indicators of regime decay pertaining to agreements concluded before 1990. This leads to infer that the stipulations before 1990 had either lost their validity or were still mostly observed.

5.4   Agreements, Period 1995-1999

TABLE 40

OSCE, A FRAMEWORK FOR ARMS CONTROL, 1996

Agreement	**Agreement 22: A Framework for Arms Control, Lisbon Document, 1996**
Attribution	CSBM cooperation cluster
Description	The 1996 OSCE Framework sets a standardized guidance for deepening and enhancing the OSCE arms control acquis. It recalls principles and prescribes goals and methods for further developing measures. It stresses the already existing 'basis for a web of interlocking and mutually-reinforcing agreements'.
Principles	• arms control, disarmament, and CSBMs integral to the OSCE's comprehensive and co-operative concept of security • enhancing military and political stability • strengthening co-operation, transparency, and predictability • complementarity between OSCE-wide and regional approaches • indivisibility of security • sovereign equality

Norms	• full implementation and further development of arms control agreements • developing new ways to deal with security concerns
Rules	• creation of a web of interlocking and mutually reinforcing arms control obligations and commitments • addressing concrete challenges and risks such as military imbalances, inter-State tensions and conflicts, internal disputes, and non-transparency • sufficiency rule • transparency through information exchange • verification • limitations on forces, constraints on military activities • evaluation of the effectiveness of existing measures • devising concrete and practical measures to reduce regional instability and military imbalances • devising arms control measures for stabilizing specific crisis situations • enhancing transparency of instruments with respect to non-signatories
Decision-Making Procedures	• key role for the FSC
Indicators of Regime Decay, Period 1995-1999	shifts in relative capabilities, divergent issue-specific interests, inequitable distribution of gains, issue linkage, internal contradictions
Evidence for Regime Decay, Period 1995-1999	During the period 1995-1999, indicators of regime decay are apparent. As part of the upgrade and further evolution of the OSCE, the agreement is an indirect product of the issue linkage between the further development of the OSCE and NATO enlargement. As described in Chapter 3, this process was characterized by shifts in relative capabilities, divergent issue-specific interests, and the Russian perception of the inequitable distribution of gains. Internal contradictions are apparent in the 'sovereign equality vs. indivisibility of security' contradiction.

TABLE 41

BOSNIA AND HERZEGOVINA, FEDERATION OF BOSNIA AND HERZEGOVINA, REPUBLIKA SRPSKA, AGREEMENT ON CONFIDENCE- AND SECURITY-BUILDING MEASURES IN BOSNIA AND HERZEGOVINA, 1996

Agreement	**Agreement 23: Agreement on Confidence- and Security-Building Measures in Bosnia and Herzegovina, 1996**
Attribution	Balkans cooperation cluster
Description	The 1995 General Framework Agreement for Peace in Bosnia and Herzegovina (Dayton Peace Agreement) committed the signatories to the 'establishment of progressive measures for regional stability and arms control'. 'Annex 1-B: Agreement on Regional Stabilization' of the Dayton accords binds parties in Article II to agree on a series of CSBMs under the auspices of the OSCE and to develop 'Measures for Sub-Regional Arms Control' (Article IV). The resulting two agreements are the first and only purely sub-regional CSBM and arms control agreements under the auspices of the OSCE. The 1996 CSBM agreement in Bosnia and Herzegovina was negotiated amongst the three internal war parties. It is designed along the lines of the VD and takes significantly forward VD provisions.
Principles	--
Norms	--
Rules	<ul><li>definitions of military equipment and force structures</li><li>exchange of information</li><li>data exchange relating to major weapon and equipment systems</li><li>demonstration of new types of major weapon and equipment systems</li><li>information on plans for the deployment of major weapon and equipment systems</li><li>information on defense related matters</li><li>notification of changes in command structure or equipment holdings</li><li>mechanism for consultation and cooperation as regards unusual military activities</li><li>cooperation as regards hazardous incidents of a military nature</li><li>notification and observation of and constraints on certain military activities</li><li>restrictions on military deployments and exercises in certain geographic areas</li><li>restraints on the reintroduction of foreign forces</li></ul>

	• measures on withdrawal of forces and heavy weapons to cantonments/barracks or other designated areas • restrictions on locations of heavy weapons • notification of disbandment of special operations and armed civilian groups • identification and monitoring of weapons manufacturing capabilities • special program of military contacts and co-operation • principles governing non-proliferation • verification and inspection regime • specific communications
Decision-Making Procedures	• creation of a Joint Consultative Commission • inclusion of the Personal Representative • consensus rule • review process at least once every two years
Indicators of Regime Decay, Period 1995-1999	--
Evidence for Regime Decay, Period 1995-1999	--

TABLE 42

BOSNIA AND HERZEGOVINA, THE REPUBLIC OF CROATIA, THE FEDERAL REPUBLIC OF YUGOSLAVIA, THE FEDERATION OF BOSNIA AND HERZEGOVINA, REPUBLIKA SRPSKA, AGREEMENT ON SUB-REGIONAL ARMS CONTROL, ARTICLE IV, 1996

Agreement	**Agreement 24: Agreement on Sub-Regional Arms Control, Article IV, 1996**
Attribution	Balkans cooperation cluster
Description	The 1996 Agreement on Sub-Regional Arms Control, Article IV (Florence Agreement) is the second agreement originating in the Dayton accords. Negotiated under the auspices of the OSCE amongst the former Yugoslav war parties, the agreement incorporates measures designed under the CFE Treaty, such as TLE categories and force limitations based on the principle of sufficiency. Together with the

217

principles of the Dayton Peace agreement and the stipulations of the 1996 Agreement on CSBMs, the Agreement on Sub-Regional Arms Control forms the foundation of a cooperation cluster on sub-regional CSBM and disarmament stipulations for the Balkans.

Principles	<ul><li>establishment of measures for regional security essential to creating a stable peace in the region</li><li>principle of sufficiency</li><li>avoid an arms race in the region</li><li>achieving greater stability and security in the region</li></ul>
Norms	<ul><li>building transparency and confidence</li><li>achieving balanced and stable defense force levels</li></ul>
Rules	<ul><li>CFE weapons categories</li><li>definitions of geography, military equipment, and force structures</li><li>specific counting rules</li><li>specific limitations and reduction periods</li><li>specific rules for armaments export</li><li>specific rules for decommissioned armaments</li><li>specific provisions for exchange of information and notifications</li><li>specific inspection provisions</li><li>specific counting rules for armored infantry fighting vehicles of internal security forces</li></ul>
Decision-Making Procedures	<ul><li>creation of a Sub-Regional Consultative Commission</li><li>inclusion of the Personal Representative</li><li>consensus rule</li><li>review process at least once every two years</li></ul>
Indicators of Regime Decay, Period 1995-1999	--
Evidence for Regime Decay, Period 1995-1999	--

TABLE 43

NATO, RUSSIA, FOUNDING ACT ON MUTUAL RELATIONS, COOPERATION AND SECURITY BETWEEN NATO AND THE RUSSIAN FEDERATION, 1997

Agreement	**Agreement 25: Founding Act on Mutual Relations, Cooperation and Security between NATO and the Russian Federation, 1997**
Attribution	NATO pol-mil cooperation cluster
Description	The 1997 NATO-Russia Founding Act is both, the recognition of a genuinely new and cordial relationship between NATO and Russia and the first expression of new competing issue-specific interests in the European security sphere. The need to give expression to this "special" relationship emerged out of the quarrels surrounding NATO enlargement. In order to cushion Russian concerns, NATO member states, led by Washington, offered Moscow a number of accommodating deals, amongst them the Founding Act. The Act lists a number of general principles and establishes the PJC. The PJC's mandate was to consult on a wide range of areas, amongst them conflict prevention, joint operations, arms control, possible cooperation on BMD, and non-proliferation efforts. Beyond that, the Founding Act declares the mutual commitment to a number of specific political-military rules. The institutional deficiencies of the PJC, conveyed in the wake of the Kosovo War, led to the subsequent creation of the NRC. The NATO-Russia Founding Act is an integral part of the multilateral cooperation cluster on political and military cooperation under the auspices of NATO, even though it is only directed at one partner nation: Russia.
Principles	<ul><li>building a lasting, stable, peaceful, inclusive, undivided Euro-Atlantic area based on democracy, cooperative security, non-inimical relationship</li><li>overcoming earlier confrontation and competition</li><li>strengthening mutual trust and cooperation</li><li>partnership based on common issue-specific interest, reciprocity, and transparency</li><li>indivisibility of security</li><li>sovereign equality</li><li>acknowledging the vital role of democracy, political pluralism, rule of law, human rights, free market economies</li><li>refraining from the threat or use of force</li></ul>
Norms	<ul><li>strengthening the OSCE</li><li>mutual transparency in creating and implementing defense policy and military doctrines</li><li>commitment to conflict prevention</li><li>support of peacekeeping operations</li><li>improving arms control regimes and CSBMs</li></ul>

Rules	• PJC built upon reciprocity and transparency • specific areas for consultation and cooperation in the PJC • intention of non-deployment of nuclear weapons and storage sites of NATO on new members' territories • commitment to adapt CFE, including lowering total amount of TLE and commitment to CFE sufficiency rule • NATO pledge not to station additional permanent substantial combat forces; Russia pledges similar restraint • expanding political-military consultations and cooperation through the PJC • implementing a program of enhanced military-to-military dialogue • reciprocal briefings on NATO and Russian military doctrine, strategy and resultant force posture • further development of a concept for joint NATO-Russia peace-keeping operations
Decision-Making Procedures	• creation of the PJC • consensus rule • consultations will not extend to internal matters of either NATO, NATO member States, or Russia • establishment of Russian Mission to NATO
Indicators of Regime Decay, Period 1995-1999	shifts in relative capabilities, divergent issue-specific interests, inequitable distribution of gains, issue linkage, negative expectations, non-compliance, internal contradictions
Evidence for Regime Decay, Period 1995-1999	During the period 1995-1999, indicators of regime decay are apparent. As with the PfP framework, the Founding Act was part of a larger deal of issue linkages which occurred with the looming NATO enlargement. As outlined in Paragraph 3.4.1, shifts in relative capabilities shaped its evolution and divergent issue-specific interests as well as the Russian perception of the inequitable distribution of gains were behind the design of Europe' security architecture which gained its full shape during those years. Negative expectations about the further cooperation process in the PJC occurred on the Russian side in conjunction with the Kosovo War (cf. Kupchan 2000: 132). Non-compliance with principles and norms occurred with the violation of the principle to build an 'inclusive' and 'undivided' Euro-Atlantic area, as NATO's expansion was seen as "drawing lines" by both, U.S. and Russian policy makers and analysts (cf. Solomon 1996, Zagorski 2011: 32). Also the norm of 'commitment to conflict prevention' was violated by Russia with the beginning of the Second Chechen War in late 1999. Internal contradictions are apparent in the 'sovereign equality vs. indivisibility of security' contradiction.

TABLE 44

NATO, PFP STATES, BASIC AGREEMENT OF THE EURO-ATLANTIC PARTNERSHIP COUNCIL, 1997

Agreement	**Agreement 26: Basic Agreement of the Euro-Atlantic Partnership Council, 1997**
Attribution	NATO pol-mil cooperation cluster
Description	The establishment of the EAPC as the successor to the NACC happened against the background of NATO's eastward enlargement and the concurrent establishment of the Founding Act and the PJC. The EAPC was established to provide the overarching framework for consultations amongst its members 'on a broad range of political and security-related issues', including PfP activities and matters. The Basic Agreement of the EAPC can be understood as the working program for the newly established EAPC and does thus contain only a limited number of principles but a broad body of rules on what issues to engage in the EAPC.
Principles	• strengthening and extending peace and stability in the Euro-Atlantic area • inclusive • self-differentiation in members' levels and areas of cooperation with NATO
Norms	--
Rules	• specific areas for consultation and cooperation in the EAPC (crisis management; regional matters; arms control issues; nuclear, WMD proliferation; international terrorism; defense planning and budgets; defense policy and strategy; security impacts of economic developments; civil emergency and disaster preparedness; armaments cooperation; nuclear safety; civil-military coordination of air traffic management and control; scientific cooperation; peace support operations)
Decision-Making Procedures	• creation of the EAPC • open to accession of other OSCE participating States • EAPC meetings in different formats ranging from plenary over limited to individual sessions • EAPC meetings on different levels ranging from Ambassadorial to Heads of State or Government sessions • SG chairs • Regular support by the Political-Military Steering Committee

	(PMSC) and the Political Committee (PC)
Indicators of Regime Decay, Period 1995-1999	shifts in relative capabilities, divergent issue-specific interests, inequitable distribution of gains, issue linkage, negative expectations, non-compliance
Evidence for Regime Decay, Period 1995-1999	During the period 1995-1999, indicators of regime decay appear with regards to the underlying political developments in the Euro-Atlantic area as outlined above (see Table 42). Non-compliance occurred with the violation of the principle of 'strengthening and extending peace and stability in the Euro-Atlantic area' in the North Caucasus from 1999 onwards.

TABLE 45

AGREEMENT ON ADAPTATION OF THE TREATY ON CONVENTIONAL ARMED FORCES IN EUROPE, 1999

Agreement	**Agreement 27: Agreement on Adaptation of the Treaty on Conventional Armed Forces in Europe, 1999**
Attribution	CAC cooperation cluster
Description	The 1999 ACFE Treaty adapts the CFE Treaty to the changed security constellation of the late 1990s. Adaptation of the treaty was requested by Russia to take account of NATO enlargement. The agreement also served the political purpose of easing Russian reservations. Accompanying the legally binding ACFE, the Istanbul Summit Declaration (Art. 19), the Final Act of the Conference of the States Parties to the Treaty on Conventional Armed Forces in Europe, and its annexes contain the so-called Istanbul commitments which became widely associated almost exclusively with the Russian politically binding pledges to withdraw excess forces and equipment from Moldova and Georgia. In 2002, NATO member states made ACFE ratification contingent upon the fulfillment of Russia's commitments, which Russia, in turn, used as justification for unilaterally suspending CFE in 2007.
Principles	• sustaining the key role of CFE as the cornerstone of European security • territorial integrity of States • refraining from the threat or use of force • prevent military conflict • strengthen stability and security in Europe

222

	<ul><li>peaceful cooperation</li><li>indivisibility of security</li><li>secure, stable and balanced overall level of conventional armed forces in Europe lower than heretofore</li><li>eliminating disparities and the capability for launching surprise attack and for initiating large-scale offensive action in Europe</li></ul>
Norms	<ul><li>further developing measures</li></ul>
Rules	<ul><li>internationally binding provisions</li><li>retaining TLE types</li><li>retaining ATTU area</li><li>retaining host nation consent rule</li><li>opening the treaty for accession on a case-by-case basis for states within the ATTU area</li><li>system of national and territorial ceilings for individual State Parties</li><li>specific rules for basic and exceptional temporary deployments</li><li>abolishment of CFE's concentric zones in the center of Europe and of the sufficiency rule</li><li>maintenance of the flank provisions as contained in the Flank Agreement</li><li>increased reporting requirements and on-site inspections</li><li>mandatory notification of the transit of major weapons</li></ul>
Decision-Making Procedures	<ul><li>retained from CFE Treaty</li></ul>
Indicators of Regime Decay, Period 1995-1999	shifts in relative capabilities, divergent issue-specific interests, inequitable distribution of gains, issue linkage, negative adaptation consequences, non-compliance
Evidence for Regime Decay, Period 1995-1999	During the period 1995-1999, indicators of regime decay appear with regards to shifts in relative capabilities and divergent issue-specific interests between the United States and Russia. Moscow saw the adaptation of the treaty above all as a means to address NATO's conventional superiority in Europe while Washington viewed CFE adaptation as a chance to cushion Russian disagreement with NATO enlargement. Issue linkage shaped ACFE's genesis with NATO enlargement being linked to adaptation of CFE. This deal resulted in the Russian perception of the inequitable distribution of gains to Moscow's detriment. Also negative adaptation consequences came to the fore with a U.S. amendment to the CFE Flank Agreement triggering the inclusion of the Russian Istanbul commitments (cf. Kühn 2009). Non-compliance occurred with Russian actions in Chechnya violating the principle of 'prevention of military conflict' and with NATO's eastward enlargement violating the principle of the 'indivisibility of security' – at least in Moscow's view.

TABLE 46

OSCE, VIENNA DOCUMENT, 1999

Agreement	**Agreement 28: Vienna Document 1999 on the Negotiations on Confidence- and Security-Building Measures, Istanbul Document, 1999**
Attribution	CSBM cooperation cluster
Description	The 1999 Vienna Document takes forward the stipulations of its predecessors, particularly through a new set of regional measures in response to the Balkan wars.
Principles	• strengthening confidence and security • achieving disarmament • refraining from the threat or use of force
Norms	--
Rules	• politically binding • annual exchange of military information, annual calendars • specific information on military forces • exchange of specific data relating to major weapon and equipment systems • information on the plans for the deployment of major weapon and equipment systems • exchange of information on defense planning • clarification, review, and dialogue on defense planning and possible additional information • mechanism for consultation and cooperation as regards unusual military activities • cooperation on hazardous incidents of a military nature • voluntary hosting of visits to dispel concerns about military activities • specific rules for military contacts • specific program on military contacts and cooperation • demonstration of new types of major weapon and equipment systems • prior notification of certain military activities • observation of certain military activities • specific constraining provisions • compliance and verification rules • evaluations and communications rules • specific regional measures

Decision-Making Procedures	• AIAM • use of OSCE Communications Network for transmission of messages
Indicators of Regime Decay, Period 1995-1999	--
Evidence for Regime Decay, Period 1995-1999	--

TABLE 47

OSCE, OPERATIONAL DOCUMENT - THE PLATFORM FOR CO-OPERATIVE SECURITY, 1999

Agreement	**Agreement 29: Operational Document - the Platform for Co-operative Security, Istanbul Document, 1999**
Attribution	--
Description	The 1999 Operational Document establishes the Platform for Co-operative Security. Its aim is to provide principles and modalities for cooperation amongst 'those organizations and institutions concerned with the promotion of comprehensive security within the OSCE area.' The Platform's principles and norms claim validity for both the OSCE and cooperating organizations and institutions. The Platform agreement is part of a package of new agreements of the OSCE at the end of the 1990s in order to adapt OSCE institutions to the changing security realities in Europe, meaning NATO enlargement.
Principles	• strengthening inter-organizational relationship
Norms	• adherence to C/OSCE principles and commitments • implementation of arms control, disarmament, and CSBM obligations • institutional transparency • institutional inclusiveness • active support of OSCE's concept of common, comprehensive, and indivisible security

Rules	• institutional readiness to support OSCE's work, particularly conflict prevention and crisis management • subscription to VD principles • transparency in OSCE's contacts and cooperation with other security organizations • use of specific instruments and mechanisms (regular contacts, including meetings; a continuous framework for dialogue; increased transparency and practical co-operation, including the identification of liaison officers or points of contact; cross-representation at appropriate meetings; and other contacts intended to increase understanding of each organization's conflict prevention tools) • development of cooperation on OSCE field operations • enhanced inter-organizational cooperation and information exchange in response to crises situations • avoidance of institutional duplication and fostering of efficient use of available resources
Decision-Making Procedures	• Chairman-in-Office to consult with participating States on process of offering OSCE as a framework for cooperation • SG to prepare annual report on relevant interactions
Indicators of Regime Decay, Period 1995-1999	shifts in relative capabilities, divergent issue-specific interests, inequitable distribution of gains, issue linkage, internal contradictions
Evidence for Regime Decay, Period 1995-1999	During the period 1995-1999, indicators of regime decay are apparent because the Platform Document was the product of a cross issue linkage between adapting the OSCE and the CFE Treaty, establishing the NATO-Russia Founding Act, and enlarging NATO. As explained above, shifts in relative capabilities, divergent issue-specific interests, and the Russian perception of the inequitable distribution of gains characterized this process. Internal contradictions occur with the norm of 'institutional inclusiveness' standing in contrast to NATO's organizational nature which is per se designed to be exclusive towards non-signatories of the Washington Treaty. Also, the norm of 'adherence to C/OSCE principles and commitments' is a general recognition of principles and recalls thus the internal contradiction of 'sovereign equality vs. indivisibility of security', even though in a clandestine manner.

TABLE 48

OSCE, CHARTER FOR EUROPEAN SECURITY, 1999

Agreement	**Agreement 30: Charter for European Security, 1999**
Attribution	--
Description	The 1999 OSCE Charter for European Security carries forward the OSCE acquis in all three security dimensions. It should be seen in a continuing line with the Helsinki Decalogue and the Charter of Paris. It symbolizes the capstone of the transitional period of adjusting the OSCE to the changed security realities of the 1990s. The Charter belongs to the package of agreements agreed at the Istanbul Summit, reflecting the changing security realities in Europe.
Principles	• sovereign equality • indivisibility of security • upholding democracy, rule of law, and respect for human rights • refraining from the threat or use of force • enhancing security and peace • strengthening confidence and cooperation among States
Norms	• implementation of OSCE commitments • promoting and further developing arms control, disarmament, and CSBMs • commitment to conflict prevention • enhancing efforts to prevent terrorism • closer cooperation among IOs • enhancing practical dialogue with other IOs • offering the OSCE as a forum for sub-regional cooperation • continuing work on CFE and VD • strengthening the instrument of Field Operations
Rules	• setting up Rapid Expert Assistance and Co-operation Teams (REACT) for conflict prevention, crisis management and post-conflict rehabilitation • setting up an Operation Centre within the Conflict Prevention Centre
Decision-Making Procedures	• consensus as the basis for OSCE decision-making • establishment of the Platform for Co-operative Security • establishment of a Preparatory Committee under the Permanent Council's direction

Indicators of Regime Decay, Period 1995-1999	shifts in relative capabilities, divergent issue-specific interests, inequitable distribution of gains, issue linkage, non-compliance, internal contradictions
Evidence for Regime Decay, Period 1995-1999	During the period 1995-1999, indicators of regime decay are apparent because the Charter was the product of a cross issue linkage between adapting the OSCE and the CFE Treaty, establishing the NATO-Russia Founding Act, and enlarging NATO. As explained above, shifts in relative capabilities, divergent issue-specific interests, and the Russian perception of the inequitable distribution of gains shaped the process. Non-compliance with principles and norms occurred with regards to 'upholding democracy, rule of law, and respect for human rights' in contrast to the realities on the ground in a number of post-Soviet states. Also, the norm of commitment to conflict prevention was violated by Russia in the North Caucasus. The internal contradiction of 'sovereign equality vs. indivisibility of security' is again present.

TABLE 49

EVALUATION OF PERIOD 1995-1999

Number of Agreements	Indicators of Regime Decay Pertaining to Agreements Concluded in 1995-1999	Ratio of Indicators of Regime Decay Per Agreement Concluded in 1995-1999	Indicators of Regime Decay Pertaining to Agreements Concluded Before 1995	Overall Number of Indicators of Decay in 1995-1999
9	34	3.77	5	39

Evidence for Indicators of Regime Decay Pertaining to Agreements Concluded before 1995	The period between 1995 and 1999 saw evidence for indicators of regime decay pertaining also to agreements concluded before 1995. **1975 Helsinki Final Act:** (non-compliance) In the Russian understanding (cf. President of Russia 2007), NATO enlargement was a violation of the Helsinki principle of the 'indivisibility of security' and therewith inconsistent behavior towards its stipulations. **1990 Charter of Paris:** (non-compliance) The Charter recalls the principle of the 'indivisibility of security'. In the Russian understanding, NATO enlargement was a violation of that principle (ibid). The Second Chechen War was a Russian violation of the principle of

'peaceful settlement of disputes'.

1990 CFE Treaty:
(non-compliance)

The treaty recalls the principle of the 'indivisibility of security'. In the Russian understanding, NATO enlargement was a violation of that principle (ibid). The Second Chechen War was a Russian violation of the principle to 'prevent military conflict'.

1991 North Atlantic Cooperation Council Statement on Dialogue, Partnership and Cooperation:
(non-compliance)

The Statement recalls the principle of the 'indivisibility of security'. In the Russian understanding, NATO enlargement was a violation of that principle (ibid).

1992 : Section V 'CSCE Forum for Security Cooperation', Helsinki Document:
(non-compliance)

Section V recalls the principle of the 'indivisibility of security'. In the Russian understanding, NATO enlargement was a violation of that principle (ibid).

The period 1995-1999 only produced nine agreements, which is half the amount of the previous period. In 1996, also the Balkans cooperation cluster started to take shape. Compared to the preceding period, indicators of regime decay pertaining to agreements concluded in 1995-1999 (35) as well as the ratio per agreement (3.88) sprang upwards. In addition, five agreements from earlier periods were violated by acts of non-compliance during that period, which leads to an overall number of 40 occurrences of indicators of regime decay in the period 1995-1999.

5.5   Agreements, Period 2000-2014

TABLE 50

OSCE, DOCUMENT ON SMALL ARMS AND LIGHT WEAPONS, 2000

Agreement	**Agreement 31: OSCE Document on Small Arms and Light Weapons, 2000**
Attribution	CSBM cooperation cluster
Description	The 2000 OSCE SALW Document addresses risks emanating from surpluses of SALW and conventional ammunition. It aims at securing the production, transfer, and stockpiling of SALW as well as the proper disposal of surpluses.
Principles	• strengthening confidence and security • cooperation on threats emanating from the spread of SALW

	- combating illicit trafficking - reduction and prevention of the accumulation and uncontrolled spread of small arms - building confidence, security, and transparency through appropriate measures on small arms
Norms	- exercising restraint - commitment to conflict prevention - developing appropriate measures at the end of armed conflicts - further developing measures - ensuring OSCE addresses issue of small arms
Rules	- politically binding - national control over manufacture of small arms - marking of small arms and record keeping - transparency measures and common export criteria - import, export, and transit procedures and documentation - control over international arms-brokering - improving cooperation in law enforcement - specific indicators of a surplus - improving national stockpile management and security - destruction and deactivation - financial and technical assistance - transparency measures on surplus weapons - procedures for assessments, recommendations, and measures related to early warning, conflict prevention, crisis management, and post-conflict rehabilitation - stockpile management and reduction in post-conflict rehabilitation
Decision-Making Procedures	- CPC main point of contact - review through the FSC
Indicators of Regime Decay, Period 2000-2014	non-compliance
Evidence for Regime Decay, Period 2000-2014	During the period 2000-2014, indicators of regime decay are apparent in the form of non-compliance because Russia and Georgia violated the norm of 'commitment to conflict prevention' in their 2008 war and because of the Russian violation of the norm in Ukraine in 2014. In the context of the Ukraine conflict and the fights between the central Ukrainian authorities and the separatist movements in East Ukraine, non-compliance occurred as the principle of 'reduction and prevention of the accumulation and uncontrolled spread of small arms' was violated by clandestine arms transfers from Russia into East Ukraine (cf. Kramer and Gordon 2014).

TABLE 51

CONCLUDING AGREEMENT OF THE NEGOTIATIONS UNDER ART. V OF ANNEX 1-B OF THE GENERAL FRAMEWORK AGREEMENT FOR PEACE IN BOSNIA AND HERZEGOVINA, 2001

Agreement	**Agreement 32: Concluding Agreement of the Negotiations Under Article V of Annex 1-B of the General Framework Agreement for Peace in Bosnia and Herzegovina, 2001**
Attribution	Balkans cooperation cluster
Description	In 2001, the third regional arms control agreement for the Balkans, called for by Article V of 'Annex 1-B: Agreement on Regional Stabilization' of the Dayton accords, emerged after two years of negotiation between 20 participating States under the auspices of the OSCE. Its politically binding provisions go beyond the provisions contained in the VD.
Principles	• sovereign equality
Norms	• adherence to the OSCE acquis and full implementation of OSCE CSBM agreements
Rules	• politically binding • encouraging exchange of defense-related information • facilitating expanded military contacts and cooperation • reducing the thresholds for military activities • offering supplementary inspections and evaluation visits • support for de-mining of areas • commitment to stop the accumulation and spread of SALW
Decision-Making Procedures	• establishment of a Commission to review Agreement • annual meetings under the auspices of the OSCE • consensus rule • liaison with the sub-table on Defence and Security Issues of Table III of the Stability Pact for South Eastern Europe
Indicators of Regime Decay, Period 2000-2014	--

TABLE 52

NATO, RUSSIAN FEDERATION, NATO-RUSSIA RELATIONS: A NEW QUALITY, 2002

Agreement	**Agreement 33: NATO-Russia Relations: A New Quality, Declaration by Heads of State and Government of NATO Member States and the Russian Federation, 2002**
Attribution	NATO pol-mil cooperation cluster
Description	In 2002, the NATO-Russia declaration of the Rome Summit established the NRC as a successor to the PJC. Following a British initiative, the NRC was created to provide a fresh stimulus to NATO-Russia relations on a more equal footing than the replaced PJC. In contrast to the 1997 Founding Act, which, amongst other stipulations contained the establishment of the PJC, the Rome declaration contains no rules but outlines the principles and norms of the working agenda of the new NRC.
Principles	• reaffirming goals, principles, and commitments set forth in the Founding Act • building together a lasting and inclusive peace in the Euro-Atlantic area • principles of democracy and cooperative security • indivisibility of security • reaffirming OSCE acquis • equal partnership
Norms	• working together in areas of common issue-specific interest • standing together against common threats and risks • strengthening cooperation in the struggle against terrorism • strengthening cooperation in crisis management • broadening and strengthening cooperation on non-proliferation of WMD • reaffirming adherence to CSBMs, A/CFE, and Open Skies • enhancing consultations on theatre missile defense • promoting cooperation on search and rescue at sea • enhancing military-to-military cooperation and cooperation on defense reform

	• enhancing mechanisms for civil emergency response • exploring possibilities for confronting new challenges and threats to the Euro-Atlantic area
Rules	--
Decision-Making Procedures	• establishment of NRC • consensus rule • NRC chaired by NATO SG • continuous meetings at all levels (including Chiefs of Staff) • establishment of a Preparatory Committee
Indicators of Regime Decay, Period 2000-2014	shifts in relative capabilities, divergent issue-specific interests, inequitable distribution of gains, negative expectations, negative spill-over, protracted negotiations, non-compliance, internal contradictions, diminished U.S. interest in cooperation
Evidence for Regime Decay, Period 2000-2014	During the period 2000-2014, indicators of decay are present with regards to shifts in relative capabilities, divergent issue-specific interests, and the Russian perception of the inequitable distribution of gains. Particularly Washington achieved its preferred issue-specific interest of restarting NATO-Russian relations, thus securing continued Russian support for the war on terrorism, while Moscow failed to achieve its preferred issue-specific interest of a say in NATO decision-making. At the same time, these issue-specific interests reveal that Washington did not view the NRC as a direct vehicle for cooperatively engaging with Moscow but as means in the war on terror (cf. Ponsard 2007). Hence, the NRC emerged against the background of the diminished U.S. interest in cooperation. Negative expectations came to the fore the more often the NRC was unable to constructively deal with the divergent issue-specific interests of the West and Russia – most vividly underscored by the suspension of the NRC after the Russian-Georgian war in 2008 and by the partial suspension of cooperation programs after the Russian annexation of Crimea in 2014. Negative spill-over can be traced from the CFE deadlock (cf. Embassy U.S. Moscow 2009a). Protracted negotiations on the NRC's working agenda came to the fore since 2008, reaching a first climax with the inability to agree on the reform agreement 'Taking the NRC Forward' (see Mission U.S. NATO 2009). Non-compliance with principles and norms occurred on several occasions with the 2008 Russian-Georgian war and with NATO's further enlargement violating the principle of the 'indivisibility of security' – at least in the Russian perception (cf. President of Russia 2007). The internal contradiction of 'sovereign equality vs. indivisibility of security' is again present with the principle of 'sovereign equality' dodging behind the reaffirmation of principles of the NATO-Russia Founding Act. Also, the principle of 'equal partnership' is practically in contradiction with the working procedure of the NRC.

TABLE 53

OSCE, STRATEGY TO ADDRESS THREATS TO SECURITY AND STABILITY IN THE TWENTY-FIRST CENTURY, 2003

Agreement	**Agreement 34: OSCE Strategy to Address Threats to Security and Stability in the Twenty-First Century, 2003**
Attribution	CSBM cooperation cluster
Description	In December 2003, the 11th OSCE Ministerial Council, held in Maastricht, adopted the Strategy to Address Threats to Security and Stability in the Twenty-First Century as a response to new forms of inter- and intra-state insecurity, in the first place terrorism and related criminal activities. The Strategy also touches upon the realm of CSBMs.
Principles	• commitment to a free, democratic, and more integrated OSCE area without dividing lines • prevention of terrorism
Norms	• compliance with OSCE norms, principles, and commitments • commitment to conflict prevention • continued relevance and validity of military factors and fighting power for the strategic security environment • implementation of instruments for conflict prevention and confidence-building essential • full implementation, timely adaptation, and further development of arms control agreements and CSBMs as key contributions to political and military stability • enhancing cooperation on issues of non-proliferation, export, and transfer control as far as illicit conventional arms transfers and transfers of SALW are concerned • expanding CSBM and arms control acquis to adjacent areas
Rules	• voluntary exchange of information on national initiatives to prevent WMD proliferation • addressing proliferation of MANPADS • addressing the risks arising from surplus stockpiles of conventional ammunition and explosives
Decision-Making Procedures	• Annual Security Review Conference to review the Strategy

Indicators of Regime Decay, Period 2000-2014	non-compliance
Evidence for Regime Decay, Period 2000-2014	During the period 2000-2014, indicators of decay are present in the realm of non-compliance with principles and norms. As examples, the principle of 'commitment to a free, democratic, and more integrated OSCE area without dividing lines' stands in contrast to the realities in a number of post-Soviet states and to NATO's eastward enlargement which can be viewed as creating dividing lines (cf. Zagorski 2011). Also the norm of 'full implementation, timely adaptation, and further development of arms control agreements and CSBMs as key contributions to political and military stability' has been contradicted by Russian as well as NATO policies directed to CFE and the OSCE's CSBM acquis. The norm of 'commitment to conflict prevention' was violated by Russia and Georgia in 2008 and by Russia in Ukraine in 2014.

TABLE 54

OSCE, DOCUMENT ON STOCKPILES OF CONVENTIONAL AMMUNITION, 2003

Agreement	**Agreement 35: OSCE Document on Stockpiles of Conventional Ammunition, 2003**
Attribution	CSBM cooperation cluster
Description	The 2003 OSCE Document on Stockpiles of Conventional Ammunition complements the OSCE Document on Small Arms and Light Weapons and addresses risks arising from surplus stockpiles of conventional ammunition, explosive material, and detonating devices.
Principles	• recognizing the risks and challenges caused by the presence of stockpiles of conventional ammunition, explosive material, and detonating devices in surplus and/or awaiting destruction
Norms	• strengthening national capacity

Rules	• politically binding • enhancing transparency through voluntary exchange of information on surplus stocks of conventional ammunition, explosive material, and detonating devices • providing participating States with a specific procedure • establishing a framework for international assistance • request for and provision of assistance takes place on a voluntary basis • possible role of OSCE Field Operations • list of specific categories of conventional ammunition • specific indicators of a surplus • specific procedures for stockpile management and security • specific procedures for transparency about needs and assistance • scope of assistance and procedure incl. Model Questionnaire • development of a "best practice" guide of techniques and procedures • regular review of agreement
Decision-Making Procedures	• CPC as point of contact
Indicators of Regime Decay, Period 2000-2014	non-compliance
Evidence for Regime Decay, Period 2000-2014	During the period 2000-2014, indicators of decay are present in the realm of non-compliance with principles and norms: Russia's policy of continued storage of conventional ammunition in the outpost of Cobasna (Transnistria) is a violation of the Document's central principle.

TABLE 55

OSCE, VIENNA DOCUMENT, 2011

Agreement	**Agreement 36: Vienna Document 2011 on Confidence- and Security-Building Measures, 2011**
Attribution	CSBM cooperation cluster
Description	The Vienna Document 2011 takes forward the stipulations of its predecessors on a very limited technical basis.

Principles	• strengthening confidence and security • achieving disarmament • refraining from the threat or use of force • recalling OSCE CSBM and arms control acquis
Norms	--
Rules	• politically binding • annual exchange of military information, annual calendars • specific information on military forces • exchange of specific data relating to major weapon and equipment systems • information on the plans for the deployment of major weapon and equipment systems • exchange of information on defense planning • clarification, review, and dialogue on defense planning and possible additional information • mechanism for consultation and cooperation as regards unusual military activities • cooperation on hazardous incidents of a military nature • voluntary hosting of visits to dispel concerns about military activities • specific rules for military contacts • specific program on military contacts and cooperation • demonstration of new types of major weapon and equipment systems • prior notification of certain military activities • observation of certain military activities • specific constraining provisions • compliance and verification rules • evaluations and communications rules • specific regional measures
Decision-Making Procedures	• FSC decisions to update VD labeled VD PLUS • special FSC meeting on the VD every five years • factual presentation by the CPC to all participating States of all CSBM information exchanged
Indicators of Regime Decay, Period 2000-2014	protracted negotiations, negative expectations, non-compliance, divergent issue-specific interests, negative spill-over

Evidence for Regime Decay, Period 2000-2014	During the period 2000-2014, indicators of decay are present. Amongst them are protracted negotiations: it took OSCE participating States eleven years to update the 1999 VD. The disappointment of the majority of states over this long process and the subsequent narrow result of the VD 2011 is stated in an interpretative statement by 39 states parties annexed to the VD (see OSCE 2011). This statement gives also evidence of the negative expectations that prevailed. Further on, non-compliance occurred during the Russian-Georgian war in 2008 and in Ukraine in 2014. Divergent issue-specific interests shaped its evolution in recent years as NATO member states were striving for more transparency on Russia's conventional forces (particularly since the beginning of the Russian military reform in 2010); a focus divergent from Moscow's issue-specific interests.[33] Negative spill-over occurred from the dysfunctionality of the cooperation cluster of conventional arms control (cf. Mission U.S. OSCE 2008).

TABLE 56

EVALUATION OF PERIOD 2000-2014

Number of Agreements	Indicators of Regime Decay Pertaining to Agreements Concluded in 2000-2014	Ratio of Indicators of Regime Decay Per Agreement Concluded in 2000-2014	Indicators of Regime Decay Pertaining to Agreements Concluded Before 2000	Overall Number of Indicators of Decay in 2000-2014
6	17	2.83	36	53

Evidence for Indicators of Regime Decay Pertaining to Agreements Concluded before 1995	The period between 2000 and 2014 saw evidence for indicators of regime decay pertaining also to agreements concluded before 2000.
	1990 CFE and 1999 ACFE Treaties:
	(protracted negotiations, 2x non-compliance, negative adaptation consequences, divergent issue-specific interests, negative expectations, issue linkage, negative spill-over, diminished U.S. interest in cooperation)
	Since the year 2000, protracted negotiations have impeded progress on the issue of ratification of ACFE. Non-compliance is apparent. Examples are the

---

33   This information was passed on to the author by an informal source.

Russian suspension of CFE, NATO's decision to make ratification of ACFE dependent on the fulfillment of Russia's Istanbul commitments, Russian and Georgian use of force in 2008 and in Ukraine in 2014, and Armenia's and Azerbaijan's non-compliance with CFE ceilings (cf. U.S. Department of State 2014: 1). In concrete, non-compliance occurred with a view to the principle of 'sustaining the key role of CFE as the cornerstone of European security', for both NATO member states and Russia did not live up to the principle through the actions of non-ratification (NATO member states) and suspension (Russia and partially NATO member states). Negative adaptation consequences came to the fore with the adaptation agreement in 1999 and its political link to the withdrawal of Russian forces and equipment from Moldova and Georgia. Divergent issue-specific interests were apparent in this regard. A diminished U.S. interest in cooperation is visible as Washington continues to insist on fulfillment of the Istanbul commitments. Negative expectations characterize the treaty at least since NATO's 2002 decision to link the issues of ACFE ratification to Russia fulfilling her Istanbul commitments. Negative spill-over effects are visible with CFE's increasing dysfunctionality affecting the further development of the cooperation clusters on CSBMs in the last decade (cf. Mission U.S. OSCE 2008) and on political and military cooperation under the auspices of NATO (cf. Ponsard 2007: 60 et seq).

1992 Treaty on Open Skies:

(protracted negotiations, divergent issue-specific interests, non-compliance)

The treaty displays a number of indicators of regime decay such as protracted negotiations in the recent years due to divergent issue-specific interests between Georgia and Russia as well as between Turkey and Greece (cf. Spitzer 2011). Non-compliance is visible with respect to the principles of 'promoting openness and transparency in military activities' and 'enhancing stability' since Russian behavior in conjunction with the Ukraine conflict was a clear violation of those two principles. Negative spill-over cannot be thoroughly verified; however, it remains a matter of fact that protracted negotiations and divergent issue-specific interests started to affect the treaty only after the Russian suspension of CFE in 2007 and the subsequent war in Georgia in 2008.

1975 Helsinki Final Act, 1990 Charter of Paris, and 1999 Charter for European Security:

(protracted negotiations, 3x non-compliance, divergent issue-specific interests, negative expectations, negative spill-over)

All three central agreements of the C/OSCE process have been affected by indicators of regime decay in the years 2000-2014. At least since the 1999 OSCE Istanbul Summit, partially protracted negotiations have come to characterize the development of OSCE institutions, particularly in the realms of CSBMs and arms control. Non-compliance occurred at various instances, most obvious in the Russian-Georgian war of 2008 and in the Ukraine conflict in 2014 where a whole range of C/OSCE core principles and norms were violated. Taking the 1999 Charter for European Security as an example, non-compliance with principles and norms occurred with regards to 'upholding democracy, rule of law, and respect for human rights' in contrast to the realities on the ground in a number of post-Soviet states. The principles of 'refraining from the threat or use of force', of 'strengthening confidence and cooperation among States', and the norms of 'implementation of OSCE commitments' as well as of the 'commitment to conflict prevention' were violated by Russia in Georgia and at Crimea. The norm of 'promoting and further developing arms control, disarmament, and CSBMs' was ignored by both the West and Russia since the dawn of the new millennium, most visibly in the CFE context. Divergent issue-specific interests in the role of the OSCE (for Russia: a pan-European security structure with central authority in the realm of "hard security"; for the United States: a political vehicle for the promotion of human rights standards) triggered increasingly negative expectations. Negative spill-over occurred from the dysfunctionality of the cooperation cluster on conventional arms control on the OSCE's 'First Basket' during the last decade (cf. Mission U.S. OSCE 2008).

1999 OSCE Platform for Co-operative Security:

(non-compliance)

Non-compliance occurred again with regards to the norms of 'adherence to C/OSCE principles and commitments' and the 'implementation of arms control, disarmament, and CSBM obligations'. The former were violated for instance by NATO enlargement as in contradiction to the principle of the 'indivisibility of security' (at least in the Russian perception) and by the Russian-Georgian war in 2008 and Russian action in Ukraine in 2014; the latter was violated by the West and Russia in the CFE context. The rule of 'enhanced inter-organizational cooperation and information exchange in response to crises situations' was ignored by NATO member states as the NRC was suspended as an answer to the Russia-Georgia war in 2008 and when all cooperation programs with Russia were stopped as a reaction to the Ukraine conflict in 2014.

1996 OSCE Framework for Arms Control:

(negative expectations, non-compliance)

Negative expectations about the OSCE's arms control acquis have come to shape Russia's stance towards the Organization's political-military dimension (see statement by Ulyanov in Mission U.S. OSCE 2010). Non-compliance occurred with the violation of the principles of 'enhancing military and political stability' and 'strengthening of co-operation, transparency, and predictability' in conjunction with the conflicts in the South Caucasus and the Ukraine conflict of 2014. As described above, the norm of 'full implementation and further development of arms control agreements' was violated in the CFE context.

1992 Section V 'CSCE Forum for Security Co-operation', Helsinki Document:

(divergent issue-specific interests, protracted negotiations, non-compliance, negative spill-over)

After a successful period of establishing a number of CSBMs, the pace of policy achievements under the FSC slowed down and almost came to an end during the last 14 years. Divergent issue-specific interests and protracted negotiations came to the fore – the years-long update of the VD being just one example. Non-compliance took over as most norms (e.g. enhancing/increasing disarmament, transparency, and predictability) were not scrupulously observed anymore. Negative spill-over occurred from the dysfunctionality of the cooperation cluster on conventional arms control (cf. Mission U.S. OSCE 2008).

1993 Stabilizing Measures for Localized Crisis Situations:

(non-compliance)

Even though the Stabilizing Measures are of a voluntary nature, their rules pertaining to the treatment of irregular forces were violated on several occasions by Russian non-compliance in conjunction with the 2014 Ukraine conflict (cf. Roulo 2014). The rule of 'careful handling of public statements' was violated on numerous occasions of open or hidden conflict in the OSCE space during the last 14 years (cf. exemplary Englund and Wan 2011).

1993 Principles Governing Conventional Arms Transfers:

(non-compliance)

With a view to the prevention of excessive arms build-ups, the example of arms acquisition in Azerbaijan in recent years (cf. Sultanova and Poghosyan 2013) depicts acts of non-compliance with norms.

1994 Code of Conduct on Politico-Military Aspects of Security:

(non-compliance)

Indicators of regime decay are apparent with regards to non-compliance with norms. The norms of 'responsible and cooperative behavior in the field of security' and 'denial of imposition of military domination of one state over any other state' were violated in the ongoing conflicts of the South Caucasus and the Ukraine conflict in 2014. The norm of 'further developing measures and institutions' with regards to the Code did not result in any update of the agreement. The norm to 'act in solidarity if norms are violated' was itself violated as no common responses were found to the violations of norms as described above. The norm of 'commitment to conflict prevention' was also violated in Georgia 2008 and Ukraine 2014. The norms of 'determining military capabilities on the basis of national democratic procedures' and 'democratic political control of military, paramilitary, internal security forces, intelligence services, and the police' have been repeatedly violated through non-democratic conduct in a number of post-Soviet states but also with respect to the dysfunctional democratic control of intelligence services in a number of Western states.

1994 Principles Governing Non-Proliferation:

(non-compliance)

Indicators of regime decay are apparent through acts of non-compliance with norms. The norms to 'strengthen existing norms' and of the 'full implementation of existing international obligations' were violated by Russia in the Ukraine conflict through the violation of the 1994 Budapest Memorandum which guaranteed the territorial integrity of Ukraine. As the Budapest Memorandum stands in close vicinity to the NPT acquis, also the non-proliferation norm associated with negative security guarantees has been violated by Russia's actions (cf. Fitzpatrick 2014: 86-7).

1994 Partnership for Peace: Framework Agreement and Invitation Agreement:

(non-compliance, negative expectations, negative spill-over)

Non-compliance is present with regards to the principles of 'enhancing security and stability in Europe'. At least in the eyes of Moscow, NATO's eastward enlargement has been undermining stability in Europe (cf. President of Russia 2007). The conflicts in the South Caucasus and the Russian annexation of Crimea are clear violations of the principle to 'refrain from the threat or use of force'. The norm of 'commitment to the CSCE acquis' has been violated on several times by a number of states. The 'fulfillment of disarmament and arms control obligations' norm has been violated by Russia's suspension of CFE and the later suspension of information exchange towards Russia under CFE by NATO member states. The norm of 'ensuring democratic control of defense forces' stands in contrast to the actual conditions in a number of post-Soviet States. Negative expectations about cooperation under PfP prevail in the NATO-Russia relationship (cf. Ponsard 2007: 60 et seq). Negative spill-over from the dysfunctionality of CFE has affected NATO's political and military cooperation with Russia (cf. ibid and Embassy U.S. Moscow 2009a).

1997 NATO-Russia Founding Act on Mutual Relations, Cooperation and Security between NATO and the Russian Federation:

(non-compliance, diminished U.S. interest in cooperation)

Non-compliance with principles and norms is widely visible. Examples are the violation of the principle to acknowledge 'the vital role of democracy, political pluralism, rule of law, [and] human rights' by infringement against basic human rights in Russia but also in the U.S. war on terror; the neglect of the principle to build a 'non-inimical relationship', as shown in the Ukraine conflict; the violation of the principle to build a partnership 'based on transparency', as in contradiction to the Russian military's policy of non-transparency in the Ukraine conflict; the violation of the principle of 'refraining from the threat or use of force' as during the Russian campaigns in Georgia (2008) and at Crimea (2014); and the mutual violation by the United States and Russia of the norm of 'improving arms control regimes and CSBMs' in the context of CFE. Diminished U.S. interest in cooperation was visible when Russia tabled the second Medvedev draft to the NRC pleading for specifying 'substantial combat forces' and Washington did not reply.

1997 Basic Agreement of the Euro-Atlantic Partnership Council:

(non-compliance)

Non-compliance occurred with the violation of the principle of 'strengthening and extending peace and stability in the Euro-Atlantic area' (see the conflicts of the South Caucasus and the Ukraine conflict).

The period 2000-2014 only produced six agreements. This is the second lowest output of all four periods. In comparison to the preceding period, the sum of indicators of regime decay pertaining to agreements concluded in 2000-2014 dropped from 33 to 16 and resulted in a lower ratio of 2.83. At the same time, indicators of regime decay pertaining to earlier agreements reached a peak with 36 occurrences and led to an overall number of occurrences of indicators of decay of 53 in the years 2000-2014. Of course, this fact may well be owed to the circumstance of the growing base of already existing agreements in the realm of cooperative arms control in Europe. The more agreements, the higher the probability of occurrences of indicators of regime decay. This pertains most of all to occurrences of non-compliance. At the same time, two events – the 2008 Russia-Georgia war and, to a larger degree, the 2014 Ukraine conflict – triggered an unprecedented high in violations of principles and norms agreed upon before (see affected agreements in Table 56 above). Hence, a total of 16 agreements of earlier periods suffered from occurrences of indicators of regime decay in this period. Most badly affected, the ACFE Treaty never came into force and the CFE Treaty practically ceased to function.

5.6   Preliminary Assessment of the Four Periods, 1975-2014

In the following preliminary assessment of the four periods only two aspects shall be scrutinized in more depth: the trend of institutionalization and the trend of occurrences of indicators of regime decay. With regards the trend of institutionalization, a high degree of volatility comes to the fore. Roughly three cycles alternate. During the fifteen years from 1975-1989, only three agreements with relevance for cooperative arms control in Europe have been concluded. In the following ten years from 1990-1999, a total of 27 agreements were concluded. In the remaining fifteen years from 2000-2014, only six agreements were concluded. Taken together, an alternating trend with a dense cycle of strong institutionalization, framed by two cycles of comparably weak institutionalization comes to the fore. Chart 34 visualized this trend, applying a polynomic trend line.

Two further aspects are worth taking note of when comparing the data to the empirical evidence collated in Chapter 3. First, the beginning and the end of the cycle of strong institutionalization correlates with two significant events. The beginning in 1990 correlates with the end of the Cold War; marked by the German reunification. The end in 1999 concurs with the last year of Boris Yeltsin's second presidency and the start of handing over of power to then-Prime Minister Vladimir Putin in late 1999. Second, the last cycle of weak institutionalization from 2000-2014 displays in itself certain volatility, as the first four years (2000-2003) have seen the conclusion of five out of the total of six agreements during those years. Here again, the third cycle's volatility correlates with a significant historical event. With the year 2003, which saw America's second intervention in Iraq, institutionalization in the realm of cooperative arms control in Europe almost comes to an end; with the exception of the Vienna Document 2011. Chart 35 visualizes occurrences of indicators of regime decay in conjunction to institutionalization during the four periods.

CHART 34

POLYNOMIC TREND OF INSTITUTIONALIZATION
(NEW AGREEMENTS CONCLUDED PER YEAR), 1975-2014

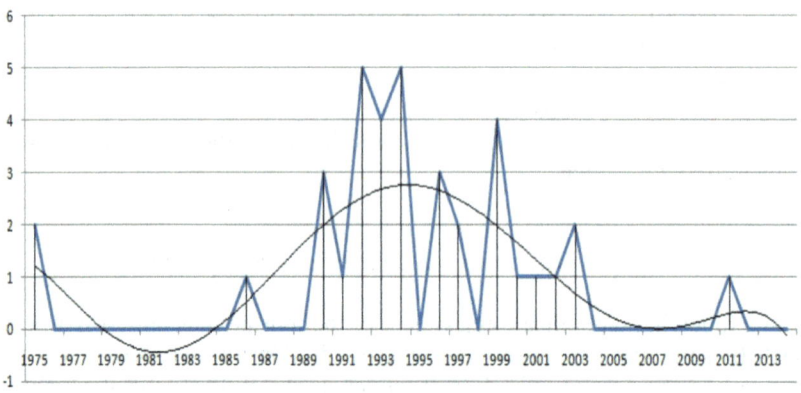

CHART 35

INDICATORS OF REGIME DECAY: TREND DYNAMICS 1975-2014

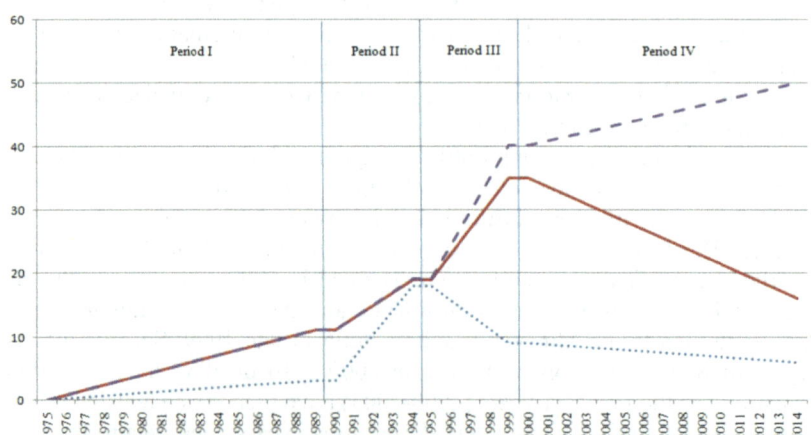

For Chart 35: dotted line = number of agreements; continuous line = indicators of regime decay pertaining to agreements concluded in corresponding period; dashed line = overall number of indicators of decay, including indicators pertaining to agreements concluded before corresponding period.

244

Visualizing a trend of occurrences of indicators of regime decay is not easy. Most indicators cannot be assigned to a certain point on the vertical time axis because they develop over time. Therefore, in Chart 35 a simplification is applied in order to allow for visualizing decay dynamics. The occurrences of indicators of regime decay during a certain period are accumulated at the end of each respective period. As an example, the period 1995-1999 saw 34 occurrences of indicators of regime decay for agreements concluded in this period. The preceding period saw only 18 occurrences. Hence, period 1995-1999 starts with the accumulated number of 18 occurrences from the preceding period and ends with the accumulated number of 34 occurrences. The same method is used with regards to the overall number of indicators of regime decay during a certain period (including occurrences of indicators of regime decay pertaining to earlier agreements).

The visualization of the trend dynamics of decay highlights four important findings.

First, occurrences of indicators of regime decay were present throughout the whole period of analysis, however, to varying degrees. While Period I (1975-1989) had eleven occurrences of indicators of regime decay pertaining to agreements concluded in that period, Period II (1990-1994) has already 18 occurrences of indicators of regime decay pertaining to agreements concluded in that period. Period III (1995-1999) then shows the most significant increase in the occurrence of indicators of regime decay with 34 cases.

Second, the increase of occurrences of indicators of regime decay pertaining to agreements concluded in Period III (1995-1999) comes in parallel with the presence of indicators of regime decay pertaining to earlier agreements. Also, the increase during Period III (1995-1999) happens only after institutionalization had reached its peak during Period II (1990-1994). Third, Period IV (2000-2014) sees the further increase of occurrences of indicators of regime decay pertaining to earlier agreements. At the same time, occurrences of indicators of regime decay pertaining to agreements concluded in Period IV (2000-2014) drop again to 17 cases.

Fourth, when calculating the ratio of occurrences of the overall number of indicators of decay per period in relation to the total number of agreements concluded so far, figures result in a value of 3.66 indicators of decay per agreement for Period I (1975-1989), 1.0 for Period II (1990-1994), 1.13 for Period III (1995-1999), and 1.47 for Period IV (2000-2014). The overall ratio of total occurrences of indicators of decay (121) in all four periods (1975-2014) in relation to the total number of agreements concluded (36) is: 3.36.

Interpreting these findings becomes possible when again comparing the data to the empirical evidence from Chapter 3. The dynamics displayed in Period III (1995-1999) all occur against the background of a number of significant historical events and developments. Those years saw the beginning of the Second Chechen War, the preparations for NATO enlargement, and the dismissal of Russia's ideas of an upgrade of the OSCE to an encompassing security organization for the Euro-Atlantic space. At the same time, the marked increase of occurrences of indicators of regime decay in Period III (1995-1999) can be partially explained with the growing basis of governing agreements. While Period II (1990-1994) had seen the strongest increase in institutionalization, the following Period III (1995-1999) saw the strongest increase in occurrences of indicators of regime decay. To put it simple: the more agreements available, the potentially more cases of decay.

With regards to Period IV (2000-2014), the historical events of the Russian-Georgian war in 2008 and the Ukraine conflict of 2014 have pushed occurrences of indicators of regime decay pertaining to earlier agreements again upwards. At the same time, occurrences of indicators of regime decay pertaining to agreements concluded in Period IV (2000-2014) dropped in comparison to Period III (1995-1999). This is owed to the fact of the different political nature of agreements established during those two periods. While Period II (1990-1994) saw the conclusion of strongly debated agreements such as the NATO-Russia Founding Act, ACFE, or the OSCE Paris Charter – all of which exhibit a strong political importance for Euro-Atlantic and U.S.-Russian security relations and all of which were reflecting competing interests – Period IV (2000-2014) saw only the establishment of the NRC as a major political endeavor. While the central agreements of Period III (1995-1999) are heavily affected by indicators of regime decay (see Tables 40, 43, 44, 45, 47, and 48), the other agreements of Period IV (2000-2014) are much lesser affected by indicators of regime decay (see Tables 50, 51, 53, and 54). This is explainable, as for instance the 2000 OSCE Document on Small Arms and Light Weapons, the 2003 OSCE Strategy to Address Threats to Security and Stability in the Twenty-First Century, or the 2003 OSCE Document on Stockpiles of Conventional Ammunition were of a lesser controversial nature.

Analyzing the trends of institutionalization and decay does nevertheless reveal only little about the forms of institutions of cooperative arms control in Europe and the reasons for decay. In the following chapter, therefore, an encompassing assessment of the regime conundrum and of the indicators of regime decay will be conducted.

6   Assessment of the First Abductive Test's Results

In the previous chapter, 36 agreements with relevance to cooperative arms control in Europe were assessed. Applying Krasner's standard typology together with the thirteen indicators of decay, a number of significant results derive. The previous and the present chapter belong together. Therefore, this chapter will summarize and assess these results as well as answer the guiding research questions to the two chapters. To recall these questions: is there clear evidence that the four cooperation clusters under the rubric of cooperative arms control in Europe are actually four regimes? If so, do those four regimes form a regime complex? Which indicators of decay are present, and to what degree?

6.1   Assessment I: Successful Multi-Regime Creation

Is there clear evidence that the four cooperation clusters under the rubric of cooperative arms control in Europe are actually four regimes? Recalling Keohane (1982: 337), regimes 'facilitate the making of substantive agreements by providing a framework of rules, norms, principles, and procedures for negotiation.' In contrast, Young (1982: 283) argues that regimes *are* agreements. According to Young, all 36 agreements assessed in the previous chapter would deserve the regime label. However, as shown in the tables above, a significant number of agreements in the CSBM cooperation cluster do not incorporate a full set of principles, norms, rules, and decision-making procedures (e.g. the 1994 CSCE Global Exchange of Military Information; see Table 34 above). Following Krasner, such agreements were no regimes.

Both approaches, Young's and Krasner's seem too formalistic when applied to the empirical evidence collated in Chapter 5. In contrast, Keohane's definition of regimes appears more flexible and encompassing because it points to the wider contractual environment in which regimes might be established. Hence, it will be important to search for the Keohanian 'framework [or frameworks] of rules, norms, principles, and procedures', which 'facilitate the making of substantive agreements'. Identifying such framework(s) should be possible by comparing which agreements are sharing which principles and norms. In a simplistic understanding, such identification follows a "bottom up" approach.

Therefore, in this paragraph an assessment will be conducted in which key principles and norms of the 36 agreements are counted and attributed to the number of agreements that incorporate those principles and norms. At the same time, those agreements will be attributed to the respective cooperation cluster and it will be assessed as to whether different agreements from different cooperation clusters share key principles and norms. A number of methodological considerations are explained first.

With regards to key principles and norms, only such principles and norms are listed that appear more than three times amongst the 36 agreements and, at the same time, in at least three different cooperation clusters. Seven agreements (no. 7, 21, 29, 32, 33, 34, and 36) are 'recalling' C/OSCE principles and norms or call for 'adherence' to C/OSCE principles and commitments. In these cases, the principles and norms of the two 1975 Helsinki accords (Tables 17 and 18 above) are taken as the reference basis and included in the data base. The 'principle of sufficiency' should not become confused with the CFE 'sufficiency rule' (Article VI, CFE 1990). The former is referred to as general sufficiency in armaments.

With regards to the number of agreements assessed, the Vienna Document represents a special case as it has recurrently been updated and only the Document's rules have been expanded to include additional provisions. If each version of the Vienna Document would be counted as a single unique agreement, the data input would be distorted. Therefore, the 1986 Stockholm Document and its successors of the Vienna Documents 1990, 1992, 1994, 1999, and 2011 are treated as one contiguous agreement. The number of agreements evaluated therewith shrinks from 36 to 31.

As regards attribution to the cooperation clusters, four agreements could not be attributed to one of the previously identified four cooperation clusters. Those agreements are the 1975 Helsinki Final Act, the 1990 Charter of Paris, the 1999 Platform for Co-operative Security, and the 1999 Charter for European Security. Those accords are basically the central political agreements of the C/OSCE process (cf. IFSH 1997-2014). Even though some of those agreements also incorporate relevant stipulations for arms control, their main provisions are more in the realm of guiding principles and norms, based on the concept of cooperative security (ibid). The decision to include these declaratory agreements is mainly based on their centrality to the process of institutionalization of cooperative arms control in Europe and their direct historical links to the evolution of the other four cooperation clusters. Table 57 groups those agreements in a column under 'C/OSCE Declaratory Cluster'. Concerning shared key principles and norms, the quantity of shared key principles and norms in a specific cluster of cooperation – e.g. for CSBM agreements – shall help to identify whether the respective agreements of the cluster in their entirety have regime quality.

TABLE 57

SHARED KEY PRINCIPLES AND NORMS OF THE 31 AGREEMENTS ASSESSED

Key Principles and Norms	CSBM Cluster	NATO Pol-Mil Cluster	CAC Cluster	C/OSCE Declaratory Cluster	Balkans Cluster	Σ
	(15)	(5)	(4)	(4)	(3)	(31)
strengthening stability	6	5	4	0	2	**17**
sovereign equality	4	4	3	4	1	**16**
promoting arms control, disarmament, and CSBMs	5	4	1	3	1	**14**
indivisibility of security	3	3	2	4	1	**13**
peaceful settlement of disputes, peaceful cooperation	2	4	2	3	1	**12**
further developing measures	6	3	3	0	0	**12**
refraining from the threat or use of force	1	3	2	3	1	**10**
implementation of arms control, disarmament, and CSBM obligations	5	3	0	1	1	**10**
strengthening confidence and security	5	3	0	0	2	**10**
commitment to conflict prevention	3	1	3	2	0	**9**
Territorial integrity of States	0	0	2	2	0	**4**

principle of sufficiency	2	1	0	0	1	**4**
Σ	**42**	**34**	**22**	**22**	**11**	**131**
Ø (per agreement)	2.8 ± 0.4	6.8 ± 1.2	5.5 ± 1.2	5.5 ± 1.2	3.6 ± 1.1	4.2

Numbers in parentheses: agreements evaluated

The dataset shows that twelve key principles and norms span over five cooperation clusters. The cluster of CSBMs under the auspices of the C/OSCE has the largest data input with fifteen agreements. The other four clusters have a markedly narrower data input. This discrepancy between the different data bases is reflected by the absolute uncertainty (±) that has been calculated for each column. For cooperation clusters with a higher number of analyzed agreements, the relative value of the uncertainty is smaller when compared with the results for other clusters. Figures show that NATO pol-mil agreements display the highest average of vertically shared principles and norms per agreement (6.8). CAC as well as C/OSCE declaratory agreements display a value of 5.5, Balkans agreements display a value of 3.6, and CSBM agreements display a value of 2.8.

Taking into account the uncertainty (±), these figures produce the first principle finding: there is clear evidence that the politics of cooperative arms control in Europe have resulted in regime creation. The average value of vertically shared principles and norms reveals a strong consistency within each cluster.[34] This leads to conclude that, in the words of Keohane (1982: 337), each cluster has a framework of shared principles and norms, which facilitate the making of the respective agreements in that cluster. Hence, what has been labeled *clusters* so far turns out to be *regimes* in the understanding of Keohane (ibid). Contrary to the previous assumption, five instead of only four regimes are present. The C/OSCE declaratory cluster is the fifth regime. Particularly the NATO pol-mil cooperation regime, the CAC regime, and the C/OSCE declaratory regime exhibit a high degree of consistency with a view to vertically shared principles and norms. Compared to the CSBM regime,

---

34   It has to be noted, however, that no common average reference value can be established for measuring from which point on the degree of vertically shared principles and norms speaks for or against general regime quality. Any artificially established common average reference value would suffer from subjectivity, as comparative case studies in this field of research are obsolete. Nevertheless, this study treats the degree of vertically shared principles and norms in all five cooperation clusters as sufficient if the average value per cluster is above half of the average value of the sum of key principles and norms per sum of agreements (4.2) to prove the regime assumption. In addition, further factors such as historical evolution and regime persistence are completing the picture.

their higher value can partly be explained by narrower data input. When compared to the Balkans regime (3.6), the explanation lies more in the exclusive arms control focus taken in the assessment which has not assessed the general stipulations of the Dayton peace accords.[35]

6.2 Assessment II: Densification to Complexity

The results of the previous paragraph lead directly to the second principle finding pertaining to regime complexity. All five regimes also share key principles and norms on a horizontal level, which means that key principles and norms are not only formative for the respective regime but that they are formative across the boundaries of single regimes. The dataset highlights this finding. Five key principles and norms are horizontally shared by all five regimes. The regimes of CSBMs, CAC, and NATO pol-mil cooperation horizontally share even eight out of twelve key principles and norms. Of the principles and norms themselves, 'strengthening stability' (17) and 'sovereign equality' (16) are most often mentioned across the five regimes. Further on, the data suggests that the five regimes are so closely interwoven on the level of key principles and norms that they might form a regime complex. Taking the number of horizontally shared principles and norms across the five regimes as a reference base to assess regime complexity is nevertheless only a first, though significant, indicator for complexity.

In their research agenda for analyzing regime complexity, Orsini, Morin and Young (2013: 32) suggest, identifying the 'links' (interactions) among the different 'nodes' (regimes). However, they miss being specific with respect to identifying concrete reference values for detecting interaction. Therefore, in the following, three reference values are established. Clearly, shared principles and norms across a set of autonomous regimes, as in the case of cooperative arms control in Europe (see Table 57 above), do represent a potential reference base. The same applies to political linkages. As analyzed in Chapter 3, various political linkages in the form of the strategy of compensation were applied during the stages of regime creation and maintenance. Some of them had synergetic and some had conflictual consequences. During the process of qualitatively assessing the 36 agreements in Chapter 5, also direct references came to the fore. In some cases, agreements from one specific regime make active textual references to an agreement from another regime. This is for instance the case for CAC. CAC agreements such as CFE and the corresponding political developments have regularly been cited in agreements from the NATO pol-mil regime and the CSBM regime. Another

---

35 In the Dayton peace accords, principles and norms of the process are set out in the 'The General Framework Agreement for Peace in Bosnia and Herzegovina' and are not as continuously repeated in the respective arms control stipulations as is the case with CSBM agreements under the auspices of the OSCE.

form of direct reference is design. Particularly the agreements of the Balkans regime have been designed according to the structure and content of the CFE Treaty and a number of CSBM agreements from the C/OSCE, such as the Vienna Document.

In the following, another test is applied in order to highlight forms of regime interaction and to either verify or falsify the complexity assumption. Three reference values for forms of regime interaction are applied. (1) The quantity of the cross-sharing of key principles and norms between the respective five regimes serves as the first reference value. Each regime will be analyzed with a view to the number of key principles and norms that it shares with any other regime. (2) Political linkages are included as the second reference value. Relying on the findings of Chapter 3 about the evolution of the politics of cooperative arms control in Europe, each regime is analyzed as to whether its inception and maintenance was bound to political linkages with any other regime. (3) Direct references amongst the five regimes is the third reference value. Each regime is assessed with a view to direct references of a textual and/or design nature with any other regime. Textual references are subdivided into active and passive references. As an example, the agreement establishing the NRC (see Table 52 above) makes direct textual references to CSBMs, CFE, and Open Skies. In that case, the textual reference will be counted as 'active' for the corresponding NATO pol-mil regime and 'passive' for the corresponding CSBM and CAC regimes. Direct references of a design nature are mentioned separately. Table 58 lists the reference values and assesses their respective occurrence. Thereby, interaction between the five regimes becomes visible.

The evaluation in Table 58 underscores once more the assumption that the five regimes form a regime complex. The NATO pol-mil cooperation and the CSBM regime cross-share the largest number of principles and norms (11), followed by the Balkans regime and the CSBM regime (9), and the Balkans regime and the NATO pol-mil cooperation regime (9). Political linkages occurred between the C/OSCE declaratory regime and the NATO pol-mil cooperation regime and therewith also between the CSBM regime and the NATO pol-mil cooperation regime during the early and mid-1990s[36] and between the CAC regime and the NATO pol-mil cooperation regime from 1995 onwards. There are no political linkages involving the Balkans regime. Direct references of a textual nature (active and passive) pertain to almost all regimes, with the exception of missing references between the NATO pol-mil cooperation regime and the Balkans regime. Direct references of a design nature pertain only to the Balkans regime, which was designed along the lines of the CFE Treaty and of a number of CSBMs, first and foremost the VD.

---

36   However, in the latter case of political linkage between the CSBM regime and the NATO pol-mil cooperation regime, the interaction was rather indirect and depended heavily on the linkage between the further evolution of the C/OSCE and NATO enlargement.

TABLE 58

COOPERATIVE ARMS CONTROL IN EUROPE: FORMS OF REGIME INTERACTION

Reference Value	Regime \\ Regime	CSBM Regime	NATO Pol-Mil Regime	CAC Regime	C/OSCE Declaratory Regime	Balkans Regime
cross-sharing of key principles and norms	CSBM Regime	/	yes (11)	yes (8)	yes (7)	yes (9)
	NATO Pol-Mil Regime	yes (11)	/	yes (8)	yes (7)	yes (9)
	CAC Regime	yes (8)	yes (8)	/	yes (7)	yes (6)
	C/OSCE Regime	yes (7)	yes (7)	yes (7)	/	yes (6)
	Balkans Regime	yes (9)	yes (9)	yes (6)	yes (6)	/
political linkages	CSBM Regime	/	yes	no	yes	no
	NATO Pol-Mil Regime	yes	/	yes	yes	no
	CAC Regime	no	yes	/	no	no
	C/OSCE Regime	yes	yes	no	/	no
	Balkans Regime	no	no	no	no	/
direct references	CSBM Regime	/	passive	active	active	passive/ design
	NATO Pol-Mil Regime	active	/	active	active	no
	CAC Regime	passive	passive	/	active	passive/ design
	C/OSCE Regime	passive	passive	passive	/	passive
	Balkans Regime	active/ design	no	active/ design	active	/

Numbers in parentheses: quantity of cross-sharing of key principles and norms

Of the twelve key principles and norms of the regime complex, five are already listed almost word by word in the 1975 CSCE Helsinki 'Declaration on Principles Guiding Relations Between Participating States'.[37] Another principle, the principle of the 'indivisibility of security' is mentioned in the 1975 preambular paragraphs. The conclusion is that the historical roots of the regime complex are in the Helsinki accords. They represent the starting point of the C/OSCE process (cf. Schlotter 1999) and function as a framework of principles and norms (cf. Keohane (1982: 337) which informed the other regimes over time. This influence on the meta-level of key principles and norms did not stop with the Helsinki stipulations but was continuously fostered through their repetition and extension in the declaratory agreements of the C/OSCE, particularly in the Charter of Paris (1990) and the European Security Charter (1999). All these agreements have so far been attributed to the C/OSCE declaratory regime in this paragraph. Indeed their significance for the overall regime complex points to a special position within this complex. Recalling Aggarval (1985: 18-20), they are less of a meta-regime in the sense of principles and norms inherent to a single regime but more of a meta-regime multiplier of principles and norms that informs a whole complex. Following such re-interpretation of the episteme of 'meta-regime' (ibid), the normative C/OSCE stipulations and their practical manifestation – the OSCE – form an overarching canon of values which frames the whole regime complex. Below this meta-regime, a dense regime complex of four regimes with a high degree of interaction among the different nodes of the complex becomes visible. Chart 36 visualizes the regime complex of cooperative arms control in Europe.

---

37   Those are: sovereign equality, refraining from the threat or use of force, territorial integrity of states, peaceful settlement of disputes, and promoting disarmament.

CHART 36

THE REGIME COMPLEX OF COOPERATIVE ARMS CONTROL IN EUROPE

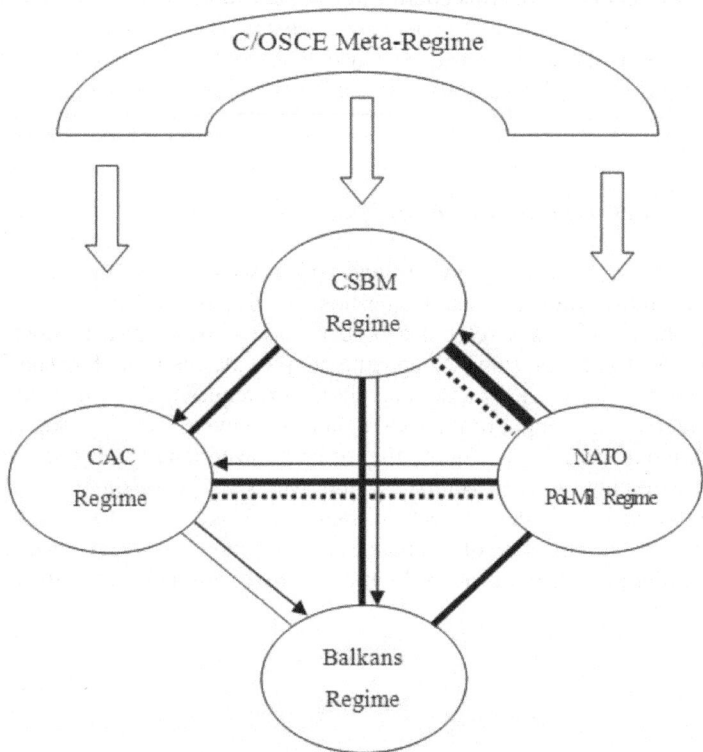

For Chart 36: The chart has been developed by the author. Arrows symbolize an active or passive direct reference of a textual and/or a design nature. Continuous lines symbolize cross-shared key principles and norms; thickness of lines indicates degree of cross-sharing. Dashed lines symbolize political linkages.

The chart highlights a vivid interaction among the elemental regimes of the complex. While the C/OSCE meta-regime sits on top of the complex, the regimes on CSBMs, CAC, and NATO pol-mil cooperation have seven links each with other regimes. The links refer to interactions at the level of cross-shared principles and norms, political linkages, and direct references. The Balkans regime has the lowest number of links (five) and is the only regime with no historical linkages and no active direct reference – a fact due to its later evolution, its top-down genesis as part of the Dayton accords, and its adopted design. In addition to regime interaction, the complexity requirement of partially overlapping membership (Orsini, Morin, and Young 2013) does apply to all four elemental regimes and the meta-regime. Further on, the complex displays a high degree of density and a low degree of centrality. On the one hand, interactions among the nodes are frequent and vivid; on the other hand, no node has considerably more links than the others. The regime complex of cooperative arms control in Europe is thus neither centralized nor fragmented but displays a high degree of density. Therewith, also the second guiding research question of the last two chapters can be answered: the five elemental regimes of cooperative arms control in Europe form a regime complex.

6.3   Assessment III: A Complex in Decay

Which indicators of decay are present, and to what degree? In order to answer the third guiding research question, all thirteen indicators of regime decay, shall serve as a reference base to assess the empirical input from Chapter 5. Again, the same 31 agreements provide the basis for data input. As in the previous case of assessing shared principles and norms (see Table 57 above), the data input of the five regimes is uneven, with a markedly larger data input for CSBMs. Again, the different sized data bases result in different uncertainties when comparing the average. The absolute uncertainty (±) has been calculated for each average value and included in Table 59. Occurrences of indicators of regime decay pertaining to agreements concluded in earlier periods (see Tables 48 and 55 above) are included in the assessment.

TABLE 59

COOPERATIVE ARMS CONTROL IN EUROPE: ASSESSING INDICATORS OF
REGIME DECAY

Indicators of Regime Decay	CSBM Regime (15)	NATO Pol/Mil Regime (5)	CAC Regime (4)	C/OSCE Meta-Regime (4)	Balkans Regime (3)	Σ (31)
non compliance	12	7	6	8	0	**33**
divergent issue-specific interests	4	5	3	4	0	**16**
issue linkage	1	4	3	4	0	**12**
Russian perception of the inequitable distri-bution of gains	1	5	2	3	0	**11**
regime-internal contradictions	3	3	1	4	0	**11**
Negative expectations	3	4	1	2	0	**10**
shifts in relative capabilities	1	5	1	2	0	**9**
protracted negotiations	3	1	2	2	0	**8**
negative spill-over	2	2	1	1	0	**6**
negative adaptation consequences	0	0	2	0	0	**2**
diminished U.S. interest in coopera-tion	0	2	1	0	0	**3**
changes in principles and norms	/	/	/	/	/	/
hegemonic practice	/	/	/	/	/	/
Σ	**30**	**38**	**23**	**30**	**0**	**121**
Ø (per agreement)	2.0 ± 0.4	7.6 ± 1.2	5.7 ± 1.2	7.5 ± 1.4	0	3.9

Numbers in parentheses: agreements evaluated

The overall number of occurrences of indicators of regime decay is 121 (combined number of Tables 20, 39, 49, and 56). Of the 31 agreements evaluated only eight show no indicators of regime decay. The Balkans regime is the only regime that is not impacted at all. The highest number of counted indicators of regime decay is in the NATO pol-mil row with 38 cases. Proportionally, the NATO pol-mil regime is most badly affected with 38 indicators of regime decay and an average of 7.6. The C/OSCE meta-regime has the second highest average value of indicators of regime decay per regime agreement (7.5). However, together with the CAC (1.2) and the C/OSCE meta-regime (1.4), the NATO pol-mil regime has a markedly higher absolute uncertainty (1.2) than the CSBM regime (0.4), which could, partially, explain the higher average value.

'Divergent issue-specific interests' (16 cases), 'issue linkage' (twelve cases), the 'perception of the inequitable distribution of gains' as well as 'regime-internal contradictions' (eleven cases of each indicator), 'negative expectations' (ten cases), and 'shifts in relative capabilities' (nine cases) are all powerful indicators of decay. In absolute terms, the indicator of 'non-compliance' is the strongest with 33 cases. Accordingly, the weakest is 'diminished U.S. interest in cooperation' with only three cases. In the following, these indicators will be interpreted separately. The aim is, to analyze the degree to which certain indicators are responsible for decay. The indicator of 'changes in principles and norms' gets addressed in Chapter 7. The indicator of 'hegemonic practice' is addressed in Chapter 8.

Non-Compliance

In absolute terms, non-compliance is omnipresent in the regime complex. To recall Zacher (1987: 174): 'occurrences of major or long-term noncompliance, particularly involving participation of or support by major actors in the system, bring into question the efficacy of regime injunctions'. The sheer number of occurrences of non-compliance (33) cannot be explained by the commonality of nonconforming behavior in connection with most social institutions (Young 1982: 278) alone. It is also in contradiction to Keohane's assumption (1984: 89 et seq) that violation or cheating becomes limited by the broader framework (in the current case a regime complex) in which regimes are nested in. While compliance is essential particularly for security regimes (cf. Levy, Young and Zürn 1995: 277), it is not so much the seriousness of the fact of non-compliance but rather the degree to which other actors in the regime interpret it as serious violation and the way the non-compliant actor communicates the act of non-compliance (cf. Kratochwil and Ruggie 1986). A good example is the Russian violation of CFE injunctions during the First Chechen War and the immediate explanations given by Boris Yeltsin, which States Parties found acceptable (see Hartmann et al 2002: 701-4).

Two factors are critical for the regime complex of cooperative arms control in Europe in conjunction with non-compliance. First, one major actor is almost always involved when it comes to non-compliance: Russia. Be it non-compliance with key principles and norms such as to 'refrain from the threat or use of force', respect for the 'territorial integrity of states', the commitment to 'further develop [cooperative] measures', or non-compliance with specific rules such as the CFE 'host nation consent rule', Russia has always been a problematic actor. This circumstance points to a general problematic stance of Russia towards the regime complex. As Chayes and Chayes (1994: 68-72) point out, it is the normative base of a regime which decides about success. If one actor is repeatedly challenging regime injunctions, the normative base is challenged as well. Hence, the relationship between the problematic actor and the nature of the normative base comes into the picture. In the current case, the important question derives whether Russian foreign and security policies are still convergent with the key principles and norms of the regime complex.

The second crucial factor is that Russian non-compliance does not occur on a constant level but has only started to skyrocket during the last ten years. The Russian-Georgian war of 2008 and the Ukraine conflict and the related Russian re-interpretations of international law (cf. Burke-White 2014) have played a critical part in contributing to an unprecedented peak in instances of non-compliance. This circumstance leads to question what reasons and developments are behind these dynamics.

CHART 37

COOPERATIVE ARMS CONTROL IN EUROPE: NON-COMPLIANCE DYNAMICS

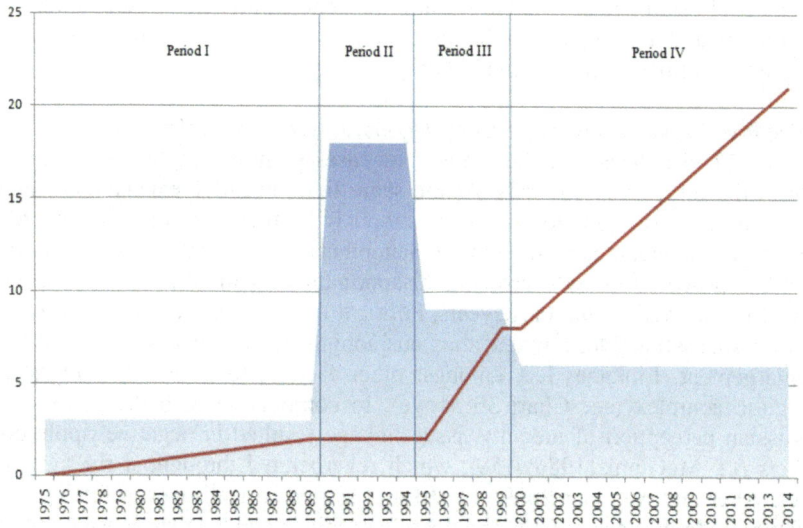

For Chart 37: colored sector = total number of agreements per period; continuous line = occurrences of non-compliance (not limited to instances of Russian non-compliance).

Divergent Issue-Specific Interests, Issue Linkage, Shifts in Relative Capabilities, and the Russian Perception of the Inequitable Distribution of Gains

While obviously Russian non-compliance is a part of the process of decay, it is nevertheless not the sole reason but rather the product of a number of sequential indicators. As analyzed in Chapter 3, divergent issue-specific interests between Washington and Moscow about the future design of Europe's security architecture prevailed throughout the 1990s with the United States' issue-specific interest of maintaining, and later enlarging, NATO structures and with Russia being in strong opposition while working towards achieving a superior role for the C/OSCE. Those divergent issue-specific interests were nevertheless present against the background of a mutual interest in cooperation that is rooted in the survival motive. At the same time, a massive shift in relative capabilities had left Russia in an extremely weak position relative to the United States (see Charts 29-33 above). On the one hand, this massive shift only made cooperation possible because it triggered the Soviet interest in cooperation (cf. Gorbachev 1996). On the other hand, against the background of this massive shift, Washington could follow through with its preferred issues-specific interest of enlarging NATO while accommodating Russia by means of cooperative security. The resulting strategy of compensation led to a number of political linkages. Even though the distribution of gains reflected roughly the relative distribution of power, it led to the Russian perception of inequity (cf. President of Russia 2014b) which did not vanish over time but increasingly affected the bilateral U.S.-Russian relationship (cf. Charap and Shapiro 2014b). When the Russian economy regained strength from 2000 onwards this minor shift in relative capabilities led the new Russian leadership under Vladimir Putin to concentrate on consolidating its economy and its influence in the direct neighborhood and to slowly withdraw from the politics of cooperative security.

Negative Expectations, Protracted Negotiations, and Negative Spill-Over

Chart 37 visualizes that the number of cases of non-compliance increases from the mid-1990s onwards. At the same time, negative expectations, and later protracted negotiations, most obviously in the cases of CFE and the Vienna Document, came to the fore. Statements by Russian delegations to the OSCE prove Moscow's growing disappointment with the way European security evolved during those years. Political linkages had served the purpose of compensating Moscow and thus cushioning Russian unease with NATO enlargement. Linkages led, amongst other factors, to a densely integrated regime complex (see Chart 36 above). In conjunction with the increasing Russian perception of inequity, issue linkage resulted in negative ripple effects (cf. McGinnis 1986: 158), which reverberated throughout the system (cf. Alter and Meunier 2009: 19-20) and started to spill-over, affecting the complex. In the case of CFE, the treaty's deadlock and later suspension led to traceable negative spill-over effects into the NATO pol-mil regime (cf.

Ponsard 2007: 60 et seq; Embassy U.S. Moscow 2009a) and the C/OSCE meta-regime (cf. Mission U.S. OSCE 2008). In the case of the C/OSCE meta-regime, spill-over effects affected the CSBM regime.

Regime-Internal Contradictions
The origins of the regime complex date back to the Helsinki days. The Helsinki principles are still part of an overarching canon of values to the complex (see Chart 36 above). Their universality mirrors their genesis as East-West accords of the lowest common denominator with a low level of issue-specification at their time of origin (cf. Schlotter 1999). Their 'symbolic' (Strange 1982: 484) and 'declaratory' (Ropers and Schlotter 1989) nature and ambivalence allowed for an understanding which reflected the Cold War realities of the 1970s. They were torn between the Soviet desire to cement the status quo and careful Western attempts at change in the human dimension. They were the prestige project of the Eastern super power and the side-project of the Western one (cf. Maresca 1988: 109).

The first Helsinki principle speaks of 'sovereign equality [and the] respect for the rights inherent in sovereignty'. This principle includes explicitly the right 'to be or not to be a party to bilateral or multilateral treaties including the right to be or not to be a party to treaties of alliance'. It follows directly after the preambular recognition of the 'indivisibility of security in Europe'. Over the years, both stipulations have become key principles of the regime complex of cooperative arms control in Europe. The former is mentioned 16 and the latter 13 times in the agreements of the regime complex (see Table 57 above). Particularly the agreements of the 1990s – most prominently in the NATO pol-mil cooperation regime – have made the principle of the 'indivisibility of security' a central declaratory element of the new political order. Even though the Cold War is long gone, 39 years after their inception, these two principles are still at the declaratory heart of the regime complex of cooperative arms control in Europe. In relation to each other, they form a classical paragon of an internal contradiction as every party could basically find any sovereign decision of any other party to join any treaty or alliance an infringement to its security and hence as contrary to the indivisibility of security. Lawyers call such discrepancy a *contradictio in adjecto* (cf. Rotfeld 2014: 57).

Internal contradictions are nothing exceptional when it comes to international agreements. Particularly negotiated principles are often the smallest common denominator and hence contradictory. As an example from the international nuclear non-proliferation regime, Brzoska (1992: 217 et seq) finds 'two contending sets of principles and norms', based on the two main 'diverging interests of types of actors in the system'. Correctly, he notes that combinations of the two sets appear to be 'uneasy' and have direct negative consequences for policy-making.[38] With regards to the two Helsinki principles, both principles fundamentally clash from a practical and a philosophical point of view[39], which was not so much the problem during the geopolitical inertia of the Cold War in Europe (cf. Rotfeld 2014: 54). However, with the end of the Cold War, the regime-internal contradiction in conjunction with the rapid shift in relative capabilities of the post-Cold War era became the buzz word for Russia's critique of NATO enlargement (cf. President of Russia 2007), the West's recognition of independence of Kosovo (cf. Lavrov 2008), or of contended NATO military initiatives such as missile defense[40].

There were almost countless occasions where Russian officials referred to the imperative of the principle (see Cliff 2012: 67). In 2010, the Russian Foreign Minister, Sergei Lavrov explained 'that there is a problem with the concept of indivisibility of security and that it will have to be tackled'. One year earlier, in 2009, he had complained to the OSCE Annual Security Review Conference that 'the main structural shortcoming lies in the fact that over a period of 20 years we have been unable to devise guarantees to ensure the observance of the principle of the indivisibility of security.' (OSCE Lavrov 2009) The tabling of Medvedev's EST proposal was openly linked by Russian officials to achieving a legal guarantee for the principle's perpetuity. 'This is a kind of test', Lavrov explained in 2010, 'if we continue to believe in what our leaders declared and subscribed to in the 90s, why cannot we make the same things legally binding.'

While the security setting had changed dramatically since 1975 in terms of relative capabilities and issue-specific interests, the principle has remained unchanged on the declaratory level. At the same time, the cases of NATO enlargement (in the Russian perception), the Russian-Georgian war of 2008, and the latest clear violations of the principle by Russia in Ukraine (cf. Freedman 2014) underscore that the principle is not consistently reflected in the operational Euro-Atlantic policies of Washington and Russia.

The fact of non-compliance with key principles and norms of the regime complex also explains to a certain degree, why the C/OSCE meta-regime is on average (7.5) so badly affected by indicators of regime decay. Particularly with a view to non-compliance, the meta-regime displays the highest average value per agreement. Every time a key principle or norm of cooperative arms control in Europe is violated, the C/OSCE meta-regime suffers indirectly. The violation of principles and norms triggers the significant question wheth-

---

38   A number of authors go as far as to see the regime-internal contradictions as being the main reason behind the ongoing political deadlock surrounding the NPT (cf. Müller 2009).

39   Of course, the two principles have much older roots than the Helsinki process and can be traced back to the Westphalian order and Kant's 'categorical imperative'.

40   As an example, Roberto Zadra, former Chairman of the NRC Missile Defence Working Group points out that the principle of 'indivisibility of security' was repeatedly 'raised by Moscow throughout the period of negotiation' on missile defense cooperation (Zadra 2014: 57).

er the declaratory level of principles and norms is still reflected at the operational level of policy-making. As the abductive test of Chapter 5 has revealed, there have been no traceable changes to principles and norms when qualitatively assessing 36 agreements. However, focusing on the operational level of policy-making might reveal differences between contemporary policies and inherited principles and norms.

Diminished U.S. Interest in Cooperation
In comparison to the other indicators, the indicator of 'diminished U.S. interest in cooperation' is the weakest in absolute terms (see Table 59 above). The indicator occurs only three times. At the same time, particularly Liberals (cf. Young 1989b: 366-74; McGinnis 1986: 165; Müller 1993a: 49) have argued that a relative loss in interest is a very powerful argument in conjunction with states disengaging from international cooperation. Because the assessment in Table 59 concentrates on decay from the endogenous perspective of regimes, the broader political spectra that drive cooperation are somewhat left out of the analysis. In addition, the period of relative U.S. disengagement from cooperation with Russia (2000-2014) has only produced six agreements of which only one – though the most significant one: establishment of the NRC – was affected by the indicator of 'diminished U.S. interest in cooperation'. Therewith, the indicator is relatively underrepresented even though it provides powerful arguments explaining regime decay. In conjunction with cooperative arms control in Europe four decisive aspects of U.S. foreign and security policy started to take shape with the beginning of the new millennium.

First, Washington's general interest in survival was not geared towards Russia anymore. Russia was neither seen as an enemy nor as a potential rival. To re-quote Kelleher (2014: 17), 'Russia […] was simply no longer relevant to the new American strategic and political preeminence.' With the events of 9/11, the U.S. general interest in survival turned even further away from Russia towards the War on Terror (cf. Daalder and Lindsay 2005). Under Obama, this policy continued; though, to a lesser degree and now with China in the direct U.S. focus (cf. Indyk, Lieberthal, and O'Hanlon 2012: 12 et seq). Second, Washington did not see an immediate need to engage on cooperative arms control in Europe (cf. Kelleher 2014: 17 et seq). The institutions of the 1990s had been set up and were largely functioning in the U.S. view (cf. Mlyn 2003). Third, in its dealings with Russia, Washington continued its policy from the 1990s which was basically non-negotiable with a view to the central Russian demands, meaning an end to NATO enlargement and a superior role for the OSCE. Fourth, America under George W. Bush was generally not very much interested in multilateralism and cooperative security (cf. Luongo 2001). Taken together, these aspects all contribute to the indicator of 'diminished U.S. interest in cooperation'. The empirical evidence collated in Chapter 3 has underscored that this factor contributed significantly to decay.

Summing up, of the thirteen indicators of regime decay, eleven indicators provide compelling indications why the regime complex is in decay. The remaining two indicators of 'hegemonic practices' and 'changes in principles and norms' remain unattended so far. The indicator of 'changes in principles and norms' will be addressed in detail in Chapter 7. The indicator of 'hegemonic practices' will be addressed in detail in Chapter 8.

6.4   Conclusions

The abductive test conducted in Chapter 5 along the lines of Krasner's regime typology has helped to explain which institutions of cooperative arms control in Europe form a regime. The thirteen indicators of regime decay provide compelling indications why the regime complex is in decay. The abductive test has proven that regime creation under the rubric of cooperative arms control in Europe has taken place. As earlier assumed, the four cooperation clusters under the rubric of cooperative arms control in Europe are actually four regimes. In addition to these four regimes, the test led to the conclusion that a fifth regime – the normative C/OSCE meta-regime – exists. As a result of the cross-sharing of key principles and norms, regime complexity comes into play, for all five regimes share a significant number of principles and norms. When further taking into account political linkages and direct references among the regimes, a regime complex, in the most recent understanding of complexity research (cf. Thakur 2013), crystallizes. Following Aggarwal's assumptions about meta-regimes (1985: 18-20), the normative stipulations of the C/OSCE form an overarching meta-regime that has strongly influenced the evolution of the regime complex. Crucial principles and norms from the 1975 Helsinki accords have survived to the very day and span across all elemental regimes of the complex.

Of the five regimes, four are affected by decay. This leads to conclude that the regime complex of cooperative arms control in Europe is characterized by decay. A number of indicators provide compelling indications why the regime complex is in decay. In absolute terms, non-compliance with principles, norms, and rules is the most visible indicator impacting the complex. Here, Russia's problematic role and the dynamics of an increase of Russian non-compliance puts into question the normative injunctions of the regime complex and Russia's stance towards the normative basis.

Visible to a comparably lesser degree, though being amongst the most important reasons for decay, is the diminished U.S. interest in cooperation with Russia since the year 2000, massive as well as minor shifts in relative capabilities – in conjunction with the end of the Cold War and, later, with the Russian economic recovery – employed strategies of issue linkage, and the Russian perception of the inequitable distribution of gains. Regime-internal contradictions in the form of the 'sovereign equality vs. indivisibility of security' paragon are a continuous reference frame for Russian claims. The former British Ambassador to the OSCE Ian Cliff observed: 'the "indivisibility of security" [is] widely regarded as code for continued Russian hostility to NATO enlargement'. (Cliff 2012: 67)

The fact of the persistence of the declaratory principle of the 'indivisibility of security' in conjunction with Moscow's dissatisfaction with the operational policies in the Euro-Atlantic security space as well as Russian non-compliance points to a significant level of tension between principles and norms of the regime complex on the one hand and operational policies on the other. It might be the case, that the normative basis of the complex – its key principles and norms – has ceased to reflect the realities of Euro-Atlantic security and is thus not valid for the operational level of policy-making anymore. Such possible result would add an important insight to explaining decay from the hitherto unattended indicator of 'changes in principles and norms' (cf. Krasner 1982: 4). In order to either verify or falsify this assumption, a second abductive test will be conducted in the following chapter.

7   A Second Abductive Test

The previous two chapters have helped to identify twelve key principles and norms that are at the heart of the regime complex of cooperative arms control in Europe. While those principles and norms are still incorporated in the respective agreements of the complex, doubts have arisen whether the operational policies of the United States and Russia are still reflecting these key principles and norms. The regime-internal contradiction of the 'sovereign equality vs. indivisibility of security' paragon and the related Russian complaints that the latter principle has been violated by the West on different occasions have hinted at a significant level of tension between principles and norms of the regime complex on the one hand and operational policies on the other. If that were the case, it would add an important stratum to explaining decay by addressing the hitherto unexplored indicator of 'changes in principles and norms' (cf. Krasner 1982: 4).

In this chapter, a second abductive test is conducted, assessing 51 statements of delegations of the United States and the Soviet Union/Russia directed to the C/OSCE during five historical periods from 1990 to 2014. The 51 statements are listed under Annex III. The aim of the test is to identify possible commonalities with and differences to the key principles and norms of the regime complex. The guiding research questions of this chapter are: to what degree are key principles and norms of the regime complex of cooperative arms control in Europe still reflected in the operational policies of the two main actors? Are there indicators for an erosion of key principles and norms of the regime complex?

7.1   Introductory Remarks

In this chapter, a second abductive test is conducted, assessing 51 statements of the United States and the Soviet Union/Russia. Assessment of the political statements of those two actors shall help to identify possible commonalities with and differences to the key principles and norms of the regime complex. The 51 statements have all been delivered as speeches to either Ministerial Councils or Summits of the C/OSCE between 1990 and 2014. The exclusive focus on the C/OSCE is due to its systemic centrality to the regime complex and its comprehensive approach toward the concept of cooperative security (cf. Krause 2003). The periodical focus of the years 1990-2014 has been chosen because only with the 1990 Paris Summit CSCE high-level meetings became a regular and continuous endeavor. The period of those 24 years is in itself again broken down into five historical periods, which resemble five of the six historical periods from Chapter 3.

For all the years, the opening statements of the Heads of Delegations are taken as empirical basis. Not all statements are publicly available.[41] Closing statements by delegations, additional U.S. or Soviet/Russian documents annexed to the respective Ministerial Journal or the Summit Document, or statements on behalf of the United States or the Russian Federation are not taken into account. This is due to their often very issue-specific nature. In contrast, opening statements allow for a broader reflection of general policy topics of the respective delegation. The method applied in this test is a mix of qualitative and quantitative content analysis (cf. Krippendorff 1980). Quantitative content analysis applies where direct references to the twelve key principles and norms of the regime complex of cooperative arms control in Europe (see Table 57 above) are counted. Qualitative content analysis applies where the general policy topics, mentioned by U.S. and Soviet/Russian delegations, are highlighted.

The test is again abductive. It combines inductive and deductive methods. The test is inductive since reflections of specific key principles and norms of the regime complex from the U.S.-Soviet/Russian statements are used to make assertions about their general continued relevance and their respective state. Key principles and norms are marked as 'contested' with an 'X' if U.S. and Soviet/Russian views are diverging at the period of delivery of speeches. As reference base for assessing divergence, the statements as well as the empirical evidence of the respective period, analyzed in Chapter 3, are applied. In some statements, key principles and norms are not directly referred to but rather indirectly. As an example, the key principle of the 'indivisibility of security' is sometimes indirectly referred to as states' imperative not to 'strengthen their own security at the expense of the security of others' (OSCE 2012). In such cases, the indirect reference of the key principle is included in the assessment.

The ensuing test is also deductive since the general policy topics on the agendas of the United States and the Soviet Union/Russia are identified and broken down to allow for assertions about their specific content in relation to the twelve key principles and norms of the regime complex (see Table 57 above). Again, general policy topics are marked as 'contested' with an 'X' if U.S.-Soviet/Russian views are diverging, based on the statements as well as on the empirical evidence analyzed in Chapter 3. In the following paragraphs, all statements are quantitatively and qualitatively assessed in a matrix displaying which of the twelve key principles and norms of the regime complex

---

41   Most of the statements are available online at www.osce.org. Copies of the statements not available online have been provided by the OSCE archive in Prague to whose staff I am extremely grateful. U.S. and Russian statements from the 1991 Moscow Additional Ministerial Meeting were not available. The Russian statement from the 1993 Rome Ministerial is also not available. The U.S. and Russian Copenhagen statements of 1997 have an OSCE+' restricted distribution status and are not publicly available as well. The Soviet and Russian statements of 1991, 1993, and 1995 were only available in Russian. In these cases, professional translations were commissioned for this book.

are detectable and contested as well as what other general policy topics are relevant and contested.

7.2   Statements, Period 1990-1994

TABLE 60

SOVIET UNION, ASSESSMENT OF STATEMENT, PARIS, 1990

Statement	Statement 1: Speech by Soviet President Mikhail Gorbachev to the Second Summit of CSCE Heads of State or Government, Paris, November 19-21, 1990

	Detectable	Contested
Key Principles And Norms	• sovereign equality • commitment to conflict prevention • territorial integrity of states • strengthening stability • promoting arms control, disarmament, and CSBMs	
Other General Policy Topics	• end of the Cold War • U.S.-Soviet partnership • universal human values • freedom and democracy • rule of law • political pluralism • building a new order for Europe • recalling Helsinki principles • economic cooperation • transforming WTO and NATO • cooperation with the European Community • political solution to the Iraq/Kuwait crisis	

TABLE 61

UNITED STATES, ASSESSMENT OF STATEMENT, PARIS, 1990

Statement	Statement 2: Speech by U.S. President George Bush to the Second Summit of CSCE Heads of State or Government, Paris, November 19-21, 1990

	Detectable	Contested
Key Principles And Norms	• peaceful settlement of disputes • promoting arms control, disarmament, and CSBMs	
Other General Policy Topics	• recalling Helsinki principles • end of the Cold War • growing nationalism • protecting minority and human rights • democracy promotion • rule of law • Iraq/Kuwait crisis	

TABLE 62

SOVIET UNION, ASSESSMENT OF STATEMENT, BERLIN, 1991

Statement	Statement 3: Statement by the Minister of Foreign Affairs of the USSR, A. A. Bessmertnykh, at the first session of the Council of Ministers of Foreign Affairs of the participating States of the CSCE, Berlin, June 19, 1991 [Unofficial Translation]

	Detectable	Contested
Key Principles And Norms	• strengthening stability • indivisibility of security • further developing measures	
Other General Policy Topics	• maintenance of NATO questionable • profound transformation of all existing organizations • CSCE process not subordinated to NATO • more work on the 'second basket' • including naval forces in the CFE • comprehensive agreement on pan-European security	X X X X

TABLE 63

UNITED STATES, ASSESSMENT OF STATEMENT, BERLIN, 1991

Statement	Statement 4: European Architecture, Remarks by Secretary of State James A. Baker, III at the First Restricted Session of the CSCE Ministerial, Berlin, June 19, 1991

	Detectable	Contested
Key Principles And Norms	• promoting arms control, disarmament, and CSBMs • commitment to conflict prevention • further developing measures	
Other General Policy Topics	• recalling Helsinki principles • growing nationalism • political and economic freedom • retaining NATO • reaching out of European Community to the East • adapting CSCE structures • non-proliferation of WMD	X

TABLE 64

RUSSIAN FEDERATION, ASSESSMENT OF STATEMENT, PRAGUE, 1992

Statement	Statement 5: Statement by Andrei V. Kozyrev, Minister of Foreign Affairs of the Russian Federation at the CSCE Council Meeting, Prague, January 30, 1992

	Detectable	Contested
Key Principles And Norms	• promoting arms control, disarmament, and CSBMs • implementation of arms control, disarmament, and CSBM obligations • further developing measures • sovereign equality	

Other General Policy Topics	• democratic transition of Russia • recalling Helsinki principles • U.S.-Russia friendship • international guarantees and reciprocal verification mechanisms for Helsinki principles • expanding CSCE structures • CSCE peacekeeping operations • strengthening economic cooperation • protecting minority and human rights • building a new order for Europe (proposal of multilateral treaty on security and cooperation in Europe) • cooperation with NATO and the European Community	X

TABLE 65

UNITED STATES, ASSESSMENT OF STATEMENT, PRAGUE, 1992

Statement	**Statement 6: CSCE: Our Community of Democratic Values, Remarks by Secretary of State James A. Baker, III, CSCE Council of Ministers Meeting, Prague, January 30, 1992**

	Detectable	*Contested*
Key Principles And Norms	• strengthening stability • commitment to conflict prevention • promoting arms control, disarmament, and CSBMs • implementation of arms control, disarmament, and CSBM obligations • further developing measures	
Other General Policy Topics	• rule of law • market economies • civil societies • growing nationalism • recalling CSCE principles • Yugoslavia crisis • promoting democracy and human rights • strengthening economic cooperation • adapting CSCE structures	

TABLE 66

RUSSIAN FEDERATION, ASSESSMENT OF STATEMENT, HELSINKI, 1992

Statement	Statement 7: Speech by President Boris N. Yeltsin of the Russian Federation to the Third Summit of CSCE Heads of State or Government, Helsinki, July 9-10, 1992

	Detectable	Contested
Key Principles And Norms	• strengthening stability	
Other General Policy Topics	• promoting freedom and democracy • growing nationalism • Yugoslavia crisis • ethnic conflicts in the CIS • CSCE peacekeeping operations • protecting human rights • recalling Helsinki principles	

TABLE 67

UNITED STATES, ASSESSMENT OF STATEMENT, HELSINKI, 1992

Statement	Statement 8: Speech by U.S. President George Bush to the Third Summit of CSCE Heads of State or Government, Helsinki, July 9-10, 1992

	Detectable	Contested
Key Principles And Norms	• commitment to conflict prevention • further developing measures	
Other General Policy Topics	• Yugoslavia crisis • Protecting human rights • Growing nationalism • Promoting democracy • Sanction violations of CSCE norms • Adapting CSCE structures • NATO contribution to CSCE peacekeeping	

272

TABLE 68

RUSSIAN FEDERATION, ASSESSMENT OF STATEMENT, STOCKHOLM, 1992

Statement	**Statement 9: Statement by the Minister for Foreign Affairs of the Russian Federation, Mr. A. V. Kozyrev at the CSCE Council Meeting, Stockholm, December 14, 1992** [Unofficial Translation]

	Detectable	Contested
Key Principles And Norms	• see footnote[42]	
Other General Policy Topics	• see footnote	

TABLE 69

UNITED STATES, ASSESSMENT OF STATEMENT, STOCKHOLM, 1992

Statement	**Statement 10: Europe in Transition: The Role of CSCE, Lawrence S. Eagleburger, Secretary of State, CSCE Council Meeting, Stockholm, December 14, 1992**

	Detectable	Contested
Key Principles And Norms	• commitment to conflict prevention • further developing measures	
Other General Policy Topics	• overcoming the Cold War legacy • promoting freedom and democracy • tackling the Yugoslavia crisis • protecting human rights • adapting CSCE structures • tackling conflicts in the CIS recalling CSCE principles	

---

42   In his statement, Kozyrev used a rhetorical device and read out a statement, which did not reflect the Russian policy but which summarized the most radical arguments of the domestic Russian opposition. He did so in order to make the other delegations aware of the threats that Russia was still facing on its way to overcome the Communist legacy. His statement did thus not contain any detectable key principles and norms or other general policy issues.

273

TABLE 70

UNITED STATES, ASSESSMENT OF STATEMENT, ROME, 1993

Statement	Statement 11: Remarks by U.S. Secretary of State Warren Christopher at the CSCE Plenary Session, Rome, November 30, 1993

	Detectable	Contested
Key Principles And Norms	• commitment to conflict prevention • strengthening stability • refraining from the threat or use of force • territorial integrity of states • further developing measures	
Other General Policy Topics	• countering nationalism • promoting democracy • protecting human rights • securing freedom of the media • tackling the Yugoslavia crisis • adapting CSCE structures • tackling conflicts in the CIS • CSCE peacekeeping operations • promoting non-proliferation of WMD • maintaining NATO • fostering free market economies	X

TABLE 71

RUSSIAN FEDERATION, ASSESSMENT OF STATEMENT, BUDAPEST, 1994

Statement	Statement 12: Address by President Yeltsin of the Russian Federation at the CSCE Summit, Budapest, December 5, 1994 [Unofficial Translation]

	Detectable	Contested
Key Principles And Norms	• peaceful settlement of disputes, peaceful cooperation • commitment to conflict prevention	

Other General Policy Topics	• recalling Helsinki principles	
	• building a new order for Europe (legal, all-European organization, new Security Model)	X
	• calling for respect of Russian interests	
	• concern over NATO enlargement	X
	• protecting human rights	
	• countering nationalism	
	• CSCE peacekeeping operations	

TABLE 72

UNITED STATES, ASSESSMENT OF STATEMENT, BUDAPEST, 1994

Statement	Statement 13: Remarks by the President of the United States William J. Clinton at the Plenary Session of the Summit of the CSCE, Budapest, December 5, 1994

	Detectable	Contested
Key Principles And Norms	• commitment to conflict prevention • indivisibility of security	
Other General Policy Topics	• promoting democracy and freedom • ensuring free markets • tackling the Yugoslavia crisis • maintaining and enlarging NATO • countering spheres of influence • protecting human rights • CSCE peacekeeping operations • tackling conflicts in the CIS • promoting economic growth	X

TABLE 73

RUSSIAN FEDERATION, ASSESSMENT OF STATEMENT, BUDAPEST, 1995

Statement	**Statement 14: 'On a New Model of Common and Comprehensive Security for Europe in the 21st Century', Statement by A. V. Kozyrev at a session of the OSCE Ministerial Council, Budapest, December 7, 1995** [Unofficial Translation]

	Detectable	*Contested*
Key Principles And Norms	• indivisibility of security • further developing measures	
Other General Policy Topics	• Security Model discussion • Europe must be free of dividing lines • setting up OSCE peacekeeping operations • streamline inter-agency work • strengthening the economic dimension • transforming and strengthening the OSCE • updating the Helsinki Decalogue • legal capacity for the OSCE	X X X

TABLE 74

UNITED STATES, ASSESSMENT OF STATEMENT, BUDAPEST, 1995

Statement	**Statement 15: Intervention of Deputy Secretary of State Strobe Talbot, OSCE Ministerial, Budapest, December 7, 1995**

	Detectable	*Contested*
Key Principles And Norms	• commitment to conflict prevention • implementation of arms control, disarmament, and CSBM obligations	X
Other General	• countering nationalism	

Policy Topics	• respecting democracy • protecting human rights • rule of law • conflict in Chechnya • tackling conflicts in the CIS • CFE compliance in the Flank region • OSCE Security Model • recalling Helsinki principles	X

TABLE 75

RUSSIAN FEDERATION, ASSESSMENT OF STATEMENT, LISBON, 1996

Statement	**Statement 16: Address of the President of Russia Boris N. Yeltsin to the Participants of the Meeting of Heads of States or Government of the OSCE Participating States, Lisbon, December 2, 1996**

	Detectable	Contested
Key Principles And Norms	• commitment to conflict prevention • further developing measures • promoting arms control, disarmament, and CSBMs	
Other General Policy Topics	• OSCE Security Model • upgrading the OSCE • legal structures of a new European security architecture • protecting human rights • adaptation of CFE	X X

TABLE 76

UNITED STATES, ASSESSMENT OF STATEMENT, LISBON, 1996

Statement	Statement 17: Transcript of Vice-President Al Gore Statement, OSCE Lisbon Summit, Lisbon, December 2, 1996

	Detectable	Contested
Key Principles And Norms	• indivisibility of security • strengthening stability • further developing measures • promoting arms control, disarmament, and CSBMs	
Other General Policy Topics	• recalling Helsinki principles • tackling conflicts in the CIS • protecting human rights • Yugoslavia crisis • no transformation of OSCE into all-responsible security organization • no legal structures for OSCE • NATO enlargement proceeds • NATO poses no threat • building strong and cooperative NATO-Russia relationship • OSCE Security Model • adaptation of CFE	X X X

TABLE 77

RUSSIAN FEDERATION, ASSESSMENT OF STATEMENT, OSLO, 1998

Statement	Statement 18: Address by Mr. Igor S. Ivanov, Minister of Foreign Affairs of the Russian Federation at the Meeting of the OSCE Ministerial Council, Oslo, December 2, 1998 [Unofficial Translation]

	Detectable	Contested
Key Principles And Norms	• indivisibility of security • commitment to conflict prevention • territorial integrity of states • sovereign equality • promoting arms control, disarmament, and CSBMs	

278

Other General Policy Topics	• achieving legal capacity for the OSCE	X
	• OSCE peacekeeping operations	X
	• security enforcement only if mandated by UN Security Council	
	• OSCE Charter on European Security	
	• Kosovo conflict	
	• critique about pace of adaptation of CFE	X

TABLE 78

UNITED STATES, ASSESSMENT OF STATEMENT, OSLO, 1998

| Statement | Statement 19: Address to the OSCE Ministerial As Delivered by U.S. Head of Delegation Under Secretary Thomas R. Pickering, Oslo, December 2, 1998 |

	Detectable	Contested
Key Principles And Norms	• promoting arms control, disarmament, and CSBMs • commitment to conflict prevention • strengthening stability • promoting arms control, disarmament, and CSBMs	
Other General Policy Topics	• critique about theoretical focus of the OSCE Security Model • strengthening human rights • tackling conflicts in the CIS • withdrawal of Russian forces from Moldova • conflict in Chechnya • non-democratic conduct in Belarus • non-democratic conduct in Kazakhstan • development of OSCE Platform for Cooperative Security • adaptation of CFE • update of Vienna Document • Kosovo conflict • promoting democracy	X X

TABLE 79

RUSSIAN FEDERATION, ASSESSMENT OF STATEMENT, ISTANBUL, 1999

Statement	Statement 20: Statement by President Boris N. Yeltsin of the Russian Federation at the OSCE Summit, Istanbul, November 18, 1999 [Unofficial Translation]

	Detectable	*Contested*
Key Principles And Norms	• strengthening stability • strengthening confidence and security • sovereign equality	
Other General Policy Topics	• new transnational threats and challenges • combating terrorism • rebuking critique about Russian actions in Chechnya • ensuring human rights • rebuking humanitarian interventions • NATO aggression against Yugoslavia • recalling Helsinki principles • compliance with international law	 X X X

TABLE 80

UNITED STATES, ASSESSMENT OF STATEMENT, ISTANBUL, 1999

Statement	Statement 21: Remarks by the President of the United States William J. Clinton at the Opening of the OSCE Summit, Istanbul, November 18, 1999

	Detectable	*Contested*
Key Principles And Norms	• commitment to conflict prevention • further developing measures	
Other General Policy Topics	• adapting OSCE • new transnational threats and challenges • Russian actions in Chechnya • combating terrorism • alleged 'NATO aggression' against Yugoslavia • recalling Helsinki principles	 X X

TABLE 81

RUSSIAN FEDERATION, ASSESSMENT OF STATEMENT, VIENNA, 2000

Statement	**Statement 22: Statement of the Minister of Foreign Affairs of the Russian Federation Mr. Igor S. Ivanov at the Eighth Meeting of the Ministerial Council of the OSCE, Vienna, November 27, 2000** [Unofficial Translation]

	Detectable	*Contested*
Key Principles And Norms	• territorial integrity of states • implementation of arms control, disarmament, and CSBMs	X
Other General Policy Topics	• recalling Helsinki principles • new transnational threats and challenges • critique about strong OSCE focus on human rights issues in the East • critique about "double standards" within the OSCE • threat of growing nationalism • OSCE role in Chechnya • Russian compliance with the CFE 'Istanbul commitments' • achieving legal capacity of the OSCE	X X X X X

TABLE 82

UNITED STATES, ASSESSMENT OF STATEMENT, VIENNA, 2000

Statement	**Statement 23: Intervention by Secretary of State Madeleine K. Albright, OSCE Ministerial, Vienna, November 27, 2000**

	Detectable	*Contested*
Key Principles And Norms	• further developing measures • implementation of arms control, disarmament, and CSBMs	X
Other General Policy Topics	• recalling Helsinki principles • ensuring human rights	

	Detectable	Contested
	• adapting OSCE instruments	
	• OSCE role in Chechnya	X
	• Russian non-compliance with the CFE 'Istanbul com- mitments'	X
	• Russian non-compliance with CFE Flank ceilings	X
	• protracted conflicts in the Caucasus	

TABLE 83

RUSSIAN FEDERATION, ASSESSMENT OF STATEMENT, BUCHAREST, 2001

Statement	**Statement 24: Statement by Igor S. Ivanov, Minister of Foreign Affairs of the Russian Federation at the Ninth OSCE Ministerial Council Meeting, Bucharest, December 3, 2001** [Unofficial Translation]

	Detectable	Contested
Key Principles And Norms	• strengthening stability • further developing measures	
Other General Policy Topics	• combating terrorism • compliance with international law • reforming the OSCE • critique about strong OSCE focus on human rights issues in the East • promoting human rights	 X X

TABLE 84

UNITED STATES, ASSESSMENT OF STATEMENT, BUCHAREST, 2001

Statement	**Statement 25: Secretary of State Colin Powell's Remarks to the 9th OSCE Ministerial Council, Bucharest, December 4, 2001**

	Detectable	Contested
Key Principles And Norms	• strengthening stability • implementation of arms control, disarmament, and CSBMs • further developing measures	

	Detectable		Contested
Other General Policy Topics	<ul><li>respect for human rights</li><li>9/11 attacks</li><li>combating terrorism</li><li>support for war in Afghanistan</li><li>recalling Helsinki principles</li><li>progress in Chechnya</li><li>progress on Russia's CFE Istanbul commitments</li><li>ensuring stability in Macedonia</li><li>elections in Kosovo</li><li>situation in Bosnia</li><li>critique of Belarus</li><li>ensuring democratic development</li><li>no legal status for the OSCE</li><li>adapting OSCE instruments</li></ul>		 X X

TABLE 85

RUSSIAN FEDERATION, ASSESSMENT OF STATEMENT, PORTO, 2002

Statement	**Statement 26: Statement by the Minister for Foreign Affairs of the Russian Federation, Igor S. Ivanov at the Tenth Meeting of the OSCE Ministerial Council, Porto, December 6, 2002** [Unofficial Translation]

	Detectable	*Contested*
Key Principles And Norms	<ul><li>further developing measures</li><li>strengthening stability</li></ul>	
Other General Policy Topics	<ul><li>strengthening role of OSCE</li><li>combating terrorism</li><li>critique about "double standards"</li><li>reforming OSCE instruments</li></ul>	X X

283

TABLE 86

UNITED STATES, ASSESSMENT OF STATEMENT, PORTO, 2002

Statement	Statement 27; Statement by U.S. Undersecretary of State for Political Affairs Marc Grossman as delivered at the Tenth Meeting of the OSCE Ministerial Council, Porto, December 6, 2002	
	Detectable	Contested
Key Principles And Norms	• further developing measures • implementation of arms control, disarmament, and CSBMs	X
Other General Policy Topics	• tackling new transnational threats and challenges • adapting OSCE structures • ensuring human rights • human rights situation in Central Asia • combating terrorism • supporting OSCE field missions • Russian non-compliance with the CFE 'Istanbul commitments' • critique of Belarus • countering anti-Semitism	X X X

TABLE 87

RUSSIAN FEDERATION, ASSESSMENT OF STATEMENT, MAASTRICHT, 2003

Statement	Statement 28: Statement by Mr. Igor S. Ivanov, Minister for Foreign Affairs of the Russian Federation at the Eleventh Meeting of the OSCE Ministerial Council, Maastricht, December 1, 2003	
	Detectable	Contested
Key Principles And Norms	• further developing measures • implementation of arms control, disarmament, and CSBMs	X
Other General Policy Topics	• tackling new transnational threats and challenges • combating terrorism • resolving protracted conflicts	

	X
• dissent about Kozak Memorandum for Transnistria	X
• concern with the OSCE 'first basket'	X
• critique of postponement of ACFE ratification	X
• critique about state of the VD	X
• critique about missing OSCE peacekeeping capability	
• critique regarding treatment of Russian-speaking minorities in the Baltics	X
• critique of "Western" visa regulations	X
• adapting the OSCE's 'second basket'	
• reforming OSCE institutions	X

TABLE 88

UNITED STATES, ASSESSMENT OF STATEMENT, MAASTRICHT, 2003

Statement	Statement 29: Remarks of The Secretary of State Colin L. Powell at the 11th Ministerial Council of the OSCE, Maastricht, December 2, 2003

	Detectable	Contested
Key Principles And Norms	• implementation of arms control, disarmament, and CSBMs	X
Other General Policy Topics	• recalling Helsinki principles • tackling new transnational threats and challenges • combating terrorism • countering intolerance • solving the conflict in Moldova • critique of Russian non-compliance with CFE Istanbul commitments • addressing protracted conflicts • critique about human rights standards in Belarus and Turkmenistan • critique about situation in Chechnya • welcoming Georgian revolution	X X X X X

TABLE 89

RUSSIAN FEDERATION, ASSESSMENT OF STATEMENT, SOFIA, 2004

Statement	Statement 30: Statement by Mr. Sergei V. Lavrov, Minister for Foreign Affairs of the Russian Federation at the Twelfth Meeting of the OSCE Ministerial Council, Sofia, December 7, 2004

	Detectable	Contested
Key Principles And Norms	• further developing measures • strengthening stability • strengthening confidence and security • implementation of arms control, disarmament, and CSBMs • promoting arms control, disarmament, and CSBMs	 X X
Other General Policy Topics	• combating terrorism • critique of postponement of ACFE ratification • calling to adapt the VD • critique about handling of Kozak Memorandum • critique of new Georgian government • proposal of conference on the energy sector • protecting Russian minorities in the Baltics • critique of OSCE "double standards" • preventing new dividing lines • need for comprehensive OSCE reform	 X X X X X X X

TABLE 90

UNITED STATES, ASSESSMENT OF STATEMENT, SOFIA, 2004

Statement	Statement 31: Remarks by Secretary of State Colin L. Powell to the Ministerial Meeting of the OSCE, Sofia, December 7, 2004

	Detectable	Contested
Key Principles And Norms	• further developing measures • implementation of arms control, disarmament, and CSBMs	 X

Other General Policy Topics	• ensuring minority rights	
	• engaging on protracted conflicts	
	• critique of Russian non-compliance with CFE Istanbul commitments	X
	• Ukraine elections	X
	• democracy deficit in Russia	X
	• dismissing "double standards"	X
	• supporting OSCE field missions	
	• respecting human rights	
	• ensuring rule of law	

TABLE 91

RUSSIAN FEDERATION, ASSESSMENT OF STATEMENT, LJUBLJANA, 2005

Statement	Statement 32: Statement by Mr. Sergei V. Lavrov, Minister for Foreign Affairs of the Russian Federation at the Thirteenth Meeting of the OSCE Ministerial Council, Ljubljana, December 5, 2005

	Detectable	Contested
Key Principles And Norms	• indivisibility of security	X
	• further developing measures	
	• implementation of arms control, disarmament, and CSBMs	X
Other General Policy Topics	• dissatisfaction with the OSCE's work	X
	• "double standards"	X
	• need to reform the OSCE	X
	• legal capacity for the OSCE	X
	• critique about the work of ODIHR	X
	• critique about strong OSCE focus on human rights issues in the East	X
	• protecting Russian minorities in the Baltics	X
	• OSCE neglects the principle of co-operation	X
	• critique of postponement of ACFE ratification	X

TABLE 92

UNITED STATES, ASSESSMENT OF STATEMENT, LJUBLJANA, 2005

Statement	Statement 33: Intervention at the Thirteenth OSCE Ministerial Council as delivered by Under Secretary for Political Affairs R. Nicholas Burns to the 13th OSCE Ministerial Council, Ljubljana, December 5, 2005

	Detectable	Contested
Key Principles And Norms	• further developing measures • implementation of arms control, disarmament, and CSBMs	X
Other General Policy Topics	• advancing human freedoms • fostering democracy • strengthening the OSCE • critique about Uzbekistan • applauding ODIHR • strengthening NGOs • addressing protracted conflicts • welcoming Georgian action plan for South Ossetia • critique of Russian non-compliance with CFE Istanbul commitments • OSCE needs no "fixing"	 X X X X X X

TABLE 93

RUSSIAN FEDERATION, ASSESSMENT OF STATEMENT, BRUSSELS, 2006

Statement	Statement 34: Address of Mr. Sergey V. Lavrov, Minister of Foreign Affairs of the Russian Federation before the 14th Meeting of the OSCE Ministerial Council, Brussels, December 4, 2006

	Detectable	Contested
Key Principles And Norms	• sovereign equality • further developing measures • implementation of arms control, disarmament, and CSBMs	X X

288

Other General Policy Topics	• efforts to revive OSCE have failed	X
	• 'first basket' becomes irrelevant	X
	• critique of postponement of ACFE ratification	X
	• critique about exclusive focus on human rights	X
	• need to reform OSCE	
	• need to reform ODIHR	X
	• OSCE misused as a vehicle to advance one-sided interests regarding protracted conflicts	X
	• recalling Helsinki principles	X

TABLE 94

UNITED STATES, ASSESSMENT OF STATEMENT, BRUSSELS, 2006

Statement	Statement 35: Statement by the Head of Delegation of the United States of America, Under Secretary of State for Political Affairs R. Nicholas Burns at the 14th OSCE Ministerial Council, Brussels, December 4, 2006

	Detectable	Contested
Key Principles And Norms	• further developing measures • sovereign equality • territorial integrity of states • implementation of arms control, disarmament, and CSBMs	X
Other General Policy Topics	• countering transnational threats and challenges • recalling OSCE principles • degradation of Helsinki principles in recent years • critique of Russian non-compliance with CFE Istanbul commitments • critique of Belarus • critique of human rights standards in certain countries • more support for Moldova and Georgia • engaging in protracted conflicts • strengthening the OSCE • dismissing attempts at OSCE reform • applauding ODIHR • strengthening human rights	X X X X X X X

TABLE 95

RUSSIAN FEDERATION, ASSESSMENT OF STATEMENT, MADRID, 2007

Statement	Statement 36: Statement by Mr. Sergei V. Lavrov, Minister for Foreign Affairs of the Russian Federation at the Fifteenth Meeting of the OSCE Ministerial Council, Madrid, November 29, 2007

	Detectable	Contested
Key Principles And Norms	• sovereign equality • implementation of arms control, disarmament, and CSBMs	X X
Other General Policy Topics	• Helsinki principles undermined • critique about Kosovo development • OSCE lacks relevance • need for legal capacity of OSCE • European architecture about to crash • "double standards" • critique of NGOs • critique of ODIHR • critique of VD development • Russian CFE suspension • countering new threats and challenges • protecting Russian minorities in the Baltics • critique about strong OSCE focus on human rights issues in the East	X X X X X X X X X X X X

TABLE 96

UNITED STATES, ASSESSMENT OF STATEMENT, MADRID, 2007

Statement	Statement 37: Intervention to the OSCE Ministerial Council, Under Secretary of State for Political Affairs Nicholas Burns, Madrid, November 29, 2007

	Detectable	Contested
Key Principles And Norms	• implementation of arms control, disarmament, and CSBMs	X

Other General Policy Topics		
	• no consensus on cooperative security	X
	• ignorance of human rights commitments	X
	• lack of democracy in some states	X
	• certain proposals undermining OSCE acquis	X
	• lack of rule of law in certain states	X
	• efforts undermining ODIHR	
	• CFE crisis	X
	• situation in Kosovo	X
	• more work in Central Asia to be done	X

TABLE 97

RUSSIAN FEDERATION, ASSESSMENT OF STATEMENT, HELSINKI, 2008

Statement	Statement 38: Statement by Mr. Sergei V. Lavrov, Minister for Foreign Affairs of the Russian Federation at the Sixteenth Meeting of the OSCE Ministerial Council, Helsinki, December 5, 2008

	Detectable	Contested
Key Principles And Norms	• sovereign equality	X
	• indivisibility of security	X
	• further developing measures	
Other General Policy Topics	• OSCE cannot prevent wars anymore (e.g. 1999 Yugoslavia, 2008 South Ossetia)	X
	• critique about OSCE field missions and ODIHR	X
	• Medvedev EST draft proposal	
	• restoring CAC	X
	• Russia-Georgia war	
	• new threats and challenges	X
	• legal capacity for the OSCE	
	• progress on protracted conflicts	X

TABLE 98

UNITED STATES, ASSESSMENT OF STATEMENT, HELSINKI, 2008

Statement	Statement 39: United States Intervention to the 2008 OSCE Ministerial Council as delivered by Under Secretary of State for Political Affairs William J. Burns to the Ministerial Council, Helsinki, December 4, 2008

	Detectable	Contested
Key Principles And Norms	• promoting arms control, disarmament, and CSBMs	X
Other General Policy Topics	• recalling Helsinki principles • addressing situation in Georgia • resolve protracted conflicts • preserve CFE • fully implementing human rights	X

7.5   Statements, Period 2009-2011

TABLE 99

RUSSIAN FEDERATION, ASSESSMENT OF STATEMENT, ATHENS, 2009

Statement	Statement 40: Statement by Mr. Sergei V. Lavrov, Minister for Foreign Affairs of the Russian Federation at the Seventeenth Meeting of the OSCE Ministerial Council, Athens, December 1, 2009

	Detectable	Contested
Key Principles And Norms	• further developing measures • promoting arms control, disarmament, and CSBMs	X
Other General Policy Topics	• overcoming dividing lines • poor state of 'first basket' • Medvedev EST draft proposal • OSCE Corfu process	X

292

		X
•	reforming OSCE	X
•	legal capacity for the OSCE	
•	updating the VD	X
•	CFE deadlock	
•	combating transnational threats and challenges	
•	inter-organizational work on human rights	X
•	striving for a visa-free regime in Europe	

TABLE 100

UNITED STATES, ASSESSMENT OF STATEMENT, ATHENS, 2009

Statement	**Statement 41: 17th OSCE Ministerial Council, Statement by Deputy Secretary of State James Steinberg, Athens, December 1, 2009**

	Detectable	Contested
Key Principles And Norms	• implementation of arms control, disarmament, and CSBM obligations • indivisibility of security • sovereign equality • promoting arms control, disarmament, and CSBMs	X X X
Other General Policy Topics	• Corfu process • Medvedev EST draft proposal • CFE principle of host nation consent • promoting conflict resolution • countering transnational threats and challenges • engaging on energy security • tackling protracted conflicts • OSCE principles and commitments were violated in the Russia-Georgia war 2008 • updating VD • CFE deadlock • protecting human rights	 X X X

TABLE 101

RUSSIAN FEDERATION, ASSESSMENT OF STATEMENT, ASTANA, 2010

Statement	Statement 42: Speech of the President of the Russian Federation D. A. Medvedev at the plenary meeting of the OSCE summit, Astana, December 1, 2010

	Detectable	Contested
Key Principles And Norms	• indivisibility of security • further developing measures • promoting arms control, disarmament, and CSBMs	X
Other General Policy Topics	• Medvedev EST draft proposal • overcoming dividing lines • recalling Helsinki principles • updating VD • CFE deadlock • securing a common information space • allow more freedom of movement (visa) • countering transnational threats and challenges • develop a set of common principles for conflict resolution • Russia-Georgia war 2008 • reform the OSCE • achieve legal capacity for the OSCE	X X X X X X X X

TABLE 102

UNITED STATES, ASSESSMENT OF STATEMENT, ASTANA, 2010

Statement	Statement 43: Remarks by Secretary of State Hillary Rodham Clinton at the OSCE Summit, Astana, December 1, 2010

	Detectable	Contested
Key Principles and Norms	• further developing measures • commitment to conflict prevention • promoting arms control, disarmament, and CSBMs	

294

Other General Policy Topics	<ul><li>recalling Helsinki principles</li><li>OSCE principles and commitments face serious challenges</li><li>supporting mutual interests in Afghanistan</li><li>situation in Georgia</li><li>tackling protracted conflicts</li><li>updating VD</li><li>engage in the human dimension</li></ul>	X

TABLE 103

RUSSIAN FEDERATION, ASSESSMENT OF STATEMENT, VILNIUS, 2011

Statement	**Statement 44: Statement by Mr. Sergei V. Lavrov, Minister for Foreign Affairs of the Russian Federation at the Eighteenth Meeting of the OSCE Ministerial Council, Vilnius, December 6, 2011**

	Detectable	Contested
Key Principles And Norms	<ul><li>indivisibility of security</li><li>commitment to conflict prevention</li><li>further developing measures</li></ul>	X
Other General Policy Topics	<ul><li>Medvedev EST draft proposal</li><li>misuse of UN Security Council resolutions</li><li>"double standards"</li><li>cooperation amongst IOs</li><li>task of establishing security community</li><li>countering transnational threats and challenges</li><li>common standards for conflict prevention and resolution</li><li>tackling protracted conflicts</li><li>growing nationalism</li><li>reforming the OSCE</li><li>achieving legal capacity for the OSCE</li></ul>	X X X X X

TABLE 104

UNITED STATES, ASSESSMENT OF STATEMENT, VILNIUS, 2011

Statement	Statement 45: Remarks by Secretary of State Hillary Rodham Clinton at the OSCE First Plenary Session, Vilnius, December 6, 2011

	Detectable	Contested
Key Principles And Norms	• strengthening stability	
Other General Policy Topics	• strengthening human rights • critique on Belarus (human rights) • critique on Ukraine (human rights) • critique on Russia (human rights and elections) • freedom of the internet • situation in the Middle East • CFE deadlock • tackling protracted conflicts	X X X X X

7.6   Statements, Period 2012-2014

TABLE 105

RUSSIAN FEDERATION, ASSESSMENT OF STATEMENT, DUBLIN, 2012

Statement	Statement 46: Statement by Mr. Sergei V. Lavrov, Minister for Foreign Affairs of the Russian Federation at the Nineteenth Meeting of the OSCE Ministerial Council, Dublin, December 6, 2012

	Detectable	Contested
Key Principles And Norms	• indivisibility of security • further developing measures • promoting arms control, disarmament, and CSBMs	X

296

Other General Policy Topics	• initiatives such as 'security community' and EST stalled due to unilateral policies	X
	• dividing lines	X
	• critique on U.S. missile defense plans for Europe	X
	• politico-military dimension in decay	
	• arms control used to achieve other political goals	X
	• countering transnational threats and challenges	X
	• economic crisis in the EU	
	• critique on visa barriers	
	• critique on "double standards" by ODIHR	X
	• continue work on CBMs for the Internet	X
	• tackling protracted conflicts	
	• reforming OSCE (legal basis)	X

TABLE 106

UNITED STATES, ASSESSMENT OF STATEMENT, DUBLIN, 2012

Statement	**Statement 47: Remarks by U.S. Secretary of State Hillary Rodham Clinton at the Intervention at the OSCE Ministerial Council First Plenary Session, Dublin, December 6, 2012**

	Detectable	Contested
Key Principles And Norms	• --	
Other General Policy Topics	• human rights are being challenged	X
	• critique on Russia, Belarus, Ukraine, Tajikistan, Turkmenistan, Uzbekistan, Kazakhstan, Hungary, Romania (human rights)	X
	• 'declaration on fundamental freedoms in the digital age' blocked	X
	• no institutional changes that would weaken the OSCE	X

TABLE 107

RUSSIAN FEDERATION, ASSESSMENT OF STATEMENT, KYIV, 2013

Statement	Statement 48: Statement by Mr. Sergei V. Lavrov, Minister for Foreign Affairs of the Russian Federation at the Twentieth Meeting of the OSCE Ministerial Council, Kyiv, December 5, 2013

	Detectable	Contested
Key Principles And Norms	• indivisibility of security • commitment to conflict prevention • further developing measures	X
Other General Policy Topics	• no progress on 'security community' • dividing lines continue • critique on visa barriers • politico-military dimension in decay • tackling transnational threats and challenges • countering protracted conflicts • continue discussion on energy security • international regulation of the Internet • critique about neoliberal interpretations of human rights • growing nationalism • achieve a legal basis for the OSCE • critique about ODIHR	X X X X X X X X

TABLE 108

UNITED STATES, ASSESSMENT OF STATEMENT, KYIV, 2013

Statement	Statement 49: Remarks by Victoria Nuland, Assistant Secretary for European and Eurasian Affairs at the OSCE Ministerial Council, Kyiv, December 5, 2013

	Detectable	Contested
Key Principles And Norms	• strengthening stability	

298

	Detectable	Contested
Other General Policy Topics	• U.S. support for Ukraine protests at Maidan • respect for human rights and fundamental freedom • human dimension in decay in a number of countries • oppression of freedom of speech • critique of Russia, Belarus, Kazakhstan, Azerbaijan, Uzbekistan, Hungary, and Turkey (human rights) • increase work in the OSCE's first dimension • addressing protracted conflicts • tackling corruption	X X X X

TABLE 109

RUSSIAN FEDERATION, ASSESSMENT OF STATEMENT, BASEL, 2014

Statement	**Statement 50: Statement by Mr. Sergei V. Lavrov, Minister for Foreign Affairs of the Russian Federation at the Twenty-First Meeting of the OSCE Ministerial Council, Basel, December 4, 2014**

	Detectable	Contested
Key Principles And Norms	• indivisibility of security • sovereign equality	X
Other General Policy Topics	• recognition of Helsinki principles • unilateral approaches and the failure to recognize mistakes have contributed to Euro-Atlantic crisis • criticizing the EU • Western support of Ukrainian 'coup d'état' • Ukrainian offensive against ethnic Russian minority • Minsk Agreements • OSCE must intensify efforts related to the SMM and participation in the Contact Group • 'European House' has been consistently undermined by unilateral actions (i.e. NATO enlargement, EPAA, EU Eastern Partnership) • support of the Helsinki+40 process • ensure freedom of movement, protect the rights of ethnic minorities and end all intolerance • OSCE must become a fully fledged international organization • establishment of Panel of Eminent Persons	 X X X X X X

TABLE 110

UNITED STATES, ASSESSMENT OF STATEMENT, BASEL, 2014

Statement	Statement 51; Remarks by Secretary of State John Kerry at OSCE Ministerial Plenary Session, Basel, December 4, 2014

	Detectable	Contested
Key Principles And Norms	• --	
Other General Policy Topics	• recalling Helsinki principles • Ukraine tested by external aggression • value of OSCE in Ukraine conflict • Russian weapons supply to Ukrainian separatists • Russian non-compliance with OSCE obligations • U.S. does not seek confrontation • Russia should take steps to end the conflict (e.g. end Crimea annexation) • Russia unwilling to abide by the rules and the principles of the OSCE • numerous violations of Helsinki principles in 2014 • repression of civil societies in a number of OSCE participating States • OSCE concentration on the Third Basket	X X X X X X X X X

7.7   Assessment of the Second Abductive Test's Results

Of the twelve key principles and norms of the regime complex, five are mentioned only very rarely in the 51 statements. Those are the principles of 'territorial integrity', 'peaceful settlement of disputes, peaceful cooperation', 'strengthening confidence and security', 'refraining from the threat or use of force', and of 'sufficiency'. All other principles and norms are mentioned regularly, though to very differing degrees. The principle to 'further develop measures' is most often mentioned (27 cases). At the same time, this principle is not contested at all. The second most often mentioned principle is the 'implementation of arms control, disarmament, and CSBM obligations' (17 cases). This principle also displays the highest degree of contention. In 15 cases, the principle was directly or indirectly debated in connection to non-compliance of either Russia or the (Russian perception of non-compliance of the) United States. Two other principles and norms are also highly contested.

One of them is the 'indivisibility of security' (eight out of 13 cases); the other is the principle of 'sovereign equality' (four out of ten cases). The rest of the principles and norms is either not contested at all or only minimally contested in the statements. Table 111 lists the twelve key principles and norms of the regime complex, arranged in descending order of the number of their being mentioned in the statements. A second row of figures quantifies occurrences of contestation.

TABLE 111

ASSESSMENT OF STATEMENTS: KEY PRINCIPLES AND NORMS MENTIONED

	detectable	contested
further developing measures	27	0
implementation of arms control, disarmament, and CSBM obligations	17	15
commitment to conflict prevention	16	0
promoting arms control, disarmament, and CSBMs	15	2
strengthening stability	14	0
indivisibility of security	13	8
sovereign equality	10	4
territorial integrity of States	5	0
peaceful settlement of disputes, peaceful cooperation	2	0
strengthening confidence and security	2	0
refraining from the threat or use of force	1	0
principle of sufficiency	0	0
total	**122**	**29**

The results of this first assessment lead to a number of conclusions. First, while some principles and norms have been mentioned regularly, others have not. There are issue-specific reasons why that is the case. The principle of 'sufficiency' (not mentioned at all) has lost most of its attention since the end of the bloc confrontation, the fulfillment of the disarmament stipulations of

CFE, shrinking national defense budgets in a number of OSCE participating States (see IISS 1973-2014), and the revolution in military affairs have led to significantly smaller national forces anyways (cf. also Chart 31 above). The principle to 'refrain from the threat or use of force' (mentioned one time) has lost certain prominence as the post-Cold War peace made international incidents of the use of force in the Euro-Atlantic area for most of the time obsolete. However, the Russian-Georgian war of 2008 and Russia's covert incursions into Ukraine in 2014 (cf. Freedman 2014) could trigger a revival of the use of the principle together with the principle of the 'territorial integrity of states'.

Second, three principles are strongly contested, which points to a high degree of divergent views. The principle of the 'indivisibility of security' has served the function of a template for accusations by Russia (cf. Cliff 2012). Almost all Russian critique directed at NATO enlargement or other relevant cases of U.S.-Russian disagreement were underpinned by quotation of the principle (ibid). A similar function applies to the principle of 'sovereign equality'. As can be seen in the tables of the previous five paragraphs, U.S. policy towards the C/OSCE was mostly dominated by concentration on human rights issues (see for example the last U.S. Statement by John Kerry, Basel 2014, Table 110 above). This fact derives from Washington's historically rooted understanding of the CSCE as a vehicle for human rights promotion in the East (cf. Schlotter 1999). With the change in presidency from William J. Clinton to George W. Bush, this pillar of U.S. foreign policy gained additional propulsion and led to an increase of instances of accusations of human rights violations in a number of eastern countries, amongst them Russia. In turn, Russia rejected such claims as violation of the principle of 'sovereign equality' or as interference in internal, Russian, affairs (see for example the last Russian statement by Sergei Lavrov, Basel 2014, Table 109 above). Last but not least, the contested state of the principle of the 'implementation of arms control, disarmament, and CSBM obligations' is a direct result of the high number of occurrences of deviant behavior in the arms control realm – most notably by Russia and in conjunction with the CFE Treaty.

Third, the large number of references to the principle of 'further developing measures' is the result of three critical motivations: (1) International institutions in general tend to be permanently concerned with advancing their governing instruments in order not to become obsolete (see Cirincione 2000b). This is a general form of institutional persistence and an indirect outcome of Keohane's (1984: 103) argument of the cost-effective maintenance of regimes. (2) During the last 25 years, Europe has experienced an unprecedented era of fundamental shifts and changes. From the peaceful management of the end of the Cold War, over violent ethnic conflicts in Yugoslavia and a number of CIS states, the emergence of transnational threats such as terrorism, to the dawning of the information age: this short era of ample change made adaptation inevitable, as can be read in most of the statements contained above. Particularly the C/OSCE with its three-dimensional approach at security (cf. Krause 2003) was always under pressure to develop timely governing instruments, addressing newly emerging threats to security (cf. IFSH 1997-2014). (3) Russia was almost always dissatisfied with the structures of the C/OSCE. Be it the contested attempt to achieve a legal capacity for the OSCE, the 1990s 'Security Model', the conclusion of the 1999 Charter for European Security, or the 2008 Medvedev EST draft and the ensuing Corfu Process, Moscow was a constant and impatient driver behind institutional adaptation.

Where there are any correlations between the normative and the policy level on the two countries' general policy agendas between 1990 and 2014? Of the multitude of different policy topics mentioned, in the following matrix, the top 15 general policy topics are assessed with a view to their occurrence and to their state of contention.[43] All in all, 13 of the 15 general policy topics were at some point contested. Only the policy topics of 'countering/addressing new transnational threats and challenges (including terrorism)' and of 'countering growing nationalism' were completely uncontested. Most often, the topic of 'reforming/transforming C/OSCE (including possibility of legal capacity and Medvedev EST)' was mentioned (60 cases). This topic, together with the topics of 'human rights critique towards specific states (including treatment of Russian minorities)' and of the CFE Treaty, was also among the top three contested topics. Table 112 lists the general policy topics and quantifies their degree of contestation.

TABLE 112

ASSESSMENT OF STATEMENTS: TOP 15 GENERAL POLICY TOPICS

	detectable	contested
reforming/transforming C/OSCE (including possibility of legal personality and Medvedev EST)	60	34
human rights critique towards specific states (including treatment of Russian minorities)	39	37
engaging on protracted conflicts	32	12
protecting/strengthening human rights	31	4

---

43 Only such general policy topics are listed that were mentioned more than seven times in the 51 statements.

CFE Treaty	28	23
recalling Helsinki principles (including mentioned cases of erosion of principles)	28	6
countering/addressing new transnational threats and challenges (including terrorism)	23	0
Yugoslavia wars/crises (including Kosovo)	16	4
promoting democracy and freedom	16	2
countering growing nationalism	11	0
debate about NATO transformation/enlargement	10	7
critique about OSCE imbalance between the three dimensions	9	7
assessment of the work of ODIHR	9	9
C/OSCE peacekeeping	9	3
critique about OSCE human rights "double standards"	8	8
total	**328**	**155**

Almost all policy topics in the above matrix were/are to different degrees a matter of contention. Correlating with the findings from Table 112, the topic of 'reforming/transforming C/OSCE (including possibility of legal personality and Medvedev EST)' is at the top spot and shows strong features of contention. This fact underscores once more that divergent issue-specific interests between the United States and Russia have shaped the institutional evolution of the C/OSCE. While the topic in all its changing facets was addressed throughout the whole of the evaluation period, most often by Russia, it was also indirectly referred to by the heavy use of the key principle of 'further developing measures' (see Table 112). The topic of 'human rights critique towards specific states (including treatment of Russian minorities)' was most often brought forward by U.S. delegations but also mentioned by Russian delegations in conjunction with Russian minorities in the Baltics and in Ukraine. As this topic was almost always directed at Russia or Russian protégé states such as Belarus, it received in turn strong criticism by Russia and is thus the most contested topic on the list. It also correlates with the key principle of 'sovereign equality' which was used by Russia to rebuke human rights criticism. The high level of contention surrounding the CFE topic correlates with the use of the key principle of the 'implementation of arms control, disarmament, and CSBM obligations' in conjunction with Russian non-compliance. Because the contested CFE Treaty is closely interwoven with the three protracted conflicts in Georgia and Moldova (through the Istanbul commitments; cf. Kühn 2009), also the general policy topic of 'engaging on protracted conflicts' shows a comparably high degree of contention.

Aside from the high degree of contention surrounding most general policy topics, an even more pronounced insight derives from assessing the trend dynamics of contestation. When counting the overall number of contested topics and principles per year, an increasing, though volatile, trend is visible. From 1990 to 2014, the number of contested general policy topics has steadily risen with two periods of heavy average increase (2000-2008 and 2011-2012), interrupted by a period of a significant drop in contested general policy topics (2008-2011). Chart 38 visualized these trend dynamics.

CHART 38

U.S.-SOVIET/RUSSIAN CONTESTED POLITICS IN C/OSCE FRAMEWORK:
TREND DYNAMICS 1990-2014

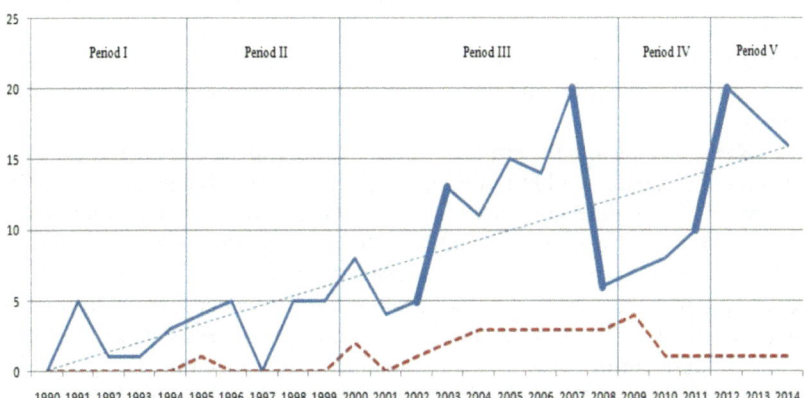

For Chart 38: dashed red line indicates trend in occurrences of contested key principles and norms of the regime complex of cooperative arms control in Europe; continuous blue line indicates trend in occurrences of contested general policy topics. Bold segments highlight periods of strong change (Δ). Please note: for the Stockholm Ministerial 1992 (see Table 68 and corresponding footnote) and for the year 1993, no Russian statements were included in the assessment. For the year 1997, no statement by either delegation was publicly available. Dashed blue line = mean trend line for occurrences of contested general policy topics.

The strong increase between 2000 and 2008 correlates with the two presidential terms of George W. Bush and the first two presidential terms of Vladimir Putin. Within this period, the year 2003 marks a peak in increase (Δ+8). As outlined in Chapter 3, these dates correlate with a change in politics in Washington and Moscow towards each other, towards the OSCE, and the 2003 Iraq War. Between 2008 and 2011 the drop in contested general policy topics correlates with the coming into office of Barack Obama in 2008 (Δ-14), the subsequent "reset" policy, the Medvedev draft EST proposals, and the OSCE Corfu Process. With the return to power of Vladimir Putin and the subsequent protests in Moscow, contested general policy topics have skyrocket in 2012 (Δ+10).

Besides this correlation with domestic political developments in the United States and Russia, the trend dynamics also correlate with the trends from Chart 35 above which displays occurrences of indicators of regime decay and from Chart 37 above, which shows occurrences of non-compliance. For all three trends it is remarkable that from the year 2000 onwards trend dynamics have considerably gone up.

7.8   Conclusions

The constant rhetorical reference by U.S. and Soviet/Russian delegations to the C/OSCE of key principles and norms, their state of contestation, the comparably higher degree of contested policies, and the high number of occurrences of non-compliance lead to conclude that the United States and Russia deal with key principles and norms at different levels and with different outcomes.

Key principles and norms are firstly dealt with at a declaratory level. This level is mostly visible in the form of references in the preambular paragraphs of the regime complex's agreements (see agreements contained in Annex II). It is also often referred to in the general introductory remarks of U.S. and Russian political statements (see statements contained in Chapter 7). Key principles and norms are also dealt with at a second, the interpretative level (cf. Rotfeld 2014: 57). This level becomes manifest in the two states' ability to agree or disagree on institutionalization based on the key principles and norms. Besides the mere ability to agreement-making, this level is also reflected in the general policies that the two states pursue and that reflects their respective interpretations of key principles and norms. At the third level, their respective interpretations of key principles and norms and the related policies flow directly into the implementation of agreements. This level becomes most visible by acts of compliance or non-compliance with certain agreements (see Chart 37 above), and thus, in an indirect way, with the underlying key principles and norms.

Not only do the two states deal with key principles and norms at three different levels, the outcome at each level differs remarkably. At the declaratory level, the key principles and norms of the regime complex of cooperative arms control in Europe remain unchanged. Without making any unsubstantiated statements about the likely processes of negotiation, they are regularly referred to in an uncontested manner. U.S. and Russian delegations have referred to the Helsinki Decalogue in 26 statements and have repeatedly made use of the key principles and norms of the regime complex of cooperative arms control in Europe in 122 cases. In only one of the 51 statements has a Russian delegation brought forward concrete arguments in favor of changing or abandoning key principles and norms. In 1995, the Russian Minister of Foreign Affairs Andrei Kozyrev stated: 'It is possible that it will be necessary to update, to a certain degree, the Helsinki Decalogue, including finding and formulating the optimum relationship between the principles of the inviolability of borders and the territorial integrity of states, on the one hand, and the right of nations to self-determination, on the other.' (OSCE 1995, Statement 14, Table 73 above) Aside from this exception from the rule, which did not result in any changes, no visible change to key principles and norms has occurred.

The picture changes when looking at the interpretative level. In 29 cases, key principles and norms have been a matter of contention between the United States and Russia. When directly linking key principles and norms to concrete policies, divergent interpretations of the meaning of principles and norms become visible. The principle of 'strengthening stability' is a good example. At the declaratory level, the principle remains uncontested. However, Russia's occupation of parts of Ukraine in 2014 (cf. Freedman 2014) has been interpreted by most Ukrainian and Western politicians as destabilizing not just for Ukraine, but also for the Russian-Ukrainian relationship as well as for NATO-Russian relations (ibid). As NATO member states pointed out at the 2014 NATO Summit, 'Russia continues to supply weapons to militants in eastern Ukraine; and it maintains thousands of combat-ready troops on its border with Ukraine. These developments undermine the security of Ukraine and have serious implications for the stability and security of the entire Euro-Atlantic area.' (NATO-Ukraine Commission 2014)

From the Russian perspective, it is the possible prospect of future NATO membership of Ukraine which is perceived as de-stabilizing. In 2008, Vladimir Putin explained to the press that NATO membership of Ukraine would 'force Russia into a situation where it has to take countermeasures [including] to target its nuclear offensive systems at Ukraine.' (President of Russia 2008) Obviously, differing interpretations of the principle of 'stability' prevail. What pertains to the international level finds its continuation at the domestic level. According to Herd (2013: 396), 'the notion that authoritarianism is the solution to instability, rather than its cause, still prevails in the minds of many [Russian] elites. According to this understanding, human rights, democracy, and humanitarian interventions undermine the stability of government and societies.'

Another example is the 'indivisibility of security'. While Moscow sees NATO enlargement as 'a serious provocation that reduces the level of mutual trust' (President of Russia 2007) and thus as contrary to the principle, the United States view enlargement as being in line with the principle and not directed at Russia (cf. OSCE 1996). While Russia criticizes the treatment of Russian minorities in the Baltics as being in conflict with the human rights approach of the OSCE, it repels U.S. claims about Russia's human rights record as being contrary to the principle of 'sovereign equality'.

While Moscow and Washington agree on the principle of the 'implementation of arms control, disarmament, and CSBM obligations', both interpret it differently when it comes to substantiation. The Kremlin interprets the CFE Istanbul commitments as 'artificial conditions that had nothing at all to do with the CFE Treaty' (OSCE 2007a). Washington and NATO insist that 'swift fulfillment of the outstanding Istanbul commitments on Georgia and Moldova […] will create the conditions for Allies and other States Parties to move forward on ratification of the Adapted CFE Treaty.' (NATO 2002)

These examples show that the United States and Russia do not share a common understanding of the meaning of key principles and norms when it comes to concrete policy implications. Rotfeld (2014: 57) concludes, 'countries in the Euro-Atlantic area have recognized the catalogue of European values agreed upon in the OSCE constitutional documents as their common foundation, but they have stuck to their own specific interpretations of these principles and values.' The result is that at the interpretative level, key principles and norms are highly contested.

Even more visible, at the implementation level, key principles and norms of the regime complex have undergone a process of active and ongoing erosion through acts of non-compliance. The 'implementation of arms control agreements' was eroded through repeated instances of non-compliance. The most serious cases are Russian non-compliance with the CFE Istanbul commitments, Washington's push for non-ratification of ACFE in 2002 (cf. Kühn 2009), and Russia's CFE suspension in 2007. From the Russian perspective, the 'indivisibility of security' was eroded through four rounds of NATO enlargement (including German reunification, cf. President of Russia 2007). 'Sovereign equality' has been eroded by Russia's incursions into Georgia in 2008 and Ukraine in 2014 (cf. Burke-White 2014). After all, both events have heavily contributed to eroding the key principles and norms of the regime complex. Almost all key principles and norms of the regime complex were violated by Russia in this context.

Last but not least, even though Washington and Moscow took constant recourse to 'further developing [the institutionalized] measures' of the regime complex, they did not agree on the concrete outcomes of reform. This leads to conclude that such references were mostly apt to generate agreement on the declaratory level while at the same time cloaking disagreement on the implementation level. All in all, the impressive number of 33 cases of non-compliance and their increasing occurrence (visualized in Chart 37 above) are indicative of a process of erosion of key principles and norms at the implementation level. Chart 39 visualizes the different policy outcomes at the different levels of U.S. and Russian reference to key principles and norms of the regime complex of cooperative arms control in Europe. The more concrete the degree of substantiation (= policies) of key principles and norms at the three reference levels get, the heavier principles and norms are negatively affected.

CHART 39

REFERENCE TO KEY PRINCIPLES AND NORMS
AT DIFFERENT LEVELS WITH DIFFERENT OUTCOMES

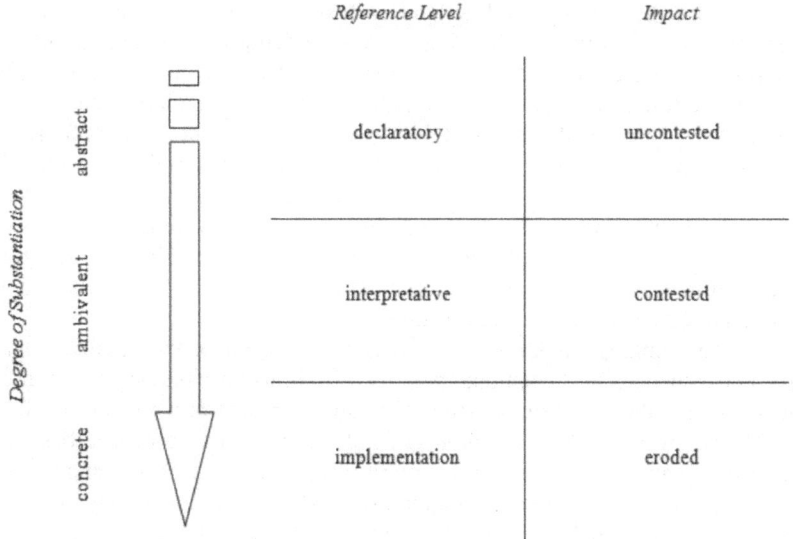

For Chart 39: The chart has been developed by the author.

Taken together, the two guiding research questions of this chapter can be answered. The key principles and norms of the regime complex of cooperative arms control in Europe are still reflected in the operational policies of the two main actors; however, to different degrees. At the declaratory level, key principles and norms are fully reflected and mostly uncontested. At the interpretative level, the United States and Russia do not follow policies that resemble a common understanding of key principles and norms. Against the background of the origin of most of the key principles and norms as lowest common denominator during the Cold War (i.e. Helsinki 1975) it is questionable whether both states ever shared a common understanding. This question shall be addressed in the ensuing chapter. Today, key principles and norms, and the respective policies are highly contested. At the implementation level, diverging interpretations of key principles and norms and the related policies trigger increasingly acts of non-compliance which have resulted over time in an erosion of key principles and norms.

Therewith, also one of the two remaining indicators of regime decay – 'changes in principles and norms' (cf. Krasner 1982:4) – can now be addressed. Analysis of the results of the second abductive test shows that there are no detectable *changes* to principles and norms of the regime complex at the declaratory level which could explain the complex's decay. Indeed, acts of non-compliance as a result of divergent *interpretations* of principles and norms in conjunction with conflicting policies, have led over time to an *erosion* of principles and norms.

Against this background, another indicator of regime decay which has been discussed before – 'regime-internal contradictions' – turns out to be less important when compared to the empirical evidence in this chapter. Even though the test conducted in this chapter has helped to underpin once more the earlier evidence of continued Russian recourse to the 'indivisibility of security' and to 'sovereign equality', their inherent contradictory nature is just one case amongst others where Russian and U.S. interpretations of key principles and norms and their related policies diverge. Adding the factors of 'divergent interpretations of principles and norms' and 'erosion of principles and norms', slowly, an encompassing picture of the reasons behind the fall of cooperative arms control in Europe takes shape.

What remains unaddressed so far is the indicator of the possible negative consequences of 'hegemonic practice'. Both, its possible negative consequences and the question whether the United States and the Soviet Union/Russia ever shared a common understanding of the normative basis of cooperative arms control in Europe point to the broader socio-political spectra which drive international cooperation. While scholars of regime have collated meaningful factors that have validity for describing the process of decay, regime theory alone cannot explain the reasons behind that process and the general periodical volatility of institutionalized cooperation (cf. Thompson and Snidal 2000: 705). This is because regime theory lacks the universality of grand theories such as Realism or Liberalism.

8   Security Communities, the English School, and Constructivist Analyses

The previous chapters unearthed a dense regime complex consisting of five regimes – one of them being a meta-regime – displaying strong signs of decay. Explaining decay, the more general question of the volatility of international institutionalized cooperation came up in conjunction with the hitherto unexplored decay indicator of the possible negative consequences of 'hegemonic practice' and the question whether the United States and the Soviet Union/Russia ever shared a common understanding of the normative basis of cooperative arms control in Europe.

In this chapter, three further theoretical approaches explaining the volatility of international institutionalized cooperation are introduced and analyzed: the concept of Security Communities, the English School, and Constructivism. The aim of this chapter is to find additional explanations for the decay of international cooperation in general and cooperative arms control in Europe in particular. The guiding research questions of this chapter are: What broader spectra of cooperation integration and dissolution drive the development of institutionalized cooperation? What are the reasons behind norm erosion? Do international institutions make a difference when it comes to the interests of the powerful?

8.1   Introductory Remarks

41 years of politics of cooperative arms control in Europe have led to an unprecedented growth of institutions and institutionalized cooperation. Now, four decades after their first tentative inception, cooperation between the United States and Russia has been reduced to a minimum (cf. Charap and Shapiro 2014b). Learning effects, cost-considerations, and repeated forms of contractual interactions, all of which are important essentials of regime scholars' assumptions of the constraining effects of institutionalized cooperation (cf. Hasenclever, Mayer, and Rittberger 1997), could not prevent this process from happening. Analysis of the empirical evidence shows that international cooperation between the United States and the Soviet Union/Russia followed a volatile evolution: from the first tentative efforts (1973-1975), followed by a longer period of stagnation (1976-1989), over the elaboration of a dense regime complex (1990-1999), to the retreat from cooperation and institutional dissolution (2000-2014). Behind these different periods, more general rationales seem to loom which make states fall in and out of love with the idea of cooperation. Regime theory is not suited to address these broader spectra. This is for several reasons.

Regime theory lacks a broader historical perspective (cf. Buzan 1993: 328; Yoshimatsu 1998: 12). Like all theoretical reflections on contemporary social interactions (cf. Carr 2009), regime theory was directly impacted by those societal developments it sought to analyze. It is thus nothing more and nothing less than a "child of its time" (cf. Strange, 1982: 479). Historically seen, regime theory is in parts a product of the Cold War (cf. Rittberger 1993a). As such, a number of critical post-1990 international developments, be it multipolarity, the perforation of the paradigm of state sovereignty by the episteme of the *responsibility to protect* (see Evans 2009), or the decay of regulatory institutions – such as the regime complex on cooperative arms control in Europe – cannot be explained from regime theory's narrow focus on institutions alone. In addition, the possibility of regime decay and cooperation dissolution runs almost contrary to the ideal of the majority of regime scholars, which view international institutionalized cooperation as improvement, in order to get away from the classical Realist state of anarchy and self-help (cf. Keeley 1990: 84). As a typical example of such understanding, Rittberger (1993: 19) argues that 'the accomplishment of international regimes as to the promotion of peace seems to lie in the effect of insulating certain issue areas against a negative "spill-over" from tensions which have arisen between and among the same actors elsewhere.' However, as this study has already shown, even sophisticated forms of successful institutionalized cooperation such as regime complexes can go into reverse or even dissolve. Current complexity research has so far missed that finding (cf. Morin and Orsini 2013). Since institutionalization is not a guarantee for the continuation of cooperation, the question comes up, what broader spectra of cooperation and non-cooperation drive the development of institutionalized cooperation in all its facets.

Another important insight from analyzing the empirical evidence pertains to the normative basis of the regime complex. As explained in Chapter 7, principles and norms of the regime complex of cooperative arms control in Europe are subject to divergent interpretations by the United States and Russia. The fact as such is not unusual at all (cf. van Kersbergen and Verbeek 2007: 221). In general, principles and norms almost never have a degree of substantiation which would allow for uniform interpretation (cf. Brzoska 1992). By their very nature of scarcity they are seldom unambiguous (cf. van Kersbergen and Verbeek 2007: 221). Their often value-laden implications ask for opposition (see Strange, 1982: 479). In the political context, they are more of a smallest common denominator, which serves the purpose of a framework that shall allow states to achieve more meaningful and concrete results (cf. Keohane 1982: 337) or leads to learning effects, socialization, and so forth.

In the case of cooperative arms control in Europe, however, divergent interpretations result in concrete U.S. and Russian foreign and security policies that are challenging the normative basis of the regime complex to a degree where the normative basis becomes eroded through repeated and increasing acts of deviant behavior, for instance in the form of non-compliance (see Chart 37). The problem with regime theory is that scholars of regime have prescribed principles and norms a certain degree of "positive" commonality (cf. exemplary Keeley 1990: 84) based on Western-centric understanding of what is morally just. This degree of commonality does neither correspond with the empirical evidence related to decay nor with critical research on norm dynamics. Various authors (cf. Acharya and Buzan 2007; Hurrell 1993: 67) have not only criticized the 'Western' claim of the universality of historically-rooted European norms, latest research has also highlighted aspects such as norm devolution (see Rosert and Schirmbeck 2007), questions pertaining to norm justice (see Müller and Wunderlich 2013), and the morality of certain norms (see Heller and Kahl 2013). Concerning cooperative arms control in Europe and the consequences of decay, the question comes up, what are the reasons behind norm erosion?

Most regime-theoretical approaches do not explore the Neorealist assumption that powerful states make use of international institutions in order to achieve their preferred interest (cf. Schweller and Priess 1997; Drezner 2007; see also Thakur 2013). As has been shown above, the cooperation volatility between the United States and Russia follows certain dynamics that correlate with changes in presidencies in the two countries as well as with certain events such as the 2003 Iraq War. These correlations lead to assume that changes in interest of those two powerful actors have a direct impact on international institutionalized cooperation frameworks. If that were the case, Neorealists would have a serious point in case for arguing that powerful states exert their power through international institutions in order to achieve their interests (cf. Drezner 2007). The question is thus, do international institutions make a difference when it comes to the interests of the powerful?

8.2   Security Communities

Research on the theoretical concept of Security Communities (SCs) has experienced a revival in latest years (see Adler 2011). Based on a concept developed in the 1950s by Karl Deutsch together with a number of further scholars, SCs can be viewed as the logical next cooperation step after the sequential establishment and operation of agreements, regimes, and regime complexes. Chart 40 illustrates this possible process. In the chart, SCs are located at the intersection of a high level of states' convergent interests and a high level of cooperation.

CHART 40

INSTITUTIONALIZED COOPERATION IN A CONTINUUM

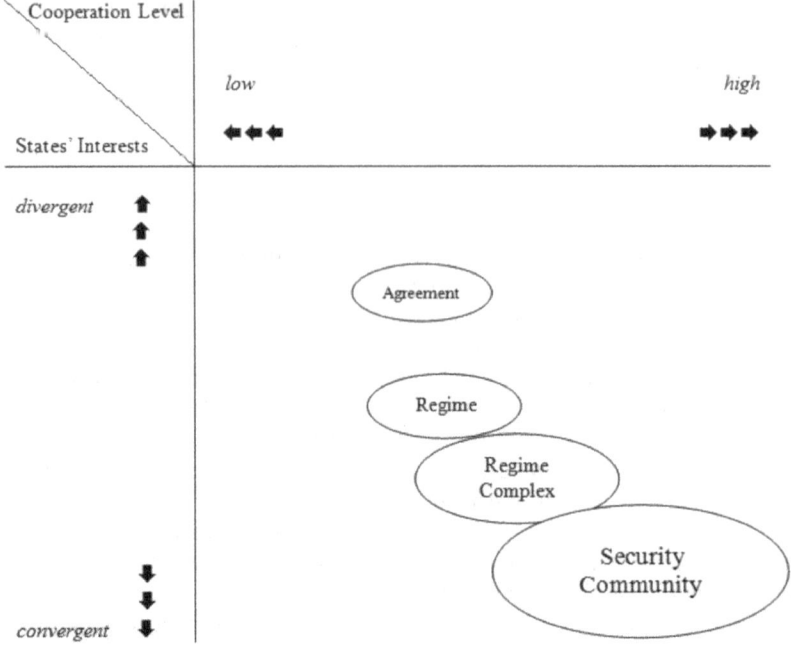

For Chart 40: The Chart has been developed by the author.

Particularly Constructivist scholars have picked up a number of assumptions by early integrationists like Deutsch (see Adler and Barnett 1998c: 11). In general, research on SCs has employed a much broader view on the cooperation-enabling preconditions that allow states to finally achieve or fail to achieve lasting cooperation and, thus, permanent peace. Because cooperative arms control in Europe is in decay, reviewing the concept of SC might help adding an additional stratum to explaining the wider cooperation spectra, regimes are embedded in. Further on, the concept has become closely associated with some declaratory political initiatives to transform the OSCE space into a Security Community, prior to the war in Eastern Ukraine (see OSCE 2010; cf. Mützenich and Karádi 2013).

8.2.1   Essentials of Security Communities

The overriding principle under which to place the various works of scholars of Security Communities was the search for a stable state of peace. In 1957,

Karl W. Deutsch and scholars released their seminal work on *Political Community and the North Atlantic Area*. Reacting to the cruelties of World War II, at the heart of the book lays the old problem of how to eliminate war (Deutsch 1957: vii). In order to search for the conditions and processes that would enable long-term or permanent peace, the authors looked at peace within the North Atlantic area (ibid: 3). The basically new approach of the group, led by Deutsch, was their broader focus on explaining *why* certain groups, such as NATO member states, have permanently stopped warring (ibid: 4). Scrutinizing specific historical periods from different centuries, the Deutsch group came to conclude that certain forms of so called 'Security Communities' existed during the last centuries. As SCs they defined

a group of people which has become "integrated". By INTEGRATION we mean the attainment, within a territory, of a "sense of community" and of institutions and practices strong enough and widespread enough to assure, for a "long" time, dependable expectations of "peaceful change" among its population. By SENSE OF COMMUNITY we mean a belief on the part of individuals in a group that they have come to agreement on at least this point: that common social problems must and can be resolved by processes of "peaceful change".

By PEACEFUL CHANGE we mean the resolution of social problems, normally by institutionalized procedures, without resort to large-scale physical force. A security-community, therefore, is one in which there is real assurance that the members of that community will not fight each other physically, but will settle their disputes in some other way. (Ibid: 5; capitalized letters as in the original)

According to their research, the state of integration differs at the state level with two distinct types of SCs: an amalgamated SC where two or more previously independent units merge into a single unit (the United States being one example) and a pluralistic SC in which the units retain their legal independence of separate governments (Norway and Sweden being another example). According to Deutsch et al, political communities become eventually successful (in the sense of ensuring peace) once they cross the integration threshold and achieve the state of a SC. However, they also note that the process can be unsuccessful 'if it ended eventually in secession or civil war'. (Ibid: 6-7)

With regards to the conditions of successful SC establishment, the authors highlight a number of 'background conditions' and 'essential requirements'. As one background condition, the authors particularly stress a 'somewhat deeper understanding of the meaning of "sense of community" [that is a] "we-feeling" [of] trust, and mutual consideration; of partial identification in terms of self-images and interests; of mutually successful predictions of behavior, and of cooperative action in accordance with it'. (Ibid: 36) This condition translates directly into the essential requirement of 'values and expectations'. For values, a compatibility of the main values held by the relevant political groups and a 'set of established or emerging habits of behavior corresponding to them' has to be present. (Ibid: 47-8) Habits of behavior should be based on the mutual predictability of behavior. With regards to expectations, joint rewards (e.g. political equality) or gains for the future had to be tangible. In addition, Deutsch et al found the presence of cores of political strength around which the integrative process develops an important condition. Political strength however turns out to be another multidimensional condition for successful SC establishment. On the one hand, the political units must have a considerable degree of capabilities ('power') to act as a political unit - the higher that degree, the better. On the other hand, they must be able to constrain their 'power' and exert 'responsiveness'.

> *More accurately, this means the ability of its political decision-makers and relevant political elites to redirect and control their own attention and behavior so as to enable rulers to receive communications from other political unites which were to be their prospective partners in the integrative process. It means, further, the ability to give these messages from other political units adequate weight in the making of their own decisions, to perceive the needs of the populations and elites of these other units, and to respond to them quickly and adequately in terms of political or economic action.* (Ibid: 37 et seq)

'Power that cannot be controlled by the governments [is likely to meet] growing external resistance; and responsiveness would remain a matter of mere intention', Deutsch et al conclude. (Ibid: 40) Explicitly, they discard the existence of a hegemonic power as of eminent importance for the formation of SCs (ibid).

According to Deutsch et al, SCs can develop into different directions: evolution, stagnation, and devolution. Devolution, or decay, occurs if one simply turns the essentials of SCs (non-violent problem resolution, compatibility of values, dependable expectations) into the other direction. Amongst the most important factors for devolution Deutsch et al note the failure of a formerly strong state 'to adjust psychologically and politically to its loss of dominance as a result of changed conditions.' (Ibid: 64)

While the concept of SC lost most of its attention in the following decades, regime theory resembles strong features of definitions of SCs. Institutionalized procedures, dependable expectations, a compatible value base, and continued habits of behavior corresponding with the value base are all elements of critical regime definitions as outlined by Krasner (1982) or Young (1982). Forty years after the inception of the SC episteme, and only shortly after regime theory started to receive comparably less scholarly attention, a second generation of IR scholars revived the concept of SC. In 1998, Adler and Barnett re-focused attention towards SCs and explicitly included the OSCE as a 'security community-building model' (Adler 1998: 119-160). The theoretical debate became elevated when the former Secretary General of the OSCE Marc Perrin de Brichambaut drove the organization's attention to-

316

wards the concept.[44] In 2010, OSCE participating States signed the Astana Commemorative Declaration which strives to achieve the vision of a Euro-Atlantic and Eurasian 'security community stretching from Vancouver to Vladivostok, rooted in agreed principles, shared commitments and common goals' (OSCE 2010). Adler concluded,

> *"[The OSCE] rather than waiting for 'the other' to change its identity and interests before it can be admitted to the security community-building institution, [...] has incorporated, from the outset, all states that express a political will to live up to the standards and norms of the security community, hoping to transform their identities and interests".* (Adler 2011: 15)

Adler and Barnett (1998b: 30) helped to refine Deutsch's concept by distinguishing between 'loosely coupled' and 'tightly coupled' pluralistic SCs. As Deutsch did, Adler and Barnett stress the importance of at least an embryonic form of "we-feeling" amongst pluralistic SCs (ibid: 30 et seq). Further on, the authors categorize SCs into 'mature', 'ascendant', and 'nascent' forms, with the United States and, to a lesser degree, the EU, having reached the highest level ('mature') of integration (ibid: 50 et seq). The authors also concentrated on the evolution of SCs and distinguish between three stages: birth, growth, and maturity. While at the stage of birth, often a form of a common threat perception helps to engage in the first cooperative efforts, at the stage of growth, the respective units develop closely interconnected institutions, particularly in the realm of military coordination and cooperation; at this stage, also collective identity in the form of "we-ness" develops. Finally, at the last stage, a common identity together with common expectations flows into a genuine Security Community.

8.2.2   Analysis and Application

The added value of the concept of SC compared to the regime episteme is its broader focus on cooperation and its inherent realism when it comes to viewing development as a continuum. While most regime scholars have a problem with decay as an inherent possibility to the development of regimes, Deutsch et al have been clear from the onset that SCs can disintegrate. When looking at the empirical evidence from 41 years of cooperative arms control in Europe, the process of institutionalization resembles strong features of the SC episteme. In that regard, the regime complex of cooperative arms control in Europe can be seen as a certain state of cooperation in the process of the eventual achievement of a SC (see Chart 40 above).

Applying Adler's and Barnett's categorization of the three stages of SC development, the empirical period between 1973 and 1989 can be seen as the

---

44   This information was passed on to the author in a private conversation with Marc Perrin de Brichambaut in 2012.

nascent phase. With regards to a common threat perception, such can be found in the omnipresent threat of unlimited nuclear war between the two superpowers, elevated by the Cuban Missile Crisis. The ensuing politics of détente would serve as framework for avoiding such outcome by approaching the problem at various layers. One layer addressing the nuclear realm, were risk reduction agreements such as establishment of a hot line, the ABM, and SALT I. A second layer addressing the conventional realm, were the MBFR talks. A third layer, at that time mostly declaratory in nature and aiming at a general understanding of mutual security, was the Helsinki CSCE. This third layer, in a Deutschean understanding, established the 'essential requirement' of a value base of principles and norms.

In contrast to Deutsch et al, the CSCE value base was less the product of a common sense of 'we-feeling' but rather the offspring of a political linkage deal between the four main issue-specific interests of territorial status quo (Soviet issue-specific interest), achievement of a CSCE (Soviet issue-specific interest), addressing human rights issues (U.S. issue-specific interest), and establishment of talks on the conventional imbalance in Europe (U.S. issue-specific interest). In 1975, the declaratory nature of the CSCE value base was not expected to directly translate into any kind of concrete habits of behavior (cf. Mützenich and Karádi 2013: 52). This changed with the end of the Cold War. The following years saw the spread of cooperative security institutions, based on the (now) commonly perceived value base. Building upon earlier agreements and cooperation processes, regimes developed and finally merged into a regime complex. This phase of ascendant SC development (1990-1994) promised, at least from an institutional perspective, the continuation of cooperation: the achievement of a tightly coupled pluralistic SC. From the mid-1990s on, the ascendant SC entered a new phase. The slow-down of institutional achievements (1995-1999) was followed by periods of stagnation (2000-2006) and devolution (2007-2014).

The volatile development of the institutionalization of cooperative arms control in Europe can thus be as well described as several stages of the overall process of SC integration and dissolution; and thus as feedback to changes in interest and perception. The previous insight that regimes and regime complexes are also subject to wider developmental processes which, by no means, have to result in a somewhat eternal state of continuous and successful cooperation, becomes further support from scholars of SCs. Beyond its aspects of evolution and devolution, the SC episteme contains relevant insights with regards to failed cooperation. Particularly two aspects are worth mentioning in conjunction with the empirical evidence: power and norms. In the normative realm, scholars of SCs ascribe paramount importance to a certain compatibility of the main values, more precisely, a partial identification in terms of self-images and interests which triggers predictability of behavior. As has been argued in the previous chapter, for most of the preceding years, compatibility of values between the United States and Russia has only been present at the declaratory level. Indeed, a certain form of "we-feeling" is completely absent (cf. Lukin 2014) and partial identification in terms of (a general) interest has mostly vanished over the course of time. As a result, unpredictable behavior prevails, as can be seen in the many instances of non-compliance (see Chart 37 above).

These insights lead to the question whether the United States and the Soviet Union/Russia ever shared a common understanding of the normative basis of cooperative arms control in Europe. For the years of the Cold War this question can be negated from the outright due to the singular nature of Communist ideology (cf. Leatherman 2003; Leffler and Westad 2010). After the Cold War, new security challenges such as secessionist conflicts, instances of "ethnic cleansing", or trans-nationally operating terrorism networks occurred. While the level of threat perception thus changed, relatively away from the scenario of nuclear holocaust, the normative base remained unchanged. Instead of engaging in efforts of 'social engineering' (Young 1982: 281) to adjust the normative base, the United States and Russia increasingly applied their own interpretations of the normative base to tackle those new challenges. Their interpretations differed remarkably with regards to tenets such as sovereign equality, territorial integrity, and the non-use of force. Examples are the two Chechen Wars (1994-1996; 1999-2000), the 1999 Kosovo War, the 2003 Iraq War, the Russian-Georgian War of 2008, the NATO-led Libya intervention in 2011, and the 2014 Ukraine conflict.

From a purely functionalist perspective (cf. Kratochwil and Ruggie 1986: 767), the question whether the United States and the Soviet Union/Russia ever shared a common understanding of the normative basis of cooperative arms control in Europe is irrelevant as long as both actors are able to bring in line their divergent interpretations. From the viewpoint of the SC episteme however, true integration cannot occur without a feeling of "we-ness". The latest rhetorical campaign by Russian politicians and researchers to negate a common value base with "the West", stressing the differences instead (see President of Russia 2013; Lukin 2014), is thus a clear departure from the integration process outlined by Deutsch et al. Whether a short window of opportunity towards a truly common understanding of shared values existed at the beginning of the 1990s (see Soviet/Russian statements between 1990 and 1994 contained in Chapter 7) remains open to debate. At least from the Russian view, it ceased to exist with the maintenance and the further enlargement of NATO (cf. President of Russia 2014b; Charap and Shapiro 2014b). Addressing this question would benefit from further research.

The second important aspect deriving from SC research relates to the realm of power (cf. Adler and Barnett 1998b: 39). While one essential requirement for the establishment of a SC, the presence of a core of political strength around which the integrative process develops, was present throughout the 'unipolar [U.S.] moment' (Krauthammer 1991) of the 1990s, a number of directly related aspects involving power were non-conducive. Obviously, the Russian Federation has failed "to adjust psychologically and politically to its loss of dominance as a result of changed conditions." (Deutsch et al 1957: 64) The famous statement by Vladimir Putin that 'the collapse of the Soviet Union was a major geopolitical disaster of the century' (President of Russia 2005, official translation), underscores this.

At the same time, analysis of the empirical evidence highlights that the United States were not willing to constrain their power and to exert 'responsiveness' towards Russian sensitivities in the way Deutsch et al saw it as necessary for successful SC establishment. Washington's refusal to allow the OSCE to become a full-fledged and encompassing regional security organization in conjunction with affirmation of NATO enlargement are the two major U.S. decisions underlining lack of power constraint and responsiveness. Walt (2014) claims that with the coming into office of the second Clinton administration, the United States became increasingly unwilling, in a Deutschean sense, to 'redirect and control their own attention and behavior so as to [...] receive communications' (Deutsch et al 1957: 37) from the Kremlin. Or as the former U.S. ambassador to NATO and one of the principle architects of enlargement, Robert Hunter, acknowledges in hindsight: 'things began to go off the rails, as the U.S. foreign policy team changed in the late 1990s [...] NATO enlargement went too far' (Hunter 2014). The result was that positive dependable expectations got lost at the Russian side. Mützenich and Karádi (2013: 50) conclude: 'In Russia, the predominant view is that the cooperative strategy of the 1990s was a failure.' As Deutsch et al (1957: 40) predicted, 'power that cannot be controlled by the governments [is likely to meet] growing external resistance'. With the first coming into office of Vladimir Putin in late 1999 supported by the ensuing recovery of the Russian economy (see Chart 29 above), this effect becomes visible.

Taken together, the SC episteme contains important theoretical insights explaining the volatility of institutionalized cooperation in the realm of cooperative arms control in Europe. The absence of an inclusive sense of "we-feeling", based on commonly agreed, equally shared, and continuously observed values, combined with the problematic handling of power accretion (United States) and dissolution (Russia) led to the decay of an institutionalized policy space which already had strong institutional features of an ascendant SC. Last but not least, the repeated use of force by certain actors, mainly Russia (cf. Freedman 2014), shows that the reality in the OSCE area is far from the state of a genuine Security Community.

8.3   The English School

Starting in the late 1950s with the discussions amongst the British Committee on the Theory of International Politics, the English School (ES) in the sense of a "school" developed around an initial core group of a handful of British scholars.[45] Their deliberations have flown into a number of emblematic texts, amongst the best known are Hedley Bull's *The Anarchical Society: A Study of Order in World Politics* (1977) and Martin Wight's *Systems of States* (1977). From the early 1990s onwards, a second wave of ES scholars, amongst them prominent figures such as Barry Buzan, Andrew Hurrell, or Tim Dunne, and from the 2000s onwards a third more globalized ES generation, sought to refine the works of their predecessors (see Green 2014: 2). In contrast to the peace-embracing episteme of Security Communities, the ES is primarily concerned with international order; that is the structures, maintenance, and instruments of order. While some proponents of the ES have been flirting with the SC concept (see Adler and Barnett 1998b: 11), there are more similarities with regime theory (see Buzan 1993; Yoshimatsu 1998), for both approaches aim at explaining the development and preservation of order in the international sphere; though, at different levels. Aside from these conceptual similarities, the ES's essentials of 'order' and 'international society' might provide explanations of additional inter-state cooperation spectra in which political institutions such as regimes are embedded.

8.3.1 Essentials of the English School

The ES starts off from the Realist assumption that international politics take place in a state of international anarchy which is lacking a centralized authority with the power to enforce rules. Proponents of the ES are quite close to Waltzian assumptions (cf. Waltz 1979) and recognize a number of structural features which they describe as arising from as well as shaping an international system. In the international system, states, much like Waltz's (1986: 343) 'shoving and shaping', recognize certain interdependence amongst each other; they do, however, lack common interests and consent of common rules (Bull 1977: 10). In order to establish a certain set of rules of behavior, the different units of the system – the states – form an 'international society' with the aim of maintaining their independence as well as preserving the states' system (ibid). Hedley Bull defines international society as follows:

> *a society of states (or international society) exists when a group of states, conscious of certain common interests and common values, form a society in the sense that they conceive themselves to be bound by a common set of rules in their relations with one another, and share in the working of common institutions.* Bull (ibid: 13)

In short, states aim at establishing and preserving order (cf. Bull 1969: 637). According to Bull (ibid: 67), the development of a sense of common interests

---

45   Prominent figures of the original school included Hedley Bull, Martin Wight, Herbert Butterfield, Alan James, C.A.W. Manning, and Adam Watson. For a good overview of the development of the ES see Green and Navari (2014).

is crucial for the operation of international society. In his writings, he outlines three crucial rules which derive from states' common interests: (1) the preservation of sovereignty which derives from a general security of life against violence and the fundamental purpose of the stability of possession; (2) reciprocity in the recognition of mutual sovereign equality which derives from the sanctity of promises and manifests itself in the principle of *pacta sunt servanda* which, anon, serves the bedrock of international law and diplomatic procedures; and (3) the maintenance of a balance of power among great powers which serves the function of prevention of system transformation into a universal empire, maintenance of states' independence, and provision of basic conditions for the operation of further institutions of international order such as agreements, organizations, and so forth. (Cf. Vincent 1988: 197-202) For Bull, war is a basic determinant of the international system.

> *War and the threat of war are not the only determinants of the shape of the international system; but they are so basic that even the terms we use to describe the system – great powers and small powers, alliances and spheres of influence, balances of power and hegemony – are scarcely intelligible except in relation to war and the threat of war.* (Bull 1977: 187)

Vincent (1988: 202) thus concludes that 'war itself might be interpreted as an institution of international society'. As such, war is in close vicinity to the balance of powers, for it is the great powers that (now) carry (additional) responsibility for managing the state of anarchy up to a point where their global interests were accommodated without the need to resort to large-scale violence or war. Bull did not view the balance of powers as an ideal state but rather as the best arrangement possible under the historic circumstances of the Cold War which were shaped by the nuclear arms race of the 1960s (cf. Bull 1961: 39).

Beyond Bull's minimalist framework of how to obtain order in the international society achieved against the background of the international system, scholars of the ES have outlined a third layer of international interaction and order, termed 'world society'. (See Wight 1991; Buzan 2004) World society exists at the personal level and includes individuals, non-state organizations, and the global population as a whole. The concept thus relates to a *Kantian* view of revolutionist or idealist thinking which envisions development towards a future state of overcoming nation state primacy. As Buzan (1993: 337) pointed out, the third layer of the trinity of system, international, and world society adds a strong liberal stratum which is particularly in conflict with Bull's tenet of the state as primary fortification against a relapse into the classical *Hobbesian* state of anarchy.

Bull's societal concepts are sometimes lacking clarity – not just in relation to war as a determining feature for either 'international system' or for both 'international system' and 'international society'. First and foremost, they leave open the question of clear-cut boundaries between the states of 'international system', 'international society', and 'world society'. The lack of an analytical framework (see Buzan 1993: 332) also prevents clear identification of when and how evolution takes place in the system. Bull's analysis that international society is subject to trends of strengthening and weakening (ibid) is not very satisfying in this regard.

Barry Buzan (ibid) has addressed these analytical shortcomings and has linked the concept of international society to regime theory and Neorealism. Starting from Wight's (1977: 33) civilizational approach which assumes that international society 'will not come into being without a degree of cultural unity among its members', he applies Tönnies' (cf. 1926) sociologic distinction between Gemeinschaft and Gesellschaft conceptions of society and links it to the *Waltzian* argument that anarchy generates 'like units' (cf. Waltz 1979: 93) of the Gesellschaft type of society whereas Wight's definition leans towards the Gemeinschaft type of society. Buzan concludes that sovereignty is central to the coming into being of international society. In international societies states recognize each other as sovereign equals (Buzan 1993: 345) and thus create like units. As a consequence of interactions among 'a group of states [that] have established by dialogue and consent common rules and institutions for the conduct of their relations, and recognize their common interest in maintaining these arrangements' (Bull and Watson 1984: 1), international law, which is central to understanding the concept of international society, develops. By linking sovereignty to a more functional (Neorealist) understanding of society as Gesellschaft, Buzan is able to make a distinction between the state of international system and international society. Mutual recognition and sovereign equality are the key distinctions drawing the line.

At the same time, by applying the Gemeinschaft type of society, Buzan is able to outline a rather fluid boundary between international society and world society. While world society rests on Wight's understanding of historically evolved shared values which establish a kind of "we-feeling" among participating states, it can develop in parallel to international society. The conduct of international relations based on international law and differently shared values leads over time to 'layers of concentric societal circles [where those] in the core circle will have more shared values, and much fuller sets of rules and institutions, than those in the outer circles.' (Buzan 1993: 345) In this core circle – and here Buzan links the ES to the regime episteme – networks of regimes are operating, thus maintaining order at the operational level. Understood in these terms, 'international society [...] might be seen as a regime of regimes', he concludes. (Buzan 1993: 350)

Buzan's 'concentric circles' represent only one manifestation of another important aspect of the ES, that is the historical expansion of international society (cf. Bull and Watson 1984). As much as the early ES and its theoretical essentials are purely European conceptions of international order and conduct, the spread of the theory as such and the developmental aspects of the episteme of international society have always included the wider spectra of global participation (cf. Bull 1977: 315-17). The global model of international society which exists in the contemporary world could have come about in two possible ways. Either, if the different centers of the ancient world would have developed in parallel, recognizing at a certain point in time that their mutual interdependence dictates a certain degree of order to manage interdependence or, closer to what actually happened, if a certain centre of power (here European) advances faster on the track of international society (through the Westphalian model) than the others and finally takes over the system as a whole (through Colonization), thus imposing its already established rules of order. (Cf. Buzan 2014: 60) Through the process of De-Colonization, the Third World finally becomes member of the international society and brings with it its inherent problems. Another important aspect of this process is the way in which the European international society got into contact with other centers of power. While early scholars of the ES paid much attention to the so called *encounter* version where the European core got in contact with other units like early China and the Ottoman Empire and failed to colonize the latter, the *standard of civilization* version (Gong 1984) concludes that from the nineteenth century onwards other non-European states had to qualify, like Japan, in order to gain entry to the European model of international society.

The important implications of the expansionist debate among scholars of the ES derive from introducing dynamism and questions of morality to the concept of international society. Regarding dynamism, Gong (1984: 90-3) sees the nineteenth century version of the standard of civilization overtaken by a more contemporary Western demand for human rights. As such, the Western states would again raise the ante of qualification for entry into the (now global) society of states, which would thus undergo a structural change in terms of common values and rules. Already Bull had voiced pessimism with regards to the further development of the international society. Amongst other reasons, he saw it weakened by its global expansion and the trend to move from the state-centric episteme of international society to the individual level of world society, most vividly brought forward in the promotion of human rights standards which might open the door for moral claims undermining the existing order (Bull 1977: 151-53). Keene (2002) argues that the ES stresses too much the aspect of order and underestimates the consequences of inequality and coercion which the ongoing evolution of the European standard of civilization model continues to trigger in third states.

Bull's as well as Buzan's findings about the further evolution of international society have in common that the concept is by no means an end to itself. Buzan (1993: 351) concludes that 'there is no guarantee that international society is a one-way process' and particularly the 'problematic agenda of intervention' (ibid) clashes with the current state-centered system of international society and human-centered world society aspirations. The same dynamics can be attributed to Buzan's 'societal circles' because it is not safe to argue that the current Western core will remain at the center or that other states are progressively heading towards the center.

8.3.2 Analysis and Application

The broad historic approach of the ES contains a number of important insights. First, it allows for a certain "downgrading" of the centrality of regimes, both from a theoretical and from an analytical point of view. As Buzan suggests, regimes are the legal tool box for close state-to-state interaction in an international society. The more regimes are interconnected and overlapping, the higher the chance that the states located at the core center of international society already share a common civilizational background (a sense of "we-feeling") in the understanding of Wight (cf. Buzan 1993: 349-51). With the cultural and societal sharing of principles and norms, often found in global sub-systems or regions such as the "Western world" or the Middle East, regimes would emerge particularly in the 'European (now Western) core' where 'states voluntarily bind themselves in pursuit of increased security, economic efficiency, environmental management, societal openness, and a range of other objectives.' (Ibid) Regimes are thus primarily a Western conception rooted in the long-term development of a Gemeinschaft type of international society which has spread both in terms of geography (though as the Gesellschaft type) and operational conduct. It follows that the study of regimes is mostly a study of the operational level embedded in a wider historically evolved spectrum of international cooperation dynamics.

The second important insight derives from tensions between the status quo impact of order preservation, best characterized by Bull's writings, and the dynamics unfolding by the historical evolution of international society. With regards the empirical evidence, the Cold War depicted the classical paragon of Bull's conceptions. Two opposing great powers which carry the additional responsibility of preserving international order (cf. Bull 1977: 200-5) have a shared interest in balancing their power (in the sense of equilibrium) through means of nuclear arms control against the permanent threat of nuclear annihilation. As both powers recognize each other as 'like units' (in the *Waltzian* sense) of an international society, they are able to manage their relations through diplomatic conduct, respect for mutual spheres of influence (the other WTO and NATO states; cf. Nye 1987: 392-3), non-intervention in internal affairs, and sporadic war at the periphery (mostly in the Third World), to the detriment of those states located at the periphery. The Helsinki Final Act is thus a classic example of an accord which stresses status quo preserving principles such as sovereign equality and non-intervention. At the same time, the West, which is a more stringently evolved international society of its own, shares a common civilizational background expressed in a common canon of values. This canon includes, amongst others, *Kantian* notions of world society which produce the imperative of individual human rights. As the Helsinki accords were only declaratory in nature and by no means enforceable, the East agreed to include the rights of individuals as a quid pro quo for status quo (cf. Schlotter 1999).

With the end of the Cold War, order was in danger of overthrow. The West – now relatively more powerful than its former adversary – and Russia recognized the danger and cooperated in establishing a new order based on the legal instruments that had guided the way so far. Even though they cooperated, both had two competing visions of order: the United States wanted to maintain NATO and wanted to include Russia in a dense network of interlocking agreements in the realm of cooperative security; Russia wanted a 'common European house' (Gorbachev 1996) where all inhabitants are equal and equally secure. The result of these two competing visions was twofold: on the one hand, a dense network of overlapping agreements, amongst them the regime complex of cooperative arms control in Europe, emerged and facilitated international conduct. On the other hand, during the early 1990s, Russia pushed towards the societal core by embracing idealist conceptions, now more forcefully voiced by Western states. At the same time, war moved from the geographical periphery to the center, most visibly in Yugoslavia. The power vacuum left by the demise of the WTO and the Soviet Union gave way to ethnic conflicts, secessions, and large-scale human rights abuses.

For three reasons this development and its consequences were crucial. First, they occurred on territories previously associated with the Soviet sphere of influence or even at the Russian territory. Second, the West was now much more willing to give expression to its own world society understanding of policies than against the previous background of nuclear deadlock (cf. Flynn and Farrell 1999). Third, Russia found itself trapped between aspirations at joining the societal Western core while at the same time remaining bound to the more classical order-preserving international society of Bull – expressed by Russian opposition to NATO enlargement.

These three conflicting realities led to different outcomes. One outcome was that increasingly the West gave its fiat to humanitarian interventions, sometimes bypassing the UN Security Council, the most visible example being the Kosovo intervention in 1999. Freedman (2014: 15) concludes, '[The Kosovo crisis] qualified the principle of non-interference in internal affairs, elevated the principle of self-determination and reduced the standing of the Security Council'. Another outcome was NATO enlargement in order to stabilize the former Soviet client states. Enlargement further contradicted the old order principle of an equilibrium balance of power and strengthened the new emerging order shaped by the West; a development criticized by Russia with the recourse to the 'indivisibility of security'. The third important outcome was that Russia, after a short period of collective interventions in the early 1990s (cf. Flynn and Farrell 1999), again started to progressively retreat from the inner core of international society and is today at the outer fringes vividly opposing the West's world society values such as the imperative of human rights in international politics. Lukin (2014: 52) states that 'the concept of the absolute priority of human rights, which forms the foundation of the West's dominant ideology [...] is alien to most other cultural traditions [including the Russian orthodox].' At the same time, Russia is now also reinterpreting older ordering principles such as territorial integrity, sovereignty, and the non-use of force, as seen in the Russian interventions in Georgia and Ukraine.

In 1993, Buzan (1993: 349) assumed that the demise of the Soviet Union had increased the cohesion of the Western international society and would propel the spread of regimes because the peer competitor had vanished. What was certainly true in 1993 appears in a totally different light some twenty years later. The opposing dynamics of Western integration towards world society on the one hand and Russian separation towards a retreat even from ordering principles of international society on the other hand has created a tension impacting the common legal framework. If regimes and regime complexes are understood as binding instruments of common orders of an international society (ibid: 351), their texture gets increasingly stretched the more the major powers involved are drifting apart to opposing poles. At a certain point, the texture yields to the centrifugal powers and falls apart. This process can be seen in the decay of the regime complex of cooperative arms control in Europe and gets elevated by the fact that the regimes composing the complex are embracing dyadic conceptions of international society (sovereignty principles) and world society (human rights principles) at the same time. Chart 41 illustrates the process.

The third important insight deals with the employment and aggregation of power in international society. Following Bull, one of the ordering principles of international society is the balance of power and thus the prevention of hegemony or world domination by one single power. In contrast, concentration of power in the hands of a single actor distorts the foundations of balance, and thus, threatens international society as a whole, as Clark (2007: 227-43) argues. It follows from ES interpretation that the post-Cold War period of the U.S. 'unipolar moment' (Krauthammer 1991) was apt to further thwart the formerly achieved order of U.S.-Soviet equilibrium balance. In reality, the end of the Cold War equilibrium state of balance of power led to two outcomes.

CHART 41

OPPOSING POLES STRETCHING COMPLEXITY TEXTURE

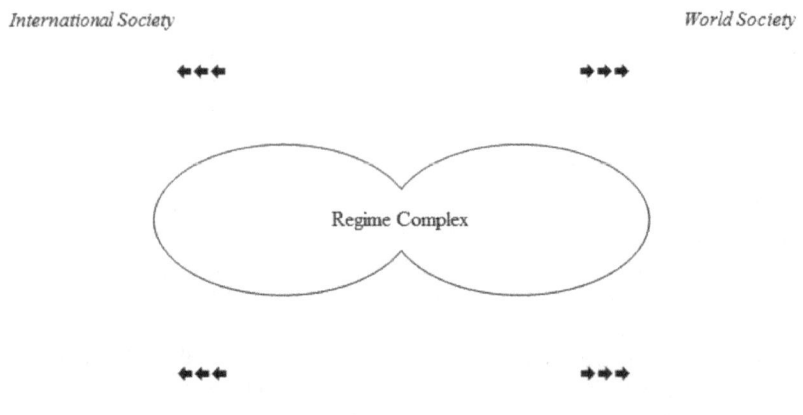

For Chart 41: The Chart has been developed by the author.

First, even though the initial years of the post-Cold War period (1990-1994) saw a significant growth in institutionalized order, the empirical evidence has revealed strong tendencies of the United States to push through its preferred issue-specific interests in the formation and scope of institutions. At least between 1990 and 2000, American power policies went almost completely unchecked. Buzan (2011: 11) adds, 'with the shift to unipolarity, the U.S. became the principle representative and exponent of the hegemonic practice by which the West continues to dominate international society.' At the same time, 'anti-hegemonism is an emergent property of post-colonial international society.' (Ibid) While post-Cold War Russia does by no means represent a post-colonial entity, it carries on the one hand historical memories of being dominated for many centuries, on the other hand, its decline from superpower status and the parallel unchecked aggregation of U.S. power triggered almost inevitably perceptions of deprivation, imperfection, and disregard on Russia's side (cf. exemplary President of Russia 2005).

The second outcome was a loss of political and moral credibility on the U.S. side. From the point of international society order as well as from the point of world society order, Washington did not practice what it preached. Regarding international society order, the United States and its NATO allies increasingly departed from the old ordering principles of respect for sovereignty and arrived at a middle position increasingly embracing ideas of world society, most notable by humanitarian interventions (cf. Luck 2003). At the same time, Washington, particularly under the eight years of the George W. Bush administration, contradicted its own ideas of world society order by the use of double standards. What Ruggie (2004) labeled 'American exemption-nalism' found its expression in 'U.S. abuses of human rights at Abu Ghraib and Guantanamo, its policy of "extraordinary renditions" and acceptance of de facto torture, as well as its fierce resistance to the International Criminal Court, [which] have gutted Washington's credibility to say much about human rights.' (Buzan 2011: 10) As such, the United States found itself increasingly in a hard to sustain position of criticizing Russian non-compliance with principles and norms of the regime complex while actively contradicting a number of principles and norms of the Helsinki acquis in other parts of the world. Not surprisingly, after the unlawful annexation of Crimea in 2014, President Putin countered Western accusations with a lengthy tirade of the West's 'transgressions' during the last fifteen years (see President of Russia 2014a). Nevertheless, the covered Russian actions in Ukraine (e.g. forces without national insignia) and the fact of the Russian rhetoric recourse to international law shows that principles and norms of the regime complex, at least those pertaining to an international society understanding of order, are still having certain constraining effects on Moscow (cf. Buzan 2011: 19).

Summing up, the ES applies a historic perspective on ordering principles among states. Its tripartite approach including *Hobbesian*, *Grotian*, and *Kantian* views on international conduct allows for understanding the diverse dynamics between integration and separation, with the concept of international society leaning more towards Neorealist and the concept of world society tending towards Liberal/Idealist conceptions (cf. Buzan 1993: 335-7). Analysis of the empirical evidence along the lines of the ES leads to two central insights. First, the downfall of the equilibrium state of balance of power disrupted the existing order. As scholars of the ES predicted, the emerging unipolar hegemony was counterproductive to efforts achieving a new stable order. Second, the civilizational difference between two understandings of international society and world society put additional strain on the newly established instruments of order. Both factors together contributed to the decay of the post-Cold War order. Beyond that, the ES allows for theoretically locating the United States and Russia in different regions of the pursuit of international order.

From an ES point of view, contemporary Russia is trapped between a classical state of the international society as outlined by Bull and the search for a new definition of international society which it can share with other participants. Moscow's latest push towards Eurasian integration and closer economic ties with China (cf. Lukin 2014) is thus not only a geopolitical game or owed to the fact of Western economic sanctions but can as well be interpreted as search for a new definition of international society which will allow Moscow to achieve its issue-specific interests against a background of ordering principles in accordance with its own issue-specific interests. Neumann (2011: 463) argues that Russia's entry into international society is shaped by its memories 'of being part of a suzerain system [of the Golden

Horde between 1240 and 1500], and that it is therefore still suspended somewhere in the outer tier of international society.' The contemporary policies of Moscow might therewith even signal a departure from the 'outer tier' towards another yet to be defined international society. Such speculation nevertheless stands on a narrow empirical base and would thus benefit from further research on the issue.

In turn, the West is progressively moving towards world society in the understanding of Wight. Its domination of world policies during the short period of the unipolar moment brings with it all the associated problems of the standard of civilization such as hubris, hegemonic practices, and inequality (cf. Gong 1984; Buzan 2014). The re-emergence of a multi-polar system (cf. Buzan 2011) thus challenges the Western conceptions of international society and particularly of world society (see BRICS 2014, particularly Paragraphs 27 and 28). It is yet too early for a sound analysis of how possible multiple future societies might interact and develop abreast (cf. Stivachtis 2014; more predictive Buzan 2011).

8.4   Constructivist Analyses of Norm Dynamics

Both theoretical approaches analyzed so far in this chapter have pointed to the complex interplay between power and the normative dimension. Both theories stress the rationale of common values as significant driver for integration, though the ES puts more effort into developing its arguments from a historical/cultural perspective. While the episteme of SC with its peace-embracing focus sees common values expressed in common norms as a product of the process of integration and cooperation and views power with more skepticism, the order-embracing ES is more nuanced in its assessment of the different societal backgrounds of the uneven evolution of values and norms and views power more positively as long as an equilibrium of power prevails (see Bull 1977). Both theories thus assume certain dynamics in the evolution of values and norms as important driving forces behind the volatility of institutionalized cooperation. Both agree that their models of cooperation (Security Communities here and International Society/World Society there) and their scope (abandoning war here and order there) are subject to dynamics and, at worst, reversible. This leads to analyzing norm dynamics and the reasons behind dynamism in more depth. The ES has a compelling point in case in arguing for different historical/civilizational developments as driving forces. Scholars of SCs lean more towards idealistic reasoning in the pursuit of peaceful conduct which clashes with classical Realist thinking. Further concentrating on norm dynamics might add additional strata explaining institutionalized cooperation integration and dissolution.

8.4.1   Norm Dynamics: Essentials of Constructivist Analyses

While norms have always been an integral part of the research agenda of IR, scholars from different schools of thought have treated the issue considerably different at different times. Initially, classical Realists treated norms as principle axioms for understanding world politics. Carr (1939: 97) claimed that 'political action must be based on a coordination of morality and power' and criticized Realisms failure to emphasize emotional appeals and moral judgment (ibid). While primarily concentrating on the struggle for power, Morgenthau (1985: 5-6) included normative factors such as nationalism and the link between morality and international law in his works. With the dawning of scientism in the 1970s (cf. Waltz 1979), Neorealists took a significant turn away from the normative dimension arguing that states comply with norms when it suits their interests and violate norms when they conflict with defined interests (cf. Gilpin 1981; Mearsheimer 1995: 340-43). Only shortly afterwards, the Neoliberal regime episteme brought back norms as an integral part of its method of describing institutionalized cooperation (cf. Krasner 1982: 2).

With the advent of Constructivism in the late 1980s and early 1990s (cf. Shannon 2000: 293), norms finally became a central reference point in the study of IR and the corresponding literature fills whole shelves by now.[46] The generally agreed and often referred to definition of norms comes from Katzenstein (1996: 5) whereas norms are 'collective expectations for the proper behavior of actors with a given identity'. The observance of norms is thus rooted in the logic of what is morally appropriate (March and Olsen 1998). Norms are not exogenously given variables but develop in a societal process. Finnemore and Sikkink (1998) present a model which has long been accepted as the standard model for norm development. In their 'norm life cycle' model, a minority group of so called 'norm entrepreneurs' advocate the advancement of a new norm in order to strengthen their specific position (ibid: 893). After a while the new norm starts spreading and more and more actors embrace the norm which leads to a crucial 'tipping point' from which onwards a 'norm cascade' develops. At this stage, already a majority of actors embrace the norm, which leads, in the end, to a quasi-universal acceptance. Norms have then achieved a 'taken-for-granted quality' (ibid: 895) of internalization.

Much in the literature about norms deals with the question of agency and structure. According to Wendt (1987: 337-8), 'the agent-structure problem has its origins in two truisms about social life which underlie most social scientific inquiry. First, human beings and their organizations are purposeful actors whose actions help reproduce or transform the society in which they live. Second, society is made up of social relationships, which structure the

---

46   For a good overview of the corresponding literature see Wunderlich 2013.

interactions between these purposeful actors'. Such ontological view was primarily aimed at creating a counter model to the individualism-centered approach of rationalistic theories. Particularly with a view to the dynamics of norm evolution, the agency/structure relationship nevertheless resulted in a one-sided account which over-emphasized structure as an idealistic quasi endpoint (see exemplary Risse-Kappen and Sikkink 1999: 33). With a pejorative undertone, Kersbergen and Verbeek (2007: 221) emphasize that 'this is all the more curious because constructivists in particular should be open to the possibility that norms are open to "social reconstruction".' Remedying this shortcoming, the so called 'second wave' (Cortell and Davis 2000: 66) of *critical* Constructivists highlighted the need to bring back agency in the discussion of norm dynamics as no compelling evidence exists that norms, once they have achieved a structural taken-for-granted quality, will eternally stay the same or trigger endless adherence (cf. Rosert and Schirmbeck 2007: 256-7). As Shannon (2000: 298) puts it very basically, 'the "message" of social structure must be received through the filter of human agency. Humans are not omniscient observers of reality; they are imperfect interpreters of it. Whether a norm's prescriptions and parameters are understood in a given situation is up to the perceiver, with all associated cognitive limits and biases.'

Departing from this crucial insight, Constructivists have contributed important insights to understanding norm dynamics, particularly norm violation and/or erosion. Starting with norm violation, Shannon (2000) argues that norms are what states and leaders make of them and places his analysis between Realist and Constructivist understandings of norm adherence. Departing from the insight that 'state leaders are not either selfish or social but both at the same time', he offers a model based on psychological research in which leaders make their choices to violate norms according to a number of variables such as the non-routine character of a situation (e.g. if adherence to a norm clashes with a perceived major national interest), the "fuzziness" of norms, meaning that the norm inherits certain ambiguities which allow for different interpretations, and the situatedness, meaning if leaders have the chance to define a situation in a way that allows socially accepted violation. If all variables can be positively answered, norm violation most likely occurs. With regards to the first variable of the non-routine character of a situation, three factors facilitate norm violation: dramatic events, a culmination of events, and changes in personnel. With regards to the second variable of the "fuzziness" of a given norm, according to Shannon, any norm has two components: prescription and parameters. The prescription tells actors what to do or not to do. The parameters inform the actor of the conditions that apply to the prescription. The more parameters a norm has and the more unspecific prescriptions and parameters are the easier to find socially acceptable grounds for violation. With regards to the situatedness, leaders need an account 'that resolves the moral dilemma in the minds of actors as well as (actors hope) the audiences to whom they feel accountable.' (Ibid: 304) Four types of accounts are usually applied: apologies, denials, excuses, and justifications.

Turning to norm erosion, Rosert and Schirmbeck (2007) point to the contemporary norm density in international relations, which is a result of international governance efforts. They conclude that the growth of governance structures naturally constrains actors' room for maneuver. Norm erosion or the removal of a given norm by another "weaker" norm thus helps to widen states' room for maneuver. Scrutinizing the norms of anti-torture and the nuclear taboo, they come to conclude that seemingly internalizes norms can indeed become watered down. They identify what they call 'norm challengers' and the act of norm-challenging speech (most notably through debates amongst elites) as important actors and means in this process and infer that norm internalization does neither work in a linear vertical way nor does it automatically works on a horizontal level including all relevant actors in a given state. Particularly in reaction to a 'domino effect of the unthinkables', which works to widen the cognitive space of what was formerly not imaginable (take 9/11), norm challengers can start questioning well-established norms and thus initiate the process of reversal (cf. also Wunderlich 2013: 35). Kahl and Heller (2013) share their assessment of the wider consequences of norm-challenging speech with regards to policies of counterterrorism. For a 'reverse cascade' (McKeown 2009) of norms to happen, certain conditions must be met: norm-challenging speech must spill over from the domestic level of one state to be echoed by other states; major powers must be involved to increase the severity of norm de-legitimation; and norm challenging behavior by major powers must occur on repeated instances to further contribute to norm de-legitimation (Kahl and Heller 2013: 420).

Kersbergen and Verbeek (2007: 218) assess that 'norms are adopted because they mean different things to different actors and that, in consequence, compliance with a norm is partly a product of the recurrence of policy differences already existing before the adoption of the norm. Actors may make strategic use of such a situation.' Concentrating on the EU subsidiarity norm, they also infer that battles over norms 'are more likely to occur if the international norms adopted in their application are expected to affect the power relations between the major actors involved.' (Ibid: 235) Adding another stratum to the debate, Wiener and Puettner (2009: 16) infer that norms undergo a process of cultural validation. Norm contestation is thus understood as relating to different cultural contexts – an understanding in close vicinity to scholars of the English School. They assert that even within an existing community 'divergence and convergence of individually perceived normative meanings' can prevail amongst the different identities of a community.

Chayes and Chayes (1994: 66) have pointed to the important realm of justice. 'The basic conception of cooperative security implies general acceptance of and compliance with binding commitments limiting military capabilities and actions. The key to compliance with such a system of norms is that it be seen as legitimate. Legitimacy, in turn, requires that the norms be promulgated by fair and accepted procedures, applied equally and without invidious discrimination, and reflect minimum substantive standards of fairness and equity.' They infer that 'to be durable, international legal norms, whether or not treaty based, must meet broad tests of legitimacy.' (Ibid: 72) Müller (2013: 6-7) adds that justice is particularly salient for arms control whereby asymmetric relations exacerbate notions of inequalities in distribution. He concludes that 'justice claims are a particularly salient type of [norm] contestation.' (Ibid: 7) Zartman helps to break down the 'meta-norm' (Müller 2013: 7) of justice to the operational politics level. 'The notion that parties first establish a formula for an agreement before they go on to apply that principle of justice to determine the disposition in detail of the items at stake is well established empirically.' (Zartman 1995: 895) Closely connected to justice is the question of the impact of power distribution. Again, Müller (2013: 12) points to this realm of constant agency-structure interactions and assumes that 'seminal changes in the distribution of international power might lead to adjustments in the normative order with a view to accommodating the priorities of rising powers at the cost of declining ones.'

Taken together, critical constructivists have collated crucial insights to better understanding norm dynamics, particularly with regards to norm violation and erosion. What is nevertheless missing is a comprehensive model capturing norm erosion processes (cf. Wunderlich 2013: 27).

8.4.2   Analysis and Application

Critical Constructivist research on norm dynamics contributes important insights when applied to the empirical evidence as well as in relation to the research design of this study. First, Constructivist research underscores the wider normative dimension in which regimes are embedded in and which they help to govern. While this study has so far concluded that regime complexes can disintegrate, scholars of critical Constructivism have highlighted that also norms can undergo a process of decay. Chapter 7 has underscored that key principles and norms of the regime complex of cooperative arms control in Europe are highly contested, subject to non-compliance, and thus caught in the process of erosion. Following the analytical understanding of Müller and Wunderlich (2013: 5, 38), regime principles and norms belong to the normative realm of regime injunctions and can thus serve as analytical reference base for assessing norm dynamics in general.[47] In the same vein,

---

47 Similarities between principles and norms in the regime concept have led some scholars of
    IR to treat the two as an entity (for a discussion see Hasenclever, Mayer, and Rittberger
    1997: 11 et seq) or to the assessment that regimes are 'systems of norms' (Wunderlich
    2013: 38). Müller (2013: 5) refers to 'metanorms' which sometimes can be called 'princi-
    ples'. Even Krasner (1982: 4) has argued that 'changes in principles and norms are chang-

Kersbergen and Verbeek (2007: 236) have rediscovered regime theory as methodological tool for better understanding the dynamics of norm acceptance and compliance. The methodological regime focus applied in this study does therewith also allow for drawing conclusions that pertain to the realm of norm dynamics. It follows that if the regime complex of cooperative arms control in Europe is in decay, so is its normative dimension.

Second, research on norm dynamics allows for better analyzing agency and structure as factors in the process of decay. Starting with structure, and here with the endogenous dimension of structure, important parts of the normative dimension of cooperative arms control in Europe are inherently vague and contradictory. Key principles and norms such as the 'indivisibility of security' or 'strengthening stability' are fuzzy and allow for a wide range of divergent interpretations. What aggravates their normative impact is the fact that their application is apt to affect the power relations between the major actors. (Kersbergen and Verbeek 2007: 235) However, even seemingly concise and historically older principles such as sovereignty and thus the non-intervention in internal affairs are prone to contestation.

At this point, the exogenous dimension of structure comes into play. As explained before, dramatic events (Shannon 2000) and a 'domino effect of the unthinkables' (Rosert and Schirmbeck 2007) have happened during the last 41 years of cooperative arms control in Europe. Amongst those unthinkable events were the dissolution of the Eastern bloc, the Yugoslavia Wars, the enlargement of NATO, 9/11, and the current war in Eastern Ukraine. All such events have triggered the constant rethinking of major national interests as well as of normative injunctions. While the crumbling of the Eastern bloc changed the power setting (cf. Müller 2013: 12) and allowed for commonly embracing norms such as the development of arms control measures and more generally of cooperative security in Europe, the Yugoslavia Wars presented a formidable challenge for the principle of sovereignty and led to a first revision of the principle towards the emerging concept of humanitarian intervention. The enlargement of NATO challenged the indivisibility of security, at least in the perception of the major power Russia. The terrorist attacks of 9/11 triggered a whole bundle of norm-challenging policies (see Rosert and Schirmbeck 2007), amongst other again challenging the principle of sovereignty. The same applies to the war in Ukraine (see Burke-White 2014). Taken together, inherently vague principles and norms and exogenous events of political magnitude have contributed to a process of norm erosion; not just affecting cooperative arms control in Europe.

Turning to agency, both principle actors in the system, the United States and the Soviet Union/Russia have played the roles of norm entrepreneurs and

---

es of the regime itself. When norms and principles are abandoned, there is either a change to a new regime or a disappearance of regimes from a given issue-area.' His unitary treatment of principles and norms points to a certain commonality between the two, which he has not specified though.

norm challengers at different times and in different contexts. With the codifying of the Helsinki Final Act, both acted as norm entrepreneurs; however, given the equilibrium state of balance of power, the rhetorical-only character of principles and norms, and the partial inherent normative vagueness, norm establishment did not have serious consequences constraining their behavior (cf. Kersbergen and Verbeek 2007: 218). With the end of the Cold War, Washington and Moscow acted as norm developers, building on the established normative base, this time also in the legally-binding sphere of agreements. With the Yugoslavia Wars and NATO enlargement, the United States turned into a norm challenger; in the former case internationally recognizable, in the latter case, mainly in the perception of Russia. From the year 2000 onwards Russia joined as norm challenger through acts of openly criticizing the uneven employment of principles and norms, non-compliance with arms control agreements, and the questioning of normative injunctions in the human dimension. Washington during those years continued its path of norm challenger, particularly with regards to sovereignty, most notably in the cases of Afghanistan, Iraq, Libya, Syria, and through the employment of targeted drone attacks in so-called failed states. Russia, in turn, challenged sovereignty in Moldova (in the CFE context), Georgia, and Ukraine.

The norm-challenging behavior of both states is the more severe because they are the two major powers in the system of cooperative arms control in Europe and because of the repeated instances of norm de-legitimation (cf. Kahl and Heller 2013: 420). Concentrating on two events, NATO enlargement and the current Ukraine conflict, both events displayed and led to norm-challenging behavior. Applying Shannon's (2000) model, NATO enlargement was triggered by dramatic events, meaning the break-up of the Eastern bloc. Changes in personnel, and hence in politics in a partisan domestic setting (cf. Wunderlich 2013: 35), from the George H. W. Bush government to Bill Clinton and later to George W. Bush facilitated the process (cf. critically Hunter 2014). Enlargement clashed with the Russian perception of the principle of indivisibility of security but was in line with the U.S. issue-specific interest and could also easily exploit the "fuzziness" of the principle. Also, the broad support in most countries of Europe as well as in NATO and in the U.S. domestic setting allowed for social acceptance. Critique, mostly by Russia, was countered on accounts of denial (cf. exemplary OSCE 1996).

Focusing on the current war in Ukraine and again applying Shannon's model, dramatic events in the form of the revolutionary ousting of President Yanukovych and the prospect of Ukraine joining closer ties with the EU and maybe, at a later stage, also NATO (cf. Putin quoted in Charap and Shapiro 2014b), triggered Russian norm-challenging behavior. Changes in personnel and the politics vis-à-vis the West from Yeltsin to Putin and Medvedev to Putin had facilitated the process. Possible adherence to the principles of strengthening stability and sovereignty clashed with a perceived major Russian issue-specific interest. However, Russian norm-challenging behavior could not that easily exploit norm "fuzziness", particularly not the principle of sovereignty. Even though broad domestic support allowed for social Russian acceptance (as shown by the independent Levada pollster; see Baczynska 2014), at the international level acceptance remained unattainable. Therefore, the Kremlin countered the critique on lengthy accounts of justifications, mainly referring to earlier norm-challenging behavior by 'the West' (President of Russia 2014a).

Critical Constructivists have also pointed to the realm of vocal contestation as an important driver of norm dynamics. While Finnemore and Sikkink (1998: 899) have found that norm entrepreneurs often draw on 'some kind of organizational platform from and through which they promote their norms' this might as well pertain to norm challengers. In the case of cooperative arms control in Europe, the OSCE was and still is the organizational platform through which Russia has expressed is dissatisfactions and to which it addressed norm-challenging speech. From the late 1990s onwards and particularly increasingly since the year 2000, Russia has employed norm-challenging speech with regards to the indivisibility of security, the realm of arms control, and the norms governing the human dimension (see Russian Statements contained in Chapter 7). If Shannon's (2000: 304) psychology-based assumption is correct that 'the process of justifying violations occurs in the actors' minds prior to committing the act', the next logical step might be vocalizing possible grounds for eventual later violation. Hence, the repeated acts of norm-challenging speech, most vividly brought forward in the 2007 Munich speech of Vladimir Putin (President of Russia 2007), might have anticipated the later cascade of norm-challenging behavior such as non-compliance with the Istanbul commitments, CFE suspension, the 2008 Russian-Georgian war, and the on-going Ukraine conflict.

Russian perceptions of the inequitable distribution of gains and massive shifts in relative capabilities have informed the development of cooperative arms control in Europe and can as well be viewed as motives for norm contestation (cf. Müller 2013). Referring to Zartman (1995: 895), international negotiators adopt 'a principle of justice as the basis of their formula for an agreement'. In the case of the Helsinki Decalogue, this principle of justice was status quo for declaratory human rights commitments (and including the linked deal to MBFR). This principle was made obsolete with the crumbling of the Eastern bloc but for Moscow it was still in place and became reflected in the formula of the 'indivisibility of security'. Russian recourse to the formula was thus a constant cognitive reflection of power shifts and perceptions of inequality.

Taken together, the empirical evidence of cooperative arms control in Europe reveals a normative 'reverse cascade' (McKeown 2009). It is extremely hard to identify a singular factor with overriding importance for the erosion of the normative base of cooperative arms control in Europe. Instead, a whole bundle of factors led to norm erosion. What can be said is that crucial indicators for norm erosion correspond significantly with crucial findings from the empirical evidence. Amongst them are inherently vague norms, power shifts, changes in personnel, dramatic events, notions of inequity and injustice, norm-challenging speech, divergent re-interpretations of norms, repeated norm-challenging behavior by the two principal actors, and non-compliance. What becomes obvious is that Washington and Moscow do not share (or never shared; Kersbergen and Verbeek 2007: 222) a common understanding of the normative basis underlying cooperative arms control in Europe. As such circumstance is not unusual or severe, more important is the question how both treated their dissatisfaction with the substantiation of norms.

Kersbergen and Verbeek (2007: 218) assess that 'norms are adopted because they mean different things to different actors and that, in consequence, compliance with a norm is partly a product of the recurrence of policy differences already existing before the adoption of the norm. Actors may make strategic use of such a situation.' When crucial national interests were at stake, both gave priority to their interests once they were able to do so – the United States after the end of the Cold War, Russia after the year 2000. Obviously, such interpretation is in very close vicinity to a Neorealist understanding whereas norms only matter as long as they serve the interests of the powerful (cf. Mearsheimer 1994/95). However, such interpretation falls short of noticing the facts that at least for Russia, a long process involving norm-challenging speech, from the mid-1990s until Russian CFE suspension in 2007 and the Russian-Georgian war in 2008, preceded the actual violation of norms. Also, the Kremlin used multiple excuses and recourses to normative injunctions to justify the most blatant forms of norm violation seen in the current Ukraine conflict (cf. President of Russia 2014a). These facts show the constraining power of norms and underline that even if crucial norms are ignored or violated, even powerful actors struggle to do so without preparing for and following up the genuine act of violation.

8.5   Conclusions

Scholars of Security Communities, the English School, and Constructivism have all contributed meaningful approaches explaining the volatility of international cooperative efforts. In contrast to regime theory, their focus is not bound to institutionalization but relates to the wider historical, cultural, and societal contexts which influence cooperative efforts. While some of their insights have underscored certain findings of this book – e.g. that massive shifts in capabilities, offensively-oriented power policies in conjunction with NATO enlargement, and the subsequent Russian perception of the inequitable distribution of gains are powerful factors behind institutional decay (cf. Deutsch et al 1957: 40; Bull 1961: 39; Müller 2013: 12) – others contain additional explanations that have not come up in this study thus far. Those explanations help to explain the volatility of the process of institutionalization of cooperative arms control in Europe.

In the following, the conclusions deriving from this chapter will be collated in the process of answering the three guiding research questions of this chapter. What broader spectra of cooperation integration and dissolution drive the development of institutionalized cooperation? Both, the English School and the concept of Security Communities are concerned with a grand idea. For the ES it is *order*, for the concept of SCs it is *peace*. While the ES was originally a rather Realist-influenced reflection of the Cold War, and order became equated with stability and the equilibrium state of balance of power (cf. Bull 1977), the concept of SCs is more of a post-World War II development with a strong idealist touch towards the elimination of war. Except for this crucial difference, both relate to each other through the basic premise of a commonly shared sense of "we-ness". Again, both treat it differently. While the ES views "we-ness" often in a utilitarian understanding of mutual recognition of governing principles such as sovereignty and international law, its idealistic concept of world society embraces "we-ness" on the individual level and comes therewith very close to the concept of a security *community* in a *Gemeinschaft* understanding. It is at this point that Constructivism with its focus on norms comes into play, analyzing how norms, the practical manifestation of "we-ness", emerge and develop.

Concerning the topic of this book, these differently, though partially overlapping, approaches allow for extrapolating three broad drivers behind cooperation: an ideational, a civilizational/cultural, and an implementational. The ideational driver reveals four turning points in the development of grand ideas (or cooperation interests) of the United States and the Soviet Union/Russia. Following the Cuban Missile Crisis, the politics of détente and arms control manifested the idea of *stability*. Both embraced this idea. The Helsinki Final Act was a byproduct of this idea. With the fall of the Berlin Wall and the crumbling of the Eastern bloc, stability became replaced by the ideas of *cooperative security, democracy, and free market economies for the former WTO states*. Again, both shared these ideas. NATO enlargement, from 1994 onwards, the bombing of Yugoslavia in 1999, and the terrorist attacks of 9/11 two years later marked the transition towards the U.S. ideas of *unipolarity, devaluation of international law, and the primacy of the universality of individual human rights*. It is important to note that these ideas were the first that were not shared by Washington and Moscow anymore. While older ideas such as cooperative security were nevertheless (institutionally) maintained, both started to give precedence to the newer ones. With the Russian-Georgian War in 2008 and the war in Eastern Ukraine in 2014, Russia pushed forward its new ideas of *consolidation of the post-Soviet space* and *rejection* of older ideas.

Summing up, it is important to notice that since the mid-1990s, the major actors did not share a common grand idea (or interest) anymore. This fact relates to a second important essential of the ES and the concept of SCs – that is the presence of an exceptional common threat perception. Since ideas can be understood as meta-answers to a common threat, the inability to develop commonly shared ideas and thus the degradation of cooperation can be seen as decline of the magnitude of mutually shared threat perceptions – be it regional instabilities or international terrorism (in the same vein, cf. Buzan 2011). Such conclusion is in line with the Realist-based assessment of Chapter 3 that from the late 1990s onwards, the United States' general interest in securing survival was not directly linked to Russia anymore (cf. Kelleher 2012).

The civilizational/cultural spectrum has best been captured by the ES and relates closely to the ideational spectrum. Applying Buzan's (1993) societal circles allows for locating Russia and the United States at different layers. While both enjoyed a short "honeymoon" at the inner core during the first years of the post-Cold War period, a common sense of "we-ness" has been absent for most of the time of the period of analysis of 41 years of cooperative arms control in Europe. Clearly, this cooperation driver has deserved the least attention in the study at hand, which is owed to the methodological circumstance of largely omitting domestic policies. Further societal research, which would also have to include a much broader historical focus, is needed to explain the civilizational/cultural differences that have triggered different emphases on different ideational concepts.

The implementational driver affects the debate about norms and norm dynamics. Norms are the somewhat grand governing lines behind institutionalization. In relation to regime theory, they consist of the key principles and norms of the regime complex. They are triggered by common interests. Their achievement becomes much easier if a sense of "we-ness" is already in place. While the Cold War brought with it a common interest (avoiding nuclear war) which translated into a common idea (stability), a common sense of "we-ness" was absent in an idealist understanding but present in a utilitarian understanding. The Helsinki Final Act managed that balancing act and devised norms that reflected the existing common idea and the non-existing idealistic common sense of "we-ness". While with the end of the Cold War, an idealistic common sense of "we-ness" started to flourish, the common idea was at first replaced and later got lost. At the same time, the common sense of "we-ness" in a utilitarian understanding became downgraded through repeated instances of intervention. In a critical Constructivist understanding, unequal norm entrepreneurs became unequal norm challengers. Through these processes of dynamism and divergence, the normative basis became increasingly eroded; the institutions that were built on that basis followed suit.

Another important aspect of the implementational driver is the role and treatment of power. The massive shifts in relative capabilities after the Cold War allowed for regime establishment not only because of an emerging core of strength (the United States) but also because the crumbling Soviet Union had an equal interest in the establishment of governing institutions. The regime complex of cooperative arms control in Europe is thus not based on imposition but on agreement. Nevertheless, the resulting institutions carried (Russian) perceptions of inequity with them which, over time, led to dissatisfaction. It was thus not only the economic recovery of Russia after the year 2000 and the emergence of multipolarity with led to decay but even more so the effects of perceived inequity. This relates directly to the decay indicator of 'hegemonic practices'. It is to a lesser degree the possibility of hegemonic decline (loss of U.S. power) but more the fact of hegemonic practices (use of U.S. power) which negatively influenced the institutions of cooperative arms control in Europe and contributed to their decay. Both, the ES and scholars of SCs were correct in their early predictions that unconstrained growth in power is to the detriment of larger cooperation efforts, particularly to those involving critical questions of power.

What are the reasons behind norm erosion? Both the United States and Russia worked as repetitive norm challengers. For a long time, Russia was a norm-preserving actor. Even though Moscow violated a number of principles and norms of the Helsinki accords in conjunction with the two Chechen Wars, one can argue that the overriding national interest of the Kremlin to preserve the unity of the Russian nation state created a problematic setting. However, with the suspension of CFE in 2007, the Russian-Georgian War in 2008, and the war in Ukraine in 2014, Russia has turned into a norm challenger. Washington, only shortly after the end of the Cold War, became a multi-dimensional norm challenger in the classical security realm, in the realm of humanitarian intervention, and in the treatment of international law. Particularly Russia employed norm-challenging speech from the late 1990s onwards in the forum of the OSCE. One of the unintended effects of norm-challenging speech is that acts of vocal dissatisfaction, even though aimed at preserving a certain norm (e.g. indivisibility of security), help to erode a norm, since the act of debate manifests the notion that something is "wrong" with the norm (cf. Rosert and Schirmbeck 2007). Aside from these agency-related reasons, multiple norms of the regime complex of cooperative arms control in Europe are "fuzzy" and allow for a wide range of interpretations. As explained before, this is the result of the Helsinki accords and the balancing act of norms related to a common idea and norms related to an obsolete common sense of "we-ness". While the end of the Cold War would have allowed for re-assessing and possibly re-crafting the normative basis, it stayed unaltered. The "fuzziness" of important norms allow the actors wide-ranging and diverging interpretations up to a point where non-compliance becomes explained with preserving the normative base.[48] Last but not least, analysis of the empirical evidence in relation to the theoretical approach contained in this chapter suggests that the United States and the Soviet Union/Russia never really shared a common understanding of the normative basis of cooperative arms control in Europe. The historical chance for such understanding was there, roughly from 1989 to 1994. However, divergent issue-specific interests prevented the development of a common sense of "we-ness" and resulted in divergent interpretations and, later, non-compliance.

Do international institutions make a difference when it comes to the interests of the powerful? The empirical evidence suggests that changed domestic interests as well as changes in personnel in Washington and Moscow had an enormous impact on the development of the institutions of cooperative arms control in Europe. They involve the Gorbachev reforms in the Soviet Union, the foreign and security policy changes initiated by the George W. Bush administration, and the changes under the first and third presidential terms of Vladimir Putin. Müller (2013: 10) observes that 'the domestic politics related to international norms have a significant impact on norm robustness and development.' With no change in meaning, the term 'norm' could be replaced by 'institutions'. According to the understanding of Neorealism, changes at the level of international institutions are only an effect of changed interests by the powerful. Mützenich and Karádi's (2013: 43) framing captures well such utilitarian understanding: 'International institutions have two functions here. On the one hand, they mirror the interests of the states involved in them: Membership of international organizations is in the interest of a state (in terms of power projection). When these interests change, so does the character of the international institution concerned. Thus, the evolution of NATO and the OSCE since 1989 illustrates the changing preferences of their members – above all those of the major states.'

As much as such framing is also true for the institutions of cooperative arms control in Europe, critical Constructivism helps to understand the processes at work once states' genuine interests collide with the political framing of international institutions. The lengthy critique, vocal contestation, and convening of special meetings preceding the Russian suspension of CFE as well as the fact that Moscow even invented the formula of 'suspension' in the CFE context to possibly return to treaty implementation at a later stage,

---

48   The U.S. decision not to ratify ACFE as long as Russia's 'Istanbul commitments' remained unfulfilled is in contradiction to the treaty's principle of 'sustaining the key role of CFE as the cornerstone of European security' and can be seen as non-compliance with the key principle of strengthening stability. This act of non-compliance was explained with strengthening the principle of 'sovereignty' by U.S. Under Secretary for Political Affairs R. Nicholas Burns: 'For us, their [the 'Istanbul commitments' fulfillment continues to be a prerequisite for the ratification of the Adapted CFE Treaty. These are not just words on paper: a basic principle of the CFE Treaty is the right of sovereign states to decide whether to allow stationing of foreign forces on their territory.' (OSCE 2005)

shows the constraining effects of international institutions. Even though, the consequences of NATO's non-ratification of ACFE were to the detriment of Russia, it took the Kremlin seven years to finally let go of the treaty. The same constraining effects, even though much lesser visible, are apparent in the on-going war in Ukraine where Russia is struggling to find an internationally acceptable formula that would allow depicting its actions as being in conformity with international law (cf. Burke-White 2014).

Therewith, one possible answer to the question is Yes and No. Yes, international institutions make a difference when it comes to the interests of the powerful because they constrain actors' abilities to go it alone. No, international institutions do not make much of a difference when it comes to the interests of the powerful if those interests are perceived as being of extraordinary magnitude, thereby often involving critical questions of national security. Another possible answer would be that international institutions can make a difference for some time. As long as the effects of international institutions (e.g. contractual environment, learning, lower transactions costs, confidence-building, etc.) help a relatively weaker state to achieve a minimum of national interest – for Russia for instance a prominent role in its dealing with NATO through the NRC – than they make a difference. Once, the underlying relative distribution of capabilities changes to the relative advantage of that state (as in the 2000s for Russia) or once their constraining effects start to collide with major national interests, international institutions might lose their appeal.

Taken together, the insights gained from this chapter allow drawing a more encompassing picture of the rise and fall of cooperative arms control in Europe. Particularly explaining decay benefits from combining Realist assumptions and assumptions from regime theorists with insights from the ES, the concept of SCs, and critical Constructivism. A normative base with a strong interpretative character, which allows for widely diverging views and norm erosion, the absence of a common sense of "we-ness", and the uneven historical/civilizational location of the two main actors heading towards different societal poles, are powerful factors that have caused the volatility of cooperative efforts.

9 Summary and Conclusions

This book has tried to answer why Europe's once unique security institutions are in decay. Focusing on the two states that most vividly shaped and continue to shape cooperative arms control in Europe between 1973 and 2014 – the United States and the Soviet Union/Russia – it was possible to explain its rise and fall as well as its institutional design.

9.1 Summary

In this study, a multi-theory approach was applied in order to comprehensively analyze and explain policies and institutions. A single-theory approach – take for instance Realism – would have been possible. However, it would have fallen short of explaining a number of additional important reasons for the rise and fall of cooperative arms control in Europe. Qualitative analysis of 41 years of U.S.-Soviet/Russian cooperative arms control in Europe policies was first conducted on the basis of Realism (see Chapter 2), which was chosen due to its inherent skepticism towards international cooperation. Given that cooperative arms control in Europe is in decay, a cooperation-skeptical approach, highlighting the impediments to successful cooperation, was deemed most valuable. Another reason in favor of Realism is Russia's foreign and security policy, which has been regularly characterized as mirroring Realist rationales.

On the basis of Realism, a model for understanding international cooperation was developed (see Paragraph 2.3) and applied to the empirical evidence of 41 years of U.S.-Soviet/Russian policies of cooperative arms control in Europe (see Chapter 3). The model helped to analyze and compare the two states' capabilities (see Annex I), interests, expectations, strategies of cooperation, and their respective evaluation of gains from cooperation over time. The analysis helped to highlight a number of significant institutional achievements in four different cooperation clusters.

On the basis of regime theory (Chapter 4), 36 agreements (see Annex II) with direct relevance to cooperative arms control in Europe were qualitatively analyzed (see Chapter 5). Regime theory was applied because previous research has constantly employed regime terminological references without presenting any empirical evidence. Regime theory provides a number of indicators for identifying regimes as well as regime decay. Those indicators were applied to the 36 agreements in a first abductive test in order to test their regime quality and their respective state. The result (see Chapter 6) was a regime complex in decay. One of the reasons behind decay was a possible tension between the normative basis of the complex and the operational policies of the United States and Russia. In order to prove this assumption, a second abductive test was conducted (see Chapter 7). For that, 51 statements by U.S.-Soviet/Russian delegations to the OSCE between 1990 and 2014 (see Annex III) were assessed by methods of qualitative and quantitative content analysis. The result was that divergent interpretations of the normative basis and subsequent national policies contributed to regime decay.

In order to complement the institution-endogenous view of regime theory with exogenous views explaining for the broader driver behind international institutionalized cooperation, three additional theoretical approaches were applied (see Chapter 8). The aim was to find potentially underexplored reasons for decay, which Realism and regime theory could not explain. The concept of Security Communities, the English School, and critical Constructivist analyses of norm dynamics helped to gain a more complete picture.

9.1.1 The Regime Complex

Qualitative analysis of the empirical evidence of 41 years of U.S.-Soviet/Russian cooperation on cooperative arms control in Europe (see Chapter 3), had led to the assumption that four cooperation clusters had developed. The first cooperation cluster evolved in the realm of declaratory or politically binding CSBMs, achieved under the auspices of the C/OSCE. It is the oldest of the four cooperation clusters. It is based on the 1975 Helsinki accords, is multilateral in nature, and gained its full shape through a whole range of agreements during the early and mid-1990s. From a purely technical point of view, it is today still largely functioning. Politically, the cluster is outdated and does not address current security challenges anymore. Its initial purpose was to provide more confidence through means of military bloc-to-bloc transparency. Later, its purpose somewhat changed to providing more stability for the newly emerging post-Soviet states.

The second cooperation cluster evolved in the realm of conventional arms control (CAC). It dates back to the early 1973 MBFR talks but only led to fruitful cooperation with the end of the Cold War and the signing of the CFE Treaty. This cluster is bilateral in nature with a strong U.S.-Soviet/Russian focus. It gained its full shape through the inclusion of additional instruments during the early 1990 and was significantly adapted during the mid- to late 1990s. It is politically deadlocked since 2002. The cluster does not address current security challenges anymore due to the Russian "suspension" of CFE and NATO's partial suspension. Its initial purpose was to prevent large-scale conventional surprise attack by establishing numerical parity and a zonal limitations system between the two blocs, to significantly downsize conventional holdings, and to provide for military transparency. Its later purpose was to achieve lower national levels of conventional equipment in conjunction with the dissolution of the Eastern bloc and NATO's eastward enlargement.

The third cooperation cluster evolved in the realm of political and military (pol-mil) cooperation under the auspices of NATO. It took off shortly after the end of the Cold War. The cluster is multilateral as well as bilateral (e.g. through the NRC) in nature and was adapted during the 1990s and the early 2000s. In its dealings with Russia it is deadlocked since the Russian annexation of Crimea. Because of the partial suspension of the NRC, the cluster is only partially addressing current security challenges. It has three purposes: achieving more stability for the newly emerging post-Soviet states; preparing for NATO enlargement; and giving Russia a prominent and visible role in its dealings with the alliance.

The fourth cooperation cluster evolved in the realm of sub-regional arms control for the Balkans. This cluster is multilateral in nature and took off during the mid-1990s. It was amended in the early 2000s and is still functioning. Its initial purpose was to achieve lower levels of conventional armaments on the Balkans, which has somewhat shifted to esuring more predictability and military transparency.

Qualitative analysis of 36 agreements (see Annex I and Chapter 5), assessed by means of a regime-methodological approach, had then led to the conclusion that those four cooperation clusters really are regimes (see Chapter 6). In addition, a fifth regime was discovered. This fifth regime evolved in the realm of declaratory and politically binding general commitments under the C/OSCE. It dates back to the 1975 Helsinki accords and is multilateral in nature. It gained its full shape in conjunction with the end of the Cold War and was adapted throughout the 1990s. It manifests itself most visibly in the organization of the OSCE. It is still mainly functioning but is characterized by internal dissent and protracted negotiations. Still today, its purpose is to provide the OSCE area with an inclusive, holistic, and consensus-oriented framework for cooperative security.

Analysis of the 36 agreements also showed that those five regimes together form a regime complex in the understanding of complexity research (cf. Thakur 2013). All regimes share a significant number of key principles and norms amongst themselves and across the five elemental regimes. Since the twelve key principles and norms of the complex are in large parts already contained in the 1975 Helsinki accords and are repeated and amended in the ensuing agreements of the declaratory C/OSCE regime, it was concluded that the declaratory C/OSCE regime forms an overarching meta-regime in the understanding of Aggarval (1985: 18-20). Thus, the C/OSCE meta-regime provides the normative basis of the regime complex. In addition, three regimes share historically-evolved political linkages. The CAC regime, the C/OSCE meta-regime, and the NATO pol-mil regime were all adapted in the wake of the first round of NATO enlargement and were part of a political compensation deal between Washington and Moscow (see Paragraph 3.4.1). Because of this development, those regimes also share a significant number of active or passive direct textual references. Concerning the Balkans regime, the regime shares passive direct references with the CAC and the CSBM regime, for it was designed along the lines of the CFE Treaty and the Vienna Document. In addition, all regimes have partially overlapping memberships. The interactions between the five regimes are frequent and vivid. The complex shows a high degree of density.

THE REGIME COMPLEX OF COOPERATIVE ARMS CONTROL IN EUROPE

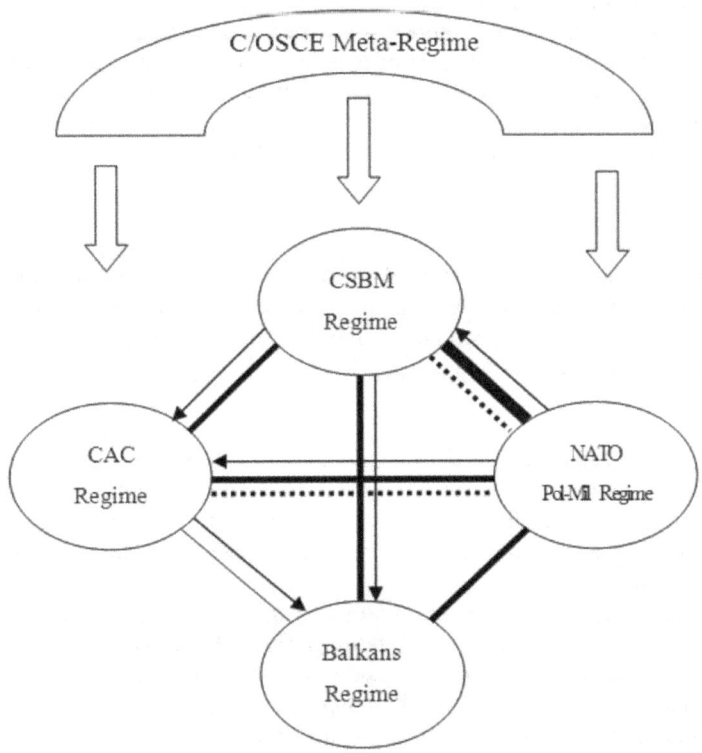

This visualization has been designed by the author. Arrows symbolize an active or passive direct reference of a textual and/or a design nature. Continuous lines symbolize cross-shared key principles and norms; thickness of lines indicates degree of cross-sharing. Dashed lines symbolize political linkages.

Analysis of the different periods of regime development shows that the complex gained its full shape during the 1990s with the years between 1992 and 1994 being especially productive in terms of the establishment of new agreements (see Chart 34 in Paragraph 5.6 above). Since the year 2000, the pace of establishment of new agreements has slowed down significantly.

During the last ten years, only one new agreement in the realm of cooperative arms control in Europe has been concluded (the Vienna Document 2011).

The findings in Chapters 5 and 6 suggest further that of the regime complex, four elemental regimes show indicators of decay, though to different degrees. Having applied thirteen indicators of regime decay to the 36 agreements, on average, each agreement in the realm of cooperative arms control in Europe is affected by 3.9 indicators of decay. Particularly the C/OSCE meta-regime, the NATO pol-mil regime, and the CAC regime are on average most strongly affected. In absolute terms, the three negative indicators of non-compliance, divergent issue-specific interests, and issue linkage are most often present. Instances of Russian non-compliance are overrepresented. Taken together, the distribution and the high number of occurrences of indicators of decay have led to the conclusion that the regime complex of cooperative arms control in Europe really is in decay.

9.1.2   Explaining Decay

The multi-theory approach applied in this volume generated a number of different avenues that directly relate to each other. Each theoretical approach stresses different indicators. Only in relation to each other, it is possible to comprehensively analyze and explain decay.

Realism
According to Realism (see Chapter 2), massive as well as minor shifts in capabilities, partially offensive orientations, a mutually diminished interest in cooperation related to the survival motive, repeated calls for re-negotiation, and increasing acts of non-compliance by major actors are indicative of and help explain decay.

According to Realism, the relative distribution of capabilities affects states' interest in cooperation (cf. Waltz 1979). The massive shift in U.S.-Soviet/Russian capabilities in conjunction with the end of the Cold War (see Paragraph 3.8.1 and Annex I) had a cooperation-enabling and, over the long term, a cooperation-disabling effect. On the one hand, it led the Soviet Union under Gorbachev to focus relatively more on the economic capabilities of the USSR than on the military. Against the background of its rapidly decreasing economic capabilities, Moscow decided to prioritize the economy and to seek cooperation with the West. Gorbachev's aim was to downsize the costly Soviet military and to get economic and financial aid from the West in return (Gorbachev 1996). On the other hand, the loss of relative capabilities on the Soviet side left Washington with relative more capabilities. Given the relative Soviet, and later Russian, weakness, the United States was able to follow its preferred policies in its dealings with Moscow. The results were Russian perceptions of inequality, dissatisfaction with the post-Cold War security design of Europe, continued calls for re-negotiation, protracted negotiations, and increasing acts of non-compliance. After another shift in economic capabilities with the relative recovery of the Russian economy during the 2000s, Russia started to (partially) exit from the institutions and policies of cooperative arms control in Europe.

Another postulate by Realism is that cooperation with offensively-oriented states is usually complicated (cf. Jervis 1999). From 1994 onwards, the United States started to show an offensive orientation, which resulted in an additional change to the existing relative distribution of power in Europe. In contrast to the Cold War, Washington was now able to succeed with that orientation. NATO enlargement led to a further shift in capabilities in three stages (1999, 2004, and 2009). According to Realism (cf. Jervis 1999), direct cooperation between Washington and Moscow on enlargement did not take place due to the offensive orientation of U.S. policy. However, tacitly, Washington sought to cushion Russian unease with enlargement through means of cooperative arms control in Europe (see Paragraph 3.4.1). The establishment of the 1997 NATO-Russia Founding Act, the adaptation of CFE, and the adaptation of the OSCE were all measures, designed to accommodate Moscow and to support the weak Yeltsin government at home. Washington rejected Russian counterproposals, such as replacing NATO with the OSCE, and linked important strands of the defensively-oriented policy of cooperative security to its enlargement policy, which was offensive in nature. These policies led to increased Russian frustrations.

States' interest in securing survival is paramount, according to Realism (cf. Waltz 1979). At the latest from the year 2001 onwards, Washington showed a diminished interest in cooperation with Russia. Both states shared a direct interest in cooperation throughout the Cold War, according to Realism because of their mutual survival concern in conjunction with the potential ramifications of MAD. This interest continued in the direct post-Cold War period, though for different reasons. For Russia, it was mainly about the economy; for the United States out of concern that Russia could backslide into authoritarianism. With the 9/11 attacks, the survival concern of Washington shifted away from Russia to the War on Terror and, later, towards China. Russia dropped out of the focus. Cooperation with Moscow was not a direct priority anymore (see Paragraph 3.5.1). In turn, Moscow, under Putin, shifted its priority towards economic recovery and consolidating its influence in the Near Abroad. This mutual diminished interest in cooperation led to the U.S. perception that issues of European security were basically non-problematic in nature and, later on, to mutually non-compromising behavior when it came to issue-specific divergent interests.

According to Realism, dissatisfied states call for re-negotiation (cf. Grieco 1988). Russian calls for re-negotiating elements of the post-Cold War security architecture or the whole system altogether are apparent from the mid-1990s onwards (see Chapter 3). These calls led to the adaptation of CFE, the adaptation of the OSCE in the second half of the 1990s, and to the establishment of the NRC in 2002. They increased in the OSCE during the 2000s and culminated in the two unsuccessfully tabled security treaty drafts of Dmitry Medvedev in 2008 and in the ensuing Corfu Process of the OSCE (see Paragraph 3.6.1). Russian calls for re-negotiation were thus partially successful. However, Moscow never achieved its overriding goal of either subordinating NATO to a higher security institution or to codify an end to enlargement. Washington and its allies continued to resist any such attempt. This fact aggravated Russian dissatisfaction.

Further on, Realists stress that the incentive to cheat is omnipresent in all cooperative efforts under anarchy (cf. Grieco 1988). Repeated acts of U.S. and Russian non-compliance with the elements of cooperative arms control in Europe start to increase from the late 1990s onwards. They involve major decisions such as NATO enlargement (in the Russian perception a violation of the Helsinki principle of the 'indivisibility of security'), NATO's 2002 decision to withhold ACFE ratification, Russian non-fulfillment of the CFE Istanbul commitments, Russian CFE "suspension" in 2007, the Russian-Georgian war in 2008, and Russia's role in the ongoing war in Ukraine. Russia was almost always involved when it came to non-compliance (see Chapter 6). According to Realism (cf. Mearsheimer 1994/95), non-compliance is a major hindrance to uphold international cooperation – an assumption fully in line with the deadlock of the cooperation cluster of conventional arms control.

Regime Theory
According to regime theory (see Chapter 4), policies of issue linkage, divergent issue-specific interests, regime-internal contradictions, protracted negotiations, divergent interpretations of principles and norms, negative adaptation consequences, Russian perceptions of the inequitable distribution of gains, negative expectations, and negative spill-over effects are indicative of and help explain decay.

Policies of issue linkage can lead to negative spill-over effects (cf. McGinnis 1986). They were present throughout most of the period of analysis. Their result was threefold. First, they helped establish cooperation through the cooperation strategy of compensation. This was the case in the MBFR/CSCE deal and particularly in the case of the deals achieved throughout the 1990s. Second, those policies were used by the Clinton administration in the process of NATO's first round of enlargement. They resulted in an unhealthy combination of offensively-oriented (enlargement) and defensively-oriented (cooperative security) policy concepts. Third, they led to close political-historical connections between some of the elemental regimes of the regime complex. When the first important agreement of the CAC regime, the CFE Treaty, came under duress, these negative developments started to spillover to other regimes and reverberated throughout the complex. Since the Russian "suspension" of CFE in 2007, such negative ripple effects can be traced towards the NATO pol-mil regime, the C/OSCE meta-regime, and the CSBM regime.

According to regime theory, divergent issue-specific interests can impede cooperation (cf. Müller 1993a: 49). Divergent issue-specific interests were present on almost all occasions of U.S.-Soviet/Russian cooperation on cooperative arms control in Europe. Nevertheless, until the new millennium they were mostly overcome by either compensation deals or because Russia shifted from an initially offensive policy orientation to a defensive orientation (see Paragraph 3.4.1). Since then, both actors insisted either on their issue-specific interests or were unwilling to set up possible compensation deals in order to offset their partially offensive orientation (see Paragraph 3.6.1).

Protracted negotiations can result in continued deadlock (cf. Aggarwal 1985: 143-82). They occur at least since 2002 when NATO member states, led by Washington, made ACFE ratification conditional on Russia fulfilling her Istanbul commitments (cf. Kühn 2009). They are symptomatic of the political process in the OSCE since more than ten years and continue to affect the NATO pol-mil regime. They led to increased negative expectations in the realm of cooperative arms control in Europe since the dawn of the new millennium.

According to regime scholars, negative adaptation consequences can hamper and even terminate institutionalized cooperation (cf. Young 1982: 281). Negative adaptation consequences occurred in the conventional arms control regime. The inclusion of the fourteen amendments of the U.S. Senate to the ratification document of the Flank Agreement and the ensuing Istanbul commitments marked a significant change, though passing mostly unnoticed at that time (cf. Kühn 2009). They led directly to ACFE non-ratification, protracted negotiations, negative expectations, Russian non-compliance with her Istanbul commitments, Russian exit from CFE, and generated effects of negative spill-over to other elemental regimes of the complex.

Regime-internal contradictions can significantly constrain successful institutionalized cooperation (cf. Young 1989: 96; Müller 1993a: 50-1). Regime-internal contradictions can be found in the 1975 Helsinki accords (see Paragraph 6.3). The accords were designed to allow for a declaratory understanding against the background of strongly divergent issue-specific interests. Since the Helsinki accords are at the heart of the normative basis of the regime complex, they continue to have declaratory validity until today. Their partially contradicting nature allows for diverse understandings and divergent interpretations of the normative base. It thus serves as a reference frame for continued Russian calls for re-negotiation and even allows justifying acts of non-compliance with reference to divergent interpretations of the normative basis.

Divergent interpretations of principles and norms (see Paragraph 6.3) can as well complicate institutionalized cooperation (Krasner 1982: 4). In fact, they are quite common in international practice (cf. Brzoska 1991).

They are not a problem as long as states are able to bring their divergent interpretations constructively in line. On cooperative arms control in Europe however, they led to justifications of divergent issue-specific interests and to acts of non-compliance, most visibly in the on-going war in Ukraine. Their roots in the regime-internal contradictions of the Helsinki accords and their almost constant occurrence since the late 1990s (see the assessment of statements contained in Chapter 7) leads to the assumption that Moscow and Washington almost never really shared a common understanding of key principles and norms of the regime complex.

The inequitable distribution of gains can lead to dissatisfaction with cooperation, according to scholars of regime (cf. Hasenclever, Mayer, and Rittberger 2004: 184). It is hard to point directly to a specific point in time from which onwards Russian perceptions of the inequitable distribution of gains occurred. At least since the year 2002, Russian statements delivered to the OSCE are full of complaints about 'double standards' and about the apparently unevenly directed critique of the organization pertaining to the so called "third basket" (see Russian statements contained in Chapter 7). The continued Russian calls for re-negotiations are indicative of the Russian perception of being treated unequally. The most prominent example of vocal dissatisfaction was the 2007 Munich Security Conference speech of Vladimir Putin (see President of Russia 2007). Negative expectations, at least on the Russian side, started to occur in conjunction with the perception of the inequitable distribution of gains.

Security Communities
According to the theoretical concept of Security Communities (see Paragraph 8.2), no common sense of "we-ness", no U.S. willingness to constrain its power and exert responsiveness towards Russia, the absence of a common threat perception, and the Russian failure to adjust to its loss of dominance are indicative of and help explain decay.

According to Deutsch et al (1957), a common sense of "we-ness" is a precondition for the establishment of a Security Community. Such sense was almost always absent between the United States and the Soviet Union/Russia throughout the entire period of analysis. Only during the short time between 1989/90 and 1994 do the statements delivered to the OSCE (see Russian statements contained in Chapter 7) show a significant, albeit only rhetorical, convergence in terms of values and policies. This window of opportunity ceased with the U.S. decisions to maintain and, later, enlarge NATO. The continuing divergence in issue-specific interests, the divergent interpretation of principles and norms of the regime complex, the increasing acts of non-compliance, and the re-emergence of war and belligerent rhetoric are a strong testament that a sense of "we-ness" is absent.

Security Communities often develop around a core of strength. A precondition is the ability of the strong state to constrain its power. The enlargement of NATO and particularly the non-cooperative policies during the eight Bush years are indicative of the unwillingness of the United States to constrain the unique amount of power that Washington enjoyed since the end of the Cold War. So is the U.S. insistence to push through its preferred issue-specific interests in conjunction with NATO enlargement and the minor role it assigned to the OSCE. The continued signs of Russian dissatisfaction are crucial signs that Washington was either not willing or not sensitive enough to exert enough responsiveness towards Russia. The result was growing frustration on the Russian side, acts of Russian non-compliance, and, over the long term, a diminished interest in cooperation with the United States.

Following to the concept of Security Communities, the presence of a common threat perception is helpful in establishing such a community. With a view to the empirical evidence, the absence of a common threat perception goes hand in hand with a mutual diminished interest in cooperation. The Cold War nuclear standoff generated a clear, though at the same time rather abstract common threat perception: MAD. In contrast, the threat perception after the Cold War was rather multi-dimensional and not so much shared anymore. It was furthered by a very diverse threat landscape that consisted of different experiences such as the economic downfall of Russia, civil wars in the OSCE area, terrorism, or the relapse of Russia into authoritarianism (see Paragraphs 3.3.1 and 3.4.1). Those diverse threat perceptions were partially overlapping, partially divergent, and partially convergent. Since the year 2001, those divergent perceptions triggered divergent national policies based on divergent issue-specific interests and divergent interpretations of principles and norms of the regime complex.

Deutsch et al (1957) have also stressed that formerly strong states have to adjust to their loss of dominance in order to facilitate Security Community establishment. The continuing Russian calls for re-negotiation, the perception of the inequitable distribution of gains, and the growing dissatisfaction and frustration are all indicative of Russia's failure to adjust to its loss of dominance. The Russian attempts to consolidate the so-called Near Abroad and to forge military and economic alliances (CSTO, Customs Union, Eurasian Union) as well as the concealed (Medvedev EST) and open (Ukraine war) attempts to halt NATO enlargement are all signs that Russia has not accepted its relative loss of power. The result is a partial incompatibility of the current Russian foreign and security policy with the principles of cooperative security because the Russian leadership employs short-term offensively-oriented policies (e.g. in Ukraine) in order to achieve the long-term goal of securing the status quo (no further NATO enlargement) in the post-Soviet space.

The English School
According to the English School (see Paragraph 8.3), the absence of a common civilizational background and a sense of "we-feeling", the loss of the ordering principle of the equilibrium state of balance of power and as a con-

sequence thereof the absence of respect for mutual spheres of influence, the emerging unipolar hegemony of the United States together with hegemonic practices, hubris, and loss of credibility, the U.S. orientation towards the concept of world society and the Russian opposition of world society values, and the mutual violations of the concept of international society are indica tive of and help explain decay.

According to the English School, historically evolved shared values help establish a kind of "we-feeling" among participants of the concept of world society (cf. Wight 1977). The absence of a sense of "we-feeling", based on the absence of a common civilizational background (cf. Neumann 2011), helps to understand why Russia and the United States are not sharing a common understanding of the normative basis of the regime complex. The consequences are incompatible policies and political discourses, which take place at different layers of the concepts of international society and/or world society.

According to Bull (1969), the maintenance of a balance of power among great powers serves as a hedge against hegemony. As is well known, the end of the Cold War brought an end to the ordering principle of the equilibrium state of the bipolar balance of power. The consequences were the unchecked rise of America and a certain disregard for the spheres of influence of the former opponent. The consequences are opposing policy concepts (NATO enlargement here vs. Near Abroad policy there), which had a direct negative impact on third states such as Ukraine and on the institutions of cooperative arms control in Europe. The emerging unipolar hegemony of the United States during the 1990s, together with hegemonic practices, hubris, and loss of credibility (see Abu Ghraib) are a product of the massive shift in relative capabilities after the end of the Cold War. Taken together, they led to policies of double standard (e.g. mutual respect for sovereignty), U.S. non-responsiveness to Russian complaints, and offensive orientations (NATO enlargement) that were softened by a parallel second U.S. policy strand of the continuation of the policies of cooperative security.

In line with an important strand in the English School, promotion of in-dividual human rights standards and moral claims, represented by the concept of world society, can help to undermine the existing order, represented by the concept of international society (Bull 1977: 151-53). The U.S. orientation towards the concept of world society and the Russian opposition thereof are a product of different civilizational backgrounds (cf. Neumann 2011). With the 1999 Yugoslavia bombing and the later recognition of the independence of Kosovo, Washington gave precedence to ideas of world society (e.g. individ-ual human rights, overcoming the primacy of the nation state, self-determination) over considerations of the concept of international society (i.e. sovereignty and non-interference in internal affairs). At the same time, Rus-sia, increasingly under the third Presidency of Putin, has started to vehement-ly oppose ideas of world society and instead relies on international relations definitions based on international society (cf. Lukin 2014). The result is another layer of practical and rhetorical incompatibility of policies. This incompatibility starts to overstretch the already strained normative basis of the regime complex the further the two states are drifting apart.

Further on, both violated the concept of international society. Examples are the circumvention of the UN Security Council in the 1999 Yugoslavia bombing, the precedent of the recognition of independence of Kosovo, the U.S.-led Iraq war, the Russian recognition of independence of South Ossetia and Abkhazia, and the annexation of Crimea. These examples are practical manifestations of the divergent interpretations of older and newer ordering principles. Their result is a loss of a common basis for understanding and conducting international affairs cooperatively.

Norm Dynamics
According to critical Constructivist analyses of norm dynamics (see Paragraph 8.4), the "fuzziness" of the Helsinki norms, Russian notions of injustice and inequality, acts of norm-challenging speech, the mutual U.S.-Russian role as norm challengers, the non-routine character of certain situations, the domestic situatedness, and changes in personnel have all facilitated norm violation and thus contributed to the erosion of the normative basis of cooperative arms control in Europe. The erosion of norms is indicative of cooperation dissolution and helps explain decay.

According to Constructivist research (see Paragraph 8.4), the erosion of norms can have a negative impact on cooperation and happens in conjunction with a number of facilitating variables (cf. Rosert and Schirmbeck 2007). First, the "fuzziness" of norms can facilitate norm violation and erosion (cf. Shannon 2000). Looking at the empirical evidence, the partial "fuzziness" of the normative basis of the Helsinki accords connects directly to the indicator of regime-internal contradictions and has helped the United States and the Soviet Union/Russia to interpret key principles and norms of the regime complex very differently (see Chapter 7). Constructivists conclude that the more "fuzzy" a norm, the easier it gets to exploit it (cf. Shannon 2000). The result is a constant Russian reference to "fuzzy" principles and norms such as the 'indivisibility of security' once issue-specific national interests lead to instances of non-compliance (see Chapter 7).

Acts of norm-challenging speech (cf. Rosert and Schirmbeck 2007) have occurred increasingly on the Russian side from the late 1990s onwards in the forum of the OSCE (see Russian Statements contained in Chapter 7). Norm-challenging speech in conjunction with justice claims are a particularly salient type of norm contestation (Müller 2013: 6-7). Russian notions of injustice and inequality pertain to NATO enlargement, the U.S. foreign and security policy which, as Russia claims, would employ double standards, and the role of the OSCE (see President of Russia 2007; 2014b). The consequences of the Russian notions of being treated unfair were increasing acts of norm-challenging speech, a (partial) retreat from the institutional structures of cooperative security, and the (partial) ignoring of the normative basis of the regime complex.

The repeated and increasing use of norm-challenging speech has actively prepared the ground for norm-challenging behavior (cf. Rosert and Schirmbeck 2007). Both, the United States and Russia have acted as norm challengers at different times. Both have challenged existing normative parts of the regime complex (see Chapter 6) in conjunction with NATO enlargement (in the Russian perception a U.S. violation of the principle of the indivisibility of security), the Yugoslavia bombing, the Russian CFE "suspension", the Russian-Georgian war, and the annexation of Crimea. Since both states are the two main actors in the system of cooperative arms control in Europe and since both acted repeatedly and increasingly, their actions are all the more severe.

The non-routine character of certain situations in conjunction with the domestic situatedness and changes in personnel (cf. Shannon 2000) has facilitated norm violation on different accounts. In conjunction with the first deliberations to enlarge NATO, the non-routine character of the dissolution of the USSR, the domestic U.S. support for enlargement, and the change in office from Bush senior to Bill Clinton have all facilitated norm violation. The same applies to the situations of the 9/11 attacks and the on-going war in Ukraine. The consequences of the political handling of these events of magnitude are that central normative pillars of cooperative European institutions were largely ignored, and therewith partially devalued. The result was a slow but increasing erosion of norms of the regime complex. With the erosion of norms, the normative basis has been considerably weakened (see Chapter 7).

9.2   Conclusions

Analysis of 41 years of U.S.-Soviet/Russian policies on cooperative arms control in Europe has shown that a dense regime complex with five elemental regimes (one being a meta-regime) developed during those years. Different theoretical IR approaches corroborate that this complex is in decay. That leads to a number of key theoretical and political conclusions, which will be summarized in the following two paragraphs.

9.2.1   Theoretical Conclusions

Previous research on cooperative arms control in Europe has failed to acknowledge the complex relationship of its various institutions (see Paragraph 1.3). Due to a lack of sound theoretical research and because of a lax use of regime terminology without any empirical evidence, scholars of IR have missed the complex form of the institutions. Explaining cooperative arms control over a long period of time (1973-2014) and including different security institutions, such as NATO and the C/OSCE, turned out to be fruitful because it helped to identify the concept's common historical-political and normative origin. That has direct bearings on the likely consequences of elemental decay and the political handling of those consequences.

The cooperative policies and institutions of NATO are an integral part of the regime complex and are much closer interwoven with other cooperative institutions than usually described in the literature (cf. Ponsard 2007). Even though previous research has successfully linked NATO's eastern policy towards the concept of cooperative security (ibid), this study shows that NATO's respective cooperative institutions are sharing the key principles and norms of the regime complex to a significant degree. Particularly the principle of the 'indivisibility of security' is a central element of the relevant NATO agreements (see Table 57). Because the institutions of NATO are an integral part of the regime complex, their policies can potentially lead to negative spill-over effects to other elemental regimes of the complex. These conclusions have a direct impact on the politics of those institutions.

The research on regime complexes is incomplete. So far, complexity research has not tried to analyze seemingly "old" security institutions based on the premises of complexity assumptions (see Thakur 2013). This study shows that the regime complex of cooperative arms control in Europe dates back to 1975. In addition, the empirical evidence has proven that even sophisticated forms of long-term successful institutionalized cooperation such as regime complexes can go into reverse or even dissolve. This empirical finding contributes significantly to theoretical complexity assumptions, which have so far missed to address the possible evolution stage of complexity decay (cf. Morin and Orsini 2013). The methods applied in Chapters 3-6 have helped to name concrete reference values for identifying the interactions ('links') between the elemental regimes ('nodes') of a complex (cf. Orsini, Morin, and Young 2013: 30). Complexity research has so far not been very specific about how to establish reference values for detecting interaction (ibid). This study introduced four novel reference values: cross-shared key principles and norms, political-historical linkages, active or passive textual references, and active or passive design links.

The multi-theory approach applied in this book was particularly helpful for analyzing the decay of cooperative arms control in Europe and the related foreign and security policies of the United States and the Soviet Union/Russia. Realism helped to identify the structural shifts in the system and their interactions with the units of the system (cf. Waltz 1979). The shifts in relative capabilities and the subsequent changes in the orientation of the United States help to explain why regime establishment in conjunction with the end of the Cold War took place and why the political deals of that time contained the seeds of future contention and institutional decay. Realism is particularly valuable for identifying issue-specific foreign and security policy orientations of states and the likely consequences for cooperation. The theory helped explain why direct U.S.-Russian cooperation on NATO enlargement never took place. It also helped to better understand certain Russian policy initiatives such as the common European house, the upgrade of the CSCE, the OSCE Security Model exercise or the Medvedev draft EST, all of which were ultimately geared, in one way or another, towards achieving an end to future rounds of NATO enlargement. It was therewith possible to identify Russia as a mainly status quo-oriented power and the United States as a power that leaves all options on the table.

On other accounts, Realism is not very helpful when it comes to addressing the reasons behind the fall of the regime complex. The Russian perception of the inequitable distribution of gains and the subsequent signs of dissatisfaction and frustration are a good example. From a Realist perspective, the distribution of gains is not "unfair" but relative to the underlying distribution of power (cf. Grieco 1988). If the gains from cooperation are not mirroring the relative distribution of power anymore, rational states will seek exit to cooperation. Such assumption is nevertheless only in line with the Russian behavior in conjunction with CFE. It does not address the negative Russian emotions and their additional consequences at all. Particularly Neorealism (cf. Waltz 1979) is too narrow in that sense. Here, Constructivist approaches (see Chapter 4 and Paragraph 8.4) seem much more valuable.

An important conclusion from the Realist approach pertains to the survival motive (cf. Waltz 1979). Since the United States and Russia are enjoying nuclear strategic parity in numerical terms of nuclear warheads and delivery vehicles (cf. New START 2011), their national survival in terms of security against direct military attack is secured as long as both deem the other to act rational in the sense of sharing an ultimate survival concern. Russian reference to NATO enlargement as a threat to national security (cf. Ministry of Defence 2010) and to the indivisibility of security are therewith part and parcel of a constant Russian construction of the survival motive. Efforts to halt enlargement, to codify the status quo, or to prevent possible future enlargement (cf. Charap and Shapiro 2014b) can thus probably be better explained in terms of power, defined in influence and status, than in terms of security. Morgenthau's (1954) classical concept of the struggle for power, complemented with Constructivist analysis of emotions of inferiority, loss, grievance, and collective memories would be a valuable approach to explaining contemporary Russian foreign and security policy towards the West. These conclusions derive only from application of the different theoretical approaches in this book. They have not led to any deeper analysis, for instance of the nuclear relationship or of domestic policies. Here, further research is needed.

Institutions and norms matter also to the powerful – but to varying degrees. The empirical evidence has shown that powerful actors such as the United States make strategic use of institutions in order to achieve their preferred issue-specific interest. America's use of the institutions of cooperative arms control in Europe during the mid-1990s in order to cushion Russian opposition to NATO enlargement is a good example. Another example was the United States pushing the Medvedev EST initiative from the NRC to the OSCE's Corfu Process (see Paragraph 3.6.1). In addition, international institutions have constraining effects. It took Russia five years to exit from CFE after NATO had made the ratification of ACFE conditional on Moscow fulfilling its Istanbul commitments. Even the Russian exit in the illegal form of a "suspension" was a sign that Russian could, under changed conditions, return to the agreement. The same applies to the OSCE. Russia has voiced its dissatisfaction with the structures and the work of the organization at least since the beginning of the 2000s (see Russian statements contained in Chapter 7). Nevertheless, Moscow has not exited from the OSCE and continues to show no such motivation (cf. Statement 50 in Chapter 7). Even in conjunction with the Russian violations of a number of key principles and norms of the regime complex in the on-going war in Ukraine, constraining effects are still visible. Russia refers to key principles and norms of the regime complex in order to justify its behavior (see President of Russia 2014a,b; cf. Burke-White 2014). On the other side, particularly the Ukraine conflict shows as much that powerful states such as Russia do not shy away from violating key principles and norms and internationally recognized agreements once they deem critical national interests at stake.

9.2.2 Political Conclusions

Analysis of America's foreign and security policy towards cooperative arms control in Europe has highlighted that Washington was not willing or capable of constraining its power from the mid-1990s onwards. The maintenance and further enlargement of NATO and the parallel policy of keeping the C/OSCE's profile comparably low are indicative of this conclusion. Analysis further suggests that different political opinions shaped the debate about NATO enlargement and the subsequent handling of the decision to enlarge (see Paragraphs 3.3.1 and 3.4.1). While the official line of argument was that NATO enlargement was seen as a stabilizing tool for the newly independent states to the East, others propagated enlargement in order to hedge against a Russian relapse into authoritarianism. The Clinton administration voted for coupling NATO enlargement with a cooperative security approach towards Russia. Quite the opposite, the Conservative majority in Congress saw close cooperation with Russia as a mistake. According to the latter, the Yeltsin government was made up of 'communists who had changed their suits from red to blue' (Lake quoted in Goldgeier and McFaul 2003: 121). The result was a policy, which could never fully conceal that it involved the potential future option of once more containing Russia – an option that has gained renewed prominence in response to the Russian annexation of Crimea. In turn, Russia has never accepted this dualistic concept and continued to view NATO as an alliance against Russia (cf. Ministry of Defence 2010). The political conclusion is that both states have not yet found, or seriously considered finding, a mutually acceptable formula to bring their contradicting power aspirations and their related policies in line with each other.

One of the results of the U.S. unwillingness to constrain its power was the strategic use of institutions of cooperative arms control in Europe in conjunction with NATO enlargement. The adaptation of CFE, the establishment of the NATO-Russia Founding Act, and the U.S. re-engagement on the OSCE during the second half of the 1990s were all measures designed to achieve a certain level of Russian acquiescence to NATO enlargement. As a result, certain decisions and institutional developments related to the concept of cooperative security are hard to distinguish from other decisions and institutions that are involving concepts, which are not consistently in line with the concept of cooperative security (cf. Bauwens et al 1994: 21). One example is CFE adaptation. While the cooperative security measure as such was also aimed at cushioning Russian unease with enlargement, it contained a clause, the Istanbul commitments, that was aimed at diminishing the Russian influence in Moldova and Georgia. Besides the more laudable goal of increasing those two countries' formal sovereignty, Russian forces withdrawal from the three break-away regions of Transnistria, South Ossetia, and Abkhazia was also a precondition for a possible future Moldovan and Georgian accession to NATO. Once this part of America's CFE policy gained the upper hand under the George W. Bush administration, the cooperative security institution of CFE became as contested as the issue of enlargement. The political conclusion is that institutions from the realm of cooperative security can become bones of contention once they become politically linked to other already contested strands of policy, which are not in line with the concept of cooperative security.

Russia has never really accepted her loss of power. The conclusions above all arise in part from the Russian leadership's inability to come to terms with the dissolution of the Soviet Union and the parallel decline in power (cf. also Deutsch et al 1957). Vladimir Putin's rhetoric has vividly underscored that point (cf. President of Russia 2005). This conclusion, in conjunction with the above noted assumption that the Russian leadership might be more struggling for power in terms of influence and status and to a lesser degree for security in its dealings with the West, makes any future re-engagement on cooperative arms control in Europe a potentially difficult endeavor. The conclusion is that any such foray would have to start by answering the question whether the West would be willing to acknowledge Russia a certain sphere of influence and, if so, under what conditions.

The institutions of cooperative arms control in Europe lack an encompassing approach that includes Russia also in terms of Moscow's issue-specific interests. Neither the OSCE nor the cooperative institutions of

NATO have a design, which reflects the difficult to fulfill Russian demand for 'equal security for all'. NATO does not have it due to the decision-making inequality between NATO members and non-NATO members. The OSCE does not have it because of its missing a legal personality and because of its non-existing authority over NATO decision-making. For most of the post-Cold War period, the two U.S. approaches towards European security – that is, cooperative security and NATO maintenance/enlargement – have co-existed in a sometimes problematic parallelism. Since the Russian annexation if Crimea, their growing incompatibility cannot be overlooked anymore. Particularly the political handling of NATO's cooperative security institutions is increasingly problematic. Suspending fora for dialogue such as the NRC at times when dialogue is most needed (2008 in conjunction with the Russian-Georgian war; 2014 in conjunction with the Ukraine conflict) is in conflict with the concept of cooperative security. This is particularly the case since those NATO institutions are an integral part of the regime complex of cooperative arms control in Europe. Even partial withdrawal or suspension of those institutions can generate negative spillover effects that could resonate throughout the whole system.

The decay of the regime complex has left Europe with comparably less institutions to tackle insecurities and uncertainties. The on-going war in Ukraine underscores this point (cf. Richter 2014). Specific aspects of the conflict, such as the Russian forces build-up on the Ukrainian boarder, could have been addressed by the CFE framework if the treaty were still in force. Other aspects of the conflict, such as the Russian strategy of hybrid warfare in the annexation of Crimea, cannot be tackled by any of the existing or dead-locked institutions without adapting them. The conclusion is that Europe lacks functioning and up-to-date security institutions. Another conclusion is that the political handling of the decay of certain elemental parts of the regime complex was not very far-sighted.

Reviving the institutions of cooperative arms control in Europe or the concept of cooperative security altogether will be extremely hard. The structures of the system have proven persistent, adaptable, and successful for a long time. They were even functioning at times when the underlying fragile political understanding had vanished. National administrations tend to cling on to already existing institutions and shy away from setting up new ones (cf. George 1980). With the war in Ukraine, the need for new security arrangements has finally arrived in the U.S. political debate (see Charap and Shapiro 2014b; Lipman 2014, Mearsheimer 2014a). Any future effort will also be extremely difficult because the institutions are so closely interwoven. It would be hard to disentangle them. A complete restart might reap larger gains. At the same time, it is extremely unlikely at this point in time.

The rise and fall of cooperative arms control in Europe is a rich field for analyzing the volatility of international cooperation. It stands symbolically for the inability of the West and Russia to craft a mutually acceptable post-

Cold War security architecture. As a result, almost three decades after the end of the Cold War, Europe has entered a new period of confrontation with Russia. The decay of cooperative arms control in Europe is deplorable. At the same time, it is even more a reason to re-engage on those issues that have led to its demise. Careful and non-biased analysis of the failures of the past might contribute to shaping a better future.

Epilogue

The annoying sound of sharp claws had come simmering through the wooden floor the entire morning. The noise had made him feel at unease; a feeling, he knew too well. For days he had felt as if it was calling for him, for a decision, for an act of personal courage. Again, he had weighed his options, carefully assessing the situation. Next, he got up and opened the cellar door, squeaking, his sweaty fingers clasped around a club.

Before the boy, a dusty stairway petering out in the dark. Beaten stairs leading the way. And the boy took each one of them in slow motion. "Don't fall", he told himself over and over again. Reaching the ground floor, he could see it. There it was, bigger and meaner than he had expected. It was the kind of monster his schoolmates would not believe, were he to tell his tale. Slowly, he approached the beast. Once it turned to the left, he followed suit. Once it was about to escape to the right, he closed the gap. There was no escape from the cellar's corner. He had it there, exactly, where he wanted it to be. A sudden flow of confidence rushed through his veins while his body tensed up, the club raised high above his head. Then...suddenly...the rat jumped at him!

This story, though slightly dramatized here, can be found in Vladimir Putin's self-portrait *First Person*. There, the now grown-up President of the Russian Federation explains how the hunt for the rat, driven to the wall, and its sudden attack on him in the cellar had taught him a lesson. It seems that Putin internalized the uneven battle. Some decades later, under the impression of America's growing influence in military, economic, and cultural terms, Russia had backed down – at least in Putin's and a majority of the Russian population's perceptions. Against the seemingly almighty NATO machinery and the economic verve of the European Union, Russia, the former bold empire, was driven to the wall. First in 2008 but more so in 2014, Russia "jumped". In a chilling metaphor, almost echoing his childhood memory, Putin confirmed that in the 2014 Ukraine context, 'Russia found itself in a position it could not retreat from. If you compress the spring all the way to its limit, it will snap back hard.'

While such portrayal is clearly painted in white, blue, and red, more than a grain of truth about the reasons for Russia's rejection of the concept of cooperative security in Europe can be found in the early 1990's years of the shaping of the continent's post-Cold War order. When Gorbachev laid down arms in an act of significant symbolism in 1988 in New York, the door opened up for a rapprochement of historical magnitude. Not few Soviet and Russian leaders, struck by the speed with which the Warsaw Pact and the Soviet Union dissolved into thin air, hoped for the subsequent dissolution of the Western military alliance. Soon, it turned out that their hopes were unrealistic. In his State of the Union Speech to Congress in 1992, George H.W.

Bush declared: 'By the grace of God, America won the Cold War.' And as is well known from a popular song: *The winner takes it all*.

This book has shown that the re-making of Europe's security order between 1989 and 1999, particularly in the crucial realm of arms control, was characterized by cooperation. However, it was cooperation amongst non-equals with almost always divergent interests. The institutional results of that process mirror this genesis. Neither did NATO dissolve nor did Washington constrain its ambitious enlargement plans. Russian complaints throughout the 1990s were heard but did not trigger any change of course. The 1975 Helsinki promise of the 'indivisibility of security' began to sound hollow in Russian ears. Moscow's very prestige project from the Cold War, the CSCE, did not evolve into a full-fledged security organization with comprehensive responsibility for the Euro-Atlantic security space. With the dawn of the new millennium, the organization underwent a process of political marginalization to which Russia contributed as well. In parallel, important institutions of cooperative arms control, such as the CFE Treaty, collapsed due to divergent interests between the United States and Russia.

Does that mean that the West is mainly responsible for the decay of cooperative security in Europe, and should therewith shoulder at least the partial blame for today's escalation in Ukraine? The answer is straightforward: it should not. Neither the United States nor its NATO allies are responsible for Russia's failure to establish a functioning democracy based on strict respect for human rights and the rule of law. They are not responsible for the Russian leadership's failure to accept the relative loss of power after the Cold War. The West is not responsible for the Kremlin's course of rejecting once agreed-upon principles and norms such as the inviolability of frontiers, the respect for the territorial integrity of states, and abstaining from the threat or use of force. Also, Western leaders are not to blame for Russia's mixed account when it comes to compliance with international arms control agreements. Therefore, some might even argue that Russian actions in Ukraine only affirm those who regularly plead for containment and not cooperation as the central goal in the West's dealings with Moscow.

However, Western policy makers and political analysts have to take the blame for two important failures of the past. First, they failed to establish a cooperative security system for Europe based on the principle of equity. Particularly the realm of cooperative arms control in Europe highlights the inability of Washington and its allies to constrain their own ambitions and interests. Since equity and thus justice are seldom real-life outcomes of international negotiations, the second failure carries even more weight: for too long and with too little appetite for cooperative solutions did policy makers in the United States and Europe stood by as the institutions of cooperative arms control eroded. As we now know, the system of interlocking agreements was much more fragile than most would have anticipated. Its passing was not the sudden product of any conscious decision. Rather, it was a slow-motion process over many years. It should have been the warning signal that something between the West and Russia was about to go terribly wrong.

So, what is next? Without any doubt, the return to confrontation harbors a number of unpleasant and unclear dangers for the West and Russia alike. Cooperative arms control instruments might regain some of their importance at some point in time. However, any future effort to rebuild substantive and also equitable institutions will encounter a much more "realistic" setting compared to the enthusiastic atmosphere at the end of the Cold War. Though, the absence of enthusiasm might turn out to be helpful in order to sharpen political senses. As an old proverb has it: *history doesn't repeat itself but it does rhyme*. In that sense, we are not entering a New Cold War. But the features of the new confrontation resemble some of the problems we were already facing some decades ago. Re-visiting the old confrontation should therefore go hand in hand with re-visiting the old instruments of cooperation. What had its merits during the Cold War has not lost its validity in today's world.

***

Annex I: Data Input (Capabilities)

1973

Country/ Military Alliance	Population	Territory (km²)	Total Armed Forces	Defense Budget	GNP
United States	**210,900,000**	**9,371,829**	**2,252,900**	**$85.2 billion**	**$1,289.1 billion**
NATO	**544,828,500**	**22,219,135**	**5,200,050**	**$125.8 billion**	-
1. Belgium	9,800,000	30,562	89,600	$990 million	-
2. Canada	22,300,000	9,971,500	83,000	$2,141 million	-
3. Denmark	5,020,000	42,994	39,800	$568 million	-
4. France	52,000,000	551,670	503,600	$8,488 million	-
5. West Germany	60,100,000	248,640	475,000	$11,083 million	-
6. Greece	8,900,000	132,608	160,000	$580 million	-
7. Iceland	213,500	102,952	-	-	-
8. Italy	54,400,000	301,217	427,500	$3,964 million	-
9. Luxembourg	345,000	2,590	550	$15 million	-
10. Netherlands	13,500,000	33,929	112,200	$2,102 million	-
11. Norway	4,000,000	323,750	35,400	$665 million	-
12. Portugal	9,200,000	94,276	204,000	$523 million	-
13. Turkey	37,900,000	766,640	455,000	$812 million	-
14. United Kingdom	56,250,000	243,978	361,500	$8,673 million	-
Soviet Union	**250,500,000**	**22,402,200**	**3,425,000**	**$88.9 billion**	**$612.5 billion[1]**
Warsaw Pact	**355,835,000**	**23,393,098**	**4,452,000**	**$95.59 billion**	-
1. Bulgaria	8,660,000	111,852	152,000	$301 million	-
2. Czechoslovakia	14,600,000	127,946	190,000	$1,336 million	-
3. East Germany	17,000,000	108,262	132,000	$2,031 million	-
4. Hungary	10,450,000	92,981	103,000	$695 million	-
5. Poland	33,725,000	312,354	280,000	$1,799 million	-
6. Romania	20,900,000	237,503	170,000	$528 million	-

1 The U.S. Dollar has been converted from Rubles at the 1973 official rate of 0.72 Rubles = $1.

1989

Country/ Military Alliance	Population	Territory (km^2)	Total Armed Forces	Defense Budget	GDP
United States	248,917,000	9,372,610	2,124,900	$290.30 billion	$5,657.7 billion
NATO	656,570,900	22,740,436	5,358,350	$435.55 billion	-
1. Belgium	9,938,000	30,510	92,400	$2.53 billion	-
2. Canada	26,065,000	9,976,140	89,000	$9.29 billion	-
3. Denmark	5,141,000	43,070	31,600	$1.86 billion	-
4. France	55,784,000	547,030	466,300	$28.83 billion	-
5. West Germany	61,214,000	248,580	494,300	$28.57 billion	-
6. Greece	10,105,000	131,940	208,500	$3.89 billion	-
7. Iceland	250,000	103,000	-	-	-
8. Italy	57,587,000	301,230	390,000	$16.22 billion	-
9. Luxem-bourg	369,000	2,586	800	$80.39 million	-
10. Nether-lands	14,800,000	37,290	103,600	$6.64 billion	-
11. Norway	4,210,900	324,220	34,100	$3.01 billion	-
12. Portugal	10,373,000	92,080	75,300	$1.25 million	-
13. Spain	39,263,000	504,750	285,000	$6.84 billion	-
14. Turkey	55,541,000	780,580	650,900	$2.93 billion	-
15. United Kingdom	57,013,000	244,820	311,650	$34.56 billion	-
Soviet Union	287,776,000	22,402,200	4,258,000	$119.44 billion[1]	$506.5 billion
Warsaw Pact	401,279,000	23,392,520	5,422,300	$139.44 billion	-
1. Bulgaria	8,985,000	110,910	117,500	$1.75 billion	-
2. Czecho-slovakia	15,624,000	127,870	199,700	$2.94 billion	-
3. East Germany	16,616,000	108,330	173,100	$12.01 billion	-
4. Hungary	10,590,000	93,030	91,000	$827.47 million	-
5. Poland	38,105,000	312,680	412,000	$1.68 billion	-
6. Romania	23,583,000	237,500	171,000	$797.48 million	-

1 Western intelligence sources still maintain that by NATO definition standards, defense spending was about twice as large as officially claimed (IISS 1990-1991: 33)

1990

Country/ Military Alliance	Population	Territory (km^2)	Total Armed Forces	Defense Budget	GDP
United States	248,855,000	9,372,610	2,117,900	$291.4 billion	$5,979.6 billion
NATO	657,101,000	22,740,436	5,247,350	$450.61 billion	-
1. Belgium	9,865,000	30,510	92,000	$2.89 billion	-
2. Canada	26,625,000	9,976,140	90,000	$10.194 billion	-
3. Denmark	5,088,000	43,070	31,700	$2.192 billion	-
4. France	56,414,000	547,030	461,250	$33.03 billion	-
5. West Germany	60,362,000	248,580	469,000	$31.02 billion	-
6. Greece	10,139,000	131,940	162,500	$3.79 billion	-
7. Iceland	255,000	103,000	-	-	-
8. Italy	57,299,000	301,230	389,600	$18.979 billion	-
9. Luxembourg	365,000	2,586	800	$90.44 million	-
10. Netherlands	14,766,000	37,290	102,600	$7.466 billion	-
11. Norway	4,200,000	324,220	34,100	$3.351 billion	-
12. Portugal	10,504,000	92,080	68,000	$1.54 billion	-
13. Spain	39,859,000	504,750	274,500	$7.98 billion	-
14. Turkey	55,860,000	780,580	647,400	$3.28 billion	-
15. United Kingdom	56,645,000	244,820	306,000	$33.405 billion	-
Soviet Union	288,561,000	22,402,200	3,988,000	$117.48 billion	$516.81 billion
Warsaw Pact	402,320,000	23,392,520	5,022,700	$136.98 billion	-
1. Bulgaria	9,062,000	110,910	129,000	$2.208 billion	-
2. Czechoslovakia	15,692,000	127,870	198,200	$3.224 billion	-
3. East Germany	16,664,000	108,330	137,700	$11.86[1] billion	-
4. Hungary	10,567,000	93,030	94,000	$716.84 million	-
5. Poland	38,479,000	312,680	312,800	$700.73 million	-
6. Romania	23,295,000	237,500	163,000	$789.98 million	-

1994

Country/ Military Alliance	Population	Territory (km²)	Total Armed Forces	Defense Budget	GDP
United States	259,533,000	9,372,610	1,650,500	$263.3 billion	$7,308.8 billion
NATO	699,773,900	22,848,766	4,197,600	$387.18 billion	-
1. Belgium	10,059,000	30,510	63,000	$2.6 billion	-
2. Canada	28,125,400	9,976,140	78,100	$8.45 billion	-
3. Denmark	5,196,600	43,070	27,000	$2.6 billion	-
4. France	57,842,400	547,030	409,600	$35.6 billion	-
5. Germany	80,974,600	356,910	367,300	$28.6 billion	-
6. Greece	10,569,500	131,940	159,300	$3.3 billion	-
7. Iceland	266,200	103,000	-	-	-
8. Italy	58,134,600	301,230	322,300	$16.1 billion	-
9. Luxem-bourg	395,200	2,586	800	$111 million	-
10. Nether-lands	15,335,000	37,290	70,900	$7.42 billion	-
11. Norway	4,322,000	324,220	33,500	$3.2 billion	-
12. Portugal	10,512,400	92,080	50,700	$1.5 billion	-
13. Spain	39,736,600	504,750	206,500	$5.8 billion	-
14. Turkey	60,641,200	780,580	503,800	$4.6 billion	-
15. United Kingdom	58,130,200	244,820	254,300	$34 billion	-
Russia	148,920,000	17,075,200	1,714,000	$79 billion	$395.09 billion
CST	226,283,800	20,975,200	1,994,700	$80.72 billion	-
1. Armenia	3,421,000	29,800	32,700	$71 million	-
2. Azerbai-jan	7,462,000	86,600	56,000	$132 million	-
3. Belarus	10,491,600	207,600	92,500	$430 million	-
4. Georgia	5,682,000	69,700	not known	$88 million	-
5. Kazakh-stan	17,407,600	2,717,300	40,000	$450 million	-
6. Kyrgyz-stan	4,684,000	198,500	12,000	$57.3 million	-
7. Tajikistan	5,897,200	143,100	2,500[1]	$115 million	-
8. Uzbeki-stan	22,318,400	447,400	45,000	$375 million	-

1 Data ranges from 2,000-3,000 total armed forces; the mean value of 2,500 has been used for calculation.

Country/ Military Alliance	Population	Territory (km²)	Total Armed Forces	Defense Budget	GDP
United States	263,119,000	9,372,610	1,547,300	$263.5 billion	$7,664.1 billion
NATO	703,150,000	22,848,766	4,057,100	$428.85 billion	-
1. Belgium	10,071,000	30,510	47,200	$3.45 billion	-
2. Canada	28,130,000	9,976,140	70,500	$8.14 billion	-
3. Denmark	5,214,000	43,070	33,100	$3.11 billion	-
4. France	58,125,000	547,030	409,000	$35.9 billion	-
5. Germany	81,109,000	356,910	339,900	$34.02 billion	-
6. Greece	10,455,000	131,940	171,300	$3.38 billion	-
7. Iceland	270,000	103,000	-	-	-
8. Italy	57,867,000	301,230	328,700	$16 billion	-
9. Luxem-bourg	406,000	2,586	800	$114 million	-
10. Nether-lands	15,446,000	37,290	74,400	$8.56 billion	-
11. Norway	4,353,000	324,220	30,000	$3.77 billion	-
12. Portugal	9,869,000	92,080	54,200	$1.60 billion	-
13. Spain	39,144,000	504,750	206,000	$6.59 billion	-
14. Turkey	61,284,000	780,580	507,800	$6.24 billion	-
15. United Kingdom	58,288,000	244,820	236,900	$34.48 billion	-
Russia	148,940,000	17,075,200	1,520,000	$63 billion[1]	$395.53 billion
CST	226,622,000	20,975,200	1,839,600	$64.01 billion	-
1. Armenia	3,800,000	29,800	60,000	$77 million	-
2. Azerbai-jan	7,640,000	86,600	86,700	$109 million	-
3. Belarus	10,372,000	207,600	98,400	$78 million	-
4. Georgia	5,441,000	69,700	not known	$56 million	-
5. Kazakh-stan	16,763,000	2,717,300	40,000	$297 million	-
6. Kyrgyz-stan	4,636,000	198,500	7,000	$13 million	-
7. Tajikistan	6,002,000	143,100	2,500[2]	$67 million	-
8. Uzbeki-stan	23,028,000	447,400	25,000	$315 million	-

1 Purchasing Power Parity (PPP) estimate
2 Data ranges from 2,000-3,000 total armed forces; the mean value of 2,500 has been used for calculation.

Country/ Military Alliance	Population	Territory (km^2)	Total Armed Forces	Defense Budget	GDP
United States	273,133,000	9,629,091	1,371,500	$292.1 billion	$9,660.6 billion
NATO	780,748,000	23,589,663	4,097,458	$447.51 billion	-
1. Belgium	10,115,000	30,510	41,750	$2.5 billion	-
2. Canada	29,236,000	9,976,140	60,600	$7.0 billion	-
3. Czech Republic	10,480,000	78,703	58,200	$1,163 million	-
4. Denmark	5,256,000	43,070	24,300	$2.6 billion	-
5. France	59,165,000	547,030	317,300	$29.5 billion	-
6. Germany	82,057,000	356,910	332,800	$25.4 billion	-
7. Greece	10,645,000	131,940	165,670	$3.4 billion	-
8. Hungary	10,028,000	93,030	43,440	$745 million	-
9. Iceland	280,000	103,000	-	-	-
10. Italy	57,917,000	301,230	265,500	$16.2 billion	-
11. Luxem-bourg	417,000	2,586	768	$102 million	-
12. Netherlands	15,724,000	37,290	56,380	$6.5 billion	-
13. Norway	4,425,000	324,220	31,000	$3.3 billion	-
14. Poland	38,854,000	312,683	240,650	$3.2 billion	-
15. Portugal	9,874,000	92,080	49,700	$1.6 billion	-
16. Spain	39,218,000	504,750	186,500	$7.4 billion	-
17. Turkey	65,161,000	780,580	639,000	$8.9 billion	-
18. United Kingdom	58,763,000	244,820	212,400	$35.9 billion	-
Russia	146,300,000	17,075,200	1,004,100	$31 billion[1]	$195.91 billion
CST	186,909,000	20,371,500	1,221,400	$31.33 billion	-
1. Armenia	3,967,000	29,800	53,400	$75 million	-
2. Belarus	10,470,000	207,600	80,900	$94 million	-
3. Kazakhstan	14,952,000	2,717,300	65,800	$117 million	-
4. Kyrgyzstan	4,600,000	198,500	9,200	$24 million	-
5. Tajikistan	6,620,000	143,100	8,000[2]	$18 million	-

1 PPP estimate
2 Data ranges from 7,000-9,000 total armed forces; the mean value of 8,000 has been used for calculation.

Country/ Military Alliance	Population	Territory (km²)	Total Armed Forces	Defense Budget	GDP
United States	275,636,000	9,629,091	1,365,800	$293.3 billion	$10,284.8 billion
NATO	784,707,000	23,594,540	3,942,329	$440.44 billion	-
1. Belgium	10,126,000	30,510	39,250	$2.5 billion	-
2. Canada	29,512,000	9,976,140	59,100	$7.6 billion	-
3. Czech Republic	10,290,000	78,866	57,700	$1,153 million	-
4. Denmark	5,267,000	43,094	21,810	$2.3 billion	-
5. France	59,425,000	547,030	294,430	$27.0 billion	-
6. Germany	82,112,000	357,021	321,000	$23.3 billion	-
7. Greece	10,692,000	131,940	159,170	$3.3 billion	-
8. Hungary	10,005,000	93,030	43,790	$791 million	-
9. Iceland	283,000	103,000	-	-	-
10. Italy	57,930,000	301,230	250,600	$16.0 billion	-
11. Luxembourg	420,000	2,586	899	$100 million	-
12. Netherlands	15,794,000	41,532	51,940	$6.2 billion	-
13. Norway	4,443,000	324,220	26,700	$2.9 billion	-
14. Poland	38,648,000	312,685	217,290	$3.2 billion	-
15. Portugal	9,875,000	92,391	44,650	$1.6 billion	-
16. Spain	39,237,000	504,782	166,050	$7.0 billion	-
17. Turkey	66,130,000	780,580	609,700	$7.7 billion	-
18. United Kingdom	58,882,000	244,820	212,450	$34.5 billion	-
Russia	146,000,000	17,075,200	1,004,100	$29 billion[1]	$259.71 billion
CST	185,805,000	20,371,500	1,208,260	$29.33 billion	-
1. Armenia	3,803,000	29,800	42,060	$96 million	-
2. Belarus	10,045,000	207,600	83,100	$75 million	-
3. Kazakhstan	15,000,000	2,717,300	64,000	$115 million	-
4. Kyrgyzstan	4,852,000	198,500	9,000	$29 million	-
5. Tajikistan	6,105,000	143,100	6,000	$19 million	-

1 PPP estimate

2008

Country/ Military Alliance	Population	Territory (km²)	Total Armed Forces	Defense Budget	GDP
United States	301,139,947	9,826,630	1,498,157	$693 billion	$14,718.6 bill.
NATO	870,645,888	24,392,848	4,019,863	$942.81 billion	-
1. Belgium	10,392,226	30,528	39,690	$3.82 billion	-
2. Bulgaria	7,322,858	110,910	40,747	$886 million	-
3. Canada	33,390,141	9,984,670	64,000	$15.9 billion	-
4. Czech Republic	10,228,744	78,866	23,092	$2.91 billion	-
5. Denmark	5,468,120	43,094	29,960	$4.10 billion	-
6. Estonia	1,315,912	45,226	4,100	$425 million	-
7. France	61,083,916	547,030	254,895	$41.1 billion	-
8. Germany	82,400,996	357,021	245,702	$39.86 billion	-
9. Greece	10,706,290	131,940	156,600	$5.62 billion	-
10. Hungary	9,956,108	93,030	32,300	$1.62 billion	-
11. Iceland	301,931	103,000	-	-	-
12. Italy	58,147,733	301,230	186,049	$20.81 billion	-
13. Latvia	2,259,810	64,589	5,696	$513 million	-
14. Lithua-nia	3,575,439	65,300	13,850	$500 million	-
15. Luxem-bourg	480,222	2,586	900	$360 million	-
16. Nether-lands	16,570,613	41,526	45,608	$10.93 billion	-
17. Norway	4,627,926	323,802	15,800	$4.83 billion	-
18. Poland	38,518,241	312,679	127,266	$8.54 billion	-
19. Portugal	10,642,836	92,391	42,910	$2.65 billion	-
20. Romania	22,276,056	237,500	74,267	$2.76 billion	-
21. Slovakia	5,447,502	48,845	17,129	$1.38 billion	-
22. Slovenia	2,009,245	20,273	5,973	$756 million	-
23. Spain	40,448,191	504,782	149,150	$11 billion	-
24. Turkey	71,158,647	780,580	510,600	$8.84 billion	-
25. UK	60,776,238	244,820	180,527	$59.7 billion	-
Russia	141,377,752	17,075,200	1,027,000	$36.35 billion	$1,660.84 bill.
CST	209,499,860	20,818,843	1,277,720	$39.16 billion	-
1. Armenia	2,971,650	29,743	42,080	$395 million	-
2. Belarus	9,724,723	207,600	72,940	$681 million	-
3. Kazakh-stan	15,284,929	2,717,300	49,000	$1.61 billion	-
4. Kyrgyz-stan	5,284,149	198,500	10,900	$46 million	-
5. Tajikistan	7,076,598	143,100	8,800	$79 million	-
6. Uzbeki-stan	27,780,059	447,400	67,000	not available	-

2009

Country/ Military Alliance	Population	Territory (km²)	Total Armed Forces	Defense Budget	GDP
United States	303,824,646	9,826,675	1,539,587	$697.8 billion	$14,418.7 bill.
NATO	**877,049,724**	**24,400,624**	**4,044,134**	**$966.94 bill**	-
1. Belgium	10,403,951	30,528	38,844	$3.97 billion	-
2. Bulgaria	7,262,65	110,879	40,747	$1.04 billion	-
3. Canada	33,212,696	9,984,670	64,371	$18.5 billion	-
4. Czech Republic	10,220,911	78,867	24,083	$2.96 billion	-
5. Denmark	5,484,723	43,094	29,550	$4.11 billion	-
6. Estonia	1,307,605	45,228	5,300	$356 million	-
7. France	64,057,790	551,500	352,771	$46 billion	-
8. Germany	82,369,548	357,022	244,324	$43.5 billion	-
9. Greece	10,722,816	131,957	156,600	$10.9 billion	-
10. Hungary	9,930,915	93,028	25,207	$1.63 billion	-
11. Iceland	304,367	103,000	-	-	-
12. Italy	58,145,321	301,340	292,983	$21.5 billion	-
13. Latvia	2,245,423	64,589	5,187	$341 million	-
14. Lithuania	3,565,205	65,300	8,850	$484 million	-
15. Luxembourg	486,006	2,586	900	$556 million	-
16. Netherlands	16,645,313	41,543	40,537	$12.1 billion	-
17. Norway	4,644,457	323,802	19,100	$5.36 billion	-
18. Poland	38,500,696	312,685	121,808	$7.36 billion	-
19. Portugal	10,676,910	92,090	42,910	$2.54 billion	-
20. Romania	22,246,862	238,391	73,200	$2.29 billion	-
21. Slovakia	5,455,407	49,035	17,445	$1.53 billion	-
22. Slovenia	2,007,711	20,273	7,200	$766 million	-
23. Spain	40,491,051	505,370	221,750	$10.9 billion	-
24. Turkey	71,892,807	783,562	510,600	$9.95 billion	-
25. UK	60,943,912	243,610	160,280	$60.5 billion	-
Russia	**140,702,094**	**17,098,242**	**1,027,000**	**$65.5 billion**	**$1,222.64 bill.**
CST	**209,534,174**	**20,850,936**	**1,277,720**	**$68.83 billion**	-
1. Armenia	2,968,586	29,743	42,080	$401 million	-
2. Belarus	9,685,768	207,600	72,940	$612 million	-
3. Kazakhstan	15,340,533	2,724,900	49,000	$948 million	-
4. Kyrgyzstan	5,356,869	199,951	10,900	$44 million	-
5. Tajikistan	7,211,884	143,100	8,800	$88 million	-
6. Uzbekistan	28,268,440	447,400	67,000	$1.24 billion	-

2011

Country/ Military Alliance	Population	Territory (km^2)	Total Armed Forces	Defense Budget	GDP
United States	317,641,087	9,826,675	1,563,996	$739.3 billion	$15,517.9 billion
NATO	908,626,894	24,485,966	3,774,186	$1,031.55 bill.	-
1. Albania	3.169.087	28.748	14.245	$136 million	-
2. Belgium	10,697,588	30,528	37,882	$3.88 billion	-
3. Bulgaria	7,497,282	110,879	31,315	$725 million	-
4. Canada	33,889,747	9,984,670	65,722	$21.5 billion	-
5. Croatia	4,409,659	56,594	18,600	$935 million	-
6. Czech Re-	10,410,786	78,867	23,441	$2.52 billion	-
7. Denmark	5,481,283	43,094	18,707	$4.91 billion	-
8. Estonia	1,339,459	45,228	5,450	$393 million	-
9. France	62,636,580	551,500	238,591	$58.8 billion	-
10. Germany	82,056,775	357,022	251,465	$44.2 billion	-
11. Greece	11,183,393	131,957	138,936	$6.83 billion	-
12. Hungary	9,973,141	93,028	29,626	$1.41 billion	-
13. Iceland	329,279	103,000	-	-	-
14. Italy	60,097,564	301,340	184,609	$21.0 billion	-
15. Latvia	2,240,265	64,589	5,745	$292 million	-
16. Lithuania	3,255,324	65,300	10,640	$425 million	-
17. Luxem-	491,772	2,586	900	$281 million	-
18. Netherlands	16,653,346	41,543	37,368	$11.7 billion	-
19. Norway	4,855,315	323,802	26,450	$6.43 billion	-
20. Poland	38,038,094	312,685	100,000	$9.43 billion	-
21. Portugal	10,732,357	92,090	43,340	$2.83 billion	-
22. Romania	21,190,154	238,391	71,745	$2.67 billion	-
23. Slovakia	5,411,640	49,035	16,531	$1.07 billion	-
24. Slovenia	2,024,912	20,273	7,600	$578 million	-
25. Spain	45,316,586	505,370	142,212	$15.3 billion	-
26. Turkey	75,705,147	783,562	510,600	$10.3 billion	-
27. UK	61,899,272	243,610	178,470	$63.7 billion	-
Russia	140,366,561	17,098,242	1,046,000	$68 billion[1]	$1,904.79 bill.
CST	209,217,720	20,850,936	1,303,210	$72.13 bill.	-
1. Armenia	3.090.379	29.743	48.570	$395 million	-
2. Belarus	9,587,940	207,600	72,940	$470 million	-
3. Kazakhstan	15,753,460	2,724,900	49,000	$1.74 billion	-
4. Kyrgyzstan	5,550,239	199,951	10,900	$33 million	-
5. Tajikistan	7,074,845	143,100	8,800	$72 million	-
6. Uzbekistan	27,794,296	447,400	67,000	$1.42 billion	-

[1] PPP estimate

Country/ Military Alliance	Population	Territory (km^2)	Total Armed Forces	Defense Budget	GDP
United States	311,050,977	9,826,675	1,569,417	$655 billion	$16,163.2 bill.
NATO	**910,138,234**	**24,485,966**	**3,771,761**	**$928.89 bill.**	
1. Albania	2,994,667	28,748	14,245	$185 million	-
2. Belgium	10,431,477	30,528	34,336	$5.27 billion	-
3. Bulgaria	7,093,635	110,879	31,315	$659 million	-
4. Canada	34,030,589	9,984,670	65,700	$18.4 billion	-
5. Croatia	4,483,804	56,594	18,600	$827 million	-
6. Czech Republic	10,190,213	78,867	25,421	$2.22 billion	-
7. Denmark	5,529,888	43,094	18,628	$4.42 billion	-
8. Estonia	1,282,963	45,228	5,750	$437 million	-
9. France	65,102,719	551,500	238,591	$50.3 billion	-
10. Germany	81,471,834	357,022	251,465	$41 billion	-
11. Greece	10,760,136	131,957	145,647	$6.68 billion	-
12. Hungary	9,976,062	93,028	22,587	$1.2 billion	-
13. Iceland	311,058	103,000	-	-	-
14. Italy	61,016,804	301,340	184,532	$24 billion	-
15. Latvia	2,204,708	64,589	4,600	$256 million	-
16. Lithuania	3,535,547	65,300	10,640	$317 million	-
17. Luxembourg	503,302	2,586	900	$267 million	-
18. Netherlands	16,653,734	41,543	37,368	$10.3 billion	-
19. Norway	4,691,849	323,802	24,450	$6.97 billion	-
20. Poland	38,441,588	312,685	100,000	$8.54 billion	-
21. Portugal	10,760,305	92,090	42,634	$2.64 billion	-
22. Romania	21,904,551	238,391	73,900	$2.21 billion	-
23. Slovakia	5,477,038	49,035	15,799	$881 million	-
24. Slovenia	2,000,092	20,273	7,600	$509 million	-
25. Spain	46,754,784	505,370	143,006	$13.9 billion	-
26. Turkey	78,785,548	783,562	510,600	$10.2 billion	-
27. UK	62,698,362	243,610	174,030	$61.3 billion	-
Russia	**138,739,892**	**17,098,242**	**956,000**	**$73 billion**[1]	**$2,017.47 bill.**
CST	**209,933,175**	**20,850,936**	**1,146,474**	**$77.97 billion**	-
1. Armenia	2,967,975	29,743	48,834	$402 million	-
2. Belarus	9,577,552	207,600	72,940	$552 million	-
3. Kazakhstan	17,304,513	2,724,900	49,000	$2.28 billion	-
4. Kyrgyzstan	5,587,443	199,951	10,900	$105 million	-
5. Tajikistan	7,627,200	143,100	8,800	$170 million	-
6. Uzbekistan	28,128,600	447,400	67,000	$1.46 billion	-

1 PPP estimate

2014

Country/Military Alliances	Population	Territory (km²)	Total Armed Forces	Defense Budget[1]	GDP[1]
United States	316,668,567	9,826,675	1,492,200	$600 billion	$16,768.1 bill.
NATO	**921,396,432**	**24,485,966**	**3,584,710**	**$873.85 bill.**	-
1. Albania	3,011,405	28,748	14,250	$182 million	-
2. Belgium	10,444,268	30,528	30,700	$5.29 billion	-
3. Bulgaria	6,981,642	110,879	31,300	$751 million	-
4. Canada	35,568,211	9,984,670	66,000	$16.4 billion	-
5. Croatia	4,475,611	56,594	16,550	$813 million	-
6. Czech Republic	10,162,921	78,867	23,650	$2.18 billion	-
7. Denmark	5,556,452	43,094	17,200	$4.51 billion	-
8. Estonia	1,266,375	45,228	5,750	$480 million	-
9. France	65,951,611	551,500	222,200	$52.4 billion	-
10. Germany	81,147,265	357,022	186,450	$44.2 billion	-
11. Greece	10,772,967	131,957	143,350	$5.68 billion	-
12. Hungary	9,939,470	93,028	26,500	$1.1 billion	-
13. Iceland	315,281	103,000	-	-	-
14. Italy	61,482,297	301,340	176,000	$25.2 billion	-
15. Latvia	2,178,443	64,589	5,310	$300 million	-
16. Lithuania	3,515,858	65,300	11,800	$355 million	-
17. Luxembourg	514,862	2,586	900	$249 million	-
18. Netherlands	16,805,037	41,543	37,400	$10.4 billion	-
19. Norway	4,722,701	323,802	25,800	$7.52 billion	-
20. Poland	38,383,809	312,685	99,300	$9.83 billion	-
21. Portugal	10,799,270	92,090	42,600	$2.77 billion	-
22. Romania	21,790,479	238,391	71,400	$2.47 billion	-
23. Slovakia	5,488,339	49,035	15,850	$995 million	-
24. Slovenia	1,992,690	20,273	7,600	$474 million	-
25. Spain	47,370,542	505,370	134,900	$11.6 billion	-
26. Turkey	80,694,485	783,562	510,600	$10.7 billion	-
27. UK	63,395,574	243,610	169,150	$57 billion	-
Russia	**142,500,482**	**17,098,242**	**845,000**	**$81.4 billion[2]**	**$2,096.78 bill.**
CST	**186,295,533**	**20,403,536**	**996,500**	**$85.01 billion**	-
1. Armenia	2,974,184	29,743	44,800	$447 million	-
2. Belarus	9,625,888	207,600	48,000	$552 million	-
3. Kazakhstan	17,736,896	2,724,900	39,000	$2.32 billion	-
4. Kyrgyzstan	5,548,042	199,951	10,900	$102 million	-
5. Tajikistan	7,910,041	143,100	8,800	$189 million	-

1 Data only available for 2013
2 PPP estimate

Annex II: List of Agreements Reviewed

Agreement 1: Conference on Security and Co-operation in Europe Final Act, Helsinki 1975: Questions relating to Security in Europe, Declaration on Principles Guiding Relations between Participating States

Agreement 2: Conference on Security and Co-operation in Europe Final Act, Helsinki 1975. Questions relating to Security in Europe, Document on confidence-building measures and certain aspects of security and disarmament

Agreement 3: Document of the Stockholm Conference on Confidence- and Security-Building Measures and Disarmament in Europe Convened in Accordance With the Relevant Provisions of the Concluding Document of the Madrid Meeting of the Conference on Security and Cooperation in Europe, 1984-1986

Agreement 4: Treaty on Conventional Armed Forces in Europe, 1990

Agreement 5: Charter of Paris for a New Europe, 1990

Agreement 6: Vienna Document 1990 of the Negotiations on Confidence- and Security-Building Measures Convened in Accordance with the Relevant Provisions of the Concluding Document of the Vienna Meeting of the CSCE

Agreement 7: North Atlantic Cooperation Council Statement on Dialogue, Partnership and Cooperation, 1991

Agreement 8: Vienna Document 1992 of the Negotiations on Confidence- and Security-Building Measures Convened in Accordance with the Relevant Provisions of the Concluding Document of the Vienna Meeting of the Conference on Security and Cooperation in Europe

Agreement 9: Treaty on Open Skies, 1992

Agreement 10: Concluding Act of the Negotiation on Personnel Strength of Conventional Armed Forces in Europe, 1992

Agreement 11: Section V "CSCE Forum for Security Cooperation", Helsinki Document 1992

Agreement 12: Programme for immediate action, Helsinki Document 1992

Agreement 13: Programme for Immediate Action Series, No. 1: Programme of Military Contacts and Co-operation, 1993

Agreement 14: Programme for Immediate Action Series, No. 2: Stabilizing Measures for Localized Crisis Situations, 1993

Agreement 15: Programme for Immediate Action Series, No. 3: Principles Governing Conventional Arms Transfers, 1993

Agreement 16: Programme for Immediate Action Series, No. 4: Defence Planning, 1993

Agreement 17: Programme for Immediate Action Series, No. 5: Global Exchange of Military Information, 1994

Agreement 18: Programme for Immediate Action Series, No. 6: Vienna Document 1994 of the Negotiations on Confidence- and Security-Building Measures, 1994

Agreement 19: Programme for Immediate Action Series, No. 7: Code of Conduct on Politico-Military Aspects of Security, 1994

Agreement 20: Programme for Immediate Action Series, No. 8: Principles Governing Non-Proliferation, 1994

Agreement 21: Partnership for Peace: Framework Document and Invitation Document, 1994

Agreement 22: A Framework for Arms Control, Lisbon Document, 1996

Agreement 23: Agreement on Confidence- and Security-Building Measures in Bosnia and Herzegovina, 1996

Agreement 24: Agreement on Sub-Regional Arms Control, Article IV, 1996

Agreement 25: Founding Act on Mutual Relations, Cooperation and Security between NATO and the Russian Federation, 1997

Agreement 26: Basic Document of the Euro-Atlantic Partnership Council, 1997

Agreement 27: Operational Document - the Platform for Co-operative Security, Istanbul Document, 1999

Agreement 28: Vienna Document 1999 on the Negotiations on Confidence- and Security-Building Measures, Istanbul Document, 1999

Agreement 29: Agreement on Adaptation of the Treaty on Conventional Armed Forces in Europe, 1999

Agreement 30: Charter for European Security, 1999

Agreement 31: OSCE Document on Small Arms and Light Weapons, 2000

Agreement 32: Concluding Document of the Negotiations Under Article V of Annex 1-B of the General Framework Agreement for Peace in Bosnia and Herzegovina, 2001

Agreement 33: NATO-Russia Relations: A New Quality, Declaration by Heads of State and Government of NATO Member States and the Russian Federation, 2002

Agreement 34: OSCE Strategy to Address Threats to Security and Stability in the Twenty-First Century, 2003

Agreement 35: OSCE Document on Stockpiles of Conventional Ammunition, 2003

Agreement 36: Vienna Document 2011 on Confidence- and Security-Building Measures, 2011

Annex III: List of Statements Reviewed

Statement 1: Speech by Soviet President Mikhail Gorbachev to the Second Summit of CSCE Heads of State or Government, Paris, November 19-21, 1990

Statement 2: Speech by U.S. President George Bush to the Second Summit of CSCE Heads of State or Government, Paris, November 19-21, 1990

Statement 3: Statement by the Minister of Foreign Affairs of the USSR, A. A. Bessmertnykh, at the first session of the Council of Ministers of Foreign Affairs of the participating States of the CSCE, Berlin, June 19, 1991 [Unofficial Translation]

Statement 4: European Architecture, Remarks by Secretary of State James A. Baker, III at the First Restricted Session of the CSCE Ministerial, Berlin, June 19, 1991

Statement 5: Statement by Andrei V. Kozyrev, Minister of Foreign Affairs of the Russian Federation at the CSCE Council Meeting, Prague, January 30, 1992

Statement 6: CSCE: Our Community of Democratic Values, Remarks by Secretary of State James A. Baker, III, CSCE Council of Ministers Meeting, Prague, January 30, 1992

Statement 7: Speech by President Boris N. Yeltsin of the Russian Federation to the Third Summit of CSCE Heads of State or Government, Helsinki, July 9-10, 1992

Statement 8: Speech by U.S. President George Bush to the Third Summit of CSCE Heads of State or Government, Helsinki, July 9-10, 1992

Statement 9: Statement by the Minister for Foreign Affairs of the Russian Federation, Mr. A. V. Kozyrev at the CSCE Council Meeting, Stockholm, December 14, 1992 [Unofficial Translation]

Statement 10: Europe in Transition: The Role of CSCE, Lawrence S. Eagleburger, Secretary of State, CSCE Council Meeting, Stockholm, December 14, 1992

Statement 11: Remarks by U.S. Secretary of State Warren Christopher at the CSCE Plenary Session, Rome, November 30, 1993

Statement 12: Address by President Yeltsin of the Russian Federation at the CSCE Summit, Budapest, December 5, 1994 [Unofficial Translation]

Statement 13: Remarks by the President of the United States William J. Clinton at the Plenary Session of the Summit of the CSCE, Budapest, December 5, 1994

Statement 14: 'On a New Model of Common and Comprehensive Security for Europe in the 21st Century', Statement by A. V. Kozyrev at a session of the OSCE Ministerial Council, Budapest, December 7, 1995 [Unofficial Translation]

Statement 15: Intervention of Deputy Secretary of State Strobe Talbot, OSCE Ministerial, Budapest, December 7, 1995

Statement 16: Address of the President of Russia Boris N. Yeltsin to the Participants of the Meeting of Heads of States or Government of the OSCE Participating States, Lisbon, December 2, 1996

Statement 17: Transcript of Vice-President Al Gore Statement, OSCE Lisbon Summit, Lisbon, December 2, 1996

Statement 18: Address by Mr. Igor S .Ivanov, Minister of Foreign Affairs of the Russian Federation at the Meeting of the OSCE Ministerial Council, Oslo, December 2, 1998 [Unofficial Translation]

Statement 19: Address to the OSCE Ministerial As Delivered by U.S. Head of Delegation Under Secretary Thomas R. Pickering, Oslo, December 2, 1998

Annex IV: References

Acharya, Amitav, and Buzan Barry. "Preface: why is there no non-Western IR theory? Reflections on and from Asia." *International relations of the Asia-Pacific* 7, no. 3 (2007): 285–286.

Adler, Emanuel. "Seeds of peaceful change: the OSCE's security community-building model." In *Security Communities*. Edited by Emanuel Adler and Michael N. Barnett, 119–60. Cambridge studies in international relations 62. Cambridge, UK, New York: Cambridge University Press, 1998.

———"The OSCE as a security community." *OSCE Magazine*, no. 1 (2011): 14–15.

Adler, Emanuel, and Michael N. Barnett. "A framework for the study of security communities." In *Security Communities*. Edited by Emanuel Adler and Michael N. Barnett, 29–65. Cambridge studies in international relations 62. Cambridge, UK, New York: Cambridge University Press, 1998.

———, eds. *Security Communities*. Cambridge studies in international relations 62. Cambridge, UK, New York: Cambridge University Press, 1998.

———"Security communities in theoretical perspective." In *Security Communities*. Edited by Emanuel Adler and Michael N. Barnett, 3–28. Cambridge studies in international relations 62. Cambridge, UK, New York: Cambridge University Press, 1998.

Adler, Emanuel, and Peter M. Haas. "Conclusion: Epistemic Communities, World Order, and the Creation of a Reflective Research Program." *International Organization* 46, no. 1 (1992): 367–390.

Aggarwal, Vinod K. *Liberal protectionism: The international politics of organized textile trade*. Studies in international political economy 13. Berkeley, Calif.: Univ. of California Press, 1985.

———. *Institutional Designs for a Complex World: Bargaining, Linkages and Nesting*. Ithaca: Cornell Univ. Press, 1998.

———"Analyzing NATO expansion: An institutional bargaining approach." *Contemporary Security Policy* 21, no. 2 (2000): 63–82.

Alcaro, Riccardo and Eric Jones, eds. *European Security and the Future of Transatlantic Relations*. IAI Research Papers. Rome: Edizioni Nuova Cultura, 2011. Accessed February 27, 2012.

Alexander, Michael. *Managing the Cold War: A view from the front line*. London: RUSI, 2005.

Alter, Karen J., and Sophie Meunier. "The Politics of International Regime Complexity." *Perspectives on Politics* 7, no. 1 (2009): 12–24.

Anstis, Christopher. "The Conference on Security and Cooperation in Europe (CSCE)." In *Disconcerted Europe: The search for a new security architecture*. Edited by Alexander Moens, 76–114. Boulder: Westview Press, 1994.

Aristotle. *Nicomachean ethics: Edited by Terence Irwin, 2. ed*. Princeton, N.J.: Hackett, 2008.

Armenia, Kazakhstan, Kyrgyzstan, The Russian Federation, Tajikistan, and Uzbekistan. "Treaty on Collective Security." In *Treaty Series*. Edited by United Nations, 314–7 Vol. 1894, 1-32307. New York, N.Y.: United Nations, Office of Legal Affairs, 1999.

Aron, Raymond. *Peace and war: a theory of international relations*. Garden City, NY: Doubleday, 1966.

Art, Robert J., and Robert Jervis. *International politics: Enduring concepts and contemporary issues*. 3rd ed. New York, NY: HarperCollins, 1992.

Asmus, Ronald D. *A little war that shook the world: Georgia, Russia, and the future of the West*. New York: Palgrave Macmillan, 2010.

Auton, Graeme P. "Multilateral Security Regimes: The Politics of CFE and CSBMs." In *The promise and reality of European security cooperation: States, interests, and institutions*. Edited by Mary M. McKenzie and Peter H. Loedel, 139–56. Westport, Conn: Praeger, 1998.

Axelrod, Robert, and Robert O. Keohane. "Achieving Cooperation under Anarchy: Strategies and Institutions." In *Cooperation Under Anarchy*. Edited by Kenneth A. Oye, 226–54. Princeton, NJ: Princeton Univ. Press, 1986.

Axelrod, Robert K. *The evolution of cooperation*. New York: Basic Books, 1984.

Baczynska, Gabriela. "After 10 years as president, Putin's ratings fly high on Ukraine." Moscow: Reuters on-line (May 7, 2014), accessed September 30, 2014. http://www.reuters.com/article/2014/05/07/us-ukraine-crisis-russia-putin-idUSBREA46OOG20140507.

Baker, James A. "Perestroika and American Foreign Policy." In *Contemporary issues in Soviet foreign policy: From Brezhnev to Gorbachev*. Edited by Frederic J. Fleron, Erik P. Hoffmann and Robbin F. Laird, 770–819. New York: A. de Gruyter, 1991.

Baldwin, David A. "Neoliberalism, Neorealism, and World Politics." In *Neorealism and Neoliberalism: The contemporary debate*. Edited by David A. Baldwin, 3–25. New directions in world politics. New York: Columbia University Press, 1993.

———, ed. *Neorealism and Neoliberalism: The contemporary debate*. New directions in world politics. New York: Columbia University Press, 1993.

———"The Concept of Security." *Review of International Studies* 23, no. 1 (1997): 5–26.

Barnett, Michael N. and Raymond Duvall, eds. *Power in global governance*. Cambridge studies in international relations 98. Cambridge, UK, New York: Cambridge University Press, 2005.

Baudissin, Wolf G. von, and Dieter S. Lutz. *Kooperative Rüstungssteuerung in Europa*. IFSH-Forschungsberichte 11. Hamburg: IFSH, 1979.

Bauwens, Werner, Bruni Colson, Wim de Haar, Koen de Feyter, Olivier Paye, and Nico Vertongen. "The CSCE and the Changing Role of NATO and the European Union." *NATO Review* 41, no. 3 (1994): 21–25.

BBC. "Yeltsin walks out on world leaders." London: BBC on-line (November 18, 1999), accessed November 4, 2014. http://news.bbc.co.uk/2/hi/europe/525839.stm.

Becher, Klaus and Andrei Zagorski, eds. *US-Raketenabwehr und russische Reaktionen*. Sozialwissenschaftliche Schriftenreihe Reihe Studien. Vienna: Internat. Inst. für Liberale Politik Wien (IILP), 2007.

Betts, Alexander. "Institutional Proliferation and the Global Refugee Regime." *Perspectives on Politics* 7, no. 1 (2009): 53–58.

Blacker, Coit D. "The MBFR Experience." In *U.S.-Soviet security cooperation: Achievements, failures, lessons*. Edited by Alexander L. George, 123–43. New York: Oxford Univ. Press, 1988.

Blake, Aaron. "Obama says Russia is just a 'regional power.' The American people disagree." Washington, D.C.: The Washington Post on-line (March 25, 2014), accessed December 28, 2014. http://www.washingtonpost.com/blogs/the-fix/wp/2014/03/25/obama-says-russia-is-just-a-regional-power-the-american-people-disagree/.

Boese, Wade. "NATO Accepts Russian CFE Compliance, But Wants More." *Arms Control Today* 32, no. 7 (2002): 22.

Borawski, John. "If Not NATO Enlargement: What Does Russia Want?" *European Security* 5, no. 3 (1996): 381–395.

Botelho, Greg, and Laura Smith-Spark. "Putin: You better not come after a nuclear-armed Russia." Washington, D.C.: CNN on-line (August 30, 2014), accessed December 28, 2014. http://edition.cnn.com/2014/08/29/world/europe/ukraine-crisis/.

Bouckaerts, Boudewijn and Gerrit de Geest, eds. *Encyclopedia of Law and Economics, Vol V: The Economics of Crime and Litigation.* Cheltenham: Edward Elgar, 2000.

Breslauer, George W. *Gorbachev and Yeltsin as leaders.* Cambridge, U.K., New York: Cambridge University Press, 2002.

BRICS. *The 6th BRICS Summit: Fortaleza Declaration.* Fortaleza, 2014. Accessed September 22, 2014. http://www.brics.utoronto.ca/docs/140715-leaders.html.

Brocking, Elisabeth. "Remember the CFE Treaty?" Washington, D.C.: The National Interest on-line (April 8, 2014), accessed December 28, 2014. http://nationalinterest.org/commentary/remember-the-cfe-treaty-10203.

Brössler, Daniel. "Putin soll Europa massiv gedroht haben." Stuttgart: Süddeutsche Zeitung on-line (September 18, 2014), accessed September 27, 2014. http://www.sueddeutsche.de/politik/berichte-des-ukrainischen-praesidenten-putin-soll-europa-massiv-gedroht-haben-1.2134168.

Brown, Michael E., Sean M. Lynn-Jones, and Steven E. Miller, eds. *The perils of anarchy: Contemporary realism and international security.* Cambridge, Mass.: MIT Press, 1995.

Brzezinski, Zbigniew. "From Hope to Audacity: Appraising Obama's Foreign Policy." *Foreign Affairs* 89, no. 1 (2010): 16–30.

Brzoska, Michael. "Is the Nuclear Non-Proliferation System a Regime? A Comment on Trevor McMorris Tate." *Journal of Peace Research* 29, no. 2 (1992): 215–220.

Bull, Hedley. *The control of the arms race: disarmament and arms control in the missile age.* Studies in international security 2. London: Institute for Strategic Studies, 1961.

———"The Twenty Years' Crisis Thirty Years On." *International Journal* 24, no. 4 (1969): 625–638.

———*The Moscow agreements and strategic arms limitation.* Canberra papers on strategy and defence 15. Canberra: Australian National University Press, 1973.

———*The Anarchical Society: A Study of Order in World Politics.* London: Macmillan, 1977.

Bull, Hedley and Adam Watson, eds. *The expansion of international society.* Oxford: Clarendon Press, 1984.

Burke-White, William W. "Crimea and the International Legal Order." *Survival* 56, no. 4 (2014): 65–80.

Buzan, Barry. *People, states & fear: An agenda for international security studies in the post-cold war era.* 2nd ed. ECPR Press classics. Colchester, UK: ECPR Press, 1991.

———— "From international system to international society: structural realism and regime theory meet the English school." *International Organization* 47, no. 3 (1993): 327–352.

————*From international to world society? English school theory and the social structure of globalization.* Cambridge studies in international relations 95. Cambridge, New York: Cambridge University Press, 2004.

———— "A World Order Without Superpowers. Decentered Globalism." *International Relations* 25, no. 1 (2011): 3–25.

———— "The Historical Expansion of International Society." In *Guide to the English School in International Studies.* Edited by Daniel M. Green and Cornelia Navari, 59 75. Chichester, England: Wiley-Blackwell, 2014.

Camisar, Adriana, Boris Diechtiareff, Bartol Letica, and Christine Switzer. "An Analysis of the Dayton Negotiations and Peace Accords: Final Research Paper." Medford, MA: The Fletcher School of Law and Diplomacy (2005), accessed November 4, 2014. http://ocw.tufts.edu/data/12/244825.pdf.

Carr, Edward Hallett. *The Twenty Years' Crisis, 1919-1939: An Introduction to the Study of International Relations.* London: Macmillan, 1939.

————*What is history?* Seoul: Basic Books, 2009.

Carter, Ashton B., William J. Perry, and John D. Steinbruner. *A New Concept of Cooperative Security.* Washington, D.C.: The Brookings Institution, 1992.

Chalmers, Hugh, Malcolm Chalmers, and Andrea Berger, eds. *A Problem Deferred? NATO's Non-Strategic Nuclear Weapons after Chicago.* Whitehall Report 4-12. London: Royal United Services Institute, 2012.

Charap, Samuel, and Jeremy Shapiro. "How to Avoid a New Cold War." *Current History* 113, no. 765 (2014): 265–271.

———— "A New European Security Order: The Ukraine Crisis and the Missing Post-Cold War Bargain." Paris (December 8, 2014), last modified December 28, 2014. http://www.frstrategie.org/barreFRS/publications/notes/2014/201415.pdf.

Chayes, Antonia H., and Abram Chayes. "Regime Architecture: Elements and Principles." In *Global engagement: Cooperation and security in the 21st century.* Edited by Janne E. Nolan, 65–130. Washington, DC: Brookings Institution, 1994.

Chung, Eunsook. "Cooperative Security Regimes: A Comparison of OSCE and ARF: Paper presented at the 5th Pan-European International Relations Conference 2004." *Sejong Policy Studies* 1, no. 1 (2005): 183–239.

CIA. "The World Factbook." Langley: CIA (1982-2014), accessed December 28, 2014. https://www.cia.gov/library/publications/the-world-factbook/.

Cirincione, Joseph. "Historical Overview and Introduction." In *Repairing the regime: Preventing the spread of weapons of mass destruction.* Edited by Joseph Cirincione, 1–14. New York, NY: Routledge, 2000.

————, ed. *Repairing the regime: Preventing the spread of weapons of mass destruction.* New York, NY: Routledge, 2000.

Clark, Ian. *Legitimacy in international society.* Oxford: Oxford University Press, 2007.

Cliff, Ian. "The Corfu Process – What Was It All About?" In *OSCE Yearbook 2011.* Edited by IFSH, 65–76. Nomos Verlagsgesellschaft Mbh & Co, 2012.

Clinton, Bill. "Promoting Trans-Atlantic Security Through NATO Enlargement: Responses by President Clinton to Questions from U.S. Senators." *U.S. Foreign Policy Agenda* 2, no. 4 (1997): 5–10.

Clinton, Hillary R. *Remarks on the Future of European Security, L'Ecole Militaire. Paris, January 29, 2010.* Accessed February 10, 2010. http://www.state.gov/secretary/rm/2010/01/136273.htm.

Cohen, Elliott A. "NATO: Dissolution, Enlargement or Either?" *International Journal on World Peace* 12, no. 2 (1995): 13–15.

Cohen, Stephen F. "Was the Soviet System Reformable?" *Slavic Review* 63, no. 3 (2004): 459–488.

Coker, Christopher. "A Farewell to Arms Control: The Irrelevance of CFE." In *In Search of Stability: Europe's Unfinished Revolution.* Edited by Gerald Frost and Andrew McHallam, 163–91. European defence and strategic studies annual 2. London: Adamantine Press, 1992.

Colby, Elbridge A. and Michael S. Gerson, eds. *Strategic stability: Contending interpretations.* Carlisle: Strategic Studies Institute, 2013.

Collina, Tom Z. "CFE Treaty Talks Stall." *Arms Control Today* 41, no. 7 (2011): 30–31.

Cortell, Andrew P., and Davis Jr., James W. "Understanding the Domestic Impact of International Norms: A Research Agenda." *International Studies Review* 2, no. 1 (2000): 65–87.

COW, Correlates of War Project. "National Material Capabilities (v4.0)." Michigan: University of Michigan 2014. http://www.correlatesofwar.org/COW2%20Data/Capabilities/nmc4.htm.

Cox, Robert W. "Social Forces, States and World Orders: Beyond International Relations Theory." *Millenium, Journal of International Studies* 10, no. 2 (1981): 126–155.

Crawford, Robert M. A. *Regime Theory in the Post-Cold War World: Rethinking Neoliberal Approaches to International Relations.* Aldershot: Dartmouth, 1996.

Crawford, Robert M. A. and Darryl S. L. Jarvis, eds. *International relations - still an American social science? Toward diversity in international thought.* SUNY series in global politics. Albany, NY: State Univ. of New York Press, 2000.

Croft, Stuart, ed. *The Conventional Armed Forces in Europe Treaty: The Cold War Endgame.* Aldershot: Dartmouth Pub. Co, 1994.

CSCE. *Charter of Paris for a New Europe.* Vienna, 1990.

Cutler, A. C., Virginia Haufler, and Tony Porter, eds. *Private authority and international affairs.* SUNY series in global politics. Albany, NY: State Univ. of New York Press, 1999.

Czempiel, Ernst-Otto. *Internationale Politik: Ein Konfliktmodell.* Uni-Taschenbücher Politische Wissenschaft. Geschichte. Soziologie 1067. Paderborn: Schöningh, 1981.

————"Foreword." In *The promise and reality of European security cooperation: States, interests, and institutions.* Edited by Mary M. McKenzie and Peter H. Loedel, ix–xii. Westport, Conn: Praeger, 1998.

Daalder, Ivo H., and James M. Lindsay. *America unbound: The Bush revolution in foreign policy.* Hoboken, N.J.: Wiley, 2005.

Daase, Christopher, Janet Mackenzie, Nikola Moosauer, and Petra Stykow. *Politikwissenschaftliche Arbeitstechniken.* Paderborn: UTB, 2008.

Darilek, Richard E. "The future of conventional arms control in Europe: A tale of two cities: Stockholm, Vienna." *Survival* 29, no. 1 (1987): 5–20.

Dean, Jonathan. "The USA and the OSCE: Still a Morganatic Union." In *OSCE Yearbook 1997.* Edited by IFSH, 39–43. Baden-Baden: Nomos Verl.-Ges., 1998.

Deep Cuts Commission. "Preparing for Deep Cuts: Options for Enhancing Euro-Atlantic and International Security." Hamburg, Moscow, Washington, D.C.: IFSH (April, 2014), accessed December 28, 2014. http://deepcuts.org/files/pdf/First_Report_of_the_Deep_Cuts_Commission_English.pdf.

Delawie, Greg. "Enhancing Security Cooperation in Europe: Remarks at the 2013 Annual Security Review Conference Working Session III: Arms Control and Confidence- and Security-Building Measures Vienna, Austria June 20, 2013." Vienna: United States State Department (June, 2013), accessed June 29, 2013. http://iipdigital.usembassy.gov/st/english/texttrans/2013/06/20130621277215.html#axzz2XbzTdq5W.

Deni, John R. "Moscow Hints at Partnership For Peace, CFE Limit Linkage." *Arms Control Today* 24, no. 5 (1994): 28.

Deutsch, Karl W. *Political community and the North Atlantic area: international organization in the light of historical experience.* Princeton, N.J.: Princeton Univ. Press, 1957.

Dewitt, David B., and Amitav Acharya. *Cooperative security and developmental assistance: The relationship between security and development with reference to Eastern Asia.* Eastern Asia policy papers 16. North York: Univ. of Toronto - York Univ. Joint Centre for Asia Pacific Studies, 1996.

Disarmament Diplomacy. "Russia Raises CFE, Nuclear Concerns Over NATO Expansion." *Disarmament Diplomacy*, no. 67 (2002): 62–63.

Drezner, Daniel W. *All politics is global: Explaining international regulatory regimes.* Princeton, N.J., Woodstock: Princeton University Press, 2008.

———"The Power and Peril of International Regime Complexity." *Perspectives on Politics* 7, no. 1 (2009): 65–70.

Duffield, John S. "What Are International Institutions?" *International Studies Review* 9, no. 1 (2007): 1–22.

Dunay, Pál. "What Has Happened to Arms Control?" In *OSCE Yearbook 2007.* Edited by IFSH, 271–9. Baden-Baden: Nomos-Verl.-Ges., 2008.

Dunay, Pál, and Wolfgang Zellner. "The Adaptation of the CFE Treaty - Between Creeping Marginalization and a New Conceptual Definition of European Arms Control." In *OSCE Yearbook 1999.* Edited by IFSH, 349–63. Baden-Baden: Nomos-Verl.-Ges., 2000.

Dunn, Lewis A. "The Role of Cooperative Security." In *Arms control and cooperative security.* Edited by Jeffrey A. Larsen and James J. Wirtz, 175–94. Boulder: Lynne Rienner Publ., 2009.

Durkalec, Jacek, Ian Kearns, and Lukasz Kulesa. "Starting the Process of Trust-Building in NATO-Russia Relations: The Arms Control Dimension." Warsaw: PISM 2013.

Dutkiewicz, Piotr and Robert J. Jackson, eds. *NATO looks East.* Westport, Conn.: Praeger, 1998.

Efinger, Manfred. "Vertrauens- und sicherheitsbildende Maßnahmen in und für Europa: Ein Schritt auf dem Weg zur Verregelung der Ost-West-Beziehungen?" In *Regime in den internationalen Beziehungen.* Edited by Beate Kohler-Koch. 1st ed., 343–84. Baden-Baden: Nomos-Verl.-Ges., 1989.

———"Preventing war in Europe through confidence- and security-building measures?" In *International regimes in East West politics.* Edited by Volker Rittberger, 117–50. London: Pinter, 1990.

Efinger, Manfred, Volker Rittberger, and Michael Zürn. *Internationale Regime in den Ost-West-Beziehungen: Ein Beitrag zur Erforschung der friedlichen Behandlung internationaler Konflikte.* Internationale Beziehungen 6. Frankfurt am Main: Haag + Herchen, 1988.

Efinger, Manfred, and Michael Zürn. "Explaining Conflict Management in East-West Relations: A Qualitative Test of Problem-Structural Typologies." In *International regimes in East West politics.* Edited by Volker Rittberger, 64–89. London: Pinter, 1990.

Eichenberg, Richard C. "Dual Track and Double Trouble: The Two-Level Politics of INF." In *Double-edged diplomacy: International bargaining and domestic politics.* Edited by Peter B. Evans, Harold K. Jacobson and Robert D. Putnam, 45–76. Studies in international political economy 25. Berkeley: University of California Press, 1993.

Eliot, Charles W., ed. *Blaise Pascal: Minor Works.* 51 vols. The Harvard Classics 48, Part 3. New York, N.Y.: P.F. Collier & Son, 1909-1914; Translated by O. W. Wright.

Embassy U.S. Moscow. *09MOSCOW1184: CFE: A Way Forward.* 2009. Accessed June 19, 2014. http://wikileaksru.wordpress.com/2009/05/08/09moscow1184-cfe-a-way-forward/.

———*09MOSCOW1541_a: Russia: Demarche on European security and the Corfu Ministerial.* 2009. Accessed November 14, 2014. https://search.wikileaks.org/plusd/cables/09MOSCOW1541_a.html.

———*09MOSCOW3056: Medvedev's Proposed European Security Treaty: How To Respond.* 2009. Accessed November 14, 2014. https://cablegatesearch.wikileaks.org/cable.php?id=09MOSCOW3056.

Englund, Will, and William Wan. "Medvedev threatens to target U.S. missile shield in Europe if no deal is reached." Washington, D.C.: The Washington Post on-line (November 23, 2011), accessed July 10, 2014.

Erickson, John. "Russia." In *Geopolitics, geography, and strategy.* Edited by Colin S. Gray and G. R. Sloan, 242–68. London: Routledge, 2013.

Erlanger, Steven, and Steven L. Myers. "NATO Allies Oppose Bush on Georgia and Ukraine." New York, NY: The New York Times on-line (April 3, 2008), accessed November 12, 2014. http://www.nytimes.com/2008/04/03/world/europe/03nato.html?pagewanted=all &_r=0.

EU Non-Proliferation and Disarmament Conference 2014. *Special Session 10: Deterrence, Non-Proliferation and Disarmament.* Brussels: EU Non-Proliferation Consortium, 2014. Accessed September 12, 2014. https://www.iiss.org/en/events/eu%20conference/sections/eu-conference-2014-4706/special-sessions-6020/special-session-10-7a22.

Euro-Atlantic Security Initiative. "Toward a Euro-Atlantic Security Community: Final Report." Washington, D.C. (February, 2012), accessed February 3, 2012.

EU-Ukraine. *Association Agreement between the European Union and the European Atomic Energy Community and Their Member States, on the One Part, and Ukraine, on the Other Part.* Brussels: European Union, 2013. Accessed December 28, 2014. http://eeas.europa.eu/ukraine/assoagreement/assoagreement-2013_en.htm.

Evans, Gareth. "The Responsibility to Protect: Ending Mass Atrocity Crimes Once and for All." *Irish Studies in International Affairs* 20, no. 1 (2009): 7–13.

Evans, Peter B., Harold K. Jacobson, and Robert D. Putnam, eds. *Double-edged diplomacy: International bargaining and domestic politics.* Studies in international political economy 25. Berkeley: University of California Press, 1993.

Evans, Tony, and Peter Wilson. "Regime Theory and the English School of International Relations: A Comparison." *Millenium, Journal of International Studies* 21, no. 3 (1992): 329–351.

Falkenrath, Richard A. *Shaping Europe's military order: The origins and consequences of the CFE Treaty.* CSIA studies in international security 6. Cambridge, Mass.: MIT Press, 1995.

———"The CFE Flank Dispute: Waiting in the Wings." *International Security* 19, no. 4 (1995): 118–144.

Fearon, James D. "Bargaining, Enforcement, and International Cooperation." *International Organization* 52, no. 02 (1998): 269–305.

Feinstein, Lee. "CFE Treaty Signed in Paris: Follow-up Negotiations Begin." *Arms Control Today* 20, no. 10 (1990): 22, 24.

Finnemore, Martha, and Kathryn Sikkink. "International Norm Dynamics and Political Change." *International Organization* 52, no. 4 (1998): 887–917.

Fitzpatrick, Mark. "The Ukraine Crisis and Nuclear Order." *Survival* 56, no. 4 (2014): 81–90.

Fleron, Frederic J., Erik P. Hoffmann, and Robbin F. Laird, eds. *Contemporary issues in Soviet foreign policy: From Brezhnev to Gorbachev.* New York: A. de Gruyter, 1991.

Flynn, Gregory, and Henry Farrell. "Piecing Together the Democratic Peace: The CSCE, Norms, and the "Construction" of Security in Post–Cold War Europe." *International Organization* 53, no. 3 (1999): 505–535.

Fong, Yuk-fai, and Jay Surti. "The optimal degree of cooperation in the repeated Prisoners' Dilemma with side payments." *Games and Economic Behavior* 67, no. 1 (2009): 277–291.

Foot, Rosemary, S. N. MacFarlane, and Michael Mastanduno, eds. *U.S. hegemony and international organizations: The United States and multilateral institutions.* Oxford, New York: Oxford University Press, 2003.

Freedman, Lawrence. "Ukraine and the Art of Crisis Management." *Survival* 56, no. 3 (2014): 7–42.

Frost, Gerald and Andrew McHallam, eds. *In Search of Stability: Europe's Unfinished Revolution.* European defence and strategic studies annual 2. London: Adamantine Press, 1992.

Fukuyama, Francis. *The end of history and the last man.* New York: Free Press, 1992.

Fund for Peace. "Fragile States Index 2014." Washington, D.C.: Fund for Peace (2014), accessed December 1, 2014. http://ffp.statesindex.org/rankings-2014.

Galtung, Johan. "The Palme Commission Report on Disarmament and Security: A Critical Comment." *Security Dialogue* 14, no. 2 (1983): 147–151.

Garthoff, Raymond L. *The great transition: American-Soviet relations and the end of the Cold War.* Washington, D.C.: Brookings Institution, 1994.

George, Alexander L. "Domestic Constraints on Regime Change in U.S. Foreign Policy: The Need for Policy Legitimacy." In *Change in the international system.* Edited by Ole R. Holsti, Randolph M. Siverson and Alexander L. George, 233–62. Boulder, Colo.: Westview Pr., 1980.

———, ed. *U.S.-Soviet security cooperation: Achievements, failures, lessons.* New York: Oxford Univ. Press, 1988.

Ghébali, Victor-Yves. "Confidence-building measures within the CSCE process: Paragraph-by-paragraph analysis of the Helsinki and Stockholm régimes." Research Papers 3, Geneva: UNIDIR 1989.

———"The Vienna Ministerial Council Meeting and Its Aftermath: Coping with the Russian Malaise." In *OSCE Yearbook 2001*. Edited by IFSH, 29–38. Baden-Baden: Nomos-Verl.-Ges., 2002.

———"Growing Pains at the OSCE: The Rise and Fall of Russia's Pan-European Expectations." *Cambridge Review of International Affairs* 18, no. 3 (2005): 375–388.

Ghébali, Victor-Yves and Daniel Warner, eds. *The reform of the OSCE 15 years after the Charter of Paris for a new Europe: Problems, challenges and risks*. PSIO occasional paper 2. Geneva: The Graduate Institute of International Studies, 2006.

Gill, Graeme J. and James Young, eds. *Routledge handbook of Russian politics and society*. Routledge handbooks. Milton Park, Abingdon, Oxon, New York: Routledge, 2012.

Gilpin, Robert. *War and change in world politics*. Cambridge: Cambridge Univ. Press, 1981.

———"The Richness of the Tradition of Political Realism." *International Organization* 38, no. 2 (1984): 287–304.

Glaser, Charles L. "Realists as Optimists: Cooperation as Self-Help." *International Security* 19, no. 3 (1994/95): 50–90.

Goldgeier, James M., and Michael McFaul. *Power and purpose: U.S. policy toward Russia after the Cold War*. Washington, D.C.: Brookings Institution Press, 2003.

Goldstein, Judith S. and Robert O. Keohane, eds. *Ideas and foreign policy: Beliefs, institutions, and political change*. Cornell studies in political economy. Ithaca: Cornell Univ. Press, 1993.

———"Ideas and Foreign Policy: An Analytical Framework." In *Ideas and foreign policy: Beliefs, institutions, and political change*. Edited by Judith S. Goldstein and Robert O. Keohane, 3–30. Cornell studies in political economy. Ithaca: Cornell Univ. Press, 1993.

Gong, Gerrit W. *The standard of "civilization" in international society*. Oxford: Clarendon Press, 1984.

Gorbachev, Mikhail S. *Memoirs*. New York: Doubleday, 1996.

———*Mikhail Gorbachev: Prophet of change: from the Cold War to a sustainable world*. Forest Row, East Sussex: Clairview, 2011.

Government of Russia. *Joint Statement by the Government of the Russian Federation and the Central Bank of the Russian Federation On the Exchange Rate Policy*. Moscow, 1998. Accessed November 4, 2014. http://www.cbr.ru/eng/press/JOINT.htm.

Gray, Colin S. and G. R. Sloan, eds. *Geopolitics, geography, and strategy*. London: Routledge, 2013.

Green, Daniel M. "Introduction to the English School in International Studies." In *Guide to the English School in International Studies*. Edited by Daniel M. Green and Cornelia Navari, 1–6. Chichester, England: Wiley-Blackwell, 2014.

Green, Daniel M. and Cornelia Navari, eds. *Guide to the English School in International Studies*. Chichester, England: Wiley-Blackwell, 2014.

Grieco, Joseph M. "Anarchy and the Limits of Cooperation: A Realist Critique of the Newest Liberal Institutionalism." *International Organization* 42, no. 3 (1988): 485–507.

Grogin, R. C. *Natural enemies: The United States and the Soviet Union in the Cold War, 1917-1991.* Lanham, Md.: Lexington Books, 2001.

Großer, Jens, Ernesto Reuben, and Agnieszka Tymula. "Political Quid Pro Quo Agreements: An Experimental Study." *American Journal of Political Science* 57, no. 3 (2013): 582–597.

Haas, Ernst B. *Beyond the Nation-State: functionalism and international organization.* Stanford, Calif.: Stanford Univ. Press, 1964.

———"Why Collaborate? Issue-Linkage and International Regimes." *World Politics* 32, no. 3 (1980): 357–405.

———"Regime decay: Conflict management and international organizations, 1945-1981." *International Organization* 37, no. 2 (1983): 189–256.

———*When knowledge is power: Three models of change in international organizations.* Studies in international political economy 22. Berkeley, Calif: Univ. of Calif. Press, 1990.

Haas, Peter M. "Epistemic Communities and the Dynamics of International Environmental Co-Operation." In *Regime theory and international relations.* Edited by Volker Rittberger, 169–201. Oxford: Clarendon, 1993.

Hækkerup, Hans. "Russia, the OSCE and Post-Cold-War European Security." *Cambridge Review of International Affairs* 18, no. 3 (2005): 371–373.

Hafner-Burton, Emilie M. "The Power Politics of Regime Complexity: Human Rights Trade Conditionality in Europe." *Perspectives on Politics* 7, no. 1 (2009): 33–37.

Haftendorn, Helga. "The link between CSCE and MBFR: two sprouts from one bulb." In *Origins of the European security system: The Helsinki process revisited, 1965-75.* Edited by Andreas Wenger, Christian Nünlist and Vojtech Mastny, 237–58. CSS studies in security and international relations. Abingdon, Oxon, New York, N.Y: Routledge, 2008.

Harrison, Mark. "Soviet Economic Growth Since 1928: The Alternative Statistics of G. I. Khanin." *Europe-Asia Studies* 45, no. 1 (1993): 141–167.

Hartmann, Rüdiger. "The Significance of Regional Arms Control Efforts for the Future of Conventional Arms Control in Europe, Exemplified by the Arms Control Negotiations in Accordance with the Dayton Agreement." In *OSCE Yearbook 1995/1996.* Edited by IFSH, 253–63. Baden-Baden: Nomos-Verl.-Ges., 1997.

———"The CFE Treaty, or: Can Europe Do Without Cooperative Security?" In *The future of conventional arms control in Europe.* Edited by Wolfgang Zellner, Hans-Joachim Schmidt and Götz Neuneck. 1st ed., 52–64. Demokratie, Sicherheit, Frieden 194. Baden-Baden: Nomos-Verl.-Ges., 2009.

Hartmann, Rüdiger, and Wolfgang Heydrich. *Die Anpassung des Vertrages über konventionelle Streitkräfte in Europa: Ursachen, Verhandlungsgeschichte, Kommentar, Dokumentation.* 1st ed. Internationale Politik und Sicherheit 53. Baden-Baden: Nomos-Verl.-Ges., 2002.

Hartmann, Rüdiger, Wolfgang Heydrich, and Nikolaus Meyer-Landrut. *Der Vertrag über konventionelle Streitkräfte in Europa: Vertragswerk, Verhandlungsgeschichte, Kommentar, Dokumentation.* 1st ed. Internationale Politik und Sicherheit 43. Baden-Baden: Nomos-Verl.-Ges., 1994.

Hasenclever, Andreas, Peter Mayer, and Volker Rittberger. *Theories of international regimes.* Cambridge studies in international relations 55. Cambridge: Cambridge Univ. Press, 1997.

————"Does Regime Robustness Require a Fair Distribution of the Gains from Cooperation?" In *Regime consequences: Methodological challenges and research strategies.* Edited by Arild Underdal and Oran R. Young, 183–216. Dordrecht: Kluwer Academic Publ, 2004.

Haufler, Virginia. "Crossing the Boundary between Public and Private: International Regimes and Non-State Actors." In *Regime theory and international relations.* Edited by Volker Rittberger, 94–111. Oxford: Clarendon, 1993.

Heller, Regina, and Martin Kahl. "Tracing and understanding "bad" norm dynamics in counterterrorism: the current debates in IR research." *Critical Studies on Terrorism* 6, no. 3 (2013): 414–428.

Herd, Graeme P. "Managing Strategic Trilemmas and Trade-Offs: The OSCE's Core Challenge?" In *OSCE Yearbook 2012.* Edited by IFSH, 391–405. Nomos Verlagsgesellschaft Mbh & Co, 2013.

Herrmann, Peter, Valérie Issarny, and Simon Shiu, eds. *Trust management: Third international conference, iTrust 2005, Paris, France, May 23-26, 2005: proceedings.* Lecture notes in computer science 3477. Berlin, New York: Springer, 2005.

Hershberg, James G. "The Cuban missile crisis." In *The Cambridge History of the Cold War.* Edited by Melvyn P. Leffler and Odd A. Westad, 65–87. Cambridge: Cambridge University Press, 2010.

Herz, John H. "Idealist Internationalism and the Security Dilemma." *World Politics* 2, no. 2 (1950): 157–180.

Hirschman, Albert O. *Exit, voice, and loyalty: Responses to decline in firms, organizations, and states.* Cambridge, Mass.: Harvard University Press, 1970.

Hobsbawm, E. J. *Nations and nationalism since 1780: Programme, myth, reality.* 2nd ed. Cambridge [England], New York: Cambridge University Press, 1992.

Hoffman, David. "Moscow Recalls NATO Delegate in Protest." *Washington Post* March 25, 1999.

Hoffmann, Stanley. *The state of war: essays on the theory and practice of international politics.* London: Pall Mall Press, 1965.

Hofmann, Stephanie C. "Overlapping Institutions in the Realm of International Security: The Case of NATO and ESDP." *Perspectives on Politics* 7, no. 1 (2009): 45–52.

Holbrooke, Richard C. "Advancing U.S. interests in Europe." *U.S. Department of State Dispatch* 6, no. 12 (1995).

Hollis, Martin, and Steve Smith. *Explaining and understanding international relations.* Oxford, New York: Clarendon Press; Oxford University Press, 1990.

Holloway, David. "Gorbachev's New Thinking." *Foreign Affairs* 68, no. 1 (1988): 66.

Holst, Johan J. "Arms Control in the Nineties: A European Perspective." *Daedalus* 120, 1, Arms Control: Thirty Years On (1991): 83–110.

Holsti, Ole R., Randolph M. Siverson, and Alexander L. George, eds. *Change in the international system.* Boulder, Colo.: Westview Pr., 1980.

Homans, George C. *Social behavior: its elementary forms.* London: Routledge & Kehan Paul, 1961.

Hopmann, P. T. "The Future Impact of the OSCE: Business as Usual or Revitalization?" In *OSCE Yearbook 2008*. Edited by IFSH, 75–90. Baden-Baden: Nomos Verl.-Ges., 2009.

Hopmann, P. T., and Daniel Druckman. "Arms Control and Arms Reduction: View I." In *International negotiation: Analysis, approaches, issues; a publication of the Processes of International Negotiations (PIN) Project*. Edited by Victor A. Kremenyuk. 1st ed., 269–87. Conflict resolution series. San Francisco: Jossey-Bass Publishers, 1991.

Horelick, Arnold L. "U.S.-Soviet Relations: Threshold of a New Era." In *Contemporary issues in Soviet foreign policy: From Brezhnev to Gorbachev*. Edited by Frederic J. Fleron, Erik P. Hoffmann and Robbin F. Laird, 623–49. New York: A. de Gruyter, 1991.

Hunter, Robert Edwards. "Enlarging NATO: Reckless or Requisite?" *U.S. Foreign Policy Agenda* 2, no. 4 (1997): 15–18.

———"Russia and the New "New World Order"" New York, NY (August, 2014), last modified September 29, 2014. http://perspectives.carnegie.org/us-russia/russia-new-world-order/.

Hurrell, Andrew. "International Society and the Study of Regimes: A Reflective Approach." In *Regime theory and international relations*. Edited by Volker Rittberger, 49–72. Oxford: Clarendon, 1993.

IFSH, ed. *OSCE Yearbook 1995/1996*. Baden-Baden: Nomos-Verl.-Ges., 1997.

———, ed. *OSCE Yearbook 1997*. Baden-Baden: Nomos Verl.-Ges., 1998.

———, ed. *OSCE Yearbook 1999*. Baden-Baden: Nomos-Verl.-Ges., 2000.

———, ed. *OSCE Yearbook 2001*. Baden-Baden: Nomos-Verl.-Ges., 2002.

———, ed. *OSCE Yearbook 2002*. Baden-Baden: Nomos Verl.-Ges., 2003.

———, ed. *OSCE Yearbook 2007*. Baden-Baden: Nomos-Verl.-Ges., 2008.

———, ed. *OSCE Yearbook 2008*. Baden-Baden: Nomos Verl.-Ges., 2009.

———, ed. *OSCE Yearbook 2009*. Baden-Baden: Nomos Verl.-Ges., 2010.

———, ed. *OSCE Yearbook 2010*. Baden-Baden: Nomos Verl.-Ges., 2011.

———, ed. *OSCE Yearbook 2011*. Nomos Verlagsgesellschaft Mbh & Co, 2012.

———, ed. *OSCE Yearbook 2012*. Nomos Verlagsgesellschaft Mbh & Co, 2013.

———, ed. *OSCE Yearbook 2013*. Baden-Baden: Nomos, 2014.

Independent International Fact-Finding Mission on the Conflict in Georgia. "Report of the Independent International Fact-Finding Mission on the Conflict in Georgia." Brussels (September 30, 2009), accessed December 28, 2014. http://www.refworld.org/docid/4ac45cd22.html.

Indyk, Martin, Kenneth Lieberthal, and Michael E. O'Hanlon. *Bending history: Barack Obama's foreign policy*. Brookings focus book. Washington, D.C.: Brookings Institution Press, 2012.

International Institute for Strategic Studies. *The military balance: the annual assessment of global military capabilities and defence economics*. London: Routledge, 1973-2014.

———"NATO enlargement and CFE Treaty: Meeting Russia's concerns." *IISS Strategic Comments* 3, no. 2 (1997): 1–2.

Ischinger, Wolfgang, Steven Pifer, and Andrei Zagorski. "Confidence Building Measures Are Now Needed More Than Ever." London: ELN (June 30, 2014), accessed September 13, 2014. http://www.europeanleadershipnetwork.org/confidence-building-measures-are-now-needed-more-than-ever_1578.html.

Jacobs, Frank. *Where Is Europe?* , 2012; The Opinion Pages *The New York Times*. Accessed December 14, 2012.
http://opinionator.blogs.nytimes.com/2012/01/09/where-is-europe/.

Jervis, Robert. "Cooperation Under the Security Dilemma." *World Politics* 30, no. 2 (1978): 167–214.

———"Security Regimes." *International Organization* 36, no. 2 (1982): 357 378.

———"Realism, Neoliberalism, and Cooperation: Understanding the Debate." *International Security* 24, no. 1 (1999): 42–63.

Jones, Peter. *Towards a regional security regime for the Middle East: Issues and options*. New ed. Solna: Stockholm International Peace Research Institute, 2011.

Jonsson, Anna. "Russia and Europe." In *Routledge handbook of Russian politics and society*. Edited by Graeme J. Gill and James Young, 444–53. Routledge handbooks. Milton Park, Abingdon, Oxon, New York: Routledge, 2012.

Jopp, Heinz D. "Regional Arms Control in Europe: The Arms Control Agreements under the Dayton Agreement (Mid-1997 until Mid-1999)." In *OSCE Yearbook 1999*. Edited by IFSH, 341–7. Baden-Baden: Nomos-Verl.-Ges., 2000.

Judt, Tony. *Ill Fares the Land: A Treatise on Our Present Discontents*. New York: Penguin Press, 2010.

Kahl, Martin. "NATO Enlargement and Security in a Transforming Eastern Europe: The Question of Adequacy." In *NATO looks East*. Edited by Piotr Dutkiewicz and Robert J. Jackson, 13–53. Westport, Conn.: Praeger, 1998.

Kahn, Alfred E. "The Tyranny of Small Decisions: Market Failures, Imperfections, and the Limit of Economics." *Kyklos* 19, no. 1 (1966): 23–47.

Kaiser, Karl, ed. *Confidence-Building Measures, Proceedings of an international symposium at Bonn, May 24-27, 1983, organized by the Forschungsinstitut der Deutschen Gesellschaft für Auswärtige Politik*. Arbeitspapiere zur Internationalen Politik 28. Bonn: Europa Union Verlag, 1983.

Karnitschnig, Matthew. "Pact With Russia Keeps NATO Bases at a Distance, But Should It?" New York, NY: The Wall Street Journal on-line (September 3, 2014), accessed September 27, 2014.
http://blogs.wsj.com/brussels/2014/09/03/qa-1997s-nato-russia-founding-act/.

Katzenstein, Peter J. *Cultural norms and national security: Police and military in postwar Japan*. Ithaca, N.Y.: Cornell University Press, 1996.

Katznelson, Ira and Helen V. Milner, eds. *Political Science: The State of the Discipline*. New York: Norton.

Kaufman, Joyce P. *NATO and the former Yugoslavia: Crisis, conflict, and the Atlantic Alliance*. Lanham: Rowman & Littlefield, 2002.

Keeley, James F. "Toward a Foucauldian analysis of international regimes." *International Organization* 44, no. 1 (1990): 83–105.

Keene, Edward. *Beyond the anarchical society: Grotius, colonialism and order in world politics*. LSE monographs in international studies. Cambridge, UK, New York, NY: Cambridge University Press, 2002.

Kelleher, Catherine M. "Cooperative Security in Europe." In *Global engagement: Cooperation and security in the 21st century*. Edited by Janne E. Nolan, 293–352. Washington, DC: Brookings Institution, 1994.

———"Cooperative Security in Europe: New Wine, New Bottles." College Park April, 2012.

http://www.cissm.umd.edu/papers/files/Cooperative%20Security%20in%20Eur
ope-New%20Wine%20New%20Bottles%20041312.pdf.

Kelleher, Catherine M., Jane M. O. Sharp, and Lawrence Freedman, eds. *The Treaty on Conventional Armed Forces in Europe: The politics of post-wall arms control.* 1st ed. Demokratie, Sicherheit, Frieden 100. Baden-Baden: Nomos-Verl.-Ges., 1996.

Keohane, Robert O. and Robert Owen, eds. *Neorealism and its critics.* The political economy of international change. New York: Columbia University Press, 1986.

Keohane, Robert O. "The demand for international regimes." *International Organization* 36, no. 2 (1982): 325–355.

——— *-After hegemony: Cooperation and discord in the world polit. economy.* Princeton, NJ: Princeton Univ. Press, 1984.

———, ed. *Neorealism and its critics.* The political economy of international change. New York: Columbia Univ. Press, 1986.

———"International Institutions: Two Approaches." *International Studies Quarterly* 32, no. 4 (1988): 379–396.

———"The Analysis of International Regimes: Towards a European-American Research Programme." In *Regime theory and international relations.* Edited by Volker Rittberger, 23–45. Oxford: Clarendon, 1993.

Keohane, Robert O., and Joseph S. Nye Jr. *Power and Interdependence: World Politics in Transition.* Boston: Little, Brown and Co., 1977.

Keohane, Robert O., and David G. Victor. "The Regime Complex for Climate Change." *Perspectives on Politics* 9, no. 1 (2011): 7–23.

Kieninger, Stephan. "Transformations versus Status Quo: The Survival of the Transformation Strategy during the Nixon Years." In *Perforating the Iron Curtain: European détente, transatlantic relations, and the Cold War, 1965 - 1985.* Edited by Poul Villaume and Odd A. Westad, 101–22. Copenhagen: Museum Tusculanum Press, 2010.

Kimball, Daryl G. "A Beginning, Not an End." *Arms Control Today* 32, June (2002): 1.

Kindleberger, Charles P. *The world in depression 1929 - 1939.* History of the world economy in the twentieth century 4. Berkeley: Univ. of California Press, 1973.

Kissinger, Henry. *Nuclear weapons and foreign policy.* Norton library. New York: W.W. Norton, 1957.

———*The White House years.* London: Weidenfeld and Nicolson, 1979.

———*Diplomacy.* New York: Simon & Schuster, 1994.

Kohler-Koch, Beate, ed. *Regime in den internationalen Beziehungen.* 1st ed. Baden-Baden: Nomos-Verl.-Ges., 1989.

Korshunov, Maxim. "Mikhail Gorbachev: I am against all walls." Moscow: Russia Beyond the Headlines (October 16, 2014), accessed December 28, 2014. http://rbth.co.uk/international/2014/10/16/mikhail_gorbachev_i_am_against_all_walls_40673.html.

Kozyrev, Andrei. "The Lagging Partnership." *Foreign Affairs* 73, no. 3 (1994): 59–71.

Kramer, Andrew E., and Michael R. Gordon. "Russia Sent Tanks to Separatists in Ukraine, U.S. Says." *New York Times* June 14, 2014. New York Edition.

Kramer, Mark. "The Myth of a No-NATO-Enlargement Pledge to Russia." *The Washington Quarterly* 32, no. 2 (2009): 39–61.

Krasner, Stephen D. "State Power and the Structure of International Trade." *World Politics* 28, no. 3 (1976): 317–347.

———"Structural Causes and Regime Consequences: Regimes as Intervening Variables." *International Organization* 36, no. 2 (1982): 185–205.

———"Sovereignty, Regimes, and Human Rights." In *Regime theory and international relations*. Edited by Volker Rittberger, 139–67. Oxford: Clarendon, 1993.

Kratochwil, Friedrich. "Contract and Regimes: Do Issue Specificity and Variations of Formality Matter?" In Rittberger, *Regime theory and international relations*, 73–93, 1993.

Kratochwil, Friedrich, and John G. Ruggie. "International Organization: A State of the Art on an Art of the State." *International Organization* 40, no. 4 (1986): 753–775.

Krause, Joachim. *The OSCE and co-operative security in Europe: Lessons for Asia.* IDSS monograph 6. Nanyang: Inst. of Defence and Strategic Studies, 2003.

Krauthammer, Charles. "The Unipolar Moment." *Foreign Affairs* 70, no. 1 (1991): 23–33.

Kremenyuk, Victor A., ed. *International negotiation: Analysis, approaches, issues; a publication of the Processes of International Negotiations (PIN) Project.* 1st ed. Conflict resolution series. San Francisco: Jossey-Bass Publishers, 1991.

———"The Emerging System of International Negotiation." In *International negotiation: Analysis, approaches, issues; a publication of the Processes of International Negotiations (PIN) Project.* Edited by Victor A. Kremenyuk. 1st ed., 22–39. Conflict resolution series. San Francisco: Jossey-Bass Publishers, 1991.

Krippendorff, Klaus. *Content Analysis: An Introduction to Its Methodology.* London: SAGE Publications, 1980.

Kropatcheva, Elena. *Russia's Ukraine policy against the background of Russian-Western competition.* Baden-Baden: Nomos, 2010.

Kühn, Ulrich. "From Capitol Hill to Istanbul: The Origins of the Current CFE Deadlock." CORE Working Paper 19, Hamburg: Centre for OSCE Research (December, 2009), accessed December 10, 2009. http://www.core-hamburg.de/documents/CORE%20Working%20Paper%2019%20%28Kuehn%29.pdf.

———"CFE: Overcoming the Impasse." *Russia in Global Affairs* 8, no. 2 (2010): 61–70.

———"Medvedev's Proposals for a New European Security Order: A Starting Point or the End of the Story?" *Connections, The Quarterly Journal* 9, no. 2 (2010): 1–16.

———"Conventional Arms Control 2.0." *The Journal of Slavic Military Studies* 26, no. 2 (2013): 189–202.

Kulebyakin, Vyacheslav. "European Security and the Treaty on Conventional Armed Forces in Europe." In *The future of conventional arms control in Europe*. Edited by Wolfgang Zellner, Hans-Joachim Schmidt and Götz Neuneck. 1st ed., 245–53. Demokratie, Sicherheit, Frieden 194. Baden-Baden: Nomos-Verl.-Ges., 2009.

Kupchan, Charles A. "The origins and future of NATO enlargement." *Contemporary Security Policy* 21, no. 2 (2000): 127–148.

————"No one's world: The West, the rising rest, and the coming global turn. New York: Oxford University Press, 2012.

Kurtov, Azhdar. "The CSTO, GUAM transformation of the post-Soviet area." *Central Asia and the Caucasus* 51-52, 3-4 (Special Issue) (2008): 262–276.

Lachowski, Zdzislaw. *Confidence- and security-building measures in the new Europe.* SIPRI Research Report 18. Oxford: Oxford Univ. Press, 2004.

Lagon, Mark P. "Promoting Democracy: The Whys and Hows for the United States and the International Community." Washington, D.C.: Council on Foreign Relations (February, 2011), accessed December 28, 2014. http://www.cfr.org/democratization/promoting-democracy-whys-hows-united-states-international-community/p24090.

Larsen, Jeffrey A. "An Introduction to Arms Control and Cooperative Security." In *Arms control and cooperative security.* Edited by Jeffrey A. Larsen and James J. Wirtz, 1–20. Boulder: Lynne Rienner Publ, 2009.

Larsen, Jeffrey A. and James J. Wirtz, eds. *Arms control and cooperative security.* Boulder: Lynne Rienner Publ, 2009.

Lavrov, Sergei. "Containing Russia: Back to the Future?" *Russia in Global Affairs* 5, no. 4 (2007): 8–22.

————"Strategic partnership between Russia and the European Union could become one of the pillars of the new Europe…": Transcript of remarks by Russian Minister of Foreign Affairs at the Myrdal Lecture, Geneva, February 12, 2008." *International Affairs, A Russian Journal of World Politics, Diplomacy and International Relations* 54, no. 3 (2008): 1–10.

————*Transcript of Speech by Russian Minister of Foreign Affairs Sergey Lavrov at the 46th Munich Security Conference, February 6, 2010.* 2010. Accessed February 10, 2010.

Leatherman, Janie. *From Cold War to democratic peace: Third parties, peaceful change, and the OSCE.* Syracuse studies on peace and conflict resolution. Syracuse, N.Y.: Syracuse University Press, 2003.

Leffler, Melvyn P. and Odd A. Westad, eds. *The Cambridge History of the Cold War.* Cambridge: Cambridge University Press, 2010.

Legvold, Robert. "The Revolution in Soviet Foreign Policy." In *Contemporary issues in Soviet foreign policy: From Brezhnev to Gorbachev.* Edited by Frederic J. Fleron, Erik P. Hoffmann and Robbin F. Laird, 357–78. New York: A. de Gruyter, 1991.

————"Managing the New Cold War." *Foreign Affairs* 93, no. 4 (2014): 74–84.

Levy, Marc A., Oran R. Young, and Michael Zürn. "The Study of International Regimes." *European Journal of International Relations* 1, no. 3 (1995): 267–330.

Lipman, Maria. "The origins of Russia's new conflict with the West." London: ECFR (October 14, 2014), accessed December 28, 2014. http://www.ecfr.eu/article/commentary_the_origins_of_russias_new_conflict_with_the_west330.

Lippman, Thomas W. "Clinton, Yeltsin Agree on Arms Cuts and NATO." *Washington Post* March 22, 1997.

Lipson, Charles. "International Cooperation in Economic and Security Affairs." *World Politics* 37, no. 1 (1984): 1–23.

Locke, John. *Two treatises of government.* Cambridge texts in the history of political thought. Cambridge [England], New York: Cambridge University Press, 1988.

Luck, Edward C. "American Exceptionalism and International Organization: Lessons from the 1990s." In *U.S. hegemony and international organizations: The United States and multilateral institutions*. Edited by Rosemary Foot, S. N. MacFarlane and Michael Mastanduno, 25–48. Oxford, New York: Oxford University Press, 2003.

Lugar, Richard, and Victoria Nuland. *Russia, its neighbors, and an enlarging NATO: Report of an independent task force*. Task Force report. New York, NY: Council on Foreign Relations, 1997.

Luhn, Alec, and Terry Macalister. "Russia signs 30-year deal worth $400bn to deliver gas to China." London: The Guardian on-line (May 21, 2014), accessed September 27, 2014. http://www.theguardian.com/world/2014/may/21/russia-30-year-400bn-gas-deal-china.

Lukin, Alexander. "Eurasian Integration and the Clash of Values." *Survival* 56, no. 3 (2014): 43–60.

Lukyanov, Fyodor. "Russia - U.S. - Back to Business?" Moscow: Russia in Global Affairs on-line edition (March 16, 2012), accessed November 11, 2014. http://eng.globalaffairs.ru/redcol/Russia---US---Back-to-Business-15490.

Luongo, Kenneth N. "The Uncertain Future of U.S.-Russian Cooperative Nuclear Security." *Arms Control Today* 31, no. 1 (2001): 3–10.

Lyne, Roderic, Strobe Talbott, and Kōji Watanabe. *Engaging with Russia: The next phase: a report to the Trilateral Commission.* Triangle papers 59. Washington, D.C., Paris, Tokyo: Trilateral Commission, 2006.

MacFarquhar, Neil, and Michael R. Gordon. "Ukraine Leader Says 'Huge Loads of Arms' Pour in From Russia." New York, NY: The New York Times on-line (August 28, 2014), accessed December 28, 2014. http://www.nytimes.com/2014/08/29/world/europe/ukraine-conflict.html?_r=0.

Makinda, Samuel. "The Role of Linkage Diplomacy in US-Soviet Relations." *Australian Journal of Politics & History* 33, no. 3 (1987): 224–236.

Mankoff, Jeffrey. *Russian foreign policy: The return of great power politics*. Lanham, Md.: Rowman & Littlefield Publishers, 2009.

March, James G., and Johan P. Olsen. "The logic of appropriateness." Oslo: ARENA, Centre for European Studies, University of Oslo 1998. https://www.sv.uio.no/arena/english/research/publications/arena-publications/workingpapers/working-papers2004/wp04_9.pdf.

Maresca, John J. "Helsinki Accord, 1975." In *U.S.-Soviet security cooperation: Achievements, failures, lessons*. Edited by Alexander L. George, 106–22. New York: Oxford Univ. Press, 1988.

Mattingly, Garrett. *Renaissance Diplomacy*. London: Cape, 1955.

Mazat, Numa, and Franklin Serrano. "An analysis of the Soviet economic growth from the 1950's to the collapse of USSR (Second Draft)." Rio de Janeiro: Universidade Federal do Rio de Janeiro, no date. http://www.indabook.org/preview/TkuysreUG0L8Pk20VGddG72cnmxve1TW7wQppJcHdtI,/An-analysis-of-the-Soviet-economic-growth-from-the.html?query=Soviet-Machine-Guns.

McDermott, Roger N. *The reform of Russia's conventional armed forces: Problems, challenges and policy implications*. Washington: The Jamestown Foundation, 2011.

McFaul, Michael, Stephen Sestanovich, and John J. Mearsheimer. "Faulty Powers: Who Started the Ukraine Crisis?" *Foreign Affairs* 93, no. 6 (2014): 167–178.

McGinnis, Michael D. "Issue Linkage and the Evolution of International Cooperation." *The Journal of Conflict Resolution* 30, no. 1 (1986): 141–170.

McKenzie, Mary M., and Peter H. Loedel. "Introduction: States and Institutions in
European Security." In *The promise and reality of European security coopera-
tion: States, interests, and institutions.* Edited by Mary M. McKenzie and Peter
H. Loedel, 1–19. Westport, Conn: Praeger, 1998.

———, eds. *The promise and reality of European security cooperation: States, interests, and institutions.* Westport, Conn: Praeger, 1998.

McKeown, Ryder. "Norm Regress: US Revisionism and the Slow Death of the Torture Norm." *International Relations* 23, no. 1 (2009): 5–25.

Mearsheimer, John J. "The False Promise of International Institutions." *International
Security* 19, no. 3 (1994/95): 5–49.

———*The tragedy of Great Power politics.* The Norton series in world politics. New
York: Norton, 2001.

———"Why the Ukraine Crisis is the West's Fault: The Liberal Delusions That
Provoked Putin." *Foreign Affairs* 93, no. 5 (2014): 77–89.

Medvedev, Dmitry. *European Security Treaty, November 29, 2009.* Accessed January 18, 2010. http://eng.kremlin.ru/text/docs/2009/11/223072.shtml.

Meister, Stefan. "Putin's plan." London: ECFR (April 17, 2014), accessed September 27, 2014. http://www.ecfr.eu/content/entry/commentary_putins_plan249.

Melvyn P. Leffler and Odd Arne Westad, eds. *Cambridge History of the Cold War,
Volume 2: Crises and Détente.* 1st ed. Cambridge: Cambridge Univ. Press,
2010.

Mihalka, Michael. "Cooperative Security in the 21st Century." *Connections, The
Quarterly Journal* 4, no. 4 (2005): 113–122.

Ministry of Defence. *The Military Doctrine of the Russian Federation, approved by
Russian Federation presidential edict on 5 February 2010*; [English transla-
tion].
http://www.carnegieendowment.org/files/2010russia_military_doctrine.pdf.

Mission U.S. NATO. *09USNATO540_a: NATO-Russia: Rogozin unclear on why
Moscow pulled the plug on NRC reform.* 2009. Accessed November 14, 2014.
https://search.wikileaks.org/plusd/cables/09USNATO540_a.html.

———*09USNATO557 Nato-russia: Deja Vu All Over Again.* 2009. Accessed July 8,
2014. https://wikileaks.org/cable/2009/11/09USNATO557.html.

———*09USNATO579 NATO-Russia: Responding to Russia's Latest Draft Treaty
Limiting the Deployment of Troops Abroad.* 2009. Accessed January 18, 2013.
http://wikileaks.org/cable/2009/12/09USNATO579.html.

———*09USNATO581_a: NATO-RUSSIA: RUSSIA "BRIEFS" NRC ON MILITARY
EXERCISES.* 2009. Accessed November 12, 2014.
https://wikileaks.org/plusd/cables/09USNATO581_a.html.

———*03USNATO595: NATO-Russia: Secretary Generals Trip to Moscow.* 2009.
Accessed September 2, 2014.
http://www.aftenposten.no/spesial/wikileaksdokumenter/21122009-NATO-
RUSSIA-SECRETARY-GENERALS-TRIP-TO-MOSCOW-5110256.html.

Mission U.S. OSCE. *08USOSCE70 Vienna Document 1999: CFE Suspension Casts
Long Shadow At German Foreign Office Seminar.* 2008. Accessed July 8, 2014.
https://wikileaks.org/cable/2008/03/08USOSCE70.html.

————*09USOSCE146_a: Scenesetter for Corfu OSCE Ministerial*. 2009. Accessed November 14, 2014.
https://search.wikileaks.org/plusd/cables/09USOSCE146_a.html.

————*10USOSCE28_a: OSCE: 1/27 FSC Responses to Russia on comprehensive approach to European security*. 2010. Accessed November 14, 2014.
https://search.wikileaks.org/plusd/cables/10USOSCE28_a.html.

————*10USOSCE28_a: OSCE: 1/27 FSC Responses to Russia on Comprehensive Approach to European Security*. 2010. Accessed June 19, 2014.
http://www.wikileaks.org/plusd/cables/10USOSCE28_a.html.

Mlyn, Eric. "The United States, Russia and the OSCE in 21st Century European Security." In *OSCE Yearbook 2002*. Edited by IFSH, 49–57. Baden-Baden: Nomos Verl.-Ges., 2003.

Moens, Alexander, ed. *Disconcerted Europe: The search for a new security architecture*. Boulder: Westview Press, 1994.

Moravcsik, Andrew. "Integrating International and Domestic Theories of International Bargaining." In *Double-edged diplomacy: International bargaining and domestic politics*. Edited by Peter B. Evans, Harold K. Jacobson and Robert D. Putnam, 3–42. Studies in international political economy 25. Berkeley: University of California Press, 1993.

Morgan, Michael C. "North America, Atlanticism, and the making of the Helsinki Final Act." In *Origins of the European security system: The Helsinki process revisited, 1965-75*. Edited by Andreas Wenger, Christian Nünlist and Vojtech Mastny, 25–45. CSS studies in security and international relations. Abingdon, Oxon, New York, N.Y: Routledge, 2008.

Morgenthau, Hans J. *Politics among nations: The struggle for power and peace (2nd ed.)*. New York: Knopf, 1954.

Morin, Jean-Frédéric, and Amandine Orsini. "Regime Complexity and Policy Coherency: Introducing a Co-adjustments Model." *Global Governance* 19, no. 1 (2013): 41–51.

Müller, Harald. *Die Chance der Kooperation: Regime in den internationalen Beziehungen*. Darmstadt: Wiss. Buchges., 1993.

————"The Internationalization of Principles, Norms, and Rules by Governments: The Case of Security Regimes." In *Regime theory and international relations*. Edited by Volker Rittberger, 361–88. Oxford: Clarendon, 1993.

————"Die Zukunft der nuklearen Ordnung." In *Die Zukunft der nuklearen Ordnung*. Edited by Michael Staack, 12–25. Schriftenreihe des Wissenschaftlichen Forums für Internationale Sicherheit e.V. (WIFIS) 27. Bremen: Edition Temmen, 2009.

————"Where It All Began." In *Norm dynamics in multilateral arms control: Interests, conflicts, and justice*. Edited by Harald Müller and Carmen Wunderlich, 1–19. Athens: University of Georgia Press, 2013.

Müller, Harald and Carmen Wunderlich, eds. *Norm dynamics in multilateral arms control: Interests, conflicts, and justice*. Athens: University of Georgia Press, 2013.

Mutschler, Max M. *Arms control in space: Exploring conditions for preventive arms control*. Palgrave studies in international relations series. Basingstoke, Hampshire: Palgrave Macmillan, 2013.

Mutz, Reinhard, ed. *Die Wiener Verhandlungen über Truppenreduzierungen in Mitteleuropa (MBFR): Chronik, Glossar, Dokumentation, Bibliogr. 1973-1982.* 1st ed. Militär, Rüstung, Sicherheit 16. Baden-Baden: Nomos Verl.-Ges., 1983.

———"Sterben in Wien: Die Abrüstung ist tot – sie lebe hoch!" Munich (February 10, 1989), last modified November 4, 2014. http://www.zeit.de/1989/07/sterben-in-wien.

Mützenich, Rolf, and Matthias Z. Karádi. "The OSCE as a Euro-Atlantic and Eurasian Security Community: Theoretical Foundations, Preconditions, and Prospects." In *OSCE Yearbook 2012.* Edited by IFSH, 43–54. Nomos Verlagsgesellschaft Mbh & Co, 2013.

Nathan, James A., and Graham Allison. "The Cuban Missile Crisis Revisited: Why It Matters Who Blinked." 91, no. 6 (2012): 163–166.

NATO. *Prague Summit Declaration issued by the Heads of State and Government participating in the meeting of the North Atlantic Council.* Brussels: NATO, 2002. Accessed December 30, 2014. http://www.nato.int/cps/en/natolive/official_texts_19552.htm

———*Bucharest Summit Declaration Issued by the Heads of State and Government participating in the meeting of the North Atlantic Council in Bucharest on 3 April 2008.* Brussels, 2008. Accessed November 11, 2014. http://www.nato.int/cps/en/natolive/official_texts_8443.htm.

———*A new strategic reality in Europe: Speech by NATO Deputy Secretary General Ambassador Alexander Vershbow to the 21st International Conference on Euro-Atlantic Security, Krakow, Poland.* Brussels, 2014. Accessed September 27, 2014. http://www.nato.int/cps/en/natolive/opinions_108889.htm.

———"NATO enlargement." Brussels (June 12, 2014), last modified December 28, 2014. http://www.nato.int/cps/en/natolive/topics_49212.htm.

———*Wales Summit Declaration, Issued by the Heads of State and Government participating in the meeting of the North Atlantic Council in Wales from 4 to 5 September 2014.* Brussels, 2014. Accessed September 27, 2014. https://www.gov.uk/government/uploads/system/uploads/attachment_data/file/3 51406/Wales_Summit_Declaration.pdf.

NATO-Russia. *Founding Act on Mutual Relations, Cooperation and Security between NATO and the Russian Federation.* Brussels: NATO, 1997. Accessed December 28, 2014. http://www.nato.int/cps/en/natolive/official_texts_25468.htm.

NATO-Ukraine Commission. *Joint Statement of the NATO-Ukraine Commission.* Brussels, 2014. Accessed September 5, 2014. https://www.gov.uk/government/publications/nato-summit-2014-joint-statement-of-the-nato-ukraine-commission/joint-statement-of-the-nato-ukraine-commission.

Neumann, Iver. "Entry into international society reconceptualised: the case of Russia." *Review of International Studies* 37, no. 2 (2011): 463–484.

Neuneck, Götz. *Die mathematische Modellierung von konventioneller Stabilität und Abrüstung.* 1st ed. Demokratie, Sicherheit, Frieden 96. Baden-Baden: Nomos-Verl.-Ges., 1995.

Nolan, Janne E., ed. *Global engagement: Cooperation and security in the 21st century.* Washington, DC: Brookings Institution, 1994.

———"The Concept of Cooperative Security." In *Global engagement: Cooperation and security in the 21st century.* Edited by Janne E. Nolan, 3–18. Washington, DC: Brookings Institution, 1994.

Nye Jr., Joseph S. "Nuclear learning and U.S.-Soviet security regimes." *International Organization* 41, no. 3 (1987): 371–402.

Odynova, Alexandra. "Relatives of Russian Soldiers Captured by Ukraine Demand Answers." New York, NY: The New York Times on-line (August 29, 2014), accessed September 27, 2014. http://www.nytimes.com/2014/08/30/world/europe/relatives-of-russian-soldiers-captured-by-ukraine-demand-answers.html.

Olson, Mancur. *Die Logik des kollektiven Handelns: Kollektivgüter und die Theorie der Gruppen (2nd Ed.)*. Die Einheit der Gesellschaftswissenschaften Bd. 10. Tübingen: Mohr, 1985.

Orsini, Amandine, Jean-Frédéric Morin, and Oran R. Young. "Regime Complexes: A Buzz, a Boom, or a Boost for Global Governance?" *Global Governance* 19, no. 1 (2013): 27–39.

OSCE. *'On a New Model of Common and Comprehensive Security for Europe in the 21st Century', Statement by A. V.* Vienna, 1995.

———*Transcript of Vice-President Al Gore Statement, OSCE Lisbon Summit, Lisbon, December 2, 1996.* Vienna, 1996.

———*Istanbul Document.* Vienna, 1999. Accessed October 26, 2014. http://www.osce.org/node/39569.

———*Intervention at the Thirteenth OSCE Ministerial Council As delivered by Under Secretary for Political Affairs R. Nicholas Burns to the 13th OSCE Ministerial Council, Ljubljana, December 5, 2005.* Vienna, 2005.

———*Extraordinary Conference of the States Parties to the CFE Treaty (CFE-EC 07.JOUR 11-15 June 2007).* Vienna, 2007.

———*Statement by Mr. Sergei V. Lavrov, Minister for Foreign Affairs of the Russian Federation at the Fifteenth Meeting of the OSCE Ministerial Council, Madrid, November 29, 2007.* Vienna, 2007.

———*Statement by Sergey Lavrov at the Opening Session of the OSCE Annual Review Conference, Vienna, 23 June 2009 (PC.DEL/480/09 English).* Vienna, 2009. Accessed July 17, 2009.

———*Astana Commemorative Declaration: Towards a Security Community.* Vienna, 2010. http://www.osce.org/cio/74985?download=true.

———*Interpretative Statement on 'Decision on Issues Relevant to the Forum for Security Cooperation', Annex to the Vienna Document 2011.* Vienna, 2011.

———*The Corfu Process.* Vienna: OSCE, 2014. Accessed December 28, 2014. http://www.osce.org/cio/108343.

———*On the road to Basel Ministerial Council, Swiss Chair launches discussion on ways to overcome the crisis of European security.* Vienna, 2014. Accessed January 4, 2015. http://www.osce.org/cio/124452.

Oxford University Press, ed. *Oxford Dictionaries.* Oxford: Oxford University Press, 2014. Accessed December 1, 2014. http://www.oxforddictionaries.com/.

Oye, Kenneth A., ed. *Cooperation Under Anarchy.* Princeton, NJ: Princeton Univ. Press, 1986.

———"Explaining Cooperation under Anarchy: Hypotheses and Strategies." In *Cooperation Under Anarchy.* Edited by Kenneth A. Oye, 1–25. Princeton, NJ: Princeton Univ. Press, 1986.

Packer, George. "The Quiet German." New York, NY: The New Yorker on-line (December 1, 2014), accessed December 28, 2014. http://www.newyorker.com/magazine/2014/12/01/quiet-german.

Palan, Ronen. *Cave! Alius Draco: There Was a Sixth Dragon!*, 2012. Accessed November 17, 2012. http://www.e-ir.info/2012/09/21/cave-alius-draco-there-was-a-sixth-dragon/.

Pascal, Blaise. "Of the Geometrical Spirit." In *Blaise Pascal: Minor Works*. Edited by Charles W. Eliot. 51 vols. The Harvard Classics 48, Part 3. New York, N.Y.: P.F. Collier & Son, 1909-1914.

Peter, Matthias and Hermann Wentker, eds. *Die KSZE im Ost-West-Konflikt: Internationale Politik und gesellschaftliche Transformation 1975 - 1990*. Schriftenreihe der Vierteljahrshefte für Zeitgeschichte Sondernummer. München: Oldenbourg, 2012.

Peters, John E. *The changing quality of stability in Europe: The Conventional Forces in Europe Treaty toward 2001*. Santa Monica, CA: Rand Corporation, 2000.

Pifer, Steven. "The INF Treaty, Russian Compliance and the U.S. Policy Response." Washington, D.C.: Brookings Institution (2014), accessed December 1, 2014. http://www.brookings.edu/research/testimony/2014/07/17-inf-treaty-russia-compliance-us-policy-response-pifer.

———"Did NATO Promise Not to Enlarge? Gorbachev Says "No"." Washington, D.C. (November 6, 2014), last modified December 28, 2014. http://www.brookings.edu/blogs/up-front/posts/2014/11/06-nato-no-promise-enlarge-gorbachev-pifer.

Ponsard, Lionel. *Russia, NATO and cooperative security: Bridging the gap*. Contemporary security studies. London: Routledge, 2007.

Powell, Robert. "Anarchy in international relations theory: the neorealist-neoliberal debate." *International Organization* 48, no. 2 (1994): 313–344.

Pradetto, August, ed. *Die zweite Runde der NATO-Osterweiterung: Zwischen postbipolarem Institutionalismus und offensivem Realismus*. Strategische Kultur Europas 2. Frankfurt am Main: Lang, 2004.

President of Russia. *Annual Address to the Federal Assembly of the Russian Federation*. Moscow, 2005. Accessed September 15, 2014. http://archive.kremlin.ru/eng/speeches/2005/04/25/2031_type70029type82912_87086.shtml.

———*Speech at the 43rd Munich Conference on Security Policy*. 2007. Accessed July 17, 2009. http://www.securityconference.de/konferenzen/rede.php?sprache=en&id=179.

———*Press Conference following Talks with President of Ukraine Viktor Yushchenko and the Second Meeting of the Russian-Ukrainian Intergovernmental Commission*. Moscow, 2008. Accessed September 5, 2014. http://archive.kremlin.ru/eng/speeches/2008/02/12/2018_type82914type82915_160088.shtml.

———*Annual Address to the Federal Assembly of the Russian Federation*. Moscow, 2013. Accessed September 16, 2014. http://eng.kremlin.ru/news/6402.

———*Address by President of the Russian Federation*. Sevastopol, 2014. Accessed September 23, 2014. http://eng.kremlin.ru/news/6889.

———*Meeting of the Valdai International Discussion Club*. Moscow, 2014. Accessed January 4, 2015. http://eng.kremlin.ru/news/23137.

Primakov, Yevgeny. *Speech to the OSCE Permanent Council, 20 September 1996 (OSCE REF.PC/587/96)*.

Putin, Vladimir V., Nataliia Gevorkian, Nataliia Timakova, A. V. Kolesnikov, and Catherine A. Fitzpatrick. *First person: An astonishingly frank self-portrait by*

Russia's president Vladimir Putin. Public Affairs reports. New York: Public Affairs, 2000.

Raustiala, Kal, and David G. Victor. "The Regime Complex for Plant Genetic Resources." *International Organization* 58, no. 2 (2004): 277–309.

Reinhard, Wolfgang. *Verstaatlichung der Welt? Europäische Staatsmodelle und außereuropäische Machtprozesse.* Schriften des Historischen Kollegs : Kolloquien 47. München: Oldenbourg, 2009.

Remnick, David. "Watching the Eclipse." New York, NY: The New Yorker on-line (August 11, 2014), accessed September 27, 2014.
http://www.newyorker.com/magazine/2014/08/11/watching-eclipse.

Renz, Bettina. "Russian Military Capabilities after 20 Years of Reform." *Survival* 56, no. 3 (2014): 61–84.

RIA Novosti. "Gorbachev criticizes Putin's hints at return to presidency." Moscow: RIA Novosti (September 21, 2009), accessed September 27, 2014.
http://en.ria.ru/russia/20090921/156201207.html.

Richter, Wolfgang. "Rüstungskontrolle und militärische Transparenz im Ukraine-Konflikt." SWP-Aktuell 59, Berlin: SWP (September, 2014), accessed September 29, 2014. http://www.swp-berlin.org/fileadmin/contents/products/aktuell/2014A59_rrw.pdf.

Risse, Thomas. "Constructivism and International Institutions: Toward Conversations Across Paradigms." In *Political Science: The State of the Discipline.* Edited by Ira Katznelson and Helen V. Milner, 597–629. New York: Norton, 2002.

Risse-Kappen, Thomas, Steve C. Ropp, and Kathryn Sikkink, eds. *The power of human rights: International norms and domestic change.* Cambridge studies in international relations 66. New York: Cambridge University Press, 1999.

Risse-Kappen, Thomas, and Kathryn Sikkink. "The Socialization of International Human Rights into Domestic Practices." In *The power of human rights: International norms and domestic change.* Edited by Thomas Risse-Kappen, Steve C. Ropp and Kathryn Sikkink, 1–37. Cambridge studies in international relations 66. New York: Cambridge University Press, 1999.

Rittberger, Volker, ed. *International regimes in East West politics.* London: Pinter, 1990.

———, ed. *Regime theory and international relations.* Oxford: Clarendon, 1993.

———"Research on International Regimes in Germany: The Adaptive Internalization of an American Social Science Concept." In *Regime theory and international relations.* Edited by Volker Rittberger, 3–22. Oxford: Clarendon, 1993.

Rittberger, Volker, Manfred Efinger, and Martin Mendler. *Confidence- and Security-Building Measures (CSBM): An Evolving East-West Security Regime?* Tübinger Arbeitspapiere zur internationalen Politik und Friedensforschung 8. Tübingen: Arbeitsgruppe Friedensforschung, 1988.

Rittberger, Volker, and Michael Zürn. "Towards Regulated Anarchy in East-West-Relations: Causes and Consequences of East-West Regimes." In *International regimes in East West politics.* Edited by Volker Rittberger, 9–63. London: Pinter, 1990.

Rochester, Martin J. "The Rise and Fall of International Organization as a Field of Study." *International Organization* 40, no. 4 (1986): 777–813.

Ropers, Norbert, and Peter Schlotter. "Regimeanalyse und KSZE-Prozess." In *Regime in den internationalen Beziehungen.* Edited by Beate Kohler-Koch. 1st ed., 315–42. Baden-Baden: Nomos-Verl.-Ges., 1989.

Rosendal, Kristin G. "Overlapping International Regimes: The Case of Biodiversity." *Global Governance* 7, no. 1 (2001): 95–117.

Rosert, Elvira, and Sonja Schirmbeck. "Zur Erosion internationaler Normen: Folterverbot und nukleares Tabu in der Diskussion." *Zeitschrift für Internationale Beziehungen* 14, no. 2 (2007): 253–288.

Rosner, Jeremy D. *The new tug-of-war: Congress, the executive branch, and national security.* A Carnegie Endowment Book, Washington, D.C.: Carnegie Endowment for International Peace, 1995.

Ross, Andrew A. G. "Coming in from the Cold: Constructivism and Emotions." *European Journal of International Relations* 12, no. 2 (2006): 197–222.

Rotfeld, Adam D. "A Euro-Atlantic and Eurasian Security Community: A New Role for the OSCE." In *OSCE Yearbook 2013.* Edited by IFSH, 53–66. Baden-Baden: Nomos, 2014.

Roulo, Claudette. "Breedlove: Russian Actions Bring Europe to Decisive Point." Washington, D.C.: American Forces Press Service, U.S. Department of Defense (June 30, 2014), accessed July 10, 2014.

Rousseau, David L. "Relative or Absolute Gains: Beliefs and Behavior in International Politics." Philadelphia: University of Pennsylvania July 1, 1999. http://www.albany.edu/~dr967231/papers/absrel5.pdf.

Rozanov, Anatoliy A., and Elena F. Dovgan. *Collective Security Treaty Organisation 2002-2009.* DCAF Regional programmes series 6. Geneva/Minsk: The Geneva Centre for the Democratic Control of Armed Forces, 2010.

Ruggie, John G. "American Exceptionalism, Exemptionalism and Global Governance." *SSRN Electronic Journal*, 2004.

Rupp, Richard E., and Mary M. McKenzie. "The Organization for Security and Cooperation in Europe: Institutional Reform and Political Reality." In *The promise and reality of European security cooperation: States, interests, and institutions.* Edited by Mary M. McKenzie and Peter H. Loedel, 119–38. Westport, Conn: Praeger, 1998.

Russett, Bruce. "The Mysterious Case of Vanishing Hegemony; or, is Mark Twain Really Dead?" *International Organization* 39, no. 2 (1985): 207–231.

Russian Federation and United States. *Joint Statement on European Security, Fourth Clinton-Yeltsin Summit.* Moscow, 1995. Accessed October 26, 2014. http://www.bits.de/NRANEU/US-Russia/A%20Official%20Docs/MoscowDecl_EuropSec.html.

Russian Security Council. *National Security Concept of the Russian Federation Approved by Presidential Decree No. 24 of 10 January 2000.* Moscow, 2000. Accessed November 12, 2014. http://www.mid.ru/bdomp/ns-osndoc.nsf/1e5f0de28fe77fdcc32575d900298676/36aba64ac09f737fc32575d9002bbf31!OpenDocument.

Sarotte, Mary E. "Not One Inch Eastward? Bush, Baker, Kohl, Genscher, Gorbachev, and the Origin of Russian Resentment toward NATO Enlargement in February 1990." *Diplomatic History, The Journal of the Society for Historians of American Foreign Relations* 34, no. 1 (January, 2010): 119–140.

———"Perpetuating U.S. Preeminence: The 1990 Deals to "Bribe the Soviets Out" and Move NATO In." *International Security* 35, no. 1 (2010): 110–137.

———"A Broken Promise? What the West Really Told Moscow About NATO Expansion." *Foreign Affairs* 90, no. 5 (2014): 90–97.

Saul, Heather. "Ukraine crisis: Russian soldiers captured in conflict area crossed border 'by accident'." London: The Independent on-line (August 26, 2014), accessed September 27, 2014.
http://www.independent.co.uk/news/world/europe/ukraine-crisis-russian-paratroopers-captured-in-conflict-area-crossed-border-by-accident-9690752.html.

Schachter, Oscar. *International law in theory and practice: general course in public international law.* Recueil des cours 178. The Hague, Boston, London: M. Nijhoff, 1982-1985.

Schelling, Thomas C., and Morton H. Halperin. *Strategy and arms control.* New York, NY: The Twentieth Century Fund, 1961.

Schieder, Siegfried and Manuela Spindler, eds. *Theorien der internationalen Beziehungen.* UTB Politikwissenschaft, Internationale Beziehungen 2315. Opladen: Budrich, 2010.

Schlotter, Peter. *Die KSZE im Ost-West-Konflikt : Wirkung einer internationalen Institution.* Studien der Hessischen Stiftung Friedens- und Konfliktforschung 32. Frankfurt am Main: Campus-Verl., 1999.

Schmidt, Hans-Joachim. *Verified transparency: New conceptual ideas for conventional arms control in Europe.* Frankfurt am Main: Peace Research Inst. Frankfurt (PRIF), 2013.

Schmidt, Hans-Joachim, and Wolfgang Zellner. "Confidence- and security-building measures." In *SIPRI Yearbook 2012: Armaments, Disarmament and International Security.* Edited by Stockholm International Peace Research Institute, 447–52. Oxford: Oxford University Press, 2012.

Schweller, Randall L. "Neorealism's status-quo bias: What security dilemma?" *Security Studies* 5, no. 3 (1996): 90–121.

Schweller, Randall L., and David Priess. "A Tale of Two Realisms: Expanding the Institutions Debate." *Mershon International Studies Review* 41, no. 1 (1997): 1–32.

Sebenius, James K. "Negotiation Arithmetic: Adding and Subtracting Issues and Parties." *International Organization* 37, no. 2 (1983): 281–316.

———"Negotiation Analysis." In *International negotiation: Analysis, approaches, issues; a publication of the Processes of International Negotiations (PIN) Project.* Edited by Victor A. Kremenyuk. 1st ed., 203–15. Conflict resolution series. San Francisco: Jossey-Bass Publishers, 1991.

Secretary of State. *09STATE59226_a: Demarche on European security and the Corfu Ministerial.* 2009. Accessed November 14, 2014.
https://search.wikileaks.org/plusd/cables/09STATE59226_a.html.

Selvage, Douglas. "The Superpowers and the Conference on Security and Cooperation in Europe, 1977-1983." In *Die KSZE im Ost-West-Konflikt: Internationale Politik und gesellschaftliche Transformation 1975 - 1990.* Edited by Matthias Peter and Hermann Wentker, 15–58. Schriftenreihe der Vierteljahrshefte für Zeitgeschichte Sondernummer. München: Oldenbourg, 2012.

Shanker, Tom. "Russian Pullback on Arms Treaty Obscures Progress, Official Says." New York, NY: The New York Times on-line (July 16, 2007), accessed November 1, 2014.
http://www.nytimes.com/2007/07/16/world/europe/16treaty.html?fta=y&_r=0.

Shannon, Vaughn P. "Norms Are What States Make of Them: The Political Psychology of Norm Violation." *International Studies Quarterly* 44, no. 2 (2000): 293–316.

Sharp, Jane M. O. "Let's make a deal: NATO and CFE." *The Bulletin of the Atomic Scientists* 51, no. 2 (1995): 19–21.

———"CFE Adaptation and Arms Control in the Balkans." In *Brassey's Defence Yearbook 1997.* Edited by Kings C. L. The Centre for Defence Studies, 325–46. London: Brassey's, 1997.

———*Striving for military stability in Europe: Negotiation, implementation and adaptation of the CFE treaty.* London: Routledge, 2006.

Sloan, Stanley R. "NATO's Future in a New Europe: An American Perspective." *International Affairs* 66, no. 3 (1990): 495–511.

Snidal, Duncan. "The Game Theory of International Politics." In *Cooperation Under Anarchy.* Edited by Kenneth A. Oye, 25–56. Princeton, NJ: Princeton Univ. Press, 1986.

Snyder, Craig A., ed. *Contemporary security and strategy.* 3rd ed. Basingstoke, Hampshire: Palgrave Macmillan, 2012.

———"Regional Security and Regional Conflict." In *Contemporary security and strategy.* Edited by Craig A. Snyder. 3rd ed., 312–29. Basingstoke, Hampshire: Palgrave Macmillan, 2012.

Sokolsky, Richard D. "Renovating U.S. Strategic Arms Control Policy." *Strategic Forum*, no. 178 (February, 2001): 1–4.

Solomon, Gerald B. *America Needs a New Russian Policy: Extension of Remarks, January 24, 1996.* Congressional Record. Washington, D.C.: U.S. Government Printing Office, 1996.

———"America's Alliance Anxieties: Prices and Pitfalls of NATO Enlargement." *Orbis* 41, no. 2 (1997): 209–222.

Spiegel on-line. "Außenminister contra EU: Steinmeier warnt vor schärferen Russland-Sanktionen." Hamburg: Spiegel on-line (December 19, 2014), accessed December 28, 2014. http://www.spiegel.de/politik/deutschland/russland-steinmeier-warnt-vor-schaerferen-sanktionen-a-1009491.html.

Spitzer, Hartwig. "Open Skies in turbulence, a well functioning treaty is endangered by outside developments." *Security and Human Rights* 22, no. 4 (2011): 373–382.

Staack, Michael, ed. *Die Zukunft der nuklearen Ordnung.* Schriftenreihe des Wissenschaftlichen Forums für Internationale Sicherheit e.V. (WIFIS) 27. Bremen: Edition Temmen, 2009.

Stares, Paul B., ed. *The new Germany and the new Europe.* Washington, DC: Brookings Inst, 1992.

Stein, Arthur A. "The Politics of Linkage." *World Politics* 33, no. 1 (1980): 62–81.

———"Coordination and collaboration: Regimes in an anarchic world." *International Organization* 36, no. 2 (1982): 299–324.

Stein, Janice G. "Detection and defection: security 'régimes' and the management of international conflict." *International Journal* 40, no. 4 (1985): 599–627.

———"Taboos and regional security regimes." *Journal of Strategic Studies* 26, no. 3 (2003): 6–18.

Steinmeier, Frank-Walter. "Von der Kooperation zur Konfrontation? Die Zukunft der Rüstungskontrolle." *Europäische Sicherheit* 57, no. 3 (2008): 29–32.

————"Foreword: The Future of Conventional Arms Control in Europe." In *The future of conventional arms control in Europe*. Edited by Wolfgang Zellner, Hans-Joachim Schmidt and Götz Neuneck. 1st ed., 11–2. Demokratie, Sicherheit, Frieden 194. Baden-Baden: Nomos-Verl.-Ges., 2009.

Stivachtis, Yannis A. "The Regional Dimension of International Society." In *Guide to the English School in International Studies*. Edited by Daniel M. Green and Cornelia Navari, 109–25. Chichester, England: Wiley-Blackwell, 2014.

Stockholm International Peace Research Institute, ed. *SIPRI Yearbook 2012: Armaments, Disarmament and International Security*. Oxford: Oxford University Press, 2012.

Strange, Susan. "Cave! hic dragones: a critique of regime analysis." *International Organization* 36, no. 2 (1982): 479–496.

Sultanova, Shahla, and Yekaterina Poghosyan. "Neighbourhood Watches as Azerbaijan Arms Up: Unable to match Baku's big spending, Armenia relies on special relationship with Moscow." CRS Issue 695, London: Institute for War & Peace Reporting (July 25, 2013), accessed July 10, 2014.

Talbott, Strobe. *The Russia hand: A memoir of presidential diplomacy*. New York: Random House, 2003.

Thakur, Ramesh, ed. *Global Governance: A Review of Multilateralism and International Organizations, Vol. 19, No. 1*. Boulder: Lynne Rienner Publ, 2013.

The Centre for Defence Studies, Kings C. L., ed. *Brassey's Defence Yearbook 1997*. London: Brassey's, 1997.

The Republic of Bosnia and Herzegovina, The Republic of Croatia, and The Federal Republic of Yugoslavia. *General Framework Agreement for Peace in Bosnia and Herzegovina (Dayton Peace Agreement)*. Dayton, 1995. Accessed May 12, 2013. http://www.ohr.int/dpa/default.asp?content_id=380.

The White House. *Address of President George H.W. Bush Before a Joint Session of the Congress on the State of the Union*. Washington, D.C.: U.S. Government Printing Office, 1992. Accessed November 1, 2014. http://www.presidency.ucsb.edu/ws/?pid=20544.

————*The President's News Conference With President Boris Yeltsin of Russia*. Washington, D.C.: U.S. Government Printing Office, 1992. Accessed October 25, 2014. http://www.presidency.ucsb.edu/ws/?pid=21101.

————*Statement by the President on Conventional Armed Forces in Europe Treaty*. Washington, D.C.: U.S. Government Printing Office, 1999. Accessed November 4, 2014. http://fas.org/nuke/control/cfe/news/991119-cfe-usia1.htm.

————*U.S.-Russia Relations: "Reset" Fact Sheet*. Washington, D.C.: U.S. Government Printing Office, 2010. Accessed November 14, 2014. http://www.whitehouse.gov/the-press-office/us-russia-relations-reset-fact-sheet.

————*Remarks by President Obama at the Brandenburg Gate*. Washington, D.C.: U.S. Government Printing Office, 2013. Accessed September 27, 2014. http://www.whitehouse.gov/the-press-office/2013/06/19/remarks-president-obama-brandenburg-gate-berlin-germany.

————*Statement by the President on Ukraine*. Washington, D.C.: U.S. Government Printing Office, 2014. Accessed December 28, 2014. http://www.whitehouse.gov/the-press-office/2014/07/29/statement-president-ukraine.

————*Remarks by President Obama to the People of Estonia, Nordea Concert Hall, Tallinn, Estonia*. Washington, D.C.: U.S. Government Printing Office, 2014.

Accessed September 5, 2014. http://www.whitehouse.gov/the-press-office/2014/09/03/remarks-president-obama-people-estonia.

Thompson, Alexander, and Duncan Snidal. "International Organization." In *Encyclopedia of Law and Economics, Vol V: The Economics of Crime and Litigation.* Edited by Boudewijn Bouckaerts and Gerrit de Geest, 692–722. Cheltenham: Edward Elgar, 2000.

Thompson, Mark. "The $5 Trillion War on Terror." New York, NY: Time on-line (June 29, 2011), accessed December 28, 2014. http://nation.time.com/2011/06/29/the-5-trillion-war-on-terror/.

Thorun, Christian. *Explaining change in Russian foreign policy: The role of ideas in post-Soviet Russia's conduct towards the West.* St Antony's series. Basingstoke, New York: Palgrave Macmillan, 2009.

Tönnies, Ferdinand. *Gemeinschaft und Gesellschaft : Grundbegriffe der reinen Soziologie, 7th Edition.* Berlin: Curtius, 1926.

Trenin, Dmitri. "Russia Leaves the West." *Foreign Affairs* 85, no. 4 (2006): 87–96.

———"The crisis in Crimea could lead the world into a second cold war." London (March 2, 2014), last modified September 27, 2014. http://www.theguardian.com/commentisfree/2014/mar/02/crimea-crisis-russia-ukraine-cold-war.

Truscott, Peter. *Russia first: Breaking with the West.* London, New York: I.B. Tauris, 1997.

Tscharner, Benedikt v., and Linus v. Castelmur. "The Work on a Security Model for Europe for the 21st Century." In *OSCE Yearbook 1995/96.* Edited by IFSH, 227–40. Baden-Baden: Nomos Verl.-Ges., 1997.

U.S. Army War College, ed. *How the Army Runs: A Senior Leader Reference Handbook 2011-2012.* Carlisle: U.S. Army War College, 2012.

U.S.-Russia. *Joint Declaration, U.S.-Russian Summit.* Camp David, 1992. Accessed October 26, 2014. http://www.bits.de/NRANEU/US-Russia/A%20Official%20Docs/Bush%20Yelt%201st%20sum%20.htm.

———*Joint Statement on European Security, Sixth Clinton-Yeltsin Summit.* Helsinki, 1997. Accessed November 3, 2014. http://www.bits.de/NRANEU/US-Russia/A%20Official%20Docs/Clint%20Yelt%206th%20sum.htm.

Ulam, Adam B. *Dangerous relations : the Soviet Union in world politics, 1970 - 1982.* 2nd ed. New York, N.Y.: Oxford Univ. Press, 1983.

Ulbert, Cornelia. "Sozialkonstruktivismus." In *Theorien der internationalen Beziehungen.* Edited by Siegfried Schieder and Manuela Spindler, 427–60. UTB Politikwissenschaft, Internationale Beziehungen 2315. Opladen: Budrich, 2010.

Umbach, Frank. "Die zweite Runde der NATO-Osterweiterung aus der Sicht Russlands." In *Die zweite Runde der NATO-Osterweiterung: Zwischen postbipolarem Institutionalismus und offensivem Realismus.* Edited by August Pradetto, 279–317. Strategische Kultur Europas 2. Frankfurt am Main: Lang, 2004.

Underdal, Arild and Oran R. Young, eds. *Regime consequences: Methodological challenges and research strategies.* Dordrecht: Kluwer Academic Publ, 2004. http://www.loc.gov/catdir/enhancements/fy0821/2004047593-t.html.

United Nations, ed. *Treaty Series* Vol. 1894, 1-32307. New York, N.Y.: United Nations, Office of Legal Affairs, 1999.

United Nations in Ukraine. "UN report details dire plight of people in eastern Ukraine." Kyiv: United Nations in Ukraine (December 15, 2014), accessed December 28, 2014. http://www.un.org.ua/en/information-centre/news/1936.

United States Department of State. *Compliance with the Treaty on Conventional Armed Forces in Europe, Condition (5) (C) Report*. 2014.

United States Senate Committee on Foreign Relations, 105th C. 1. S. *Flank Document Agreement to the CFE Treaty (Exec. Rept. 105-1). Report together with Additional Views [To accompany Treaty Doc. #105-5]*. Washington, D.C.: Library of Congress, 1997.

United States State Department. *Fact Sheet: NATO Partnership for Peace*. Washington, D.C.: Bureau of Public Affairs, 1995. Accessed January 14, 2013. https://www.fas.org/man/nato/offdocs/us_95/dos950519.htm.

———*Implementation of the Treaty on Conventional Armed Forces In Europe: Press Statement Victoria Nuland*. Washington, D.C., 2011. Accessed February 20, 2012. http://www.state.gov/r/pa/prs/ps/2011/11/177630.htm.

van Kersbergen, Kees, and Bertjan Verbeek. "The Politics of International Norms: Subsidiarity and the Imperfect Competence Regime of the European Union." *European Journal of International Relations* 13, no. 2 (2007): 217–238.

Vetschera, Heinz. "The Agreement on Sub-regional Arms Control (Florence Agreement)." In *The future of conventional arms control in Europe*. Edited by Wolfgang Zellner, Hans-Joachim Schmidt and Götz Neuneck. 1st ed., 450–64. Demokratie, Sicherheit, Frieden 194. Baden-Baden: Nomos-Verl.-Ges., 2009.

Villaume, Poul and Odd A. Westad, eds. *Perforating the Iron Curtain: European détente, transatlantic relations, and the Cold War, 1965 - 1985*. Copenhagen: Museum Tusculanum Press, 2010.

Vincent, R. J. "Hedley Bull and Order in International Politics." *Millennium - Journal of International Studies* 17, no. 2 (1988): 195–213.

Voronkov, Vladimir. "The OSCE Summit and the European Security Treaty." In *OSCE Yearbook 2010*. Edited by IFSH, 35–44. Baden-Baden: Nomos Verl.-Ges., 2011.

Waever, Ole. "The Sociology of a Not So International Discipline: American and European Developments in International Relations." *International Organization* 52, no. 4 (1998): 687–727.

Walker, Dinah. "Trends in U.S. Military Spending." Washington, D.C.: Council on Foreign Relations (July 15, 2014), accessed December 28, 2014. http://www.cfr.org/defense-budget/trends-us-military-spending/p28855.

Walker, Jenonne. *Security and arms control in post-confrontation Europe*. Strategic issue papers. Oxford: Oxford Univ. Press, 1994.

Wallander, Celeste A. "Russia's Strategic Priorities." *Arms Control Today* 32, January/February (2002): 4–7.

Walt, Stephen M. *The origins of alliances*. Cornell studies in security affairs. Ithaca: Cornell University Press, 1987.

———"The Way We Were." Washington, D.C. (September 12, 2014), last modified September 13, 2014. http://www.foreignpolicy.com/articles/2014/09/12/the_way_we_were_obama_b ush_clinton_foreign_policy.

Waltz, Kenneth N. *Man, the state, and war;: A theoretical analysis*. Topical studies in international relations. New York: Columbia University Press, 1959.

———*Theory of international politics*. 1st ed. Boston: McGraw-Hill, 1979.

—————"Laws and Theories." In *Neorealism and its critics*. Edited by Robert O. Keohane, 27–45. The political economy of international change. New York: Columbia Univ. Press, 1986.

—————"Reflections on Theory of International Politics: A Response to My Critics." In *Neorealism and its critics*. Edited by Robert O. Keohane, 322–43. The political economy of international change. New York: Columbia Univ. Press, 1986.

—————"Realist Thought and Neorealist Theory." *Journal of International Affairs* 44, no. 1 (1990): 21–37.

Wendt, Alexander. "Anarchy is what states make of it: the social construction of power politics." *International Organization* 46, no. 2 (1992): 391–425.

Wendt, Alexander E. "The Agent-Structure Problem in International Relations Theory." *International Organization* 41, no. 3 (1987): 335–370.

Wenger, Andreas, Christian Nünlist, and Vojtech Mastny, eds. *Origins of the European security system: The Helsinki process revisited, 1965-75*. CSS studies in security and international relations. Abingdon, Oxon, New York, N.Y: Routledge, 2008.

Wiener, Antje, and Uwe Puettner. "The Quality of Norms is What Actors Make of It Critical Constructivist Research on Norms." *Journal of International Law and International Relations* 5, no. 1 (2009): 1–16.

Wight, Martin. *Systems of states*. Leicester: Leicester University Press, 1977.

—————*International theory: The three traditions*. Leicester: Leicester University Press for the Royal Institute of International Affairs, 1991.

Wilcox, Mark R. "Russia and the Treaty on Conventional Armed Forces in Europe (CFE Treaty)—A Paradigm Change?" *The Journal of Slavic Military Studies* 24, no. 4 (2011): 567–581.

Winning, Alexander, and Vladimir Abramov. "Russian ruble suffers steepest drop in 16 years." Moscow: Reuters on-line (December 16, 2014), accessed December 28, 2014. http://www.reuters.com/article/2014/12/16/us-russia-rouble-exchange-idUSKBN0JU0KO20141216.

Wisotzki, Simone. *Between morality and military interests: Norm setting in humanitarian arms control*. Prif reports 92. Frankfurt am Main: Peace Research Inst. Frankfurt (PRIF), 2010.

Wolf, Klaus D., and Michael Zürn. "'International Regimes' und Theorien der internationalen Politik." *Politische Vierteljahresschrift* 27, no. 2 (1986): 201–221.

Wolfers, Arnold. ""National Security" as an Ambiguous Symbol." *Political Science Quarterly* 67, no. 4 (1952): 481–502.

World Bank. *Data GDP (current US$)*. Washington, D.C.: World Bank. Accessed October 23, 2014. http://data.worldbank.org/indicator/NY.GDP.MKTP.CD/countries?page=4&display=default.

—————"Data Base GDP (current US$)." Washington, D.C. (1989-2013), last modified December 28, 2014. http://data.worldbank.org/indicator/NY.GDP.MKTP.CD/countries?page=4&display=default.

—————"World Bank Revises Its Growth Projections for Russia for 2015 and 2016." Washington, D.C. (December 9, 2014), last modified December 28, 2014. http://www.worldbank.org/en/news/press-release/2014/12/08/world-bank-revises-its-growth-projections-for-russia-for-2015-and-2016.

Wörner, Manfred. *Address by Secretary General, Manfred Wörner to the Bremer Tabaks Collegium, Brussels, 17 May 1990*. Accessed February 18, 2010. http://www.nato.int/docu/speech/1990/s900517a_e.htm.

Wright, Kevin. *Arms control and security: The changing role of conventional arms control in Europe*. Aldershot: Ashgate, 2000.

Wunderlich, Carmen. "Theoretical Approaches in Norm Dynamics." In *Norm dynamics in multilateral arms control: Interests, conflicts, and justice*. Edited by Harald Müller and Carmen Wunderlich, 20–47. Athens: University of Georgia Press, 2013.

Yeltsin, Boris N. *Midnight diaries*. London: Phoenix, 2001.

Yoshimatsu, Hidetaka. "International Regimes, International Society, and Theoretical Relations." Kitakyushu: The International Centre for the Study of East Asian Development, Kitakyushu May, (1998), accessed September 16, 2014. http://www.icsead.or.jp/user03/825_182_20110620203449.pdf.

Young, Oran R. "Regime dynamics: the rise and fall of international regimes." *International Organization* 36, no. 2 (1982): 277–297.

———"International Regimes: Toward a New Theory of Institutions." *World Politics* 39, no. 1 (1986): 104–122.

———*International cooperation: Building regimes for natural resources and the environment*. Cornell studies in political economy. Ithaca, NY: Cornell Univ. Press, 1989.

———"The Politics of international regime formation: managing natural resources and the environment." *International Organization* 43, no. 3 (1989): 349–376.

———"Institutional Linkages in International Society: Polar Perspectives." *Global Governance* 2, no. 1 (1996): 1–24.

Zacher, Mark W. "Trade gaps, analytical gaps: regime analysis and international commodity trade regulation." *International Organization* 41, no. 2 (1987): 173 202.

Zadra, Roberto. "NATO, Russia and Missile Defence." *Survival* 56, no. 4 (2014): 51–61.

Zagorski, Andrei. "The OSCE and Cooperative Security." *Security and Human Rights* 21, no. 1 (2010): 58–63.

———"The Astana Summit Has Left the OSCE in a State of Limbo." In *OSCE Yearbook 2010*. Edited by IFSH, 31–4. Baden-Baden: Nomos Verl.-Ges., 2011.

Zakaria, Fareed. *From wealth to power: The unusual origins of America's world role*. Princeton studies in international history and politics. Princeton, N.J.: Princeton University Press, 1998.

Zangl, Bernhard. "Politik auf zwei Ebenen: Hypothesen zur Bildung internationaler Regime." *Zeitschrift für Internationale Beziehungen* 1, no. 2 (1994): 279–312.

———"Regimetheorie." In *Theorien der internationalen Beziehungen*. Edited by Siegfried Schieder and Manuela Spindler, 131–55. UTB Politikwissenschaft, Internationale Beziehungen 2315. Opladen: Budrich, 2010.

Zartman, I. W. "The Structure of Negotiation." In *International negotiation: Analysis, approaches, issues; a publication of the Processes of International Negotiations (PIN) Project*. Edited by Victor A. Kremenyuk. 1st ed., 65–77. Conflict resolution series. San Francisco: Jossey-Bass Publishers, 1991.

———"The Role of Justice in Global Security Negotiations." *The American Behavioral Scientist* 38, no. 6 (1995): 889–903.

Zelikow, Philip. "NATO Expansion Wasn't Ruled Out." New York, NY: The New York Times on-line (August 10, 1995), accessed December 28, 2014. http://www.nytimes.com/1995/08/10/opinion/10iht-edzel.t.html.

Zellner, Wolfgang. "Can This Treaty Be Saved? Breaking the Stalemate on Conventional Forces in Europe." *Arms Control Today* 39, no. 7 (2009): 12–18.

———"Cooperative Security - principle and reality." *Security and Human Rights* 21, no. 1 (2010): 64–68.

———"Conventional Arms Control in Europe: Is There a Last Chance?" *Arms Control Today* 42, no. 2 (2012): 14–18.

Zellner, Wolfgang, Hans-Joachim Schmidt, and Götz Neuneck, eds. *The future of conventional arms control in Europe.* 1st ed. Demokratie, Sicherheit, Frieden 194. Baden-Baden: Nomos-Verl.-Ges., 2009.